Lecture Notes in Artificial Intelligence 1934

Subseries of Lecture Notes in Computer Science
Edited by J. G. Carbonell and J. Siekmann

W0246262

Lecture Notes in Computer Science

Edited by G. Goos, J. Hartmanis and J. van Leeuwen

Springer
Berlin
Heidelberg
New York
Barcelona
Hong Kong
London
Milan
Paris
Singapore
Tokyo

John S. White   (Ed.)

Envisioning Machine Translation in the Information Future

4th Conference of the Association
for Machine Translation in the Americas, AMTA 2000
Cuernavaca, Mexico, October 10-14, 2000
Proceedings

 Springer

Series Editors

Jaime G. Carbonell, Carnegie Mellon University, Pittsburgh, PA, USA
Jörg Siekmann, University of Saarland, Saarbrücken, Germany

Volume Editor

John S. White
Litton PRC
1500 PRC Drive, McLean, VA 22102, USA
E-mail: white_john@prc.com

Cataloging-in-Publication Data applied for

Die Deutsche Bibliothek - CIP-Einheitsaufnahme

Envisioning machine translation in the information future :
Cuernavaca, Mexico, October 10 - 14, 2000 / John S. White (ed.). -
Berlin ; Heidelberg ; New York ; Barcelona ; Hong Kong ; London ;
Milan ; Paris ; Singapore ; Tokyo : Springer, 2000
  (... Conference of Association for Machine Translation in the
  Americas, AMTA ... ; 4. 2000)
  (Lecture notes in computer science ;
  Vol. 1934 : Lecture notes in artificial intelligence)
  ISBN 3-540-41117-8

CR Subject Classification (1998): I.2.7, H.3, F.4.3, H.5, J.5

ISBN 3-540-41117-8 Springer-Verlag Berlin Heidelberg New York

Springer-Verlag Berlin Heidelberg New York
a member of BertelsmannSpringer Science+Business Media GmbH
© Springer-Verlag Berlin Heidelberg 2000
Printed in Germany

Typesetting: Camera-ready by author, data conversion by PTP-Berlin, Stefan Sossna
Printed on acid-free paper   SPIN: 10781226   06/3142   5 4 3 2 1 0

Preface

Envisioning Machine Translation in the Information Future

When the organizing committee of AMTA-2000 began planning, it was in that brief moment in history when we were absorbed in contemplation of the passing of the century and the millennium. Nearly everyone was comparing lists of the most important accomplishments and people of the last 10, 100, or 1000 years, imagining the radical changes likely over just the next few years, and at least mildly anxious about the potential Y2K apocalypse.

The millennial theme for the conference, "Envisioning MT in the Information Future," arose from this period. The year 2000 has now come, and nothing terrible has happened (yet) to our electronic infrastructure. Our musings about great people and events probably did not ennoble us much, and whatever sense of jubilee we held has since dissipated. So it may seem a bit obsolete or anachronistic to cast this AMTA conference into visionary themes.

But the millennial concepts remain pertinent to MT because of what it is and what will be expected of it. Like the printing press, that archetypal breakthrough invention of the last millennium, MT will make information available to everyone, breaking open the language-bound cloisters of ideas. Like printing and publishing, MT has and will evolve from a tool that can only be calibrated and operated by skilled people to one which anyone can directly operate, even while the demand for the professionally developed product continues to grow. Like the printing press, in short, MT will create its own demand, and will go from a capability that we never thought we would need to one we cannot do without.

This process has begun. The papers in this volume capture the state of MT in the year 2000, and they will continue to be of value for researchers, developers, users, translators, and information consumers for many years to come. They cover breakthrough approaches to the science of knowledge representation, statistical modeling, interlinguas and transfer strategies, and deployment of systems. They express the ingenious application of MT systems and techniques to the demands of actual translation environments, and the collection and reuse of corpora. They delve into the visions of future needs, programs, and expectations, along with the means by which we will evaluate change.

The AMTA-2000 Program Committee deserves the credit for capturing the essence of the state of MT at the turn of the millennium. The members of the Program Committee are:

Jeff Allen, Softissimo
Robert Cain, Foreign Broadcast Information Service
Gary Coen, Boeing Phantom Works
Jennifer DeCamp, MITRE Corp.
Jennifer Doyon, Litton PRC
Ulrich Germann, University of Southern California Information Science Institute
Stephen Helmreich, New Mexico State University Computing Research Laboratory
Doug Jones, National Institute of Standards and Technology

Kevin Knight, University of Southern California Information Science Institute
Marjorie Leon, Pan American Health Organization
Dan Loehr, MITRE Corp.
Jackie Murgida, Lernout & Hauspie
Kathryn Taylor, Georgetown University

My thanks also go to the organizers of AMTA-2000: Ed Hovy, Muriel Vasconcellos, Laurie Gerber, and Dave Farwell, who picked up my sundry dropped balls, helped with reviews, and set the tone for a successful conference and proceedings volume. The venue of the conference, arranged masterfully by Muriel Vasconcellos, Marina Urquidi, and Nena Uranga, is the ancient and beautiful city of Cuernavaca, Mexico. The tutorials and workshops were organized by Laurie Gerber, who built balanced programs evocative of the issues on the edge of MT in this new century. Kimberly Kellogg Belvin continues in her polished, professional role as exhibits coordinator. My good friends Ed Hovy (AMTA President) and Dave Farwell (AMTA-2000 Conference Chair) have provided much needed support, vision, and hortatory expressions to stimulate the development of the program represented in this volume.

I wish to thank especially Florence Reeder of MITRE Corporation, whose command of the quaint art of LaTeX stitchery made the assembly of this volume possible for me, who had heretofore presumed that WYSIWYG word processing was, like indoor plumbing, an ordinary expectation.

Whatever the vision of the future holds, whether ubiquitous information access, information appliances that we wear, or whole new metaphors of what it means to communicate, two things should be clear: our predictions will be wrong (including this one), and variation in human language will remain. In this light, I hope that both the present and future reader of this volume will benefit from these papers, both in the context of today and across the changes that the future will have brought to the field of machine translation.

August, 2000   John S. White

Tutorial Descriptions

Ontological Semantics

Sergei Nirenburg
Computing Research Laboratory, New Mexico State University

In computational linguistics the term ontology has come to denote a world model used for specifying the meaning of lexical units in a language. Elements of the ontology, thus, can be viewed as the lexis of a metalanguage for describing the lexical semantics of a particular language. Once the ontological approach is chosen for describing lexical meaning, the lexicon and the ontology become coupled. Depending on the type of computational linguistic application that a lexicon is supposed to support, the ontology that underlies its semantic component will contain different (though possibly compatible) information. Among the possible applications are: knowledge-based machine translation (MT); lexical disambiguation as a module in transfer-based MT or in an information extraction (IE) system; text summarization; human-computer interaction; planning and plan recognition for a society of software and human agents; object and scene recognition; and others. To illustrate the application-oriented differences in ontology content, the work on agents requires detailed statements about "workflow scripts" that these agents follow as well as domain-related plans, both realizable as complex events, while the work on knowledge-based MT typically does not. Lexical disambiguation is often considered feasible without ontological underpinnings in the lexicon but based on a set of semantic features assigned to a lexical item (if not based entirely on corpus-based co-occurrence calculations).

The application on which we will concentrate will be knowledge-based MT. In the framework of knowledge-based MT, ontology supplies major chunks of the metalanguage not only for the semantic component of the lexicon but also for the language in which the meaning of texts is represented. The latter language (called TMR, for Text Meaning Representation) is the interlingua in the KBMT system.

The tutorial will include the following topics:

Design of an MT system based on ontological semantics

The Static Knowledge Sources for KBMT: the TMR, the Ontology and the Lexicon

   The TMR
   - a) The TMR content
   - b) The TMR format

   The Ontology
   - c) The syntax of the ontology entry
   - d) The content of the ontology
   - e) A brief comparison with other ontologies used for language processing, notably, CYC, WordNet and Sensus.

Ontology Acquisition
   - a) The acquisition methodology
   - b) Examples of concept acquisition

The Lexicon
> a) The analysis lexicon
> b) The generation lexicon
> c) The onomasticon

Lexicon Acquisition
> a) The acquisition methodology
> b) Examples of lexicon entry acquisition

Interaction among the TMR, the Ontology and the Lexicon in Mikrokosmos
Ontological support for **applications other than MT** (IE, summarization, agents).

The tutorial is intended for computational lexicographers, designers and implementers of NLP systems, including MT, IE, IR, and text summarizers.

A Gentle Introduction to MT: Theory and Current Practice

Eduard Hovy

Information Sciences Institute of the University of Southern California

This tutorial provides a non-technical introduction to machine translation. It reviews the whole scope of MT, outlining briefly its history and the major application areas today, and describing the various kinds of MT techniques that have been invented--- from direct replacement through transfer to the holy grail of interlinguas. It briefly outlines the difficult questions of MT evaluation and provides an introduction to the newest statistics-based techniques (which are the topic of another tutorial).

Topics include:
- History and development of MT
- Theoretical foundations of MT
- Traditional and modern MT techniques
- Latest MT research
- Thorny questions of evaluating MT systems

Eduard Hovy is the director of the Natural Language Group at the Information Sciences Institute of the University of Southern California, and is a member of the Computer Science Departments of USC and of the University of Waterloo. His research focuses on machine translation, automated text summarization, automated question answering, multilingual information retrieval, and the semi-automated construction of large lexicons and terminology banks. He is the author or editor of four books and over 100 technical articles. Currently Dr. Hovy serves as the President of the Association of Machine Translation in the Americas (AMTA) and as Vice President of the ACL and as President-Elect of the International Association of Machine Translation (IAMT). Dr. Hovy regularly co-teaches a course in the new Master's Degree Program in Computational Linguistics at the University of Southern California, as well as occasional short courses on MT and other topics at universities and conferences.

Controlled Languages

Teruko Mitamura and Eric Nyberg
Carnegie Mellon University

The notion of Controlled Language (CL) is becoming increasingly important for both authors and translators working a large-scale document production environment. Good design, process and implementation of a Controlled Language can provide higher-quality documentation and more productive translation. Even so, there are some issues associated with introducing Controlled Language into document production environment which must be considered carefully. The goal of this tutorial is to introduce the concept of Controlled Language, to discuss design and deployment issues, and to summarize the state of the art in CL development.

Intended audience: MT users, Authors, Translators, anyone who would be interested in learning about CL.

- Introduction
    - What is Controlled Language?
    - Goals of Controlled Language
- History of Controlled Language & Applications
    - Human Communications
    - Document Authoring
    - Document Translation
- Designing a Controlled Vocabulary
- Designing a Controlled Grammar
- How To Build and Deploy a Controlled Language
    - For authoring only
    - For authoring and MT
- Evaluating the Use of Controlled Language
    - Author's Perspective
    - Translator's Perspective
    - Developer's Perspective
- Current Status of Controlled Language
- The Future of Controlled Language

Statistical Machine Translation

Kevin Knight
Information Sciences Institute of the University of Southern California

The statistical approach to machine translation (MT) seeks to extract translation knowledge automatically from online bilingual texts (e.g., publications of the Canadian or Hong Kong governments). This idea can be traced back to suggestions made by Warren Weaver in the 1940s. It was pioneered at IBM in the 1990s and continues to be inspired by relative successes in statistical speech recognition. We will present an accessible but technical tutorial that will cover the statistical MT literature to date. We will use graphical influence diagrams to explain statistical translation models used in different research projects around the world. We will also cover language models and "decoding" algorithms that perform online translations.

Outline:

- Introduction
  - History of statistical MT
  - Substitution ciphers, light probability, noisy channel framework
  - Substitution ciphers, light probability, noisy channel framework
  - Transliteration: a case study of MT as codebreaking
  - Sketch of a complete statistical MT system (training/translation modules)
- Building Blocks
  - Acquisition and cleaning of training data
    - monolingual and bilingual text corpora
    - sentence alignment
    - preprocessing
    - comparable text corpora
  - Language modeling and training
    - ngram models and smoothing
    - structured models
  - Translation modeling and training
    - word-internal translation models
    - word-for-word replacement and transposition models
    - phrase-for-phrase replacement and transposition models
    - tree-based models
  - Online translation ("decoding")
  - computational complexity and heuristics
  - word-for-word models, phrase-for-phrase models, tree-based models
- Assessment
  - Empirical results: does it work?
  - Strengths and weaknesses of statistical MT
  - Related applications
  - Immediate and long-term prospects
- Resources
  - Available software and text corpora
  - Full bibliography

The Diversity and Distribution of Languages

Laurie Gerber
Information Sciences Institute of the University of Southern California

Funding agencies and the market are placing greater emphasis on less common languages. Rapid response and short development times are crucial as economic or political events bring diverse regions and their languages to the front of the international stage. However, most MT development groups have worked on a relatively small set of languages - namely Indo-European. Even where other languages are addressed, the frameworks and architectures within which such development takes place were only designed to cover this relatively homogeneous group. Can extensions to existing paradigms cover the full diversity of the world's estimated 6,000 languages? Is it possible to build a single architecture that can handle the full range of diversity? How weird does it get? And are there any regularities that can be exploited in tackling the great diversity we face?

Outline:

- Classification methods:
    - What constitutes a language?
    - morphological, genetic, and word-order classification systems
        - *types of morphology
        - language families and areal contact
        - word order tendencies
    - variations in POS inventory... "Do all languages have nouns?"
- What's out there?
    - Where are 6,000 languages hiding?
    - Regional distribution and frequency of typological traits
        - or, How often will I have to worry about polysynthetic morphology and other exotic pheonomena?
- How can I use this information?
    - - Are there any useful universals?
    - What statistical tendencies and implicational universals can help in designing NLP systems?

MTranslatability

Arendse Bernth and Claudia Gdaniec
IBM T.J. Watson Research Center

Current MT systems are often unable to produce high-quality output on arbitrary, unseen input. The output frequently does not meet user needs and requirements. We will address some of the reasons for the unsatisfactory quality of MT output, ways to improve translatability, and ways to measure the translatability of a document.

Intended audience: MT users and consultants, people in charge of information development.

Presenters: Arendse Bernth & Claudia Gdaniec, IBM T.J. Watson Research Center. The presenters have worked in the MT field for many years. Both have also worked on MT-related tools -- for pre-editing, and for automatically estimating the quality of MT output.

Outline

- Introduction
    - Why is MT output not better?
    - What aspects can the MT user control?
    - Is it possible to predict the output quality for given input automatically?
- Ways to Improve Translatability
    - Grammar Checkers
    - Controlled Language Checkers
- Other Helpful Tools
- Ways to Measure Translatability
    - Automatic readability scoring
    - Automatic detection of lexical inadequacies
    - Automatic MTranslatability scoring
- Conclusion
- Discussion of a Special Interest Group on Translatability

Table of Contents

Technical Papers

Building a Chinese-English Mapping between Verb Concepts for......................... 1
MultilingualApplications
Bonnie J. Dorr, Gina-Anne Levow, and Dekang Lin

Applying Machine Translation to Two-Stage Cross-Language Information 13
Retrieval
Atsushi Fujii and Tetsuya Ishikawa

Mixed-Initiative Translation of Web Pages 25
Michael Fleming and Robin Cohen

A Self-Learning Method of Parallel Texts Alignment 30
António Ribeiro, Gabriel Lopes, and João Mexia

Handling Structural Divergences and Recovering Dropped Arguments in a 40
Korean/English Machine Translation System
Chung-hye Han, Benoit Lavoie, Martha Palmer, Owen Rambow,
Richard Kittredge, Tanya Korelsky, Nari Kim, and Myunghee Kim

A Machine Translation System from English to American Sign Language 54
Liwei Zhao, Karin Kipper, William Schuler, Christian Vogler, Norman Badler, and
Martha Palmer

Oxygen: A Language Independent Linearization Engine 68
Nizar Habash

Information Structure Transfer: Bridging the Information Gap in Structurally........ 80
Different Languages
Margo Budzikowska

The Effect of Source Analysis on Translation Confidence 89
Arendse Bernth and Michael C. McCord

Contemplating Automatic MT Evaluation 100
John S. White

How Are You Doing? A Look at MT Evaluation 109
Michelle Vanni and Florence Reeder

Recycling Annotated Parallel Corpora for Bilingual Document Composition 117
Arantza Casillas, Joseba Abaitua, and Raquel Martínez

Combining Invertible Example-Based Machine Translation with 127
Translation Memory Technology
Michael Carl

What's Been Forgotten in Translation Memory 137
Elliot Macklovitch and Graham Russell

Understanding Politics by Studying Weather: A Cognitive Approach to.............. 147
Representation of Polish Verbs of Motion, Appearance, and Existence
Barbara Gawronska and Hanna Duczak

Small but Efficient: The Misconception of High-Frequency Words in 158
Scandinavian Translation
Pernilla Danielsson and Katarina Mühlenbock

Challenges in Adapting an Interlingua for Bidirectional English-Italian 169
Translation
Violetta Cavalli-Sforza, Krzysztof Czuba, Teruko Mitamura, and Eric Nyberg

Text Meaning Representation as a Basis for Representation of Text 179
Interpretation
Stephen Helmreich and David Farwell

System Descriptions

MT-Based Transparent Arabization of the Internet TARJIM.COM 189
Achraf Chalabi

The KANTOO Machine Translation Environment 192
Eric Nyberg and Teruko Mitamura

Pacific Rim Portable Translator 196
John Weisgerber, Jin Yang, and Pete Fisher

LabelTool: A Localization Application for Devices with Restricted 202
Display Areas
Jimmy C.M. Lu, Lars Åkerman, and Karin Spalink

The LogoVista ES Translation System 209
Nan Decker

L&H Lexicography Toolkit for Machine Translation 213
Timothy Meekhof and David Clements

A New Look for the PAHO MT System 219
Marjorie León

User Studies

Is MT Software Documentation Appropriate for MT Users? 223
David Mowatt and Harold Somers

Evaluating Embedded Machine Translation in Military Field Exercises 239
M. Holland, C. Schlesiger, and C. Tate

Machine Translation Systems: E-K, K-E, J-K, K-J 248
*Yu Seop Kim, Sung Dong Kim, Seong Bae Park, Jong Woo Lee,
Jeong Ho Chang, Kyu Baek Hwang, Min O Jang, and Yung Taek Kim*

Author Index 253

Building a Chinese-English Mapping Between Verb Concepts for Multilingual Applications

Bonnie J. Dorr[1], Gina-Anne Levow[1] and Dekang Lin[2]

[1] Institute for Advanced Computer Studies
University of Maryland
College Park, MD, 20742
{bonnie,gina}@umiacs.umd.edu
[2] Department of Computing Science
University of Alberta
Edmonton, Alberta, Canada, T6G 2H1
lindek@cs.ualberta.ca

Abstract. This paper addresses the problem of building conceptual resources for multilingual applications. We describe new techniques for large-scale construction of a Chinese-English lexicon for verbs, using thematic-role information to create links between Chinese and English conceptual information. We then present an approach to compensating for gaps in the existing resources. The resulting lexicon is used for multilingual applications such as machine translation and cross-language information retrieval.

1 Introduction

With the advent of the web and increasingly more global interconnectivity, the need for online multilingual information has grown significantly in the last 5–10 years. This is accompanied by a growing need for rapid construction of lexical resources. Creating resources by human labor alone has become infeasible, thus motivating the development of automatic and semi-automatic approaches to resource acquisition. This paper addresses large-scale construction of a Chinese-English lexicon for verbs, including an approach to compensating for gaps in the existing resources.

The lexicons resulting from our acquisition approach are used for semantic analysis in applications such as machine translation and cross-language information retrieval. The importance of semantic analysis in either of these two applications is clear when one considers the degree of inaccuracy that might result from using a weak alternative, such as access to a bilingual word list.

Our starting point is an existing classification of English verbs called EVCA (English Verbs Classes and Alternations) [11]. We couple this with a Chinese conceptual database called HowNet [23–25] (http://www.how-nct.com), from which we extract thematic-role information (e.g., a mapping between the HowNet "Patient" and the EVCA-based "Th(eme)") to create links between Chinese and

J.S. White (Ed.): AMTA 2000, LNAI 1934, pp. 1–12, 2000.

English conceptual information. HowNet currently contains no English translations; thus, we also use a large machine-readable Chinese-English dictionary called Optilex to produce candidate English translations.[1] Although later versions of HowNet are expected to include the English translations, these are not openly available—only the binary versions have been promised and these will be accessible solely through the use of (purchasable) HowNet software. Moreover, we expect our techniques to be generally applicable to *other* foreign language semantic hierarchies where English translations are not available. We predict this will occur more and more frequently, as online (non-bilingual) linguistic resources continue to be made available in multiple languages.

Several researchers have investigated the problem of assigning class-based senses to verbs [2, 17, 18] using a variety of online resources including Longman's Dictionary of Contemporary English (LDOCE) [19], EVCA [11], and WordNet [14]. Translation of English classes into other languages has proven difficult [7, 15, 21], but regularities between different language classifications can be found in some online resources [1, 4, 16].

This work extends previous work which used a concept space to produce a hierarchical organization of Chinese verbs [18]. We adopt a technique that is similar in flavor to that of [1] for partitioning English verbs into refined classes using WordNet, with the following extensions: (1) The use of the entire EVCA database rather than a small set of verbs (the *break* class); (2) The provision of a thematic-role based filter for a more refined version of verb-class assignments; (3) Concept alignment across two different language hierarchies (Chinese and English); and (4) Mappings between Chinese and English thematic roles.

This work relies on an augmented set of EVCA classes which include 26 new classes [2]. There are 500 total classes in the extended set, each hand-tagged with semantic representations, thematic-role information, and WordNet synset numbers. We will demonstrate that it is possible to produce a lexicon by associating 709 Chinese HowNet concepts with 500 EVCA classes, with a clear concept-to-class correspondence in a large majority of the cases.[2]

Figure 1 illustrates the relation between existing resources and the mappings we produced. Solid lines represent pre-existing mappings; dotted lines are ones resulting from the application of our techniques. The most critical of these is the one labeled θ-roles (shorthand for "thematic roles"), which associates EVCA classes with HowNet Concepts. The remaining two dotted-line mappings are "transitive closure" biproducts of the other mappings: Once the thematic-role mapping associates EVCA verbs with HowNet verbs, each HowNet verb is associated with Optilex-based English *glosses* (translations) and WordNet 1.6 Senses.

---

[1] Optilex is a large (600k entries) machine-readable version of the CETA Chinese-English dictionary, licensed from the MRM corporation, Kensington, MD.

[2] HowNet contains 815 verb HowNet concepts altogether. However, we are not including the 106 HowNet concepts that are not associated with any Chinese words; these are "higher level" conceptual nodes with no Chinese realization (e.g., V.1 |static|).

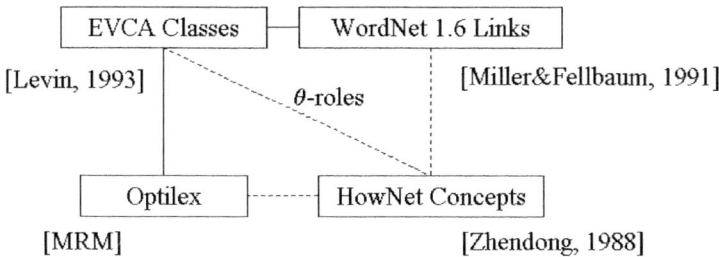

Fig. 1. Relation Between Existing Resources and New Mappings

We will describe how these correspondences are derived and we will show how this process has provided a framework for compensating for gaps in our online resources.

2 Multilingual Applications

The semantic representations produced semi-automatically for our multilingual resources are used in machine translation (MT) and cross-language information retrieval (CLIR) applications. Both applications rely on the use of a parser for mapping the input sentence into a syntactic tree. The parser output is semantically analyzed, producing an encoding of semantic and argument-structure information.

The MT approach is interlingual, where the target-language lexicon is searched for appropriate lexical items matching argument-structure information [3]. A screen snapshot of a MT example is shown in Figure 2. The CLIR approach relies on the same interlingual representation to transform a user's query into the document language for information retrieval [5, 12].

In both of these applications, thematic roles facilitate the selection of appropriate target-language words. For example, the Chinese verb 拉 (la) corresponds to a wide range of English translations—even if we examine only the verb translations: *slash, cut, chat, pull, drag, transport, move, raise, help, implicate, involve, defecate, pressgang.*[4] Our approach provides a framework for disambiguation of such cases. Certain of these possibilities—*transport* and *move*— are analyzed as one semantic representation corresponding to thematic roles

---

[3] The Chinese verbs are additionally associated (for free) with WordNet senses from our previously tagged EVCA verbs. More details are given in [6].

[4] The ambiguity in the word 拉 (la) can often be resolved if it is combined with other characters. For example, 拉车 (la che) unambiguously means *pull a cart*. However, since object dropping is a frequently phenomenon in Chinese, it is not uncommon for verbs like 'la' to appear without an argument that easily disambiguates the word. Thus, our approach must allow for multiple possibilities in the lexicon.

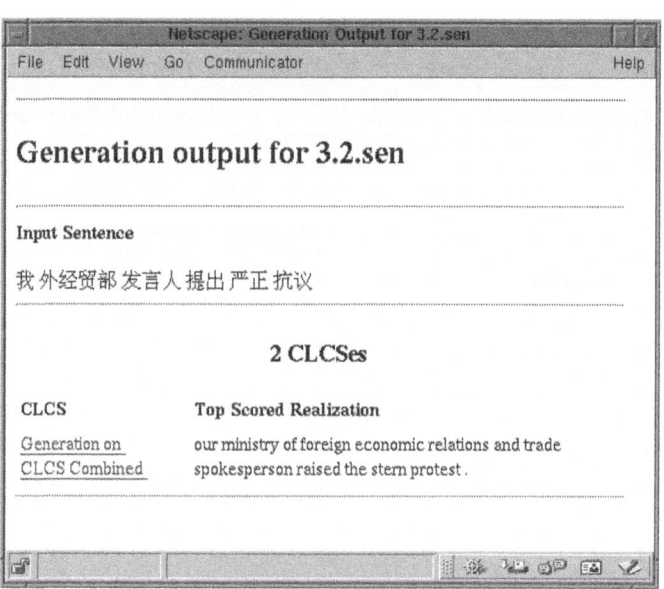

Fig. 2. Translation of a Chinese sentence into English

1. Associate English Optilex glosses with all 12342 Chinese verbs in HowNet, producing 41,324 Chinese-English pairs.

2. Associate each verb-to-concept candidate with at least one of the 500 EVCA classes.[3]

3. For each HowNet concept, partition the associated Chinese-English pairs into groups whose English glosses correspond to EVCA classes.

Fig. 3. Mapping Chinese HowNet Concepts to English EVCA Classes

(`agent,theme,goal,source`). Other possibilities—*help*—are analyzed as a different semantic representation corresponding to thematic roles (`agent,theme,mod-poss`).

3   Mapping Between Chinese HowNet and English EVCA

Our technique for mapping between Chinese HowNet concepts and English EVCA classes involves associating HowNet thematic roles with those in EVCA. Each HowNet concept (and each EVCA class) is paired with a list of thematic roles, which we call a thematic *grid*. For example, the HowNet concept |Cure| is paired with the grid (`agent,patient,content,tool`), as in *The doctor(agent) cured the man(patient) of pneumonia(content) using antibiotics(tool)*. The corresponding grid in our EVCA database is (`ag,th,mod-poss(of)`). Although the HowNet and EVCA roles are not in a one-to-one correspondence, they can still be used for a "closest match" prioritization of candidate HowNet-EVCA associations, as we will see shortly.

The three top-level tasks involved in mapping Chinese HowNet concepts to and English EVCA classes are given in Figure 3. (See [6] for more details.) For the purposes of this discussion, we focus on the last of these three tasks, which involves a massive filtering of spurious class assignments. This task involves three steps:

- Order the candidate EVCA classes so that the highest-ranking classes are those that contain the highest number of English verbs matching the Optilex glosses.
- In cases where a tie-breaker is needed, reorder the candidate EVCA classes according to the degree to which the thematic grid in HowNet concept matches that of the relevant EVCA class. The matching procedure relies on correlations derived from approximately 200 seed mappings.[5] Figure 4 shows a small subset of these mappings.
- For each Chinese-English entry associated with the HowNet concept, assign the highest ranking candidate EVCA class.

Consider the case of the multiply ambiguous Chinese verb 拉 (la). Two of the HowNet concepts associated with this verb are |Help| and |Transport|. The thematic grid associated with |Help| is (agent,patient,scope) (as in *John helped him with his work*). This grid most closely matches that of the Equip EVCA Class (where 拉 (la) is translated as *help*) which has the grid _ag_th,mod-poss(with); thus, the |Help| HowNet concept is associated with the Equip EVCA Class, and the mapping between the two is (agent->ag), (patient->th), (scope->mod-poss).

On the other hand, the |Transport| HowNet concept is associated with the thematic grid (agent,patient,LocationIni,LocationFin,direction) (as in *John transported the goods from Boston to New York (westward)*). This grid most closely matches that of the Send EVCA Class (where 拉 (la) is translated as *transport*); thus, the |Transport| HowNet concept is associated with the Send EVCA class, and the mapping between the two is (agent->ag), (patient->th), (LocationIni->src), (LocationFin->goal). The end result is that the English glosses associated with 拉 (la) are filtered down to *help* in the EVCA's Equip class and *transport* in EVCA's Send class; the corresponding semantic representations are assigned from the EVCA database.

The massive filtering of spurious assignments is evident when we examine each individual HowNet concept. Consider the |Establish| HowNet concept. This concept is ultimately associated with only two EVCA classes, 29.2.c and 26.4.a (Characterize and Create), but it initially had 29 potential EVCA class assignments. One EVCA class that was ruled out is the Change of State class, 45.4.a, associated with the Optilex translation *colonize* for the Chinese verb

---

[5] The seed mappings were done by hand at a rate of approximately 50 mappings per hour; these were verified by a native Chinese speaker in a half day.

Hownet Roles	EVCA-Based Roles														
	ag	th	exp	goal	src	perc	loc	info	pred	prop	Instr	Poss	Pred	Purp	Ben
agent	278	77	32	1	2	3	0	0	0	0	4	7	0	11	4
beneficiary	0	0	0	0	0	0	0	0	0	0	0	0	0	0	4
content	0	31	1	2	2	14	0	20	3	6	3	0	1	3	1
experiencer	13	32	33	0	0	0	0	0	0	0	0	0	0	0	0
patient	0	122	7	7	0	8	0	0	0	0	0	0	0	0	0
source	0	4	0	0	16	0	0	0	0	0	0	0	0	0	1
target	0	7	12	27	1	17	0	0	0	3	0	2	0	0	1

Fig. 4. Seed Table for mapping HowNet Roles into EVCA Roles

殖民 (zhimin). Although this is a perfectly valid EVCA class assignment for the HowNet concept |Colonize|, it is not appropriate for the |Establish| HowNet concept. Because this class is ranked 8th for |Establish|—as opposed to 1st and 2nd place ranking for 29.2.c and 26.4.a, respectively—this assignment is ruled out by our algorithm.

4   Compensating for Resource Deficiencies

As part of our effort to produce a complete alignment between HowNet and EVCA, we built an EVCA-based canonical specification for each of the 709 HowNet concepts so that we could compensate for certain types of resource deficiencies. The canonical specification consists of an EVCA class coupled with its associated prototype verb. These canonical specifications provide a mapping between a HowNet concept and an EVCA class/prototype-verb pair.

Each canonical specification was automatically generated according to the highest ranking EVCA class using steps 3.a and 3.b in Section 2. All such specifications were hand-verified (at a rate of 80 per hour for 709 classes). In most cases, the prototype verb names the HowNet concept, e.g., *transport* for the |Transport| HowNet concept. In other cases—where the HowNet concept is not an English word—the prototype word is a realization of that concept, e.g., *belittle* for the |PlayDown| HowNet concept. A sample of the canonical specifications is given in Figure 5.

We use these canonical specifications to compensate for gaps that arise in our three online resources: (1) EVCA, (2) Optilex, and (3) HowNet.

4.1   EVCA Gaps

An EVCA gap is detected when an Optilex verb gloss for a Chinese verb does not occur in EVCA. When this occurs, the canonical specification for the Chinese verb is automatically used to assign the verb an appropriate EVCA class. For example, one Optilex gloss associated with the HowNet concept |Establish| (for the verb 重建 (chongjian)) is *reconstruct*, which does not occur in EVCA. Our technique associates this Chinese verb with the canonical specification "29.2.c Characterize, *establish*," and the Chinese verb is then linked with the word sense associated with *establish*.

HowNet Concept	Canonical Specification
|Transport|	11.1 Send, *transport*
|BeNot|	22.2.a Amalgamate, *oppose*
|Help|	13.4.2 Equip, *help*
|Moisten|	45.4.a Change of State, *facilitate*
|Excrete|	40.1.2 Breathe, *bleed*
|Apologize|	32.2.a Long, *apologize*
|PlayDown|	33.b Judgment, *belittle*
|Naming|	29.3 Dub, *name*
|Choose|	29.2.c, *choose*
|Announce|	37.7.b Say, *announce*
|Mean|	37.7.a Say, *signify*
|Communicate|	37.9.c Advise *inform*

Fig. 5. Sample of Canonical Specifications for Filling Resource Gaps

An interesting byproduct of the handling of EVCA gaps is that it allows us to enhance our EVCA resource. For example the verb *reconstruct* can now be added to EVCA Class 29.2.c, on a par with the previously classified EVCA verb *establish*.

4.2   Optilex Gaps

An Optilex gap occurs when a particular translation for a Chinese verb is missing. For example, the verb 摆布 (baibu) has only one Optilex gloss: *manipulate*. However, the word 摆布 is associated with two HowNet concepts, \|Decorate\| and \|Control\|. This gloss is only appropriate for the \|Control\| concept. The *decorate* meaning of 摆布 (baibu) is omitted in Optilex.

Such gaps are detected by means of two types of information: (1) HowNet and EVCA thematic grid; and (2) correlations between the gloss under question and *other* HowNet concepts. In this particular example, the thematic grid for *manipulate* in EVCA is (ag,exp,instr), which is ranked low (11th out of 28) with respect to the roles (agent,patient) associated with the HowNet \|Decorate\| concept. By contrast, this same EVCA class has a high ranking (2nd out of 22) with respect to the HowNet \|Control\| concept due to a close match between (ag,exp,instr) and the HowNet thematic roles (agent,patient,ResultEvent). In addition, the correlation of the gloss *manipulate* is much higher for HowNet's \|Control\| concept than it is for HowNet's \|Decorate\| concept (4 occurrences compared to 0). From these two types of information, we can conclude that the *decorate* sense of 摆布 (baibu) is missing from Optilex. As in the case with EVCA gaps, our technique associates the Chinese verb with the canonical specification "9.8.b Fill, *decorate*" to compensate for this Optilex gap.

In addition to their usefulness in handling of gaps in our lexical resources, the canonical specifications proved useful for assigning EVCA classes to Chinese verbs whose Optilex gloss was not "parsable" by our gloss extraction procedure. For example, the Chinese verb 挨打 (aida) has only a single Optilex translation: *take a beating*. This verb is associated with the HowNet concept |Suffer|, which has as its canonical specification "31.3.d Marvel, *suffer*." Thus, our technique associates 挨打 verb with this canonical specification.

A similar approach is used for unknown or misspelled words. For example, the translation of 输送 (shusong) as in Optilex is misspelled as *tranport*. Because this verb is associated with HowNet's |Transport| concept, we associated this verb with the canonical specification "11.1 Send, *transport*."

4.3   HowNet Gaps

In some cases, the HowNet hierarchy incorrectly associates a Chinese word with a particular concept. For example, HowNet incorrectly associates the two Chinese verbs 扎花 (zhahua) and 绣花 (xiuhua) with the |Decorate| concept. These two verbs are translated as *embroider* in EVCA class 26.1.b (Build), but their meaning is closer to *sew flowers*. That is, the patient is incorporated into the verb, which means the thematic grid _ag_th_goal(into),ben(for) does not match that of the HowNet concept (agent,possession,source).

Discrepancies in HowNet are detected by means of EVCA-class frequency for a particular HowNet concept. Out of the 17 verbs associated with HowNet's |Decorate| concept, only two of them (the two miscategorized Chinese verbs) are associated with an EVCA class that is not 9.9 or 9.8. As in the gap-recovery described approaches above, our technique associates the miscategorized verbs with the canonical specification "9.8.b Fill, *decorate*."[6]

5   Results

Preliminary results of our classification scheme were reported in [6]. This earlier work resulted in 8089 EVCA-classified Chinese entries—about 43% of the number of potential entries. The remaining 10441 entries were accounted for through the compensation techniques described above. Using the canonical specifications, we have achieved a more refined EVCA-to-HowNet mapping, providing an increase in EVCA-classified Chinese words from the previous 8089 entries to the current expanded set of 17284 EVCA-classified Chinese words. The histogram in Figure 6 characterizes the number of EVCA classes required for coverage of 709 HowNet concepts.

Examples of the HowNet partitionings into EVCA classes are given in Figure 7, with a focus on the cases where 1 partition was found. Percentages are given with respect to the number of Chinese verbs associated with each EVCA class.

---

[6] Ultimately, the miscategorized verbs should be disassociated from the HowNet concept, but there is currently no way to tease apart such cases from the Optilex gaps. Thus, the two are treated identically.

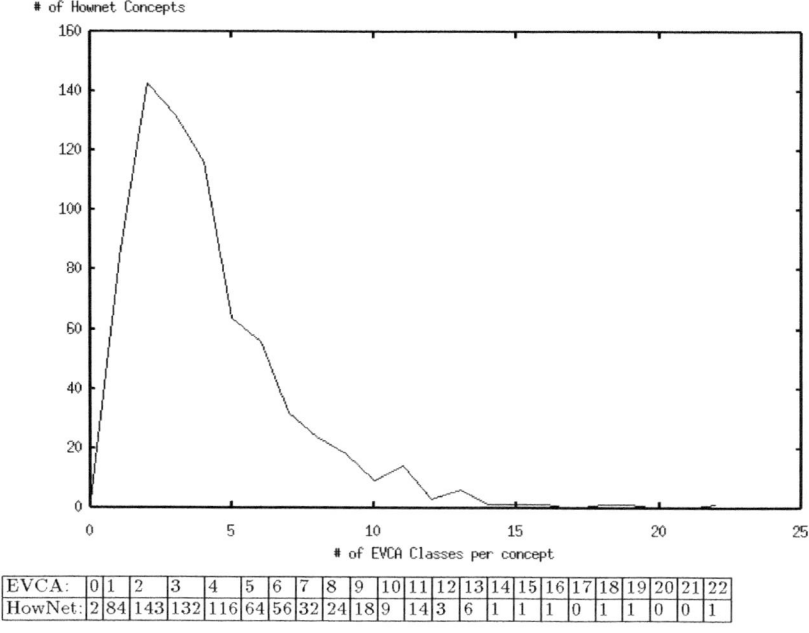

EVCA:	0	1	2	3	4	5	6	7	8	9	10	11	12	13	14	15	16	17	18	19	20	21	22
HowNet:	2	84	143	132	116	64	56	32	24	18	9	14	3	6	1	1	1	0	1	1	0	0	1

Fig. 6. Distribution of HowNet Concepts by Number of Intersecting EVCA Classes using Canonical Specifications

We consider the approach to be a success for several reasons: (1) In 359 cases (50% of the HowNet concepts), the partitioning corresponded to 3 or fewer EVCA classes; (2) Most HowNet concepts with 2 or more partitions had a very heavy association with a single EVCA class (60% or higher), with most other partitions falling around 20% or lower; (3) Only 2 cases did not correspond to any EVCA class (i.e., degenerate HowNet concepts for which no correlations with EVCA could be found); (4) There were virtually no partitionings (a handful of single HowNet concepts) exceeding 13 EVCA classes.

6   Summary and Future Work

We have presented an approach to aligning two large-scale online resources, HowNet and EVCA. The lexicon resulting from this approach is large-scale, containing 18530 Chinese entries. The technique for producing these links involves matching thematic grids in HowNet with those in EVCA. Our results indicate that the correspondence is very high between the 709 Chinese HowNet concepts and the 500 EVCA classes. We see our techniques as the first step toward a general approach to building repositories for interlingual-based NLP applications.

HowNet Concept	EVCA Class(es)
|Transport|	11.1 Send
|Help|	13.4.2 Equip
|Apologize|	32.2.a Long
|Naming|	29.3 Dub
|Judge|	29.4 Declare
|Moisten|	45.4.a Change of State
|Excrete|	40.1.2 Breathe
|TakeVehicle|	51.4.2.a.ii Motion by Vehicle
|PlayDown|	33.b Judgment (75%), 31.2.a Admire (25%)
|Establish|	29.2.c Characterize (90%), 26.4.a Create (19%)
|Decorate|	9.8.b Fill (50%), 26.1.b Build (43%), 9.9.ii Butter (25%)
|Buy|	10.5 Steal (08%), 13.5.1.a Get (30%), 13.5.1.b.ii Get (54%), 13.5.2.d Get (46%)
|Teach|	29.2.c Characterize (24%), 33.b Judgment (71%), 37.9.a Advise (29%), 37.1.a Transfer Message (45%), 31.1.a Amuse (19%)

Fig. 7. Examples of HowNet Partitionings with Respect to EVCA

We are currently investigating the use of the lexicon for word-sense disambiguation in machine-translation and cross-language information retrieval. As we saw above the Chinese verb 拉 (la) has several possible translations, but not all of these will be appropriate in every context. If we can determine which HowNet concept corresponds to 拉 (la), then we will translate it appropriately. For example, if the HowNet concept is |Transport|, the translation would be *ship* or *transport*, but not *slash*, *chat*, *implicate*, etc. We can detect which HowNet concept is appropriate by examining the other words in the sentence. If those words co-occur with *other* Chinese verbs associated with a particular HowNet concept (as determined through a corpus analysis), then it is likely that that HowNet concept is the appropriate one for the Chinese verb. That is, if we find other verbs from a given HowNet concept occurring in the same context, then we can hypothesize that this particular verb has the meaning of this HowNet concept.

The algorithm for mapping between HowNet concepts and EVCA classes requires a "training" step—i.e., the seed mappings given earlier. However, it is possible to produce a ranked mapping between thematic grids by counting correspondences between EVCA-based roles and the HowNet-based roles across the entire concept space. This approach is also currently under investigation.

Another area of investigation is the use of a WordNet-based distance metric (e.g., the information-content approach of [20]) for additional pruning power in the HowNet-to-EVCA alignment. Because each of the entries in the EVCA classification is associated with a WordNet sense [14], it is possible to rule out certain class assignments for a given HowNet concept by examining semantic distance between the Optilex glosses for a particular Chinese word and the glosses for other words associated with that concept.

Acknowledgements

The University of Maryland authors are supported, in part, by PFF/PECASE Award IRI-9629108, DOD Contract MDA904-96-C-1250, and DARPA/ITO Contract N66001-97-C-8540. Dekang Lin is supported by Natural Sciences and Engineering Research Council of Canada grant OGP121338. We are indebted to an astute anonymous reviewer for catching several errors and inconsistencies in the original draft. We also thank Nizar Habash, Maria Katsova, and Scott Thomas for their assistance with experimental runs on the data and their useful commentary and aid in the preparation of this document.

References

1. Dang, H.T. Kipper, K., Palmer, M., Rosenzweig, J.: Investigating Regular Sense Extensions Based on Intersective Levin. In: ACL/COLING 98, Proceedings of the 36th Annual Meeting of the Association for Computational Linguistics. (1998) 293–299
2. Dorr, B.J.: Large-Scale Acquisition of LCS-Based Lexicons for Foreign Language Tutoring. Proceedings of the ACL Fifth Conference on Applied Natural Language Processing (ANLP). (1997) 139–146
3. Dorr, B.J., Habash, N., Traum,D.: A Thematic Hierarchy for Efficient Generation from Lexical-Conceptual Structure. In: Proceedings of the Third Conference of the Association for Machine Translation in the Americas, AMTA-98, in: Lecture Notes in Artificial Intelligence, 1529. (1998) 333–343
4. Dorr, B.J., Jones, D.: Acquisition of semantic lexicons: Using word sense disambiguation to improve precision. In: Viegas, E.(ed.): Breadth and Depth of Semantic Lexicons. (1999)
5. Dorr, B.J., Katsova, M.: Lexical Selection for Cross-Language Applications: Combining LCS with WordNet. In: Proceedings of the Third Conference of the Association for Machine Translation in the Americas, AMTA-98, in Lecture Notes in Artificial Intelligence, 1529. (1998) 438–447
6. Dorr, B.J., Levow, G.-A., Lin, D., Thomas, S.: Chinese-English Semantic Resource Construction. In: Proceedings of the 2nd International Conference on Language Resources and Evaluation (LREC2000). (2000)
7. Jones, D., Berwick, R., Cho, F., Khan, Z., Kohl, K., Nomura, N., Radhakrishnan, A., Sauerland, U., Ulicny, B.: Verb Classes and Alternations in Bangla, German, English, and Korean. Technical report, Massachusetts Institute of Technology (1994)
8. Langkilde, I., Knight, K.: Generating Word Lattices from Abstract Meaning Representation. Technical report, Information Science Institute, University of Southern California (1998)
9. Langkilde, I., Knight, K.: Generation that Exploits Corpus-Based Statistical Knowledge. In: Proceedings of COLING-ACL '98. (1998) 704–710
10. Langkilde, I., Knight, K.: The Practical Value of N-Grams in Generation. In: International Natural Language Generation Workshop. (1998)
11. Levin, B.: English Verb Classes and Alternations: A Preliminary Investigation. University of Chicago Press, Chicago, IL (1993)

12. Levow, G.-A., Dorr, B., Katsova, M.: Construction of Chinese-English Semantic Hierarchy for Cross-Language Retrieval. In: Proceedings of the Workshop on English-Chinese Cross Language Information Retrieval, International Conference on Chinese Language Computing. (2000)
13. Lin, D.: Dependency-based Evaluation of MINIPAR. In: Proceedings of the Workshop on the Evaluation of Parsing Systems, First International Conference on Language Resources and Evaluation. (1998)
14. Miller, G.A., Fellbaum, C.: Semantic Networks of English. In: Levin, B., Pinker,S. (eds): Lexical and Conceptual Semantics, Cognition Special Issue. Elsevier Science Publishers B.V., Amsterdam, The Netherlands (1991) 197–229
15. Nomura, N., Jones, D.A., Berwick, R.C.: An architecture for a universal lexicon: A case study on shared syntactic information in Japanese, Hindi, Ben Gali, Greek, and English. In: Proceedings of COLING-94. (1994) 243–249
16. Olsen, M.B., Dorr, B.J., Thomas, S.C.: Enhancing Automatic Acquisition of Thematic Structure in a Large-Scale Lexicon for Mandarin Chinese. In: Proceedings of the Third Conference of the Association for Machine Translation in the Americas, AMTA-98, in: Lecture Notes in Artificial Intelligence, 1529. (1998) 41–50
17. Palmer, M., Rosenzweig,J.: Capturing motion verb generalizations with synchronous tags. In: Proceedings of the Second Conference of the Association for Machine Translation in the Americas. (1996)
18. Palmer, M., Wu, Z.: Verb Semantics for English-Chinese Translation. Machine Translation. 10(1–2) (1995) 59–92
19. Procter, P.: Longman Dictionary of Contemporary English. Longman, London (1978)
20. Resnik, P.: Using information content to evaluate semantic similarity in a taxonomy. In: Proceedings of IJCAI-95 (1995) 448–453
21. Saint-Dizier, P.: Semantic Verb Classes Based on 'Alternations' and on WordNet-like Semantic Criteria: A Powerful Convergence. In: Proceedings of the Workshop on Predicative Forms in Natural Language and Lexical Knowledge Bases. (1996) 62–70
22. Weinberg, A., Garman, J., Martin, J., Merlo, P.: Principle-Based Parser for Foreign Language Training in German and Arabic. In: Holland, M., Kaplan, J., Sams, M. (eds.): Intelligent Language Tutors: Theory Shaping Technology. Lawrence Erlbaum Associates, Hillsdale, NJ (1995) 23–44
23. Dong, Z. Enlightment and Challenge of Machine Translation. Shanghai Journal of Translators for Science and Technology. 1 (1998) 9–15
24. Dong, Z.: Knowledge Description: What, How and Who? In: Proceedings of International Symposium on Electronic Dictionary. (1988) 18
25. Dong, Z.: MT Research in China. In: Proceedings of International Conference on New Directions in Machine Translation (1988) 85–91

Applying Machine Translation to Two-Stage Cross-Language Information Retrieval

Atsushi Fujii and Tetsuya Ishikawa

University of Library and Information Science
1-2 Kasuga, Tsukuba, 305-8550, Japan
E-mail: fujii@ulis.ac.jp

Abstract. Cross-language information retrieval (CLIR), where queries and documents are in different languages, needs a translation of queries and/or documents, so as to standardize both of them into a common representation. For this purpose, the use of machine translation is an effective approach. However, computational cost is prohibitive in translating large-scale document collections. To resolve this problem, we propose a two-stage CLIR method. First, we translate a given query into the document language, and retrieve a limited number of foreign documents. Second, we machine translate only those documents into the user language, and re-rank them based on the translation result. We also show the effectiveness of our method by way of experiments using Japanese queries and English technical documents.

1 Introduction

The number of machine readable texts accessible via CD-ROMs and the World Wide Web has been rapidly growing. However, since the content of each text is usually provided in a limited number of languages, the notion of information retrieval (IR) has been expanded so that users can retrieve textual information (i.e., documents) across languages. One application, commonly termed "cross-language information retrieval (CLIR)", is the retrieval task where the user presents queries in one language to retrieve documents in another language. Thus, as can be predicted, CLIR needs to standardize queries and documents into a common representation, so that monolingual IR techniques can be applied. From this point of view, existing CLIR can be classified into three approaches.

The first approach translates queries into the document language [2,4,5,16], while the second approach translates documents into the query language [13, 17]. The third approach projects both queries and documents into a language-independent representation by way of thesaurus classes [6,18] and latent semantic indexing [3,11].

Although extensive comparative experiments among different approaches in a rigorous manner are difficult and expensive, a few cases can be found in past CLIR literature.

Oard [17] compared the query and document translation methods. For the purpose of English-German CLIR experiments, he used the 21 English queries

J.S. White (Ed.): AMTA 2000, LNAI 1934, pp. 13–24, 2000.

and SDA/NZZ German collection consisting of 251,840 newswire articles, contained in the TREC-6 CLIR collection. Then, he showed that the MT-based query translation with the Logos system was more effective than various types of dictionary-based query translation methods, and that the MT-based document translation method further outperformed the MT-based query translation method. Those findings were salient especially when the length of queries was large.

McCarley [13] conducted English/French bidirectional CLIR experiments, where the 141,656 AP English documents and 212,918 SDA French documents in the TREC-6 and TREC-7 collections were used, and applied a statistical MT method to both query and document translation methods. He showed that the relative superiority between query and document translation methods varied depending on the source and target language pair. To put it more precisely, in his case, the quality of French-English translation was better than that of English-French translation, for both query and document translations.

In addition, he showed that a hybrid method, where the relevance degree of each document (i.e., the "score") is the mean of those obtained with query and document translation methods, outperformed methods based on either query or document translation, irrespective of the source and target language pair. Possible rationales include that since machine translation is not an invertible operation, query and document translations mutually enhance the possibility that query terms correspond to appropriate translations in documents.

To sum up, the MT-based document translation approach is potentially effective in terms of retrieval accuracy. Besides this, since retrieved documents are mostly in a user's non-native language, the document translation approach is significantly effective for browsing and interactive retrieval.

However, a major drawback of this approach is that the full translation on large-scale collections is prohibitive in terms of computational cost. In fact, Oard [17], for example, spent approximately ten machine-months in translating the SDA/NZZ collection. This problem is especially crucial in the case where the number of user languages is large, and documents are frequently updated as in the Web. Although a fast MT method [14] was proposed, this method is currently limited to MT within European languages, which are relatively similar to one another.

In view of the above discussions, we propose a method to minimize the computational cost required for the MT-based document translation, which is fundamentally twofold. First, we translate the query into the document language, and retrieve a fixed number of top-ranked documents (one thousand, for example). Second, we machine translate those documents into the query language, and then re-rank those documents based on the score, combining those individually obtained with query and document translation methods. Consequently, it is expected that the retrieval accuracy is improved with a minimal MT cost.

From a different perspective, our method can be classified as a *two-stage* retrieval principle. However, in the monolingual two-stage IR, the second stage usually involves re-calculation of term weights and local feedback so as to increase the number of relevant documents in the final result [10], and that in the case of existing two-stage CLIR, multiple stages are used to improve the quality of query translation [1,4].

Section 2 describes our two-stage CLIR system, where we elaborate mainly on the MT-based re-ranking method. Section 3 then evaluates the performance of our system, using the NACSIS test collection [8], which consists of 39 Japanese queries and approximately 330,000 technical abstracts in English and Japanese.

2   System Description

2.1   Overview

Figure 1 depicts the overall design of our Japanese/English bidirectional CLIR system, in which we combined query and document translation modules with a monolingual retrieval system. In this section, we explain the retrieval process based on this figure.

First, given a query in the source language (S), a query translation is performed to output a translation in the target language (T). In this phase, we use two alternative methods. The first method is the use of an MT system, for which we use the Transer Japanese/English MT system.[1] This MT system uses a general bilingual dictionary consisting of 230,000 entries, and 19 optional technical dictionaries, among which a computer terminology dictionary consisting of 100,000 entries is combined with our system.

However, since in most cases, queries consist of a small number of keywords and phrases, word/phrased-based translation methods are expected to be comparable with MT systems, in terms of query translation. Thus, for the second method, we use the Japanese/English phrase-based translation method proposed by Fujii and Ishikawa [5], which uses general/technical dictionaries to derive possible word/phrase translations, and resolves translation ambiguity based on statistical information obtained from the target document collection. In addition, for words unlisted in dictionaries, transliteration is performed to identify phonetic equivalents in the target language.

Second, the monolingual retrieval system searches a collection for documents relevant to the translated query, and sorts them according to the degree of relevance (i.e., the score), in descending order. For English documents, we use the SMART system [19], where the augmented TF·IDF term weighting method ("atc") is used for both queries and documents, and the score is computed based on the similarity between the query and each document in a term vector space. For Japanese documents, we implemented a retrieval system based on the vector space model.

Consequently, only the top N documents are selected as an intermediate retrieval result, where N is a parametric constant.

Third, the top N documents are translated into the source language. Note that unlike the query translation phase, we use solely the Transer MT system,

---

[1] Developed by NOVA, Inc.

because translations are aimed primarily at human users, and thus the phrase-based translation method potentially degrades readability of retrieval results.

Finally, the N documents translated are *re*-ranked according to the new score. To accomplish this task, we compute the similarity score between the source query (submitted by the user) and each translated document in the term vector space, as performed in the first retrieval stage. We then compute the new score by averaging those obtained independently with English and Japanese monolingual similarity computations. We will elaborate on this process in Section 2.2.

Note that by decreasing the value of N, we can decrease the computational cost required for machine translation. However, this also decreases the number of relevant documents contained in the top N set, and potentially dilutes the effectiveness of the re-ranking. For example, in an extreme case where the top N set contains no relevant document, the re-ranking procedure does not change the retrieval accuracy.

The re-ranking procedure is similar to McCarley's hybrid method [13], in the sense that his method also combines scores obtained with query and document translations. However, unlike McCarley's method, which needs to translate the entire document collection prior to the retrieval, in our method the overhead for translating documents is minimized and can be distributed to each user. In other words, the second stage can be performed on each client (i.e., users' computers or Web browsers). In fact, there are a number of commercial Web browsers combined with MT systems, and thus it is feasible to additionally introduce the re-ranking function to those browsers. Besides this, we can easily replace the MT system with a newer version or those for other language pairs.

2.2   MT-Based Re-ranking Method

First, given the top N documents retrieved and translated into the source language, we first compute the similarity score between each document and the source query provided by the user. Following the vector space model, both queries and documents are represented by a vector consisting of statistical factors associated with indexed terms (i.e., term weights).

In conventional retrieval systems, documents are indexed to produce an inverted file, prior to the retrieval, so that documents containing query terms can efficiently be retrieved even from a large-scale collection. However, in the case of our re-ranking process, since (a) the number of target documents is limited, and (b) real-time indexing degrades the time efficiency, we prefer to use a simple pattern matching method, instead of the inverted file.

For term weighting, we tentatively use a variation of TF·IDF [20,23], as shown in Equation (1).

$$
\begin{aligned}
TF &= 1 + \log(f_{t,d}) \\
IDF &= \log \frac{N}{n_t}
\end{aligned}
\tag{1}
$$

Here, $f_{t,d}$ denotes the frequency that term t appears in document d. Note that unlike the common IDF formula, N denotes the number of documents retrieved

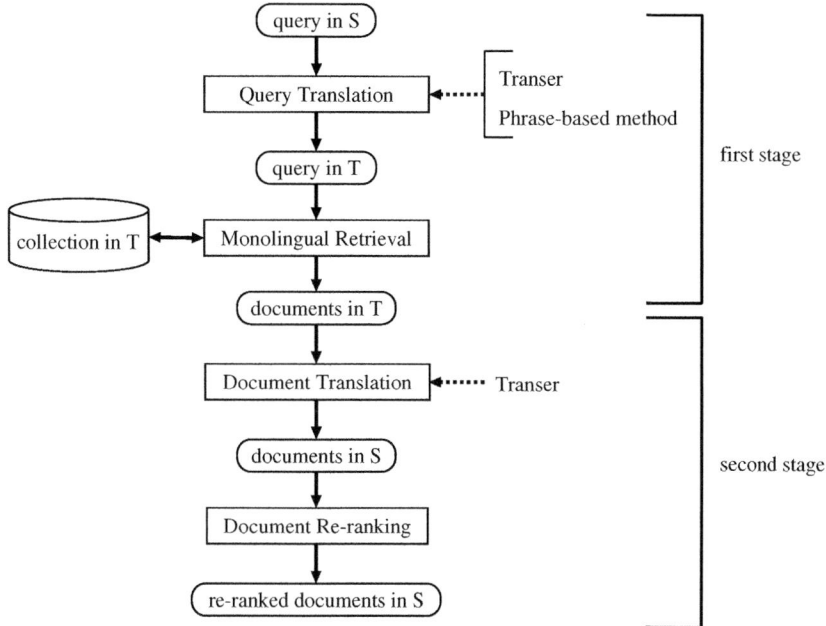

Fig. 1. The overall design of our CLIR system.

in the first stage (see Section 2.1), and n_t denotes the number of documents containing term t, out of N documents.

One may argue that since in our case where the number of target documents is considerably smaller than that of the entire collection, a different term weighting method is needed. For example, the IDF formula proposed for large-scale document collections may be less effective for a limited number of documents. However, a preliminary experiment showed that the use of IDF marginally improved the performance obtained without IDF. On the other hand, since the preliminary experiment showed that the use of document length considerably degraded the performance, we compute the similarity between the query and each document, as the inner product (instead of the cosine of the angle) between their associated vectors.

Thereafter, for each document, we combine two similarity scores obtained in English-English and Japanese-Japanese retrieval processes. We shall call them $ESIM$ and $JSIM$, respectively. Since those two similarity scores have different ranges, we use a geometric mean, instead of an arithmetic mean, as shown in Equation (2).

$$SIM = ESIM^\alpha \cdot JSIM^\beta \qquad (2)$$

Here, SIM is the final similarity score with which we re-rank the top N documents, and α and β are parametric constants used to control the degree to which $ESIM$ and $JSIM$ affect the computation of SIM. However, in the case where either $ESIM$ or $JSIM$ is zero, the value of SIM always becomes zero, disregarding the value of the other similarity score. To avoid this problem, in such a case we arbitrarily assign the value 0.0001 to either $ESIM$ or $JSIM$ that takes zero.

Possible factors to set values of α and β include the quality of Japanese-English and English-Japanese translations. In the case where the quality of one of the translations is considerably lower, α and β must be properly set so as to decrease the effect of the similarity score through the lower quality translation. Generally speaking, the quality of English-Japanese translation is higher than that of Japanese-English translation, because morphological and syntactic analyses for Japanese are usually more crucial than those for English. However, we empirically set $\alpha = \beta = 1$, that is, we consider $ESIM$ and $JSIM$ equally in the re-ranking process.

3   Experimentation

3.1   Methodology

We investigated the performance of several versions of our system in terms of Japanese-English CLIR, where each system outputs the top 1,000 documents, and the TREC evaluation software was used to calculate 11-point non-interpolated average precision values.

For the purpose of our experiments, we used the official version of the NACSIS test collection [8]. This collection consists of 39 Japanese queries and approximately 330,000 documents (in either a combination of English and Japanese or either of the languages individually), collected from technical papers published by 65 Japanese associations for various fields.

Each document consists of the document ID, title, name(s) of author(s), name/date of conference, hosting organization, abstract and keywords, from which titles, abstracts and keywords were indexed by the SMART system. We used as target documents 187,081 entries that are in both English and Japanese.

Each query consists of the query ID, title of the topic, description, narrative and list of synonyms, from which we used only the description. Figure 2 shows example descriptions (translated into English by one of the authors).

The NACSIS collection was produced for a TREC-type (CL)IR workshop held by NACSIS (National Center for Science Information Systems, Japan) in 1999.[2] In this workshop, each participant was allowed to submit more than one retrieval result using different methods. However, at least one result had to be gained with only the description field in queries. According to experimental results reported in the proceedings of the workshop [15], in the case where only the description field was used, average precision values ranged from 0.021 to 0.182.

---

[2] See http://www.rd.nacsis.ac.jp/~ntcadm/workshop/work-en.html for details of the NACSIS workshop.

Relevance assessment was performed based on the pooling method [22]. To put it more precisely, candidates for relevant documents were first pooled by multiple retrieval systems (primarily systems that participated in the NACSIS workshop). Thereafter, for each candidate document, human expert(s) assigned one of three ranks of relevance, that is, "relevant", "partially relevant" and "irrelevant". The average number of candidate documents pooled for each query is 2,509, among which the number of relevant and partially relevant documents are approximately 21 and 6, respectively. In our experiments, we did not regard "partially relevant" documents as relevant ones, because interpretation of "partially relevant" is not fully clear to the authors. Note that since the NACSIS collection does not contain English queries, we cannot estimate a baseline for Japanese-English CLIR performance using English-English IR.

In the following two sections, we will show experimental results in terms of the first and second stages (i.e., query translation methods and the MT-based re-ranking method), respectively.

ID	Description
0032	middleware construction in network collaboration
0035	digital libraries in distributed systems
0036	problems related to groupwares in mobile communication
0062	life-long education and volunteer
0065	image retrieval based on genetic algorithm

Fig. 2. Example query descriptions in the NACSIS collection.

3.2 Evaluation of Query Translation Methods

The primal objective in this section is to compare the effectiveness of the phrase-based translation method proposed by Fujii and Ishikawa [5] and one based on the Transer MT system, in terms of Japanese-English query translation. While the former method is aimed solely at words and phrases, the MT system can also be used for full sentences. In addition, since both methods are, to some extent, complementary to each other, we theoretically gain a query expansion effect, combining query terms translated by individual methods. In view of those above factors, we compared the following query translation methods:

- the use of the Transer MT system for full sentences contained in the description field ("MTS"),
- the use of the Transer MT system for content words and phrases extracted from the description field, for which the ChaSen morphological analyzer [12] was used ("MTP"),
- the phrase-based translation method applied to the same words and phrases as used for the MTP method ("PBT"),

  – the use of query terms obtained with both MTP and PBT, where terms
    outputed by both methods are considered to appear twice in the query
    ("MPBT").

Table 1 shows the 11-point non-interpolated average precision values, averaged
over the 39 queries, for different query translation methods listed above. The
second column denotes the average number of query terms provided with each
translation method, some of which were potentially discarded as stopwords by
the SMART system. The third column denotes average precision values for different query translation methods. We will explain the fourth and fifth columns
in Section 3.3.

  Looking at this table, one can see that while two MT-based methods, that is,
MTS and MTP, were quite comparable in performance, and that PBT outperformed both of them. In the case of PBT, the transliteration successfully identified
English equivalents for *katakana* words unlisted in the word dictionary, such as
"*coraboreishon* (collaboration)" and "*mobairu* (mobile)", which the MT-based
methods failed to translate. Another reason was due to the difference in dictionaries used. Generally speaking, PBT tended to output technical words more
than the MT-based methods. For example, for Japanese phrases "*fukusuu-deeta*"
and "*sekitsui-doubutsu*", PBT outputed "multiple data" and "craniate", while
MTS/MTP outputed "more than one data" and "vertebrate", respectively. Note
that this effect was evident partially because the NACSIS collection consists of
technical documents. In addition, MPBT further improved the performance of
PBT. Although the difference between PBT and MPBT was marginal, it is worth
utilizing both the MT-based and phrase-based methods, if available, for query
translation.

Table 1. 11-point non-interpolated average precision values, averaged over the 39
queries.

Query Translation			Avg. Precision with Re-ranking	
Method	# of Terms	Avg. Precision	MT	HT
MTS	16.6	0.1124	0.1770 (+57.5%)	0.2297 (+104.3%)
MTP	8.7	0.1134	0.1746 (+54.0%)	0.2217 (+95.5%)
PBT	6.1	0.1403	0.2013 (+43.5%)	0.2295 (+63.6%)
MPBT	13.1	0.1426	0.1986 (+39.3%)	0.2356 (+65.2%)

  To validate those above results in a thorough manner, we used the non-
parametric Wilcoxon matched-pairs signed-test for statistical testing (at the 5%
level), which investigates whether the difference in average precision is meaningful or simply due to chance [7,9,21]. We found that differences in average precision
values for pairs "MTP versus MTS", "MPBT versus MTS", and "MPBT versus
MTP" were significant, although for other pairs, we could not obtain sufficient
evidence to conclude a statistical significance. To sum up, we concluded that
in query translation, a combination of MT-based and phrase-based translation
methods was more effective than a method relying solely on the MT system.

3.3   Evaluation of the MT-Based Re-ranking Method

First, we consider Table 1 again, where the fourth column "MT" denotes the average precision values for each query translation method, combined with the MT-based re-ranking method. Throughout our experimentation in this paper, the best average precision value by an automatic method was 0.2013 (i.e., one obtained by PBT combined with the MT-based re-ranking method), which is relatively high, when compared with average precision values reported in the NACSIS workshop (ranging from 0.021 to 0.182).

For each query translation method, the improvement in average precision from one without the re-ranking, which is generally noticeable, is indicated in parentheses. In fact, we used the Wilcoxon test again, as conducted in Section 3.2, and confirmed that every improvement was statistically significant. To sum up, the MT-based re-ranking method we proposed was generally effective, irrespective of the query translation method combined, in terms of CLIR performance.

Second, we conducted an error analysis for queries for which the re-ranking method degraded the average precision, and found that roughly two thirds of errors were due to ambiguity in the document translation. For example, the English word "library" was often incorrectly translated into "*raiburari* (library as a software)", whereas the original query was intended to "*toshokan* (library as an institution)".

Third, to estimate the upper bound of the re-ranking method, as denoted in the fifth column "HT", we used as human translations Japanese documents comparable to English ones in the NACSIS collection. By comparing the results of "MT" and "HT", one can see that MT systems with a higher quality, if available, are expected to further improve our CLIR system. In fact, when we manually corrected inappropriate translations in translated documents, such as "library (*raiburari/toshokan*)" above, the average precision of "MT" became almost equivalent to that of "HT".

Noted that when combined with the re-ranking method, differences among query translation methods in average precision were relatively overshadowed. In the case of "MT", the Wilcoxon test showed that differences in only pairs "MPBT versus MTS" and "MPBT versus MTP" were significant, while in the case of "HT", none of the differences were identified as significant.

Fourth, we investigated how the number of documents retrieved in the first stage (i.e., the value of N in Section 2) affected the performance of the re-ranking method. As discussed in Section 2.1, in real world usage, one has to consider the trade-off between the retrieval accuracy (i.e., average precision in our case) and overhead required for the document translation.

Table 2 shows the results, where average precision values in the column "1,000" correspond to those in Table 1. By comparing average precision values for each of four query translation methods (i.e., MTS, MTP, PBT and MPBT) and those suffixed with "+MT" and "+HT" in Table 2, one can see that the re-ranking methods were effective, irrespective of the number of documents retrieved. In other words, it is expected that we can minimize the overhead in translating documents, without decreasing the retrieval accuracy.

Table 3 shows CPU time (sec.) required for the document translation and re-ranking procedures, averaged over four different query translation methods. In the case of $N = 1,000$, the total CPU time was approximately three minutes, which is perhaps not tolerable for a real-time usage. However, for small values of N (e.g., 50 and 100), the CPU time was more acceptable and practical, maintaining the improvement of retrieval accuracy.

Table 2. The relation between the number of documents retrieved in the first stage and 11-point non-interpolated average precision values, averaged over the 39 queries.

Method	# of Documents Retrieved (N)						
	50	100	200	400	600	800	1,000
MTS	0.0949	0.1017	0.1074	0.1101	0.1112	0.1119	0.1124
MTS+MT	0.1341	0.1556	0.1673	0.1698	0.1720	0.1736	0.1770
MTS+HT	0.1666	0.1901	0.2070	0.2173	0.2230	0.2259	0.2297
MTP	0.0953	0.1020	0.1085	0.1113	0.1123	0.1131	0.1134
MTP+MT	0.1449	0.1584	0.1692	0.1711	0.1728	0.1750	0.1746
MTP+HT	0.1619	0.1819	0.2017	0.2105	0.2165	0.2203	0.2217
PBT	0.1215	0.1301	0.1355	0.1385	0.1394	0.1399	0.1403
PBT+MT	0.1553	0.1723	0.1866	0.1954	0.1978	0.2005	0.2013
PBT+HT	0.1722	0.1915	0.2097	0.2212	0.2241	0.2279	0.2295
MPBT	0.1229	0.1305	0.1376	0.1405	0.1416	0.1421	0.1426
MPBT+MT	0.1690	0.1766	0.1901	0.1946	0.1958	0.1967	0.1986
MPBT+HT	0.1814	0.1968	0.2142	0.2242	0.2301	0.2319	0.2356

Table 3. CPU time for document translation and re-ranking (sec.).

	# of Documents Retrieved (N)						
	50	100	200	400	600	800	1,000
translation	9.5	17.7	33.3	65.6	106.2	139.3	175.1
re-ranking	0.2	0.3	0.6	1.2	1.8	2.4	3.0
total	9.7	18.0	33.9	66.8	108.0	141.7	178.1

(Pentium III 700MHz)

4   Conclusion

Reflecting the rapid growth in the utilization of machine readable texts, cross-language information retrieval (CLIR) has variously been explored in order to facilitate retrieving information across languages.

In brief, existing CLIR systems are classified into three approaches: (a) translating queries into the document language, (b) translating documents into the query language, and (c) representing both queries and documents in a language-independent space. Among these approaches, the second approach, based on machine translation, is effective in terms of retrieval accuracy and user interaction. However, the computational cost in translating large-scale document collections is prohibitive.

To resolve this problem, we proposed a two-stage CLIR method, in which we first used a query translation method to retrieve a fixed number of documents, and then applied machine translation only to those documents, instead of the entire collection, to improve the document ranking.

Through Japanese-English CLIR experiments using the NACSIS collection, we showed that our two-stage method significantly improved average precision values obtained solely with query translation methods. We also showed that our method performed reasonably, even in the case where the number of retrieved documents was relatively small.

Acknowledgments. The authors would like to thank NOVA, Inc. for their support with the Transer MT system, and Noriko Kando (National Institute of Informatics, Japan) for her support with the NACSIS collection.

References

1. Ballesteros, L. and Croft, W. B.: Phrasal translation and query expansion techniques for cross-language information retrieval. In Proceedings of the 20th Annual International ACM SIGIR Conference on Research and Development in Information Retrieval. (1997) 84–91
2. Ballesteros, L. and Croft, W. B.: Resolving ambiguity for cross-language retrieval. In Proceedings of the 21st Annual International ACM SIGIR Conference on Research and Development in Information Retrieval. (1998) 64–71
3. Carbonell, J., Yang, Y., Frederking, R., Brown, R., Geng, Y. and Lee, D.: Translingual information retrieval: A comparative evaluation. In Proceedings of the 15th International Joint Conference on Artificial Intelligence. (1997) 708–714
4. Davis, M. and Ogden, W.: QUILT: Implementing a large-scale cross-language text retrieval system. In Proceedings of the 20th Annual International ACM SIGIR Conference on Research and Development in Information Retrieval. (1997) 92–98
5. Fujii, A. and Ishikawa, T.: Cross-language information retrieval for technical documents. In Proceedings of the Joint ACL SIGDAT Conference on Empirical Methods in Natural Language Processing and Very Large Corpora. (1999) 29–37
6. Gonzalo, J., Verdejo, F., Peters, C. and Calzolari, N.: Applying EuroWordNet to cross-language text retrieval. Computers and the Humanities. **32** (1998) 185–207
7. Hull, D.: Using statistical testing in the evaluation of retrieval experiments. In Proceedings of the 16th Annual International ACM SIGIR Conference on Research and Development in Information Retrieval. (1993) 329–338
8. Kando, N., Kuriyama, K. and Nozue, T.: NACSIS test collection workshop (NTCIR-1). In Proceedings of the 22nd Annual International ACM SIGIR Conference on Research and Development in Information Retrieval. (1999) 299–300
9. Keen, E. M.: Presenting results of experimental retrieval comparisons. Information Processing & Management. **28(4)** (1992) 491–502

10. Kwok, K. L. and Chan, M.: Improving two-stage ad-hoc retrieval for short queries. In Proceedings of the 21st Annual International ACM SIGIR Conference on Research and Development in Information Retrieval. (1998) 250–256
11. Littman, M., Dumais, S. and Landauer, T.: Automatic cross-language information retrieval using latent semantic indexing. In Gregory Grefenstette, editor, Cross-Language Information Retrieval. Kluwer Academic Publishers. (1998) 51–62
12. Matsumoto, Y., Kitauchi, A., Yamashita, T., Imaichi, O. and Imamura, T.: Japanese morphological analysis system ChaSen manual. Technical Report NAIST-IS-TR97007, NAIST. (1997) (In Japanese)
13. McCarley, J.S.: Should we translate the documents or the queries in cross-language information retrieval? In Proceedings of the 36th Annual Meeting of the Association for Computational Linguistics. (1999) 208–214
14. McCarley, J.S. and Roukos, S.: Fast document translation for cross-language information retrieval. In Proceedings of the 3rd Conference of the Association for Machine Translation in the Americas. (1998) 150–157
15. National Center for Science Information Systems. Proceedings of the 1st NTCIR Workshop on Research in Japanese Text Retrieval and Term Recognition. (1999)
16. Nie J.Y., Simard, M., Isabelle, P. and Durand, R.: Cross-language information retrieval based on parallel texts and automatic mining of parallel texts from the Web. In Proceedings of the 22nd Annual International ACM SIGIR Conference on Research and Development in Information Retrieval. (1999) 74–81
17. Oard, D.: A comparative study of query and document translation for cross-language information retrieval. In Proceedings of the 3rd Conference of the Association for Machine Translation in the Americas. (1998) 472–483
18. Salton, G.: Automatic processing of foreign language documents. Journal of the American Society for Information Science. $21(3)$ (1970) 187–194
19. Salton, G.: The SMART Retrieval System: Experiments in Automatic Document Processing. Prentice-Hall (1971)
20. Salton, G. and Buckley, C.: Term-weighting approaches in automatic text retrieval. Information Processing & Management. $24(5)$ (1988) 513–523
21. Srinivasan, P.: A comparison of two-poisson, inverse document frequency and discrimination value models of document representation. Information Processing & Management. $26(2)$ (1990) 269–278
22. Voorhees, E.: Variations in relevance judgments and the measurement of retrieval effectiveness. In Proceedings of the 21st Annual International ACM SIGIR Conference on Research and Development in Information Retrieval. (1998) 315–323
23. Zobel, J. and Moffat, A.: Exploring the similarity space. ACM SIGIR FORUM. $32(1)$ (1998) 18–34

Mixed-Initiative Translation of Web Pages

Michael Fleming and Robin Cohen

Department of Computer Science,
University of Waterloo,
Waterloo, Ontario, Canada N2L 3G1
{mwflemin,rcohen}@uwaterloo.ca

Abstract. A mixed-initiative system is one which allows more interactivity between the system and user, as the system is reasoning. We
present some observations on the task of translating Web pages for users
and suggest that a more interactive approach to this problem may be
desirable. The aim is to interact with the user who is requesting the
translation and the challenge is to determine the circumstances under
which the user should be able to take the initiative to direct the processing or the system should be able to take the initiative to solicit further
input from the user. In fact, we envision a need to support interactive
translation of Web pages as the World Wide Web becomes more accessible to people with varying needs and abilities throughout the world.

1 Overview

Our main research interest is in the development of guidelines for the designers
of mixed-initiative artificial intelligence systems. Mixed-initiative systems are
ones where the system can take the initiative to solicit further input from the
user or where the user can take the initiative to interrupt the processing of the
system to provide additional input (see [11]). Mixed-initiative systems contrast
with other AI systems which perform automated reasoning given input from a
user, producing output without further interactivity.

To date, the design of mixed-initiative AI systems has been largely done
independently by researchers in various subareas of AI, including intelligent tutoring systems ([1], [14]), planning systems ([2], [5], [7]) and interface agents
([6], [8], [13]). Our aim is to determine some guiding influences to direct the
design of mixed-initiative AI systems in a more principled manner. To this end,
our plan is to study the requirements of various kinds of mixed-initiative applications.

One area which we feel is promising for our study is that of machine translation – in particular, an environment where machine translation is being used to
translate web pages for a user. Below we describe our view of this problem and
how it should be addressed. We include some comparison to related work and
some discussion on how such a system could be evaluated.

J.S. White (Ed.): AMTA 2000, LNAI 1934, pp. 25–29, 2000.

2   Translating Web Pages

Our view of the task of translating web pages for users is as follows. First, we feel that users do in fact want translations of web pages – that there is a need for supporting this task. Moreover, we are concerned that the task of translating the entire web page, using a general purpose machine translation (MT) system, is too difficult. We feel that users are probably requesting translations of web pages because they have a specific interest in that web page – there is a particular piece of information being sought within the web page, so that not all of the web page needs to be translated for them. One suggestion is to have a summary of the web page presented to the user first, instead of a full translation – we mean here a translated summary. If a translated summary is desired, one must decide whether to summarize within the language of the text and then translate or to do a rough translation of the entire page and then apply summarization; we hypothesize that summarizing first would be more effective – this is in a scenario where the tool to achieve summarization is more robust that the tool to do translation. In order to produce a summary which maximizes the possible benefit to the user, it would be worthwhile to interact with the user, to determine the reason he is interested in the web page. (Note that this may be true of doing summarization without translation as well).

Some translation systems like Babelfish[1] produce crude translations with some obvious errors. Figure 1 shows some examples of phrases from an original web page and its translation into French, using Babelfish, indicating in the third column various types of errors which were produced in the translation. The question is whether the user can put up with the errors, reading through them to some extent to get the information he requires from the page. In the case of the web page translated in Figure 1, the user requesting the translation had some facility in both languages, so was not adversely affected by the errors. However, in many cases, the user would not know the source language and may be confused by mistakes such as literal translations and incorrect choices of word sense. In any case, there were significant segments of the translation which were acceptable. It is worth noting that the translation system used to produce this output does not model the grammar of the target language,[2] hence the cause of some of the errors.

A related question is whether the gist of the translation is really all that a user needs to take away. Resnik [15] in fact claims that getting the gist of a document is often sufficient for a user, who can then decide whether to use other resources to get help with a complete translation. Another question is whether there is more room for interactivity with this kind of a translation process (again, this is the case where perhaps the entire page is translated (or an attempt is made to do so)).

---

[1] http://babelfish.altavista.com
[2] This information is based on a personal conversation with Elliott Macklovitch at the University of Montreal in 1999.

English text	French translation	Type of error
In the very near future, I hope to nail down what my thesis topic will be.	À très court terme, j'espère **clouer en bas** de ce que sera mon sujet de thèse.	Literal translation; does not capture the use of metaphor.
I'm a big fan of the Montreal Montréal Canadiens · · ·	Je suis un grand **ventilateur** de Canadiens · · ·	Incorrect choice of word sense.
· · · while my mother, Linda, is · · ·	· · · tandis que **mon** mère, Linda, · · ·	Possessive adjective should be **ma**; mère has feminine gender in French.
· · · I attended Tantramar Regional High School · · ·	· · · **I est allé** au lycée régional de Tantramar · · ·	Unable to recognize 'I' as a common personal pronoun.
My father, Berkeley, is a Professor of Sociology · · ·	Mon père, Berkeley, **un professeur sociologie** · · ·	Fails to include words corresponding to is and of.
My main research interests are in mixed-initiative interaction, · · ·	Mes intérêts principaux de recherches sont dans l'interaction **d'mélanger-initiative**, · · ·	Use of apostrophe in front of a consonant is incorrect.
Last updated: May 6, 1999	Dernier mis à jour: **Mai 6, 1999**	Incorrect date format in French.

Fig. 1. Examples of translation errors

3 Interactivity in Machine Translation

In general, we are interested in exploring the possibilities for mixed-initiative interaction within machine translation. There have been some efforts in designing interactive translation systems but so far these efforts have been limited in one way or another – e.g. there are systems which allow the author of a text to help in disambiguating words in the text for the translation system ([4], [17]) **or** there are systems which interact with a human translator, providing more of an assistance with machine aided human translation ([9], [12]). Our aim is to see the potential role for interacting with a user who is **requesting** a translation. In addition to soliciting further information from the user to direct the initial translation, it may also be useful to allow for "relevance feedback" from the user, in response to the system's processing.

4 Next Steps

In order to investigate a mixed-initiative approach to translating web pages, interacting with a user requesting a translation, we will need to identify the circumstances under which a system may solicit further input from the user or the user may choose to offer more input to the system. Some general variables we are investigating within our study of mixed-initiative include: (i) the extent to which the solution should be user-specific (i.e. should the question of when initiative can change between the two parties be fixed for all possible users or not?) and (ii) an estimation of the cost of having a system communicate with a user (i.e. trying to estimate the likelihood of successful communication before communication is even attempted).

It is important to note that evaluating the performance of a mixed-initiative system is also a challenging topic. There are tradeoffs between user satisfaction and efficiency, as discussed in [16]. If a system performs quite well, but in a scenario where a user has had to participate very actively, is this really more successful than a system which is slower or more error prone but has not needed to bother the user? The question of whether a user would welcome the opportunity to interact or would be bothered by it is another influencing factor in deciding where initiative should take place within interactive translation systems. Work such as [8], which calculates a bother factor, [3], which incorporates an estimate of the user's annoyance level, or [10], which discusses a principle of minimal disruption, may therefore be useful as well.

5 Summary

We feel that the area of interactive MT of web pages is a worthwhile application to use as part of our study of what makes an effective mixed-initiative system; we are in fact curious to discover whether machine translation is amenable to mixed-initiative design. This particular topic area will lead us to explore issues of user information need as well as system information need (when coping with ambiguous interpretations).

References

1. Aist, G.S.: Challenges for a mixed initiative spoken dialog system for oral reading tutoring. In Papers from the 1997 AAAI Symposium on Computational Models for Mixed Initiative Interaction. AAAI Press (1997) 1–6
2. Allen, J.: Mixed-initiative planning: Position paper. Presented at the ARPA/Rome Labs Planning Initiative Workshop. Available on the World Wide Web at http://www.cs.rochester.edu/research/trains/mip (1994)
3. Bauer, M., Dengler, D., Meyer, M. and Paul, G.: Instructible information agents for web mining. In Proceedings of the 2000 International Conference on Intelligent User Interfaces. (2000)
4. Boitet, C.: Towards personal MT: general design, dialogue structure, potential role of speech. In COLING-90: Papers presented to the 13th International Conference on Computational Linguistics. (1990)
5. Burstein, M. and McDermott, D.: Issues in the development of human-computer mixed-initiative planning. In B. Gorayska and J.L. Mey, (eds.): In Search of a Humane Interface. Elsevier Science B.V. (1996) 285–303
6. Cesta, A. and D'Aloisi, D.: Mixed-initiative issues in an agent-based meeting scheduler. User Modeling and User-Adapted Interaction. 9(1-2) (1999) 45–78
7. Cox, M. and Veloso, M.: Controlling for unexpected goals when planning in a mixed-initiative setting. In Proceedings of the 8th Portuguese AI Conference, Coimbra, Portugal. (1997) 309–318
8. Fleming, M. and Cohen, R.: User modeling in the design of interactive interface agents. In Proceedings of the Seventh International Conference on User Modeling, Banff, Alberta, Canada. (1999) 67–76
9. Foster, G., Isabelle, P. and Plamondon, P.: Target-text mediated interactive machine translation. Machine Translation. 12(1–2) (1997) 175–194
10. Godden, K.: The evolution of CASL controlled authoring at general motors. In Proceedings: The 3rd International Workshop on Controlled Language Applications. (2000)
11. Haller, S., McRoy, S. and Kobsa, A., eds.: Computational Models of Mixed-Initiative Interaction. Kluwer Academic Publishers (1999)

12. Isabelle, P., Dymetman, M., Foster, G., Jutras, J.M., Macklovitch, E., Perrault, F., Ren, X. and Simard, M.: Translation analysis and translation automation. In Proceedings of the Fifth International Conference on Theoretical and Methodological Issues in Machine Translation. (1993)
13. Lesh, N., Rich, C. and Sidner, C.L.: Using plan recognition in human-computer collaboration. In Proceedings of the Seventh International Conference on User Modeling, Banff, Alberta, Canada. (1999) 23–32
14. Lester, J.C., Stone, B.A. and Stelling, G.D.: Lifelike pedagogical agents for mixed-initiative problem solving in constructivist learning environments. User Modeling and User-Adapted Interaction. **9(1–2)** (1999) 1–44
15. Resnik, P.: Evaluating multilingual gisting of web pages. In Papers from the 1997 AAAI Symposium on Cross-Language Text and Speech Retrieval, Stanford, CA. (1997) 189–195
16. Walker, M., Litman, D., Kamm, C. and Abella, A.: PARADISE: A framework for evaluating spoken dialogue agents. In Proceedings of the 35th Annual Meeting of the Association of Computational Linguistics. (1997)
17. Whitelock, P.J., Wood, M.M., Chandler, B.J., Holden, N. and Horsfall, H.J.: Strategies for interactive machine translation: The experience and implications of the UMIST Japanese project. In Proceedings of the 11th International Conference on Computational Linguistics. (1986) 25–29

A Self-Learning Method of Parallel Texts Alignment

António Ribeiro[1], Gabriel Lopes[1], and João Mexia[2]

[1] Universidade Nova de Lisboa, Faculdade de Ciências e Tecnologia,
Departamento de Informática, Quinta da Torre,
P-2825-114 Monte da Caparica, Portugal
{ambar,gpl}@di.fct.unl.pt
[2] Universidade Nova de Lisboa, Faculdade de Ciências e Tecnologia,
Departamento de Matemática, Quinta da Torre,
P-2825-114 Monte da Caparica, Portugal

Abstract. This paper describes a language independent method for alignment of parallel texts that re-uses acquired knowledge. The system extracts word translation equivalents and re-uses them as correspondence points in order to enhance the alignment of parallel texts. Points that may cause misalignment are filtered using confidence bands of linear regression analysis instead of heuristics, which are not theoretically reliable. Homographs bootstrap the alignment process so as to build the primary word translation lexicon. At each step, the previously acquired lexicon is re-used so as to repeatedly make finer-grained alignments and produce more reliable translation lexicons.

1 Introduction

In order to compile bilingual dictionaries automatically, either for cross-language information retrieval, machine translation or lexicography research, *parallel texts* (texts that are mutual translations) have proven to be valuable sources of information. These texts are *aligned* first, i.e. the various pieces of text are put into correspondence. This is usually done by finding *correspondence points* – sequences of characters with the same form in both texts (*homographs*, e.g. numbers, proper names, punctuation marks), similar forms (*cognates*, e.g. *Comissão* and *Comisión*) or even previously known translations (e.g. *data* and *fecha*).

An alignment algorithm is presented in [5] that uses term translations as correspondence points between English and Chinese. In [8], texts are aligned using correspondence points taken either from orthographic cognates [13] or from a seed translation lexicon. However, both approaches use statistically unsupported heuristics to filter noisy points. Although the heuristics may be intuitively quite acceptable and may improve the alignment precision, they are just heuristics without a theoretical background. This is a recurrent problem in previous work ([5], [8], [14]).

[11] proposes a method to filter candidate correspondence points generated from homograph words which occur with equal frequencies in parallel text segments. It

J.S. White (Ed.): AMTA 2000, LNAI 1934, pp. 30–39, 2000.
© Springer-Verlag Berlin Heidelberg 2000

uses the *statistically defined* Confidence Bands [15] of Linear Regression Lines formed by the candidate correspondence points, recurring to no heuristic filters as in previous work. It extends previous work in [9] and [10].

In this paper, we will present a method of re-using extracted word[1] equivalents in order to generate further candidate correspondence points for parallel texts alignment. The method becomes recursive as the newly acquired word translation equivalents may be re-used by the alignment method. Noisy points are filtered out when they lie outside the *confidence bands*. In this way, we are able to enhance the alignment and the extracted bilingual lexicon.

The following section will discuss related work. The method is described in sections 3 and 4. We evaluate and compare the results in section 5. Finally, we present the conclusions and future work.

2 Background

There have been two mainstreams for parallel text alignment. One assumes that translations have proportional sizes; the other tries to use lexical information in parallel texts to generate candidate correspondence points. Both use some notion of correspondence points.

In early work, [1] and [6], sentences were aligned till they had a proportional number of words and characters, respectively. However, these algorithms tended to break down when sentence boundaries were not clearly marked. Full stops do not always mark sentence boundaries.

Using lexical information, [2] showed that *cheap* alignment of text segments was still possible exploiting orthographic cognates [13] instead of sentence delimiters. They became the new candidate correspondence points. During the alignment, some were discarded because they lied outside an *empirically* estimated bounded search space, required for time and space reasons.

[7] also needed clearly delimited sentences. Words with *similar distributions* become the candidate correspondence points. Two sentences were aligned if the number of correspondence points associating them was greater than an *empirically* defined threshold: "[...] more than some minimum number of times [...]" ([7], p.128).

The requirement for clear sentence boundaries was dropped in [4] on a case-study for English-Chinese. Instead, they used vectors that stored distances between consecutive occurrences of a word (DK-vec's). Candidate correspondence points were identified from words with *similar* distance vectors and noisy points were filtered using some *heuristics*. Later, in [5], the algorithm used extracted terms to compile a list of reliable pairs of translations. Those pairs whose distribution similarity is above a *threshold* become candidate correspondence points (named potential anchor points). These points are further constrained not to be "too far away" from the diagonal of a rectangle whose sides sizes are proportional to the lengths of the texts in each language.

---

[1] It is not the purpose of this paper to handle term equivalents.

Sentences were aligned in [14] using isolated cognates as candidate correspondence points, i.e. cognates that were not mistaken for others within a text window. Some were filtered out if they either lied outside an *empirically* defined search space, named a corridor, or were "not in line" with their neighbours.

Candidate correspondence points obtained from orthographic cognates were also filtered in [8]. A maximum point ambiguity level filters points outside a search space, a maximum point dispersion filters points too distant from a line formed by candidate correspondence points and a maximum angle deviation filters points that tend to slope this line too much.

Whether the filtering of candidate correspondence points is done prior to alignment or during it, we all want to find reliable correspondence points. They provide the basic means for extracting reliable information from parallel texts. However, as far as we learned from the above papers, current methods have repeatedly used *statistically unsupported heuristics* to filter out noisy points. For instance, the "golden translation diagonal" is mentioned in all of them but none attempts filtering noisy points using *statistically* defined confidence bands.

3   Correspondence Points Filters

3.1   Source Parallel Texts

We worked with a mixed parallel corpus consisting of texts selected at random from the Official Journal of the European Communities[2] [3] and from The Court of Justice of the European Communities (http://curia.eu.int) in eleven languages[3].

Table 1. Words per sub-corpus (average per text inside brackets; markups discarded)[4].

Language	Written Questions	Debates	Judgements	Total
		Sub-corpus		
da	259k (52k)	2,0M (395k)	16k (3k)	2250k
de	234k (47k)	1,8M (368k)	15k (3k)	2088k
el	272k (54k)	1,9M (387k)	16k (3k)	2222k
en	263k (53k)	2,1M (417k)	16k (3k)	2364k
es	292k (58k)	2,2M (439k)	18k (4k)	2507k
fi	---	---	13k (3k)	13k
fr	310k (62k)	2,2M (447k)	19k (4k)	2564k
it	279k (56k)	1,9M (375k)	17k (3k)	2171k
nl	275k (55k)	2,1M (428k)	16k (3k)	2431k
pt	284k (57k)	2,1M (416k)	17k (3k)	2381k
sv	---	---	15k (3k)	15k
Total	2468k (55k)	18,4M (408k)	177k (3k)	21005k

For each language, we included:

---

[2] Danish (da), Dutch (nl), English (en), French (fr), German (de), Greek (el), Italian (it), Portuguese (pt) and Spanish (es).

[3] The same languages as those in footnote 2 plus Finnish (fi) and Swedish (sv).

[4] No Written Questions and Debates texts for Finnish and Swedish are available in ELRA (1997) since the respective countries were not still part of the European Union in 1992-4.

- five texts with Written Questions asked by members of the European Parliament to the European Commission and their corresponding answers (average: about 60k words or 100 pages / text);
- five texts with records of the Debates in the European Parliament (average: about 400k words or more than 600 pages / text);
- five texts with judgements of The Court of Justice of the European Communities (average: about 3k words or 5 pages / text).

In order to reduce the number of possible pairs of parallel texts from 110 sets (11 languages×10) to a more manageable size of 10 sets, we decided to take Portuguese as the kernel language of all pairs.

3.2   Generating Candidate Correspondence Points

We bootstrap the alignment process generating candidate correspondence points from *homographs with equal frequencies* in two parallel texts segments. Homographs, as a naive and particular form of cognate words, are likely translations (e.g. *México* in some European languages).

Table 2. Average number of homographs with equal frequencies per pair of parallel texts (average percentage of homographs inside brackets).

Pair	Written Questions	Debates	Judgements	Average
pt-da	2,8k (4,9%)	2,5k (0,6%)	0,3k (8,1%)	2,5k (1,1%)
pt-de	2,7k (5,1%)	4,2k (1,0%)	0,4k (7,9%)	4,0k (1,5%)
pt-el	2,3k (4,0%)	1,9k (0,5%)	0,3k (6,9%)	1,9k (0,8%)
pt-en	2,7k (4,8%)	2,8k (0,7%)	0,3k (6,2%)	2,7k (1,1%)
pt-es	4,1k (7,1%)	7,8k (1,9%)	0,7k (15,2%)	7,4k (2,5%)
pt-fi	---	---	0,2k (5,2%)	0,2k (5,2%)
pt-fr	2,9k (5,0%)	5,1k (1,2%)	0,4k (9,4%)	4,8k (1,6%)
pt-it	3,1k (5,5%)	5,4k (1,3%)	0,4k (9,6%)	5,2k (1,8%)
pt-nl	2,6k (4,5%)	4,9k (1,2%)	0,3k (8,3%)	4,7k (1,6%)
pt-sv	---	---	0,3k (6,9%)	0,3k (6,9%)
Average	2,9k (5,1%)	4,4k (1,1%)	0,4k (8,4%)	4,2k (1,5%)

(Sub-corpus spans the Written Questions, Debates, and Judgements columns.)

For average size texts (e.g. the Written Questions), these words account for about 5% of the total (about 3k words / text) and varies according to language similarity. These words end up being mainly numbers and names. Here are a few examples from a parallel Portuguese–Spanish text: *2002* (numbers, dates), *Euratom* (acronyms), *Carlos* (proper names), *Portugal* (names of countries), *Guadalajara* (names of cities), *p* (abbreviations), *República* (common vocabulary words).

Each pair of texts gives a set of candidate correspondence points from which we draw a line based on linear regression. Points are defined using the co-ordinates of the word positions in each parallel text. For example, if the first occurrence of the homograph word *México* occurs at word position 60311 in the Portuguese text and at 61940 in the Spanish parallel text, then the point co-ordinates are (60311,61940). Points may adjust themselves well to the linear regression line or may be dispersed around it. So, we use firstly a simple filter based on the histogram of the distances between the expected and real positions to remove extreme points. After that, we use a finer-grained filter based on *statistically* defined confidence bands of linear regression lines.

3.3 Eliminating Extreme Points

In Fig. 1, there are noisy points because their respective homographs appear in positions quite apart, e.g. the word *último* in pt word position 940 (Point A) was paired with the es word position 2810:

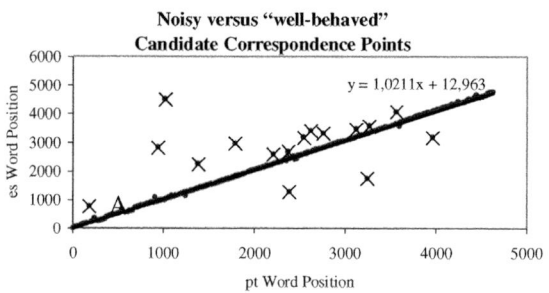

Fig. 1. Noisy candidate correspondence points (marked with an ×) versus "well-behaved" candidate correspondence points "in line". The linear regression equation is shown on the top right corner.

We should feel reluctant to accept these pairings and that is what the first filter does. It filters out those points which are clearly quite far apart from their *expected* positions to be considered as reliable correspondence points.

Table 3. A sample of the distances between expected and real positions of the noisy points.

		Positions		
Word	pt	es	es Expected	Distance
940	último	2810	973	1837
1793	mediante	2965	1844	112
2371	para	2668	2434	234

Expected distances are computed from the linear regression line equation $y = ax + b$, where a is the line slope and b is the Y-axis intercept (the value of y when x is 0), substituting x for the Portuguese word position. For Fig. 1, the expected word position for the word *último* at pt word position 940 is $1.0211 \times 940 + 12.963 = 973$ and the distance between its expected and real positions is $| 973 - 2810 | = 1837$.

If we draw a histogram ranging from the smallest to the largest distance, we get:

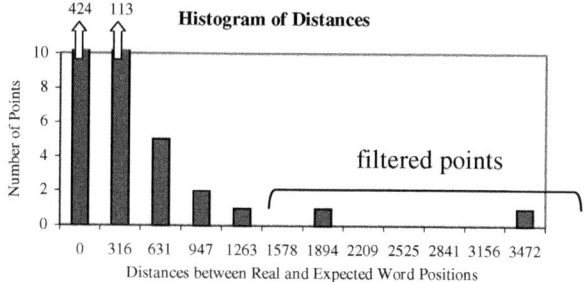

Fig. 2. Histogram of the distances between expected and real word positions.

With this histogram, we are able to identify those words which are too far apart from their expected positions and filter them out of the candidate correspondence points set.

3.4 Linear Regression Line Confidence Bands

Confidence bands of linear regression lines [15] help us to identify reliable points, i.e. points which belong to regression line with a great confidence level (99.9%).
The figure below shows an example of filtering using the confidence band:

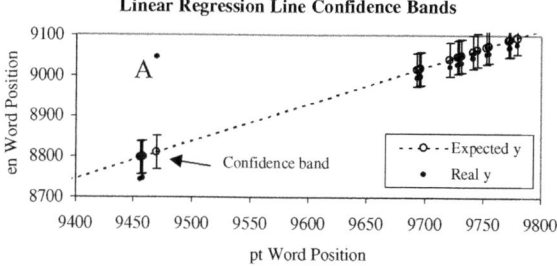

Fig. 3. Confidence bands. Point A lies outside the confidence band. It will be filtered out.

The confidence band is the *error* admitted at an x co-ordinate of a linear regression line. A point (x,y) is considered outside a linear regression line with a confidence level of 99.9% if its y co-ordinate does not lie within [$ax + b - error(x)$; $ax + b + error(x)$], where $ax + b$ is the linear regression line equation and $error(x)$ is the error admitted at the x co-ordinate. The upper and lower limits of the interval are given by an equation given in [15], p. 385.

Here is a summary of the recursive alignment algorithm:
1. Take two parallel texts A and B;
2. Define the texts' beginnings – the point (0,0) – and ends – the point (length of text A, length of text B) – as the extremes of the initial parallel text segment;

3. Consider as candidate correspondence points those defined both by homograph and equivalent words (if an extracted bilingual word lexicon is already available) which occur with the same frequency within the parallel text segment;
4. Filter out extreme points using the Histogram technique;
5. Filter out points which lie outside the confidence bands of the regression line;
6. For each sub-segment defined by two consecutive correspondence points, repeat steps 3 to 6;
7. Extract translation equivalents from the aligned parallel text segments into a bilingual lexicon;
8. Repeat from step 2.

4 Extracting Translation Equivalents

The key issue in the extraction of translation equivalents is to find a correlation between the occurrences of terms in parallel texts. In general, if two terms appear more often together than isolated, then they should be equivalents.

We start by building a contingency table for each pair of Portuguese–Spanish words (see Table 4). These tables store the *number of segments* that contain (a) both words, (b) the Portuguese word but not the Spanish word, (c) the Spanish word but not the Portuguese word and (d) neither word:

Table 4. Contingency table for *Comissão – Comisión. n* is the total number of segments.

n:1671	*Comisión* (25)	× *Comisión*
Comissão (23)	(a) 16	(b) 7
× *Comissão*	(c) 9	(d) 1639

Recent experiments with more than twenty measures of similarity have shown that the following measures give more correct translation equivalent.

Table 5. Performance of the best measures of similarity.

Measure of Similarity	Precision Equivalent	+Near Misses
Average Mutual Information	75,6%	79,6%
Weighted Mutual Information	75,6%	81,2%
Likelihood Ratio	75,6%	80,8%

Table 6 shows a sample of the top 50 using the Likelihood Ratio. Although the algorithm finds many correct equivalents out of the 100 best ranked pairs (about 90%), there are still "near misses". A "near miss" is a pair of words which are not mutual translations but which belongs to a collocation that is a translation equivalent. E.g. *DO* belongs to the collocation *ACORDÃO DO TRIBUNAL DE JUSTIÇA* ('Judgement of the Court') and *SENTENCIA* belongs to *SENTENCIA DEL TRIBUNAL DE JUSTICIA*, which are mutual translations.

Table 6. Sample of word translation equivalents. f(pt,es) is the joint frequency of occurrence.

pt Word	es Word	f(pt,es)	f(pt)	f(es)
¶	¶	168	206	214
ACÓRDÃO	SENTENCIA	1	1	1
DO	SENTENCIA	1	1	1
TRIBUNAL	TRIBUNAL	3	3	3
DE	DE	3	3	3
Setembro	septiembre	2	2	2
Incumprimento	Incumplimiento	1	1	1
do	del	15	22	29
processo	procedimiento	2	3	2
Não	Por	2	4	2

5   Evaluation

We ran our alignment algorithm on the parallel texts of 10 language pairs as described in section 3.1, using only homographs with equal frequencies:

Table 7. Average number of correspondence points in the first non-misalignment (average ratio of filtered and initial candidate correspondence points inside brackets).

Pair	Written Questions	Debates	Judgements	Average
pt-da	128 (5%)	56 (2%)	114 (35%)	63 (2%)
pt-de	124 (5%)	99 (2%)	53 (15%)	102 (3%)
pt-el	118 (5%)	115 (6%)	60 (20%)	115 (6%)
pt-en	88 (3%)	102 (4%)	50 (19%)	101 (4%)
pt-es	59 (1%)	55 (1%)	143 (21%)	56 (1%)
pt-fi	---	---	60 (26%)	60 (26%)
pt-fr	148 (5%)	113 (2%)	212 (49%)	117 (2%)
pt-it	117 (4%)	104 (2%)	25 (6%)	105 (2%)
pt-nl	120 (5%)	73 (1%)	53 (15%)	77 (2%)
pt-sv	---	---	74 (23%)	74 (23%)
Average	113 (4%)	90 (2%)	84 (23%)	92 (2%)

We then proceeded the alignment algorithm with a smaller set of files for which we could extract translation equivalents.

Table 8. Variation in the number of words / segment for a set of Portuguese–Spanish texts.

Filename	Previous	Current	Variation
C-170-98 pt.txt	2,8	2,0	-27%
C-171-96 pt.txt	2,9	2,1	-27%
C-233-97 pt.txt	2,5	1,7	-32%
C-368-97 pt.txt	2,5	1,9	-22%
C-431-97 pt.txt	2,4	1,8	-25%
Average	2,7	2,0	-27%

After one more step, we compared the results with the ones reported in [10] and found that, for the set of files we used, we got an average of about 40% more correspondence points with a single "re-feed" of the extracted lexicon (see Table 8).

6 Conclusions

Confidence bands of linear regression lines help us identify reliable correspondence points without using empirically found or statistically unsupported heuristics. This paper presents a purely statistical approach to the selection of candidate correspondence points parallel texts alignment without recurring to heuristics as in previous work. The alignment is not restricted to sentence or paragraph level for which clearly delimited boundaries markers would be needed.

Moreover, the methodology does not depend on the way candidate correspondence points are generated, i.e. although we used homographs and extracted word translation equivalents which occur with equal frequencies in parallel texts, we could have also bootstrapped the process using a small bilingual lexicon to identify equivalents of words or expressions ([16], 5], [8]). When it comes to distant languages like English and Chinese where the number of homographs is reduced, the extraction of translation equivalents becomes more important. In this paper, we have proposed a set of similarity measures that have proven to select reliable translation equivalents.

As this alignment algorithm is not restricted to paragraphs or sentences, 100% alignment precision may be degraded by language specific term order policies in small segments. The method is language and character-set independent and does not assume any a priori language knowledge (namely, small bilingual lexicons), text tagging, well defined sentence or paragraph boundaries nor one-to-one translation of sentences.

7 Future Work

We plan to work on the extraction of multiword units translation equivalents from parallel Portuguese–Chinese texts. We intend to use two different approaches: one based on the comparison of multiword units extracted from each parallel text individually using a methodology described in [11] and on the reconstruction of multiword units translation equivalents based on the "near misses".

8 Acknowledgements

This research was partially supported by a grant from Fundação para a Ciência e Tecnologia / Praxis XXI. We would like to thank the anonymous referees for their valuable comments on the paper.

References

1. Brown, P., Lai, J., Mercer, R.: Aligning Sentences in Parallel Corpora. In: Proceedings of the 29th Annual Meeting of the Association for Computational Linguistics, Berkeley, California, U.S.A. (1991) 169–176
2. Church, K.: Char_align: A Program for Aligning Parallel Texts at the Character Level. In: Proceedings of the 31st Annual Meeting of the Association for Computational Linguistics, Columbus, Ohio, U.S.A. (1993) 1–8
3. ELRA (European Language Resources Association) (1997) Multilingual Corpora for Co-operation, Disk 2 of 2, Paris, France
4. Fung, P., McKeown, K.: Aligning Noisy Parallel Corpora across Language Groups: Word Pair Feature Matching by Dynamic Time Warping. In: Technology Partnerships for Crossing the Language Barrier: Proceedings of the First Conference of the Association for Machine Translation in the Americas, Columbia, Maryland, U.S.A. (1994) 81–88
5. Fung, P., McKeown, K.: A Technical Word- and Term-Translation Aid Using Noisy Parallel Corpora across Language Groups. In: Machine Translation, Vol. 12, numbers 1–2 (Special issue) (1997) 53–87
6. Gale, W., Church, K.: A Program for Aligning Sentences in Bilingual Corpora. In: Proceedings of the 29th Annual Meeting of the Association for Computational Linguistics, Berkeley, California, U.S.A. (1991) 177–184 (short version). Also in: Computational Linguistics, Vol. 19, number 1 (1993) 75–102 (long version)
7. Kay, M., Röscheisen, M.: Text-Translation Alignment. In: Computational Linguistics, Vol. 19, number 1 (1993) 121–142
8. Melamed, I.: Bitext Maps and Alignment via Pattern Recognition. In: Computational Linguistics, Vol. 25, number 1 (1999) 107–130
9. Ribeiro, A., Lopes, G., Mexia, J.: Using Confidence Bands for Alignment with Hapaxes. In: Proceedings of the 2000 International Conference on Artificial Intelligence (IC-AI' 2000), Las Vegas, U.S.A.. CSREA Press, U.S.A. (2000)
10. Ribeiro, A., Lopes, G., Mexia, J.: Linear Regression Based Alignment of Parallel Texts Using Homograph Words. In: Horn, W. (ed.): ECAI 2000. Proceedings of the 14th European Conference on Artificial Intelligence, Berlin, Germany. IOS Press, Amsterdam, Netherlands (2000)
11. Ribeiro, A., Lopes, G., Mexia, J.: Using Confidence Bands for Parallel Texts Alignment. In: Proceedings of the 38th Annual Meeting of the Association for Computational Linguistics (ACL 2000) (2000, to appear)
12. da Silva, J., Dias, G., Guilloré, S., Lopes, J.: Using Localmaxs Algorithms for the Extraction of Contiguous and Non-contiguous Multiword Lexical Units. In: Barahona, P., Alferes, J. (eds.): Progress in Artificial Intelligence – Lecture Notes in Artificial Intelligence, Vol. 1695. Springer-Verlag, Berlin Heidelberg New York (1999) 113–132
13. Simard, M., Foster, G., Isabelle, P.: Using Cognates to Align Sentences in Bilingual Corpora. In: Proceedings of the Fourth International Conference on Theoretical and Methodological Issues in Machine Translation TMI-92, Montreal, Canada (1992) 67–81
14. Simard, M., Plamondon, P.: Bilingual Sentence Alignment: Balancing Robustness and Accuracy. In: Machine Translation, Vol. 13, number 1 (1998) 59–80
15. Wonnacott, T., Wonnacott, R.: Introductory Statistics, 5th edition, John Wiley & Sons, New York Chichester Brisbane Toronto Singapore (1990)
16. Wu, D.: Aligning a Parallel English–Chinese Corpus Statistically with Lexical Criteria. In: Proceedings of the 32nd Annual Conference of the Association for Computational Linguistics, Las Cruces, New Mexico, U.S.A. (1994) 80–87

Handling Structural Divergences and Recovering Dropped Arguments in a Korean/English Machine Translation System*

Chung-hye Han[1], Benoit Lavoie[2], Martha Palmer[1], Owen Rambow[3],
Richard Kittredge[2], Tanya Korelsky[2], Nari Kim[4], and Myunghee Kim[2]

[1] Dept. of Computer and Information Sciences/IRCS
Univ. of Pennsylvania, Philadelphia, PA 19104, USA
{chunghye, mpalmer}@linc.cis.upenn.edu
[2] CoGenTex, Inc., Ithaca, NY 14850-1589, USA
{benoit, richard, tanya, myunghee}@cogentex.com
[3] ATT Labs-Research, B233, Florham Park, NJ 07932, USA
rambow@research.att.com
[4] Konan Technology, Inc., Seoul 135-090, Korea
nari@konantech.co.kr

Abstract. This paper describes an approach for handling structural divergences and recovering dropped arguments in an implemented Korean to English machine translation system. The approach relies on canonical predicate-argument structures (or dependency structures), which provide a suitable pivot representation for the handling of structural divergences and the recovery of dropped arguments. It can also be converted to and from the interface representations of many off-the-shelf parsers and generators.

1 Introduction

This paper describes an approach for handling structural divergences ([1,3,4, 8]) and recovering dropped arguments for Korean to English translation. Given that the two languages are very different from each other in structure, many challenging problems arise, demanding sophisticated linguistic modeling. The basic elements of our approach include:

- Transfer rules based on syntactic lexico-structural transfer ([8]);
- Conversion rules using a Korean predicate-argument lexicon for converting parsed syntactic structures produced by an off the-shelf Korean parser ([12]) to the syntactic structures used for transfer;

---

* The work reported in this paper was supported by contract DAAD 17-99-C-0008 awarded by the Army Research Lab to CoGenTex, Inc., with the University of Pennsylvania as a subcontractor and NSF Grant - VerbNet, IIS 98-00658. Owen Rambow's contribution to this paper was made when he was with CoGenTex, Inc. and Nari Kim's contribution was made when she was a visiting researcher at IRCS, UPenn.

J.S. White (Ed.): AMTA 2000, LNAI 1934, pp. 40–53, 2000.

– Generation rules using an English realization lexicon for recovering dropped arguments after transfer.

The current implementation and processing of the transfer, conversion and generation rules is done uniformly, using a syntactic lexico-structural based framework ([5]). Declarative transformation specifications indicate how the lexemes and their relevant syntactic structures (essentially, their syntactic projection along with syntactic/semantic features) are mapped from one level to another. A similar approach was used in previous work for English to Arabic and English to French translations ([8,9]).

The corpus for this project is a set of Korean/English parallel texts that consist of battle scenario message traffic and military language training manual. These contain information on typical military events such as troop movement, intelligence gathering, and equipment supplies, among others. Each half has roughly 50,000 word tokens, and 6000 sentences.

This paper is structured as follows. In section 2, we introduce some linguistic issues that pose problems for Korean/English MT. In section 3, we present a brief overview of the implemented system. Section 4 presents the linguistic knowledge bases used for conversion, transfer and argument recovery. We conclude with sections 5 and 6 with a brief comparison to different approaches in other MT systems (e.g., LCS and CCLINC) and a discussion of future work. Although our system handles transfer in both Korean-to-English and English-to-Korean directions, in this paper we mainly concentrate on the Korean-to-English direction for the sake of exposition.

2   Some Linguistic Issues in Korean/English Machine Translation

While English canonically has rigid subject-verb-object (SVO) order, Korean is a verb-final language with free word order. For instance, ditransitive sentences in English have 'subject-verb-indirect object-direct object' order, as shown in the target sentence in Table 1. The corresponding Korean sentence can have 'direct object-indirect object-subject-verb' order, as shown in the source sentence in Table 1.[1] In our system, the grammatical functions of argument NPs are identified by the use of Yoon's Korean parser and conversion rules using the predicate-argument lexicon.

Unlike English, argument NPs can be deleted in Korean. For instance, in the source sentence in Table 2, which is a conditional sentence, the subject NP in the *if*-clause has been deleted and the subject NP and the object NP in the main clause have been deleted. Ideally, all the missing arguments should be identified in the output as in the target sentence in Table 2. With the addition of a discourse component, the references of the missing arguments can be restored.

---

[1] Korean examples in this paper are romanized for convenience.

Table 1. Word Order

SOURCE: chuka kongkwupmul-eul 103 ceonwiciweontaetae-eke saryeongpu-ka cueossta.	
GLOSS: additional supply-Acc 103 FSB-Dat headquarter-Nom gave	
TARGET: Headquarters gave 103rd FSB additional supplies.	
OUTPUT: Headquarters gave an additional supply to a 103 forward support battalion.	

In our system, the dropped arguments are recovered for the English translation output using English generation rules.[2]

Table 2. Dropped Arguments and Morphology

SOURCE: IBP hwail-eul keomsaekhaci moshaess-tamyeon cikeum tasi ponaekessta.	
GLOSS: IBP file-Acc retrieve could_not-if now again will_send	
TARGET: if (NP1) could not retrieve IBP file, (NP2) will send (NP3) again now.	
OUTPUT: If one can not retrieve an IBP file, one will send it again now.	

In addition to word order difference and dropped argument recovery, there are many transfer issues that arise from structural divergences, some of which will be presented in section 4.3.

3 Overview of the System

Figure 1 illustrates the major transformation steps in our system. Korean or English sentences (depending on what the source language is) are first parsed. The parser output is then reformatted and converted into *Deep Syntactic Structure* (DSyntS) based on Meaning Text Theory (MTT) ([7]) (See below for more details). These Korean or English DSyntSs are then transferred respectively into English or Korean DSyntS (depending on what the target language is) that are finally realized as English or Korean sentences.

The DSyntS representations are composed of nodes labeled by lexemes which correspond to meaning-bearing words (nouns, verbs, adjectives, adverbs) and directed arcs with dependency relation labels. The subject is labeled as 'I', the direct object as 'II' and the indirect object as 'III'; label 'ATTR' covers all adjuncts. Function words such as determiners, semantically empty auxiliary verbs, and grammatical morphology are represented through features on the node labels. This level of representation is well suited to MT since it abstracts away

---

[2] As the anonymous reviewer correctly pointed out, the reference of *one* in the antecedent clause and the reference of *one* in the consequent clause must be different.

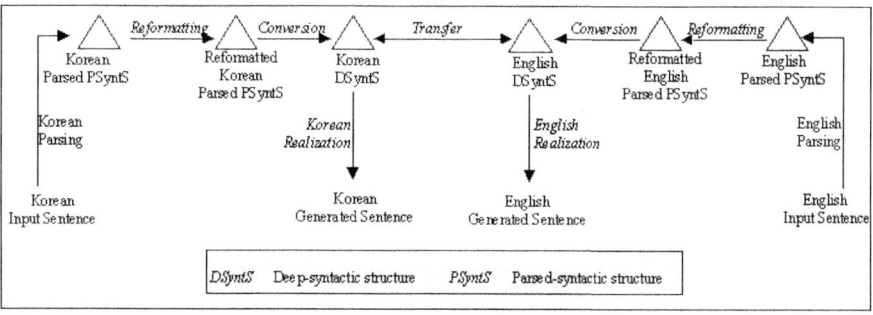

Fig. 1. Main Translation Steps

from superficial grammatical differences between languages, such as linear order and the usage of function words. For the sake of illustration, a DSyntS representation corresponding to the sentence *John often eats beans* is given in tree format below.

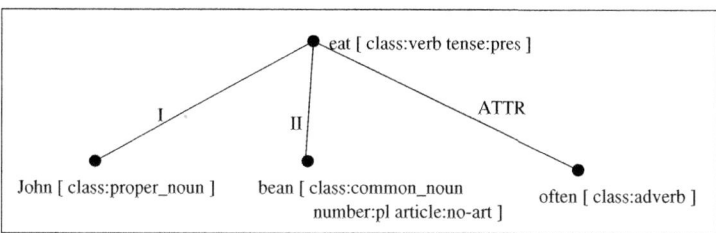

Fig. 2. DSyntS for *John often eats beans*

In our system, the conversion, transfer and realization is done uniformly via lexico-structural processing ([5]). The Korean parsing is done using Yoon's statistical Korean dependency parser ([12]), the English parsing is done using the Collins parser ([2]) and the Korean and English realization is done using RealPro ([6]).

4   Linguistic Knowledge Base

4.1   Predicate-Argument Lexicon

The predicate-argument lexicon contains subcategorization information for verbs and adjectives. The types of arguments (actants) include subjects (NP_0), direct objects (NP_1), indirect objects (NP_2), sentential complements (S_1) and optional arguments.

Example entries in the Korean predicate-argument lexicon are illustrated graphically in Figure 3. NP arguments are listed with case or adverbial postpositions as features: e.g., [case:] or [adv-case:]. Case postpositions include nominative and accusative case inflections and adverbial postpositions include those inflections that roughly correspond to English prepositions: e.g. {e-Ke} ('to'), {Ro} ('to'), {Kwa} ('with'), {e-Seo} ('from'). Sentential complements are listed with the relevant verbal inflectional morphology as a feature [mode-string:]. Actants with an asterisk (e.g., NP_1*) are optional arguments, and they count as arguments only when they are present in the sentence. In contrast, actants without an asterisk are obligatory arguments, and when they are missing from sentences, they are counted as dropped arguments. Example entries in the Korean predicate-argument lexicon are illustrated graphically in Figure 3.

In principle, all arguments are syntactically optional in Korean given that they can be dropped in the appropriate discourse context. Having said this, what we mean by optional/obligatory arguments are those that are optional/obligatory in the predicate-argument structure. Under this definition, for instance, in *John left for Paris, John* is an obligatory argument, but *for Paris* is an optional argument.

As will be described in Section 4.2, the Korean predicate-argument lexicon is used as a guide for making argument/adjunct distinctions in the DSyntS representations which are the input to the transfer component. The English predicate argument lexicon plays an important role in recovering arguments in English translation output when the corresponding input Korean sentence has dropped arguments, as will be discussed in section 4.4.

4.2   Conversion Rules

As mentioned in section 3, the source structures used for the transfer consist of MTT-based DSyntS. In our previous system we were able to utilize off-the-shelf English parsers and convert their output to our transfer lexicon requirements ([9]). The same approach has worked here, this time with a pre-existing Korean parser ([12]). This parser assigns dependencies between two words using lexical association values estimated on the basis of co-occurrence data extracted from a 30 million word corpus. The co-occurrence data consist of pairs of nouns for compound noun analysis, and triplets of a verb, an associated noun and the postposition on the noun for dependency analysis of verbs and nouns.

Although Yoon's Korean parser was not designed with DSyntS in mind, the generic dependency structure it produces is often isomorphic to the corresponding DSyntS. When it is not isomorphic, lexico-structural transformations can

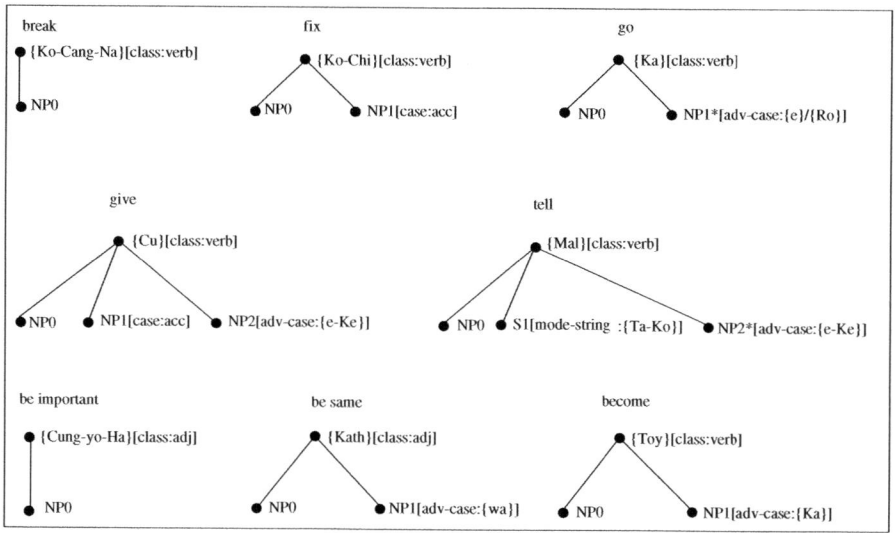

Fig. 3. Predicate-argument Lexicon for Korean

be used to fix the discrepancies. The tree on the left in Figure 4 illustrates Yoon's parser output for the source sentence in Table 2 formatted using a tree notation. The tree on the right in Figure 4 illustrates the corresponding DSyntS used for transfer.

The transformation, or conversion, necessary to produce the DSyntS from the Korean parser output illustrated in Figure 4 takes place in three separate stages:

- *Rewriting feature labels*: Where our system requires different feature labels, preprocessing rules such as those in Figure 5 simply replace the feature 'ppca:{Reul}' with 'case:acc'.
- *Making dependency relationships more explicit*: In Figure 4, Yoon's parser only specifies one relation (the relation 'OBJ' between '{Keom-Saek-Ha}' and '{Hwa-il}'). The Korean predicate-argument lexicon (defined in section 4.1) is used as a guide for more explicit dependency relationships. The rule in Figure 6 sets the dependency relation between 'Keom-Saek-Ha' and 'X' to 'II' if 'X' has accusative case.
- *Promoting features to lexemes and vice versa*: Some of the features found in Yoon's Korean parser are represented as lexemes in the corresponding DSyntS. In Figure 7, the features 'enco2:{Ta-Myeon}' and 'ax:{Mos-Ha}' in Yoon's parser output are transformed to lexemes '{Ta-Myeon}' and '{Mos-Ha}' in the corresponding DSyntS. The rule in Figure 7 promotes the feature 'enco2:{Ta-Myeon}' to a lexeme. Predicate-specific lexico-structural grammar rules are used to map Yoon's argument structure onto ours.

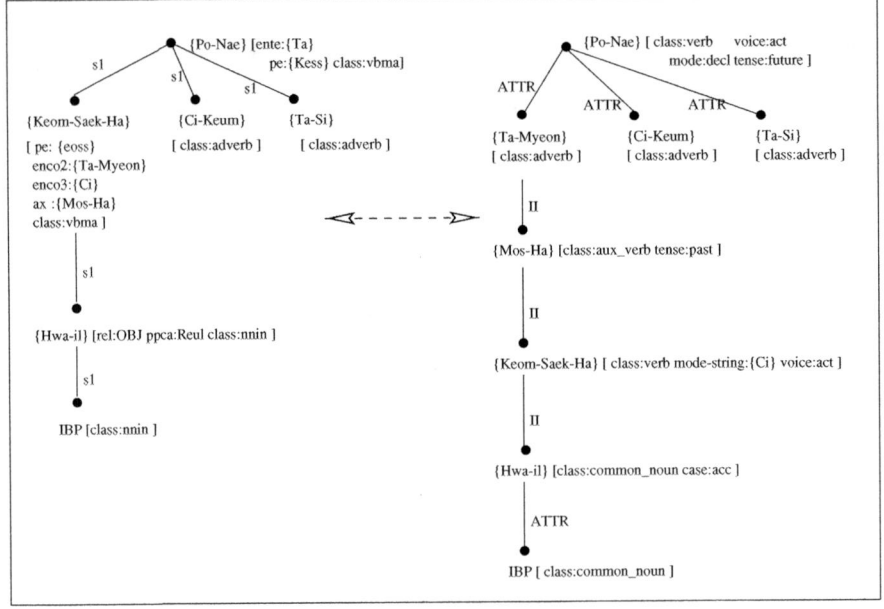

Fig. 4. Conversion from Reformatted Korean Parser Output to DSyntS

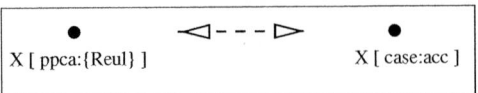

Fig. 5. Rewriting Feature Labels

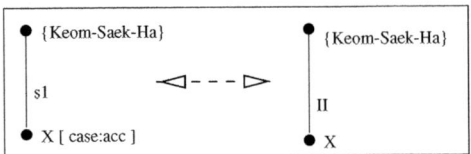

Fig. 6. Identifying the Dependency Relation

This conversion process has thus provided the additional argument/adjunct distinctions that allow the parser output to be matched against our transfer lexicon, by referencing the Korean predicate-argument lexicon.

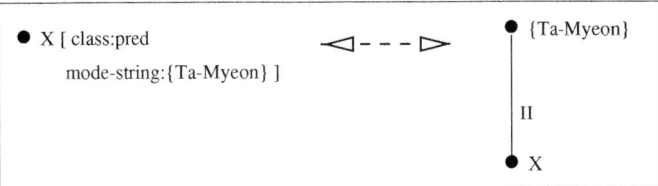

Fig. 7. Promoting Features to Lexemes and Vice Versa

4.3   Transfer Lexicon

The transfer formalism is based on DSyntS grammars that are independently motivated by source and target languages, and was previously used for transfer from English to French and English to Arabic ([8]). It relates DSyntS subtrees, anchored by lexemes of different languages, with projections that represent a context in which the source language lexeme is translated into the target language lexeme. Transfer is carried out by replacing a subtree in the source language DSyntS with another to which it is linked in the target language DSyntS. In the simplest case, the related subtrees are reduced to a single node: the root of the tree. The following example shows a relation between the Korean verb {*Po-Nae*} and the corresponding English verb *send*.

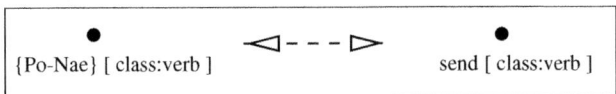

Fig. 8. Transferring Lexemes Directly

Additional contextual information is not required in this case since the two verbs share a common subcategorization frame. When applying such a rule for transfer, the nodes that are not present in the rule will remain unchanged after application of the rule. The target language realization grammars ensure that the proper word order for the target language is followed.

Multi-Word Transfer. When the translation of a lexeme (or a group of lexemes) results in a syntactically divergent structure in the target language, this divergence is represented in the transfer lexicon by including contextual information in the related subtrees.

For instance, a predicative adjective in Korean translates to copular *be* and the corresponding adjective in English: e.g., {*Cak-Ta*} ↔ *be small*. Such divergence necessitates a transfer rule that relates a single node anchored to one

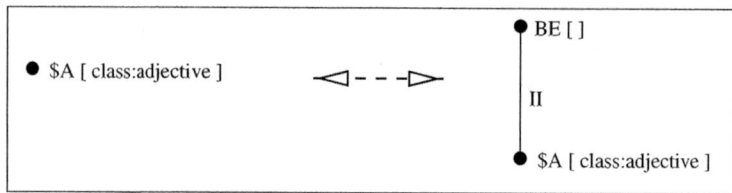

Fig. 9. Transferring Predicative Adjectives

lexeme and a subtree with more than one node. The rule given in Figure 9 handles the transfer between predicative adjectives in Korean and English.

Another example of syntactic divergence has to do with cases in which an inflection in one language translates to a lexical item in another language. For example, in Korean, the main verb in complement clauses has a verbal inflection which corresponds to the complementizer *that* in English. Our transfer rule that handles this divergence along with an example translation that uses this rule are given in Figure 10. We represent the verbal inflection as a feature [mode-string:Ta-Ko] on the verb node in the subordinate clause ($V2) and this node maps onto the corresponding verb and complementizer *that* in English.

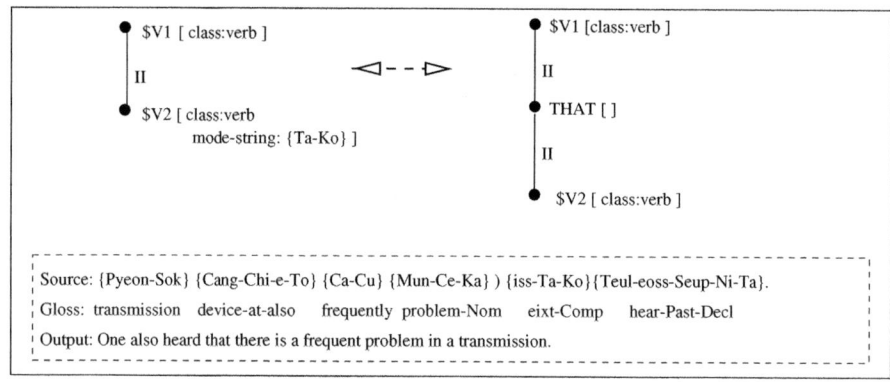

Fig. 10. Transferring Complementizer Inflection

An example of a more complicated structural divergence involves transferring a Korean complex NP whose head noun is lexicalized as an auxiliary noun {*Keos*} in the context of a copular to an English *to*-infinitive.[3] Our transfer rule that handles this divergence along with an example translation using this rule are given in Figure 11.

---

[3] Nouns that cannot stand alone are called *auxiliary nouns*. They must be modified by a clause or other nouns.

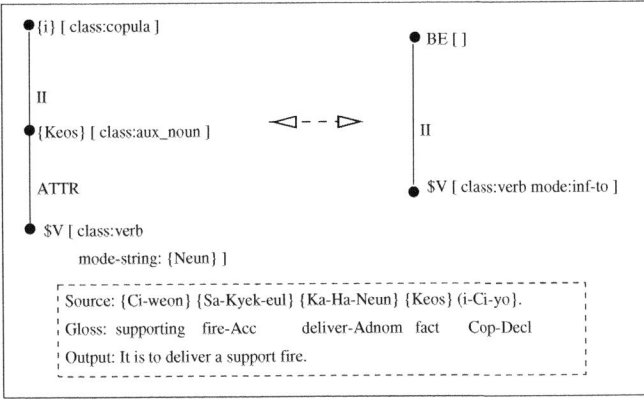

Fig. 11. Transferring Complex NP with Auxiliary Noun

Transfer rules can have variables (e.g., $V1, $V2 in Figure 10) instead of lexemes as nodes, allowing generalization of the rule application. Moreover, constraints on rule application can be introduced in the subtrees by means of features on the nodes. For instance, the feature [mode-string:{Neun}] in the transfer rule represented in Figure 11 restricts the rule application to source sentences containing a verb with inflectional morphology {-*Neun*}, which is an adnominal morpheme.

4.4 Argument Recovery Rules

In Korean, argument NPs can be dropped. When translating from Korean to English, the dropped arguments must be recovered in order to obtain grammatical English sentences. It is generally assumed that accurate translation of dropped arguments requires a discourse model. However, what type of discourse model is needed is not yet well understood. Our current translation model for Korean to English is based only on individual sentences and does not use a discourse model. Instead, we recover generic cases of dropped arguments by adding default pronouns for missing arguments using grammatical and lexical knowledge. For example, in Table 2, the three pronouns in the English translation, missing in the Korean sentence, have been recovered using only English grammatical and lexical knowledge: *If* **one** *can not retrieve an IBP file,* **one** *will send* **it** *again now.*

The recovery of dropped generic arguments is performed just before English realization, by preprocessing the English DSyntS obtained from the transfer of the corresponding Korean DSyntS. Figure 12 illustrates the result of the argument recovery processing applied to the English DSyntS generated after the transfer rules have applied to the example sentence in Table 2. Once again, the predicate-argument lexicon can be used as a reference to indicate the type of missing argument.

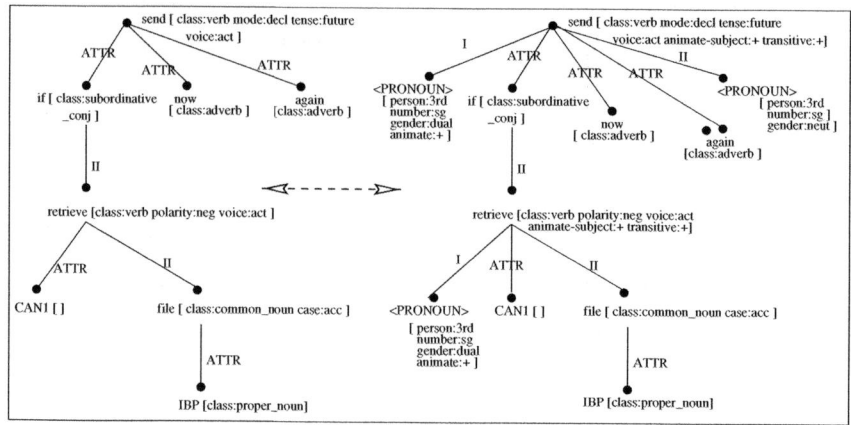

Fig. 12. Argument Recovery Transformation

Providing a filter for the argument is performed by using the following types of transformations, which currently do not take into account anaphoric dependencies:

- *Insertion of Missing Actant I*: This transformation involves adding, if missing, a 3rd person singular pronoun as actant I to a verb with mood indicative. Figure 13 illustrates a general case where a missing actant I can be recovered. Such a transformation is used in Figure 12 to add the actant I of 'retrieve' and 'send' (*If* **one/it** *can not retrieve ...* **one/it** *will send ...*). (Another rule determines whether or not the pronouns must be animate.)

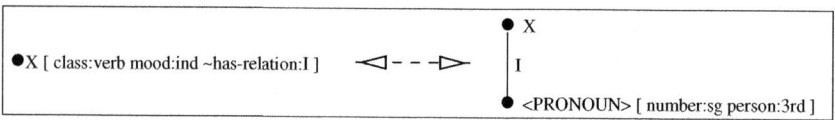

Fig. 13. Recovering Missing Actant I

- *Insertion of Missing Actant II*: This transformation involves adding, if missing, a 3rd person singular pronoun as actant II to a transitive verb of indicative mood and active voice. Figure 14 illustrates how a missing actant II can be recovered. Such a transformation is used in Figure 12 in order to add the actant II of 'send' (*... one will send* **it** *...*).
- *Determining Whether Pronouns are Animate or Not*: This transformation involves setting the animate feature of a pronoun in the subject position. Figure 15 illustrates how the animate feature associated with a recovered

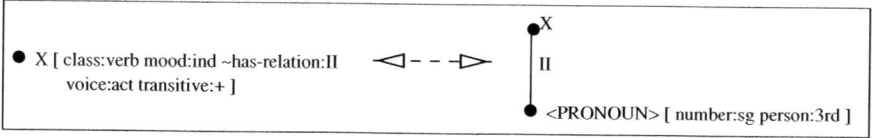

Fig. 14. Recovering Missing Actant II

pronoun can be determined in general. The transformation rule indicates how by unification, the value '?A' of the feature 'animate-subject:?A' assigned to a verb is passed to the pronoun. Such a transformation is used in Figure 12 to assign the feature 'animate:+' to the actant I of 'retrieve' and 'send' (*If* **one** *can not retrieve* ... **one** *will send* ...).

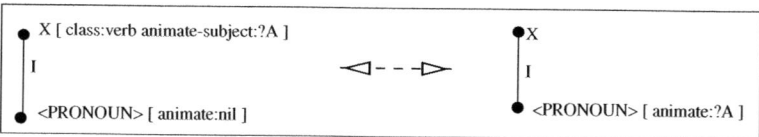

Fig. 15. Recovering of Animacy

4.5 Coverage

The current coverage of our linguistic knowledge base can be summarized as follows. Both the Korean and English predicate-argument lexicons cover 100% of the verbs and adjectives from our corpus. The transfer lexicon covers 100% of the word-to-word mappings, and 20% of these have currently been enriched for structural mapping and evaluated for the quality of the translations they produce. We should have 80% coverage by the end of August. In addition, we have a 20,000+ word bilingual lexicon for Korean/English provided by Systran, which contains subcategorization frame information for Korean, and word-to-word mappings to English. We will be enriching the Systran verb and adjective entries with the type of argument links that have been presented here.

The coverage for the Conversion Rules and Argument Recovery Rules is 100% of the small base set we tested for transfer (representing 20% of the corpus), although extension of the rules will be needed to cover the rest of the corpus. Since we have a parallel corpus, we have a Gold Standard for our target translations, and consider the translation is of suitable quality if it has the correct predicate argument structure, the expected lexemes and is grammatical.

5   Comparison to Other Approaches

A crucial part of an interlingua-based approach to MT, such as the LCS approach at the University of Maryland ([3]), and CCLINC at MIT's Lincoln Labs ([10]), is the mapping of a source language sentence to a language-independent intermediate representation, which serves as the basis for generating an output in the target language. The abstract interlingua has been argued to facilitate the development of a multilingual system, and to facilitate the handling of structural divergences. However, a disadvantage of the interlingua approach is the difficulty of reaching a consensus on criteria for truly language-independent representations. It is also necessary to develop special purpose language-specific parsers that can map the source language sentence onto the appropriate interlingua representation.

With our approach, there is no extra level of representation that mediates between source and target sentences. Instead, the source dependency parse tree is directly mapped to the target dependency tree. However, by basing our transfer rules on canonical predicate-argument structures with feature specifications, we provide a level of representation that can still capture the same structural divergences and many of the semantic generalizations traditionally associated with interlinguas ([8]). Our predicate-argument structures are in fact quite similar to the CCLINC "semantic frames," although somewhat flatter than LCS representations ([8]). In addition, we can much more readily utilize off-the-shelf parsers, as described above, and can also exploit statistical techniques for analyzing corpora and finding automatic alignments between parallel words and phrases ([9]). This provides the basis for our current experiments with the extraction of transfer lexicons from annotated bilingual corpora by decomposing tree structures into lexicalized subtrees ([11]).

6   Conclusion

We have described an approach for handling structural divergences and recovering dropped arguments for Korean to English machine translation. The common reliance on canonical predicate argument structure representations of lexical items provides the basis for our treatment of structural divergences and recovery of dropped arguments.

Our future plans include the development of a Korean TreeBank for our corpus which will be based on the hand corrected output of our Korean parser. We will also use the Korean and English parsers to help us construct a parallel, syntactically annotated corpus for automatic extraction of our lexico-structure transfer rules. The explicit annotation of empty arguments as well as the incorporation of a discourse model will allow a more principled recovery of implicit arguments.

Finally, we will extend the conversion rules and argument recovery rules to better cover the corpus, and enhance the machinery to improve the processing with larger knowledge bases.

References

1. Abeillé, A., Schabes, Y. and Joshi, A.K.: Using Lexicalized Tags for Machine Translation. In Proceedings of the International Conference on Computational Linguistics (COLING '90), Helsinki, Finland. (1990)
2. Collins, M.: Three Generative, Lexicalized Models for Statistical Parsing. In Proceedings of the 35th Annual Meeting of the Association for Computational Linguistics, Madrid, Spain. (1997)
3. Dorr, B. J.: Machine Translation: a View from the Lexicon. MIT Press, Boston, Mass. (1993)
4. Dorr, B. J.: Machine translation divergences: a formal description and proposed solution. Computational Linguistics **20(4):** (1994) 597–635
5. Lavoie, B., Kittredge, R., Korelsky, T. and Rambow, O.: A Framework for MT and Multilingual NLG Systems Based on Uniform Lexico-Structural Processing. In Proceedings of ANLP/NAACL 2000, Seattle, Washington. (2000)
6. Lavoie, B. and Rambow, O.: A Fast and Portable Realizer for Text Generation Systems. In Proceedings of the Conference on Applied Natural Language Processing (ANLP'97), Washington, DC. (1997)
7. Mel'čuk, I. A.: Dependency Syntax: Theory and Practice. State University of New York Press, New York. (1988)
8. Nasr, A., Rambow, O., Palmer, M. and Rosenzweig, J.: Enriching Lexical Transfer with Cross-Linguistic Semantic Features. In Proceedings of the Interlingua Workshop at the MT Summit, San Diego, California. (1997)
9. Palmer, M., Rambow, O. and Nasr, A.: Rapid prototyping of domain-specific machine translation system. In Proceedings of AMTA-98, Langhorne, PA, October. (1998)
10. Weinstein, C. J., Lee, Y. S., Seneff, S., Carlson, D. R. Carlson, B., Lynch, J. T., Hwang, J. T. and Kukolich, L. C.: Automated English/Korean Translation for Enhanced Coalition Communications. Lincoln Laboratory Journal. **10(1)** (1997) 35–60
11. Xia, F.: Extracting Tree Adjoining Grammars from Bracketed Corpora. In Proceedings of 5th Natural Language Processing Pacific Rim Symposium (NLPRS-99), Beijing, China. (1999)
12. Yoon, J., Kim, S. and Song, M.: New Parsing Method Using Global Association Table. In Proceedings of International Workshop on Parsing Technology. (1997)

A Machine Translation System
from English to American Sign Language

Liwei Zhao, Karin Kipper, William Schuler,
Christian Vogler, Norman Badler, and Martha Palmer

Department of Computer and Information Science
University of Pennsylvania, Philadelphia PA 19104-6389 USA
{lwzhao,kipper,schuler,cvogler,badler,mpalmer}@graphics.cis.upenn.edu

Abstract. Research in computational linguistics, computer graphics
and autonomous agents has led to the development of increasingly sophisticated communicative agents over the past few years, bringing new
perspective to machine translation research. The engineering of language-
based smooth, expressive, natural-looking human gestures can give us
useful insights into the design principles that have evolved in natural
communication between people. In this paper we prototype a machine
translation system from English to American Sign Language (ASL), taking into account not only linguistic but also visual and spatial information associated with ASL signs.

1   Introduction

As the third or fourth most widely used language in the United States [23],
American Sign Language (ASL) is the primary communication means used by
members of the North American deaf community. There is linguistic, psycholin-
guistic, and neurological evidence in favor of ASL being a fully developed natural
language [18]. It is not a derivative of English – it is a complete language with
its own unique grammar [11,28,30].

While the last ten years have seen an ever increasing development of machine translation systems for translating between major spoken natural languages, translation to and from ASL is virtually ignored by the machine translation community. Yet, ASL translation systems are very important to the deaf.
Systems that simply render spoken language as text are inadequate for two reasons: First, many deaf people in the United States have difficulties with reading
and writing English; in fact, some do not read above the fourth-grade level. A
text-based system would make it impossible for these people to follow and understand a conversation in real-time. Second, if spoken language is rendered as
text, all the information on intonation, pitch, and timing is lost, even though
this information is important (e.g., the reason why people prefer dubbed movies over subtitled movies). ASL, on the other hand, is capable of conveying
this information through the intensity of the signs and facial expressions. As a
result, a fully-functional ASL machine translation system would be far superior

J.S. White (Ed.): AMTA 2000, LNAI 1934, pp. 54–67, 2000.

to a text-based system when it comes to conveying all the nuances of spoken language.

ASL machine translation systems have been neglected largely because of the specialty of ASL as a natural language. Not so long ago ASL was still looked upon as 'merely gestures' – non-linguistic, pantomimic presentations of concrete concepts. For several years some researchers believed that ASL lacked any rigid structure on the sentence-level, which obviously made it very hard to translate any other natural language into ASL. To make things worse, ASL is produced in a modality (or channel) that is greatly different from English: ASL is a signed language; it cannot be spoken; and there is currently no accepted form of written ASL [30]. The earlier commonly-used means of referring to signs in writing is *glosses* notation, whereby signs are represented in their natural order by uppercase words taken from their nearest spoken counterparts. A major drawback of this representation is that it does not show what the translated signs look like.[1] More recent methods use relatively iconic, picture-like symbols to represent the positions and movements of the hands, as well as the facial expressions, but failing to incorporate spatial elements into the representation, this kind of writing system can still cause confusion in complex signs. An ideal approach would use three dimensional (3D) representations of ASL signs being performed, allowing examination from different perspectives, and making accurate understanding and imitation more feasible. This clearly imposes a severe constraint on the target language generation of a machine translation system, however.

Our approach involves two steps: (1) a translation from an input English sentence into an intermediate representation, taking into account aspects of syntactic, grammatical and morphological information; (2) an interpretation of the intermediate representation as a motion representation with a small set of qualitative parameters which can be further converted to a large set of low-level quantitative parameters that actually control the human model to produce ASL signs.

For the intermediate representation, we use *glosses* notation with embedded parameters. To generate the intermediate representation from the input sentence, we need to (i) analyze the word order and figure out which sign order is more appropriate, and (ii) generate the *glosses* and embed parameters indicating grammatical information, such as sentence types, facial expressions, and morphological information. We use a Synchronous Tree Adjoining Grammar (STAG) [21,20] for mapping this information from English to ASL.

A sign synthesizer is employed for the second step. It assumes that the embedded *glosses* representation is already in correct sign order with appropriately assigned grammatical and morphological parameters. For each sign, it first uses the *gloss* as an index to look up a sign dictionary, which stores the parameterized motion templates for all available ASL signs; then uses the embedded parameters to modify the default parameters defined in the motion template to get the effective parameters. The sign synthesizer employs Parallel Transition

---

[1] Although the system described in this paper does use *glosses* in its internal intermediate representation, it does not use them in the final output.

Networks (PaT-Nets) [3] to achieve the smooth transitions between signs. PaT-Nets in turn call *Jack Toolkit* and *Jack Visualizer* functions to generate the final animation [8].

We implemented this system and called it TEAM (Translation from English to ASL by Machine). The major contributions of this work are:

- To our knowledge, this is the first machine translation system from English to 3D animated ASL, taking into consideration not only linguistic but also visual and spatial information associated with ASL.
- It demonstrates that a machine translation system for ASL that uses full natural language processing and full graphics in real time is feasible.
- Our system is not limited to ASL only. Its flexibility allows it to be easily expanded to other signed languages.

2   Graphics Modeling

In order to output true ASL we need a fully articulated 3D human model. The model should have finely articulated hands, highly expressive arms and body, as well as controllable facial expressions. In addition, we need a fast computational model to procedurally generate a wide range of natural-looking ASL signs.

2.1   Human Model

Our human model (shown in Figure 2.2) has 80 joints with a total of 135 degrees of freedom [8]. The torso is composed of 17 joints in the spine between the waist and the neck. A forward kinematics algorithm is employed to position the torso towards a specified set of joint angles. The movements of the arms are specified through key time and end-effector positions (keypoints). An analytical inverse kinematics algorithm computes shoulder and elbow rotations given a specified keypoint.[2] The hand is finely articulated. We use a left/right-independent library of joint angles to shape the hand into a variety of pre-determined positions. Currently we use MIRALab's Face model [17] for animating facial expressions. Facial expressions play an important role in ASL's grammatical process.

2.2   Effort and Shape

Our approach in generating ASL signs and dynamically changing their motion characteristics is based on recent work [6,31] on building computational models of a particularly important system called Laban Movement Analysis (LMA). LMA has four major components — Body, Space, Shape, and Effort. The components of LMA that we cover are Effort and Shape [4]. Effort comprises four motion

---

[2] An inverse kinematics algorithm computes a set of joint angles that satisfies some constraints, given a desired position and orientation of the end-effector, i.e., the hand. The algorithm we are using is made suitable for an anthropomorphic arm [27].

factors: Space (S), Weight (W), Time (T), and Flow (F). Each motion factor is a continuum between two extremes: (1) *indulging* in the quality and (2) *fighting* against the quality. These extreme Effort elements are seen as basic, 'irreducible' qualities, which means that they are the smallest units of change in an observed movement. Table 2.2 shows the LMA Effort elements – the extremes for each motion factor. The Shape dimensions in LMA are Horizontal (H), Vertical (V), Sagittal (S), and Flow (Fl). The terms used to describe the extreme attitudes towards these dimensions are Spreading and Enclosing, Rising and Sinking, Advancing and Retreating, Opening and Closing, respectively. In general, Shape changes occur in affinities with corresponding Efforts (Table 2 [4]).

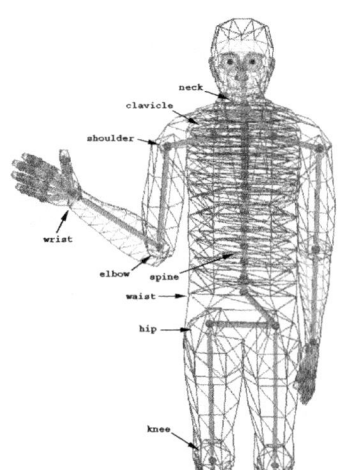

Fig. 1. Human Model

Table 1. Effort Elements

Effort	Indulging	Fighting
Space	Indirect	Direct
Weight	Light	Strong
Time	Sustained	Sudden
Flow	Free	Bound

Table 2. Effort and Shape Affinities

Dimension	Shape	Effort
Vertical	Rising	Weight-Light
	Sinking	Weight-Strong
Horizontal	Enclosing	Space-Direct
	Spreading	Space-Indirect
Sagittal	Retreating	Time-Sudden
	Advancing	Time-Sustained

Effort and Shape qualities are expressed using numeric parameters that can vary along distinct scales. Each dimension of Effort and Shape is associated with a scale ranging from -1 to $+1$. Effort parameters are translated into low-level movement parameters which affect the dynamics of the underlying movement, while Shape parameters are used to modify key pose information, which affect the dimensions of space of the underlying movement. For more technical details about Effort and Shape see [6].

3   ASL Linguistics

3.1   ASL Phonology

William Stokoe was the first linguist to recognize and analyze ASL as a language in its own right. In his seminal work [24,25] a notational system (now called

"Stokoe notation") was devised to analyze each ASL sign into three phonological [3] components: *handshape, location* (place of articulation), and *movement.* Battison [5] and Frishberg [10] presented evidence that these aspects of the sign, along with *orientation* of the palm of the hand, are internal phonological parameters that are necessary for a complete and efficient description of ASL signs. Changing any of these parameters of a sign may make a new sign and therefore change the meaning of the sign.

Simultaneity and Sequentiality. Siple [22] and Kilma and Bellugi [15] have pointed out that the phonological components in ASL exhibit a high degree of simultaneity — they are not produced sequentially. All of the components should be simultaneously present when the signs are produced. However, this does not necessarily mean that sequentiality is not at all incorporated in the phonology of ASL. Linguists [16] proposed that the sequential production of components did indeed need to be represented in ASL phonology, for example, ASL signs move to and from locations.

3D Modeling ASL Phonology. Under the analysis above, it is safe to say ASL signs can be sequentially segmented into one or more phonologically significant units, which are simultaneously associated with certain handshapes, locations, and orientations. In order to accurately model an ASL sign, we need to take into consideration all these phonological parameters, as well as the simultaneity and sequentiality characteristics.

Seamless Solutions^{TM} [1] created some interactive 3D avatars that can communicate in ASL, but they did not take into account the phonological information and their avatars basically perform in signed English rather than ASL. SignSynth [12] uses Perl CGIs (Common Gateway Interfaces) to generate 3D animation in VRML format from a phonological specification, but currently only the finger-spelling module is reported to be working. The lack of a good inverse kinematics procedure prevents it from realizing the remaining and more important modules (arm movement, etc.).

Our approach is phonologically-based and more comprehensive. The location and movement for a specific sign are specified by keypoints, which are relative to the human model's shoulders. Keypoints can be either *Goal* or *Via* keypoints. *Goal* keypoints define a general movement path; the hand follows a path which pauses at each *Goal* keypoint. *Via* keypoints direct the motion between *Goal* keypoints without pausing. A fast analytical inverse kinematics algorithm computes the shoulder and elbow rotations, given a keypoint specified by three-dimensional position coordinates and an elbow swivel angel [27]. The base of the wrist acts as the end-effector indicating the keypoints. Wrist orientations (which decide the palm orientations) and handshapes can also be specified.

---

[3] The terms *phonology* and *phonological* are used to describe ASL sign formation, even though these terms are derived from speech-related phenomena. They are widely used in ASL linguistics research.

3.2   ASL Morphology

ASL differs dramatically from English in the *mechanisms* – inflections and derivations – by which its phonological units are modified.

ASL Inflectional Morphology. ASL exhibits a very rich set of inflectional variations [15]. Rather than affix-like sequential additions to signs, inflections in ASL involve superimposed spatial and temporal contrasts affecting the phonological movement. There are quite a few different inflectional processes in ASL. In this paper we focus on inflections for *temporal* aspect, reflecting distinctions such as *frequently, slowly,* and *quickly;* inflections for *manner,* such as *carefully,* and *haphazardly;* and inflections for *degree,* such as *very* and *a little bit.* The nuances of meaning expressed by these reflectional processes represent a considerable range of semantic distinctions.

ASL Derivational Morphology. In addition to inflectional processes, ASL has a wide variety of methods that expand the phonology by regular systematic changes in the phonological root and result in the formation of related phonological units. At present, we focus on the so-called *paired noun-verbs* [15,26] which are pairs of noun and verb that share the same phonological characteristics and semantic meaning (for example, *FLY* and *AIRPLANE, SIT* and *CHAIR*). To a non-signer the distinction between paired noun-verb may not be readily apparent unless the two are performed consecutively. However, there is a consistent and standardized distinction between them in directionality, manner, frequency, tension, and/or evenness of the underlying movement.

Systematic Changes Underlying Inflectional and Derivational Processes. As mentioned, inflectional and derivational morphology can be achieved by systematically changing Effort and Shape parameters. In the following, we show an example of how to embed Effort parameters.

```
TOP-LEVEL
sign / SIGN / SPACE WEIGHT TIME FLOW

SPACE                                   WEIGHT
_[directly]    / _( 0.2, _, _, _)       _[strongly]   / _(_,  0.2, _, _)
_[indirectly] / _(-0.2, _, _, _)        _[lightly]    / _(_, -0.2, _, _)
_              / _( 0.0, _, _, _)       _             / _(_,  0.0, _, _)

TIME                                    FLOW
_[slowly]     / _(_, _, -0.2, _)        _[freely]     / _(_, _, _, -0.2)
_[quickly]    / _(_, _,  0.2, _)        _[boundly]    / _(_, _, _,  0.2)
_             / _(_, _,  0.0, _)        _             / _(_, _, _,  0.0)
```

In this example, *sign slowly,* is translated into embedded *glosses* notation SIGN(0.0, 0.0, -0.2, 0.0). [4] Other inflections as well as derivations can be

---

[4] The parameter values are set arbitrarily, for example, −0.2 stands for a noticeable change in the Sustained quality.

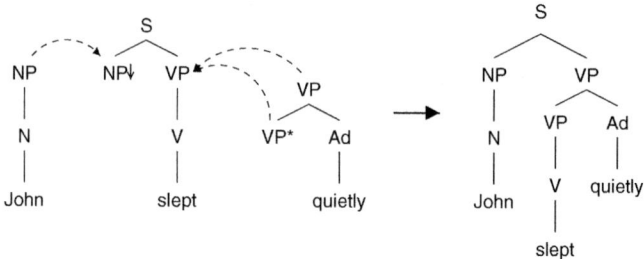

Fig. 2. Substituting and adjoining TAG trees.

done similarly. For example, because the nouns in the paired noun-verbs consistently have a smaller movement that is restrained in dimensions of space, we may assign smaller Shape (or Effort) parameter values to derive the nouns from their associated verbs. Our parameterized representation on the phonology level offers us the advantage that we do not have to list paired nouns and verbs as independent items in the dictionary but can derive one from the other consistently. Our approach also complies with the hypothesis shared by linguistic researchers: that is, the underlying forms of roots may be abstract items that do not occur as surface forms in the language [7].

4   Translating English Sentences

4.1   Synchronous Grammar

We use a Lexicalized Tree Adjoining Grammar based system for translating between English sentences and ASL *glosses*. A Tree-Adjoining Grammar (TAG) is a tree rewriting system [14], the primitive elements of which are *elementary trees* (see Figure 2). In a Lexicalized TAG, these elementary trees are anchored by lexical items, such as nouns and verbs [21]. The elementary trees also have argument positions for the subjects and objects of verbs, adjectives, and other predicates, which constrain the way they can be combined, and which determine the predicate-argument structure of the input sentence. Elementary trees are combined by the operations of *substitution* and *adjunction*, where substituting elementary trees (such as the noun tree for 'John' in Figure 2) are attached at the frontier nodes of other elementary trees (designated with ↓), and adjoining elementary trees (such as the modifier tree for 'quietly') are attached at internal nodes of other elementary trees by removing the part of the host tree below the adjunction site and reattaching it at one of the frontier nodes of the adjoining tree (designated with ∗). A source-language sentence can be parsed using these constrained operations in polynomial time. As the source-language sentence is parsed, a target-language tree can be simultaneously assembled, using Synchronous TAGs [21,20], by associating one or more target-language elementary trees with each source-language elementary tree, and associating the nodes at which

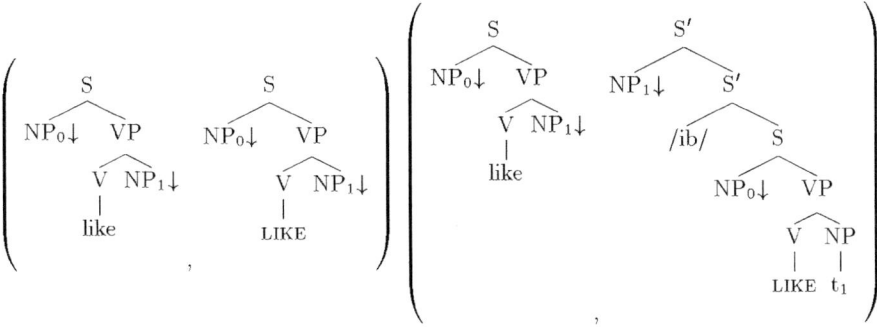

Fig. 3. Untopicalized tree and topicalized tree for pronouns

subsequent substitutions or adjunctions can take place. For example, the associated source and target trees in Figure 3, for the English and ASL translations of 'like,' have links (denoted by subscripts) between the designated sites for substitutions of noun trees (like 'John' in the previous example), which will function as the subjects in each sentence. Recognizing a complete parse on the source (English) side therefore means building a complete parse on the target (ASL) side. Synchronous TAGs have been used for machine translation between spoken languages [2] but this is the first application to a signed language.

The input sentence brings with it grammatical information such as sentence types and morphological marks such as tense. This information is expressed in ASL through non-manual signals which have to be incorporated into the target derivation tree.

4.2   Grammar Patterns

Although ASL seems to have a freer word order than English, Fisher [9] claims that the underlying structure of ASL is based on subject-verb-object (SVO) order and when other patterns are used, they need to be marked by 'intonational breaks' (e.g., pauses, head tilts, raising of eyebrows). Topicalized ordering is preferred when the sentence has pronouns or when the discourse referents are present.

Intransitive and transitive verbs can be represented either in SVO or in topicalized order; the choice of order depends heavily on the use of nouns and/or pronouns. Translations (1) and (2) show the sentences in English and the respective ASL *glosses* with the addition of an *intonation break* (/ib/) which is mapped to the non-manual signs for topicalization in the animation system. Figure 3 shows the tree mappings for these two pairs of sentences.

(1) *John likes the girl*
    JOHN LIKE GIRL

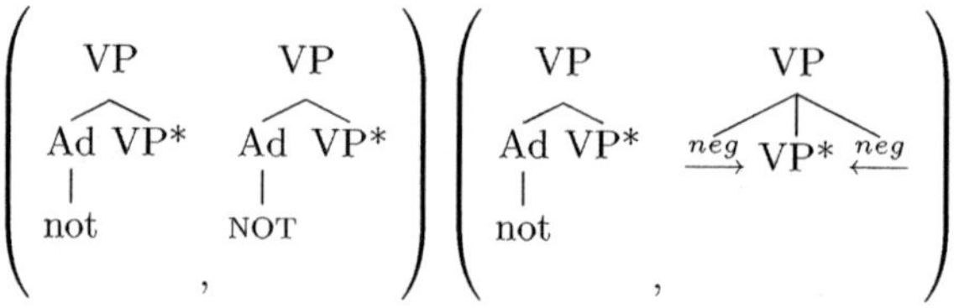

$$\left(\begin{array}{cc} \text{VP} & \text{VP} \\ \overbrace{\text{Ad VP*}} & \overbrace{\text{Ad VP*}} \\ | & | \\ \text{not} & \text{NOT} \end{array}\right), \left(\begin{array}{cc} \text{VP} & \text{VP} \\ \overbrace{\text{Ad VP*}} & \overbrace{\xrightarrow{neg}\text{VP*}\xleftarrow{neg}} \\ | & \\ \text{not} & \end{array}\right),$$

Fig. 4. Synchronous tree pairs for manual and nonmanual negation

(2) *I like the girl*
   GIRL */intonation_break/* I LIKE

Predicative constructions in English which have nouns and adjectives as descriptors are mapped to ASL sentences without verbs. The translation in (3) is an example of this construction which also allows for topicalization.

(3) *They are doctors*
   DOCTOR */intonation_break/* HE SHE

Negation in ASL may include the *gloss* NOT or simply movement of the head side-to-side to express the idea of negation. It is usually accompanied by a nonneutral facial expression, such as a frown. We use the top line notation to specify the scope of the non-manual signs to be performed by the animation system. The mapping between English and ASL shown in Figure 4 includes the beginning ($\xrightarrow{neg}$) and ending ($\xleftarrow{neg}$) marks for these signs in the ASL tree. In a sentence such as (4), the non-manual signs expressing negation are performed throughout the VP, "NOT BUY DOG."

(4) *The woman is not buying a dog*

$$\overline{\hspace{2cm}\text{neg}\hspace{2cm}}$$
   WOMAN NOT BUY DOG

A declarative sentence, a yes/no question and an imperative sentence may all map to the same *glosses* in ASL. The translations in (5), (6), and (7) show how these three sentence types are distinguished by the way they are presented by the signer through the use of non-manual signals. The declarative sentence in (5) is delivered at a normal rate and with a neutral face; the yes/no question in (6) is delivered with a question sign at the end, which means it requires a head tilt and eyebrows raised to convey the question idea and also the arms do not go back to a neutral position immediately after; and the imperative sentence in (7) is delivered with lower eyebrows and eyes slightly squinted, and the verb is signed with more force, which we map using the Effort parameters. PAST is a sign gesture with the hand above the shoulder.

(5) *I left the cat in the house*
   PAST */intonation_break/* LEAVE CAT IN HOUSE

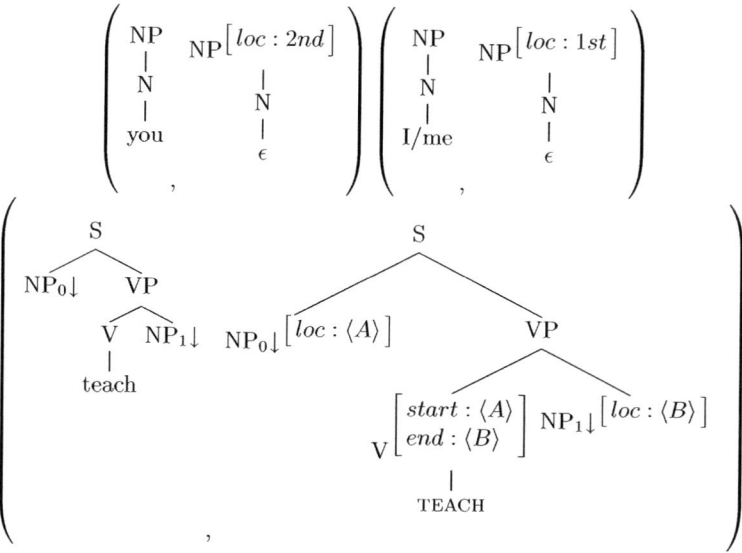

Fig. 5. Synchronous tree pairs for "I teach you," and "you teach me"

(6) *Did you leave the cat in the house?*

$$\text{PAST } /intonation\_break/ \overline{\text{LEAVE CAT IN HOUSE}}^{\text{q}}$$

(7) *Leave the cat in the house*
    LEAVE(0,0.5,0.2,0.2) CAT IN HOUSE

There are different classes of verbs in ASL. One distinction is between *non-directional* and *directional* verbs. In the first case, the sign is always the same and cannot be changed without altering its meaning. If a nondirectional verb is accompanied by pronouns, these need to be mapped explicitly and must be present as *glosses* in ASL. Examples of these verbs include KNOW, FORGET, EAT, and TRUST. For directional verbs, such as ASK, GIVE, WAIT, and TEACH, the start and end points of the verb sign depend on the pronouns used (1st, 2nd or 3rd person). For example, TEACH has a different orientation for *You teach me* (8) than for *I teach you* (9). In this case, we map the pronouns to ϵ (empty arguments) and have features identifying their locations in space which are used as start and end points for the verb sign. Other classes of verbs also exist, such as location verbs, where only the direct object is referred to; we treat these the same as directional verbs but with the start point in neutral position.

(8) *I teach you*
    $_1$TEACH$_2$

(9) *You teach me*
    $_2$TEACH$_1$

64   L. Zhao et al.

For multi-directional verbs such as *teach*, the translation must match the start- and end-points of the sign for the verb with the locations of the signs for the subject and object. This behavior, which closely resembles subject-verb agreement in spoken languages such as English, is modeled using essentially the same mechanism used for subject-verb agreement in existing grammars [13]. We handle this using features in the paired grammar which coindex the location of the verb's subject and object signs with features on the verb sign, which are interpreted as parameters for the start and end points of the sign in the parameterized gesture system (Figure 5).

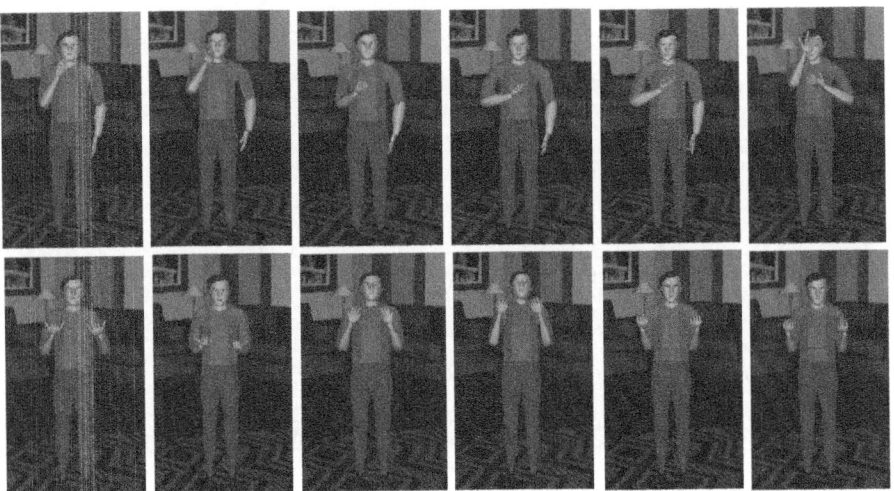

Fig. 6. An ASL Animation Example: "RECENTLY I-SICK NOW I-WELL"

Incorporation of number, size and shape, manner, and location, among others, occurs frequently in ASL. These phenomena present problems for translation, since they are frequently dependent on the signer's understanding of the sentence.[5] We use the Effort-Shape parameters discussed in (2.2) to handle inflections for *temporal aspect, manner,* and *degree.* The example translation in (10) shows the mapping of the adverb *slowly* to the appropriate parameters that modify the way the sign OPEN is performed.

(10) *John opened the door slowly*
     JOHN OPEN(0,0,-0.2,0) DOOR

Conditional sentences are expressed in English by using the lexical item *if.* In ASL one way to express a conditional sentence is by marking the condition

---

[5] For example, in the signed version of the English sentence *He picked up the dead fish and threw it in the trash* it is likely that the *gloss* FISH will be signed as far as possible from the signer's body.

as a question and the consequent as a statement. Examples of this can be seen in (11) and (12).

(11) *If it rains tomorrow, I will not go to the beach*

$$\underline{\qquad\qquad q\qquad\qquad}\ \underline{\qquad\qquad neg\qquad\qquad}$$
TOMORROW RAIN ME NOT GO BEACH

(12) *If it rains tomorrow, are you going to the beach?*

$$\underline{\qquad\qquad q\qquad\qquad}\ \underline{\qquad\qquad q\qquad\qquad}$$
TOMORROW RAIN YOU GO BEACH

5 Sign Synthesizer

In most cases, the transitions between the signs should be smooth. A simple and straightforward approach for the smoothness is to have the beginning and ending of every sign performed in the same standard posture. While this approach offers smooth continuous transitions, beginning and ending each sign in the same 'neutral' position is very unnatural. An awkward, computationally expensive approach is to define transitions between every pair of possible motions. NYU's Improv project [19] uses a technique called *motion blending* to automatically generate smooth transitions between isolated motions. This approach succeeds in avoiding returning to a required 'neutral' pose, but it does not necessarily guarantee natural and rational transitions.

We are using PaT-Nets (Parallel Transition Networks) to solve the motion blending problems. A PaT-Net is a simultaneously executing finite state automata in which the nodes are associated with actions and connections between the nodes are associated with transition conditions. PaT-Nets make it very easy to wait on completion of actions before moving onto the next action, to execute actions in parallel or in sequence, and to dynamically extend the action structure by invoking other PaT-Nets from nodes of the current one [3].

To demonstrate the power of PaT-Nets and the integration of our TEAM system, we create an ASL animation example with English input "recently I was sick but now I am well" (Figure 6). The animation was generated in real time.

6 Conclusion and Future Work

We have described a prototype machine translation system from English to American Sign Language, taking into account not only linguistic but also visual and spatial information associated with ASL signs. Currently we focus on translation from English to ASL, but translating the other way around from ASL to English is an even more interesting challenge. If we can create an ASL recognizer [29] and parser as we have for English, we would be able to translate signed ASL to spoken English sentences and back again to allow real-time interaction on the Internet.

Acknowledgments. This research is partially supported by U.S. Air Force F41624-97-D-5002, Office of Naval Research K-5-55043/3916-1552793, DURIP N0001497-1-0396, and AASERTs N00014-97-1-0603 & N0014-97-1-0605, DARPA SB-MDA-97-2951001, NSF IRI95-04372, SBR-8900230, IIS99-00297, and EIA-98-09209, Army Research Office ASSERT DAA 655-981-0147, NASA NRA NAG 5-3990, AFOSR F49620-98-1-0434 and Engineering Animation Inc. (EAI).

References

1. Seamless Solution Inc. (1998) http://www.seamless-solutions.com.
2. Abeillé, A., Schabes, Y. and Joshi, A.: Using lexicalized tree adjoining grammars for machine translation. In Proc. of the 13th International Conference on Computational Linguistics (COLING '90), Helsinki, Finland. (1990)
3. Norman Badler, Martha Palmer, and Bindiganavale, R.: Animation control for real-time virtual humans. Communications of the ACM. (1999) **42(8)** 65–73
4. Bartenieff, I. and Lewis, D.: Coping With the Environment. Gordon and Breach Science Publishers, New York. (1980)
5. Battison, R.. Phonological deletion in American Sign Language. Sign Language Studies. **5** (1974) 1–19
6. Chi, D., Costa, M., Zhao, L. and Badler, N.: The EMOTE model for Effort and Shape. In Proceedings of ACM Computer Graphics Annual Conference (SIGGRAPH), New Orleans, LA. (2000)
7. Chomsky, N. and Halle, M.: The Sound Pattern of English. Harper, New York, NY. (1968)
8. Engineering Animation Inc. Jack Toolkit 2.2 Reference Guide. (1999)
9. Fisher, S.: Influences in word order change in ASL. In C. Li, (ed.), Word order and word order change. Univ. of Texas Press, Austin, TX. (1975) 1–25.
10. Frishberg, N.: Arbitrariness and iconicity: Historical change in American Sign Language. Language. **51(3)** (1975) 696–719
11. Fromkin, V.: Sign language: Evidence for language universals and the linguistic capacity of the human brain. Sign Language Studies. **59** (1988) 115–127
12. Grieve-Smith, A.: Sign synthesis and sign phonology. In Proceedings of the First High Desert Student Conference in Linguistics, New Mexico. (1998)
13. XTAG Research Group.: A lexicalized tree adjoining grammar for english. Technical report, University of Pennsylvania. (1998)
14. Joshi, A.: An introduction to tree adjoining grammars. In A. Manaster-Ramer, (ed.), Mathematics of Language. John Benjamins, Amsterdam. (1987)
15. Klima, E. and Bellugi, U.: The Signs of Language. Harvard University Press. (1979)
16. Liddell, S.K. and Johnson, R.E.: American Sign Language: The phonological base. Sign Language Studies. **64** (1989) 195–277
17. Magnenat-Thalmann, N., Kalra, P. and Escher, M.: Face to virtual face. Proceedings of the IEEE. **86(5)** (1998)
18. Messing, L. and Campbell, R.: Gesture, Speech and Sign. Oxford University Press (1999)
19. Perlin, K.: Real time responsive animation with personality. IEEE Transactions on Visualization and Computer Graphics. **1(1)** (1995) 5–15
20. Shieber, S.: Restricting the weak-generative capability of synchronous tree adjoining grammars. Computational Intelligence. **10(4)** (1994)

21. Shieber, S. and Schabes, Y.: Synchronous tree adjoining grammars. In Proceedings of the 13th International Conference on Computational Linguistics (COLING '90), Helsinki, Finland. (1990)
22. Siple, P.: Understanding Language Through Sign Language Research. Academic Press. (1976)
23. Sternberg, M.: The American Sign Language Dictionary. Multicom. (1996)
24. Stokoe, W.: Sign language structure. Studies in Linguistics: Occasional Paper 8. Buffalo, New York. (1960)
25. Stokoe, W., Casterline, D. and Croneberg, C.: A Dictionary of American Sign Language on Linguistic Principles. Gallaudet College Press, Washington, DC. (1965, 1976 (2nd ed.))
26. Supalla, T. and Newport, E.: How many seats in a chair? The derivation of nouns and verbs in American Sign Language. In P. Siple, (ed.) Understanding Language through Sign Language Research. Academic Press, New York, NY. (1978)
27. Tolani, D. Inverse Kinematics Methods for Human Modeling and Simulation. PhD thesis, University of Pennsylvania. (1998)
28. Valli, C. and Lucas, C.: Linguistics of ASL: An Introduction. Gallaudet University Press (1995)
29. Vogler, C. and Metaxas, D.: A framework for recognizing the simultaneous aspects of American Sign Language. To appear in Computer Vision and Image Understanding.
30. Wilcox, S. and Wilcox, P.: Learning to See. Gallaudet University Press, Washington, DC. (1996)
31. Zhao, L., Costa, M. and Badler, N.: Interpreting movement manner. In Computer Animation 2000. IEEE Computer Graphics Society. (2000)

Oxygen: A Language Independent Linearization Engine

Nizar Habash

Institute for Advanced Computer Studies
University of Maryland
College Park, MD 20740
phone: +1 (301) 405-6768
fax: +1 (301) 314-9658
habash@umiacs.umd.edu
http://umiacs.umd.edu/labs/CLIP

Abstract. This paper describes a language independent linearization engine, oxyGen. This system compiles target language grammars into programs that take feature graphs as inputs and generate word lattices that can be passed along to the statistical extraction module of the generation system Nitrogen. The grammars are written using a flexible and powerful language, oxyL, that has the power of a programming language but focuses on natural language realization. This engine has been used successfully in creating an English linearization program that is currently employed as part of a Chinese-English machine translation system.

1 Introduction

This paper describes a language independent realization engine, oxyGen. The system compiles linearization grammars into programs that run independent of the grammar and the compilation engine. The grammars are written in oxyL, a powerful and flexible natural language grammar description language. The syntax of oxyL is described in the paper. Currently, the input to the compiled grammar is a feature graph and the output is a word lattice to be fed into the statistical extraction module of the generation engine Nitrogen [3,4,5].

2 Research Context

The work described in this paper has been developed as part of an interlingual Chinese-English Machine Translation (MT) system at the University of Maryland College Park. [1,7]. The focus of this paper is only on the linearization sub-module of the realization module in the generation component of the MT system. The realization module discussed is Nitrogen, a hybrid rule-based/statistical realization engine [2,3,4,5]. The system consists of two components, Linearization and Statistical Extraction (Fig. 1). First, a Feature Graph

J.S. White (Ed.): AMTA 2000, LNAI 1934, pp. 68–79, 2000.
© Springer-Verlag Berlin Heidelberg 2000

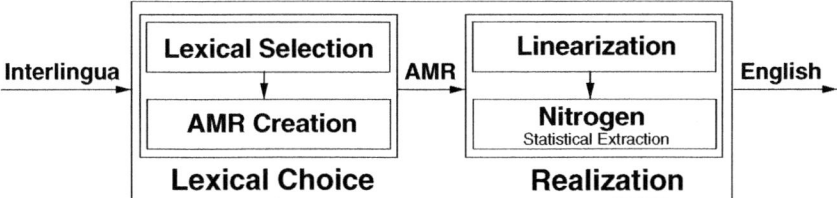

Fig. 1. Generation System Overview

(FG) representation of the sentence is converted into a word lattice of possible word sequences, i.e. linearized. Then, uni and bigram statistics are used to determine the most probable set of paths across the word lattice.

The particular form of FGs exemplified in this paper is a modified version of Nitrogen's Abstract Meaning Representation for the MT system's purposes [1]. AMRs are labeled directed feature graphs written using the syntax of the Penman Sentence Plan Language [6]:

(1) `<AMR>    ::= ( <label> {<role> <value>}+ )`
     `<value> ::= <AMR> || <terminal>`

Every node in an AMR has a label and one or more role-value pairs. Roles, i.e. features, are marked by a colon prefix except for the default role, `:inst` (*instance*), which can be represented as a forward slash `/`. Values may be meaning bearing terminal tokens or AMR nodes. These terminal tokens can be semantic concepts such as `|china|` or `|love|`, syntactic categories such as `N` or `V`, or plain surface text strings such as "Once upon a time". The roles and concepts of AMRs are a mix of syntactic and semantic significance: there are thematic roles such as `:AG` and `:TH` (agent and theme) and syntactic categories such as `ADV`. The following is an example AMR for the sentence *The United States unilaterally reduced the China textile export quota* :

```
(2)  (a1 / |reduce|
         :CAT V
         :AG (a2 / |united states| :CAT N)
         :TH (a3 / |quota|
                 :CAT N
                 :MOD-THING (a4 / |china|   :CAT N)
                 :MOD-THING (a5 / |textile| :CAT N)
                 :MOD-THING (a6 / |export|  :CAT N))
                 :MOD-MANNER (a8 / |unilaterally| :CAT ADV))
```

In this example, `(a2 / |united states|  :CAT N)` is the agent of the concept `|reduce|`. And similarly, `N` is the category of the concept `|united states|`.

The basic role :inst or / is always present in a non-ambiguous AMR. An ambiguous AMR, i.e., a conglomeration of different AMRs has one or more role-value pairs using the special role :OR. For example, a variant of the above AMR in which the root concept is three way ambiguous would look as follows at the top node:

```
(3)   (# :OR (# / |reduce| . . . )
         :OR (# / |cut| . . . )
         :OR (# / |decrease| . . . ))
```

Since such ambiguity can occur anywhere in an AMR, it presents a challenge to writing simple linearization rules whose application is conditional upon specific AMR role combinations at different depths. This issue is addressed later in this paper. The output of the linearization module is a word lattice of possible word sequence renderings. It includes ambiguous paths resulting from underspecified features, such as definiteness, and undetermined relative word orders, such as that of modifiers. The following is a possible word lattice corresponding to (2).

```
(4)   (SEQ (WRD "*start-sentence*" BOS)
           (WRD "united states" NOUN)
           (WRD "unilaterally" ADJ)
           (WRD "reduced" VERB)
           (OR (WRD "the" ART) (WRD "a" ART) (WRD "an" ART))
           (WRD "china" ADJ)
           (OR (SEQ (WRD "export" ADJ) (WRD "textile" ADJ))
               (SEQ (WRD "textile" ADJ) (WRD "export" ADJ)))
           (WRD "quota" NOUN) (WRD "*end-sentence*" EOS))
```

Finally, the statistical extraction module evaluates the different paths represented in the word lattice and orders the different word renderings using uni and bigram statistics:

(5)

```
united states unilaterally reduced the china textile export quota.
united states unilaterally reduced a china textile export quota.
united states unilaterally reduced the china export textile quota.
united states unilaterally reduced a china export textile quota.
united states unilaterally reduced an china textile export quota.
united states unilaterally reduced an china export textile quota.
```

The focus of this paper is on the implementation techniques of the linearization module of the realization system.

3   Motivation

The linearization module is basically an implementation of a set of rules, a grammar, that governs the relative word ordering (syntax) and word form (morphology) of a target language. A linearization grammar can be implemented declaratively or procedurally. In the declarative approach, the system contains a grammar description formalism and a linearization engine that interprets the grammar on-line and applies its rules to the input sentence representation. The advantages of this approach are reusability, easy extendibility and language independence. Its main drawback is slow speed. Nitrogen's Linearization module is an example of this approach. It provides rules to decompose an AMR and order the results linearly. The Nitrogen grammar description formalism uses a recasting mechanism to transform AMRs into other AMRs. Besides the slowness inherited from the paradigm of its implementation, Nitrogen's grammar formalism is limited and inflexible:

- Rule application is conditional upon equality of concepts or existence of roles at the top level of an AMR only. This makes it impossible to write a single rule that is conditioned upon a combination of features at different levels. Cascading features is a solution to this problem that only increases the size of the grammar and aggravates the speed problem.
- Recasting operations are limited to adding feature-value pairs and introducing new nodes. Implementing a thematic hierarchy ordering in which thematic roles such as agent and theme are recast as syntactic roles such as subject and object cannot be implemented in a single recast operation. Again, cascading of features is the only way to do this. An implementation of thematic hierarchies using cascading features is discussed in [1].
- There is no mechanism to perform range-unbounded or computationally complex transformations. For example, number formatting is a transformation problem that requires access to functions such as multiplication and addition which are not available to the grammar. One instance of this problem appeared in our system when translating Chinese numbers represented as multiples units of 10,000. For example, 80,000 is the concept |8| modified by the concept |10,000|. Multiplying Chinese number concepts and formatting them into English number sequences was necessary and is impossible to do using recasting without enumerating all combinations.

The procedural approach to linearization grammars uses a programming language to implement the rules of the grammar. The main advantages of this approach are flexibility, power and speed. Having access to the full computing power of a programming language opens a lot of possibilities for efficient implementation. It also frees the linearizer's designer from the restrictions of a limited declarative grammar by providing access to the operating system, databases, the web, etc. However, a major disadvantage of this approach is that the linguistic knowledge is coupled with the programming code. This hard-coding of grammar rules makes the system rather redundant, difficult to understand and debug, non-reusable and language specific.

4 Oxygen

The oxyGen approach to implementing the linearization module is a hybrid implementation between the declarative and procedural paradigms. oxyGen uses a linearization grammar description language to write declarative grammar rules which are then compiled into a programming language for efficient performance. oxyGen contains three elements: a linearization grammar description language (oxyL), an oxyL to Lisp compiler (oxyCompile) and a run-time support library (oxyRun). Target language linearization grammars written in oxyL are compiled off-line into oxyGen Linearizers using oxyCompile (Fig.2).

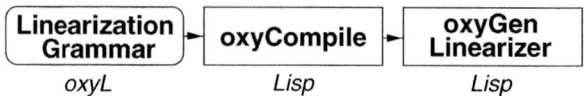

Fig. 2. oxyGen Compilation Step

oxyGen Linearizers are Lisp programs that require the oxyRun library of basic functions in order to execute (Fig. 3). They take AMRs as input and create word lattices that are passed on to some Statistical Extraction unit.

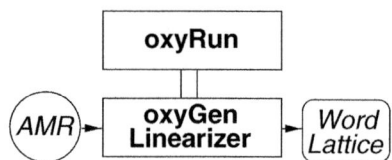

Fig. 3. oxyGen Runtime Step

This implementation maximizes the advantages and minimizes the disadvantages inherent in the declarative and procedural paradigms: The separation between the linearization engine (oxyCompile and oxyRun) and the linearization grammar (oxyL) combines in one system the best of two worlds: the simplicity and focus of a declarative grammar with the power and efficiency of a procedural implementation. It also provides language independence and reusability since needs of the target language are only addressed in its specific oxyL grammar. Secondly, The run-time separation between language-specific code (compiled oxyL file – oxyGen Linearizer) and language-independent code (oxyRun) allows for an efficient resource-sharing implementation especially when running multiple linearizers for different languages at the same time as in multilingual generation. Finally, oxyGen's linearization grammar description language, oxyL, is as powerful as a regular programming language but with the focus on linearization needs. This is accomplished through providing powerful linearization mechanisms for the most common needs of a linearization grammar and also by allowing embedding of code in a standard programming language (Lisp). This allows for efficient implementation of the more language specific realization problems (e.g., Chinese number formatting). oxyL linearization grammars are also simple, clear, concise and easily extendible. An example of the simplicity of oxyL grammars is that redundancy issues such as the handling of :OR ambiguities are hidden from the linearization grammar designer and are treated only in the compiler and support library. The following section describes oxyL's syntax and the mechanism of application of oxyL rules.

5   Oxyl

In many ways, oxyL is similar to the language Nitrogen grammars are written in; however, it has several special features that makes it more powerful. First, oxyL linearization rules can be conditionally applied using general Boolean expressions and embedded if-then-else control flow structures which allows for powerful and compact linearization grammars. Second, oxyL provides accessibility functions that can return the value of any descendant of the AMR. Contrast these two features with Nitrogen's grammar's conditions of application which are flat if-then structures and use only equality of roles or role-value combinations at the top level of the AMR. Third, oxyL provides recasting mechanisms that are more powerful than Nitrogen's. For example, a thematic hierarchy recast in oxyL is implemented in a single rule whereas it requires as many rules as the number of hierarchy slots in Nitrogen. For more information on Thematic Hierarchies, see [1]. Finally, oxyL can embed calls to Lisp functions that can be included in the oxyL file. This feature provides oxyL linearization grammars with access to all the tools available to a programming language. The rest of this section will describe oxyL's syntax.

5.1   OxyL Basic Tokens

The function of different tokens in oxyL is marked through their form using a prefix symbol: variables are prefixed with a dollar sign (e.g. $form, $tense), role-names are prefixed with a colon (e.g. :agent, :cat) and functions are prefixed with an ampersand (e.g. &eq, &ProperNameHash). Some of oxyL's functions resemble Lisp functions (e.g. &eq and eq). However, their implementation is different in oxyGen since ambiguity has to be handled. For example, &eq is aware of the existence of :ORed AMRs in which matching one of the possible values is enough to return true, whereas Lisp eq is not.

In addition to general functions, oxyL has a special class of functions called referential functions. These functions, which are prefixed with an *at* sign (e.g. @goal, @this), are used to access values corresponding to specific roles of the current AMR. For example, @goal returns the value corresponding to the role :goal. If the current AMR is (2) in section 2, @AG returns (a2 / |united states| :cat n). The instance role, /, is returned using the special referential function @inst. A referential function can specify the path from the current AMR's root to any value under it by concatenating the references along such path. For instance, if the current AMR is (2), @AG.CAT returns N. If the current AMR contains multiple instances of the same role as in :MOD-THING in 2, the values are combined in an :OR structure. For example, if the current AMR is (2), @TH.MOD-THING.INST gives (# :OR |china| :OR |textile| :OR |export|). Access to the full current AMR is provided through the self-referential function @this. For example, @this.AG is equal to @AG.

The last oxyL basic token type is Macros, which are prefixed with a circumflex (e.g. ^NP-NOM). Macros are treated like variables except that while variables appear as is in the compiled grammar, macros are substituted in the compiler. The use of macros makes the grammar description more concise. For example, if a set of role-value pairs is very commonly used such as (:Form NP :Case NOM), they can be referred to using a single macro, ^NP-NOM.

5.2   Oxyl File

An oxyL file contains the a set of declarations. Some are obligatory (marked below with an asterisk) for proper compilation into Lisp code. Others introduce symbols that could be eventually used in the grammar rules such as global variables or special Lisp functions. The following is a list of these declarations:

Table 1. oxyL Declarations

Declaration	Function	Example
:Language*	Name of generated grammar	:Language "English"
:Code	User-defined Lisp functions	:Code (<Lisp code>)
:Include	Lisp file to load at runtime	:Include "EnglMorph.lisp"
:Class	Defines a class of roles	:Class :THETA (:AG :TH :GOAL)
:Global	Declares a global variable	:Global $MODE HTML
:Macro	Declares a macro	:Macro ^NP-ACC (:CAT N :CASE ACC)
:Morph*	Defines the morphological generation function	:Morph (&morph @word @morphemes)
:Rules*	Defines the grammar	:Rules <Linearization-Grammar>

All Lisp supporting code introduced through :Include or :Code need all interfacing functions to be prefixed with an & like oxyL general functions.

A :Class is a "super" role. It is a cover symbol that can be used to reference different classes of roles. For example, :THETA can be defined to refer to all thematic roles and :MOD can refer to all types of modifiers. Once defined, referential functions can be used for it. Internally, class roles and regular roles are processed differently but that is hidden from the user.

The syntax of the oxyL grammar rules declared using :RULES is described in the next section.

5.3   Oxyl Target Language Grammar

```
(6)   <GRAMMAR>  ::= <RULE>+
      <RULE>     ::= ([== <ASSIGN>]
                      {?? <COND>
                       -> <RESULT>}*
                      [-> <RESULT>] )
      <ASSIGN>   ::= ((<variable> <value>)+)
      <COND>     ::= <Boolean Expression>
      <RESULT>   ::= <RULE> || <SEQUENCE>
      <SEQUENCE>::= ({<AMR>||<RECAST>}+}) ||
                    (OR <SEQUENCE> <SEQUENCE>+)
      <RECAST>   ::= (<AMR> {<RECAST-OP> <RECAST-OP-ARGS>}+)
```

The above BNF describes the syntax of an oxyL grammar. A grammar consists of a set of ordered rules each of which is considered for application over the current AMR. Each rule has an optional assignment section, introduced with ==, in which local variables are defined. The second part of a rule is an optional condition and result pair that can be repeated multiple times. Conditions are introduced with ?? and results are introduced with ->. And finally an optional result that is treated as the default when all conditions fail. A result can be a rule in itself with all of the portions described above or it can be a sequence of AMRs or AMR-returning tokens such as variables or functions. The ability to embed rules within rules and declare local variable with deep scope allows users to limit the size of the grammar and increase the speed of its application logarithmically. The linear order of AMRs in the result specifies the linear order of the surface forms corresponding to these AMRs. The grammar is run recursively over each one of the different AMRs. This process continues until terminal values, i.e. surface forms, are reached. Consider the following oversimplified rule:

```
(7)   (== (($form @form))
      ?? (&eq $form S)
      -> (?? (&eq @voice Passive)
         -> (@object (&passivize @inst) "by" @subject)
         -> (@subject @inst @object)))
```

Initially, this rule takes the value of the role :form in the current AMR and assigns it to the variable $form. In the case the value of $form equals S, a second check on the voice of the current AMR is done. If the voice is passive, the passive word order is realized. Otherwise, the active voice word order is realized. The grammar is then called recursively over the AMRs of @subject, @object and @inst. The function &passivize takes the AMR of @inst as input and can return a passive verb AMR that gets processed by the grammar or a terminal word sequence. In addition to AMRs, a linearization sequence can contain AMR recast operations. A recast operation is made out of an AMR followed by one or more pairs of recast operator and recast operator arguments. Recast operations modify AMRs before they are recursively run through the grammar. The recast mechanism is very useful in restructuring the current AMR or any of its components. For example, the ++ recast operator adds role-value pairs to an AMR. This is useful in cases such as adding case marking roles on the subject and object AMRs where such case markers are not specified in the original, more semantic, representation. The rule described above, (7) could be modified to specify case as follows:

(8)   (== (($form @form))
       ?? (&eq $form S)
       -> (?? (&eq @voice Passive)
          -> ((@object ++ (:case nom)) (&passivize @inst)
             "by" (@subject ++ (:case gen)))
          -> ((@subject ++ (:case nom)) @inst
             (@object ++ (:case acc)))))))

The following is a list of oxyL recast operators with their usage formalism and functionality. Note that the use of / in recast operations is different from its role as a shorthand for :inst.

Table 2. oxyL Recast Operators

Name	Op	Usage	Function
Add	++	(AMR ++ $role_0 value_0$ $role_1 value_1$ ...)	Add role-value pairs to AMR
Delete	--	(AMR -- ($role_0$ $role_1$ ...))	Remove all $role_n$-value pairs
Replace	&&	(AMR && ($role_0 value_0$ $role_1 value_1$ ...))	Replace values of $role_n$
Simple Recast	<<	(AMR << ($role_{new}$ / $role_0$ $role_1$ ...))	Rename all existing $role_n$ as $role_n ew$
Hierarchy Recast	<	(AMR <! ($role_{new_0}$ $role_{new_1}$ .../ $role_0$ $role_1$ ...))	Hierarchically rename available $role_n$ as $role_{new_n}$
Morph	+-	(AMR +- morpheme)	Invoke the morphological generation function on the AMR if it is a value, or on its instance value

6 Evaluation

In this section, oxyGen is evaluated based on Speed of performance, Size of grammar, Expressiveness of the grammar description language, Reusability and Readability/Writability. The evaluation context is provided by comparing an oxyGen linearization grammar for English to two other implementations, one procedural (using Lisp) and one declarative (using Nitrogen Linearization module). Three comparable linearization grammars are used to calculate speed and size. All three were actually implemented at different stages of development in the Chinese-English MT system mentioned in section 2.

Speed: Two tests were performed. The first test uses a small corpus of 100 simple AMRs of an average of 17 particles (label, role or terminal value) per AMR. The second test uses a corpus of 213 AMRs representing translated Chinese news article sentences. These averaged 463 particles and 7 :ORs per AMR. The following table contains the times spent on average per system in milliseconds. The Lisp implementation is the fastest followed by oxyGen. Nitrogen lags behind considerably.

Table 3. Speed Evaluation

	Procedural (Lisp)	oxyGen	Declarative (Nitrogen)
Test 1	3.84 ms	37.67 ms	630.56 ms
Test 2	11.50 ms	278.45 ms	17028.00 ms

Size: The following table contains the size of code in lines of code (*loc*) of the three implementations. The oxyGen code size is the sum of the oxyL grammar (190 loc) and the Lisp English support functions (62 loc). The Nitrogen code size is the sum of Nitrogen's English grammar (1655 loc) and an extension grammar to make it compatible with our system (375 loc). Clearly, oxyGen performs the best.

Table 4. Size Evaluation

	Procedural (Lisp)	oxyGen	Declarative (Nitrogen)
Size	763 loc	252 loc	2030 loc

Expressiveness: Lisp and oxyGen are equally expressive in the sense of their accessibility to computational tools as described earlier. Whereas Nitrogen falls behind.

Reusability: Both Nitrogen and oxyGen are language independent, an advantage over any procedural implementation.

Readability/Writability: All three approaches need a certain amount of training. However, oxyGen's simple syntax is an advantage over Lisp (for linearization purposes, that is). Its compact powerful rules are an advantage over Nitrogen's simple rule mechanisms.

Overall: oxyGen has the best overall performance of the three systems:

Table 5. Overall Evaluation

	Procedural (Lisp)	oxyGen	Declarative (Nitrogen)
Speed	+	0	-
Size	0	+	-
Expressiveness	+	+	-
Reusability	-	+	+
Readability/ Writability	-	+	-

7   Future Work

This project is still in its initial phases and more work is still needed. As far as the oxyL language definition and the runtime library support, oxyRun, more tools and function libraries are needed such as meta-level functions that return information about the current AMR, e.g., its role under its parent AMR, the number of theta roles or modifiers in it, its total depth, etc. Such information can be very helpful for sentence planning purposes. Other function libraries can be created to handle generation of specific domains such as time/date formatting, newspaper titles, etc. As for oxyCompile, more debugging tools and error handling routines are needed to make the system more robust and user-friendly. Independently of the engine itself, more oxyL grammars for other languages are needed to test the systems extendibility. Chinese, Arabic and Spanish generation are especially under consideration.

A possible extension to the oxyGen suite could be to allow different input formats yet still use the same common engine. Other possible input formats besides Penman sentence planning include NMSU F-Structures, XML and CycL. Such an endeavor would require a higher level of separation between the compiler and the input format which has to be specified to the compiler through some input language definition grammar.

Another area for possible future work is to use oxyGen as part of NLP applications besides machine translation such as text summarization.

8   Conclusion

I have presented a language independent linearization engine that compiles target language grammars into programs that take abstract meaning representations as input and generate word lattice that can be passed along to a statistical extraction module. The grammars are written using a flexible and powerful language, oxyL, that has the power of a programming language but focuses on natural language realization. This approach was evaluated to be more efficient than other purely declarative or purely procedural approaches.

Acknowledgements. This work has been supported by NSA Contract MDA904-96-C-1250 and NSF PFF/PECASE Award IRI-9629108. I would like to thank members of the CLIP lab for helpful conversations and advice and especially Bonnie Dorr, Philip Resnik, David Traum and Amy Weinberg. I would also like to thank Kevin Knight and Irene Langkilde for making the Nitrogen system available and help with understanding the Nitrogen grammar formalism.

References

1. Dorr, B., Habash, N. and Traum, D.: A Thematic Hierarchy for Efficient Generation from Lexical-Conceptual Structure. In Proceedings of the Third Conference of the Association for Machine Translation in the Americas (AMTA-98). Langhorne, PA, (1998) 333–343
2. Knight, K. and Hatzivassiloglou, V.: Two-Level, Many-Paths Generation. In Proceedings of ACL-91. (1991) 143–151
3. Langkilde, I. and Knight, K.: Generating Word Lattices from Abstract Meaning Representation. Technical report, Information Science Institute, University of Southern California (1998)
4. Langkilde, I. and Knight, K.: Generation that Exploits Corpus-Based Statistical Knowledge. In Proceedings of COLING-ACL '98. (1998) 704–710
5. Langkilde, I. and Knight, K.: The Practical Value of N-Grams in Generation. In International Natural Language Generation Workshop. (1998)
6. Penman.: The Penman Reference Manual. Information Sciences Institute, University of Southern California. (1989)
7. Traum, D. and Habash, N.: Generation from Lexical Conceptual Structures. In Proceedings of the Workshop on Applied Interlinguas, NAACL/ANLP 2000, Seattle, WA. (2000)

Information Structure Transfer: Bridging the Information Gap in Structurally Different Languages

Margo Budzikowska

Conversational Machines Department
IBM T. J. Watson Research Center,
30 Saw Mill River Rd, Hawthorne, NY 10532, USA
sml@us.ibm.com

Abstract. This paper presents the implementation part of my doctoral research at the University of Cambridge. It provides a description of the Information Structure Transfer (IST), a machine translation prototype designed within the framework of the Spoken Language Translator (SLT by SRI, Cambridge/Palo Alto) and based on the Core Language Engine ([1]). The IST includes two discourse-processing modules: the pre-transfer Information Structure Activator (ISA) and the post-transfer Information Structure Generator (ISG). The IST prototype calculates and processes vital features of information structure explored in context of structural differences between positional and non-positional languages. It offers algorithmic solutions and an implementation framework for local discourse processing in machine translation. Under scrutiny is a web of interrelated factors such as pronominalization, anaphora resolution, zero anaphors, definiteness and constituent order.

1 Introduction

This paper describes some of the efforts behind my doctoral research undertaken at the University of Cambridge. It explores an experimental implementation of the Information Structure Transfer (IST), a machine translation prototype designed within the framework of the Spoken Language Translator (SLT by SRI, Cambridge/Palo Alto) and based on the Core Language Engine ([1]).

The IST is a prototype system calculating and processing vital features of information structure explored in context of structural differences between positional and non-positional languages. Under scrutiny is a web of interrelated factors such as pronominalization, anaphora resolution, zero anaphors, definiteness and constituent order.

The development environment used for the IST was the Quintus Prolog Compiler (release 3.1.3) for the Sun Unix operating system. The theoretical basis for the interpretation of the input was provided by the Multi-Centering constituting an adaptation of Centering ([5]). The generation drew from the functional studies of language initiated by the Prague Circle of Linguists ([15]).

J.S. White (Ed.): AMTA 2000, LNAI 1934, pp. 80-88, 2000.
© Springer-Verlag Berlin Heidelberg 2000

2 Overview of IST Architecture

IST architecture (Figure 1 q.v.) consisted of two central engines: the Information Structure Activator (ISA) and the Information Structure Generator (ISG), two modules implementing Centering and Ordering constraints, respectively. English analysis was based on the CLE ([8]) resulting in a quasi-logical form (QLF) which was then traversed in search of relevant contextual and non-contextual information. This traversal and feature assignment constituted the **Information Structure Activator** which operated on a pre-transfer basis and was compiled with the English part of the IST. It was responsible for assigning center values and additional features to each term within the bounds of successive clauses. QLF-based **transfer** incorporates a number of unification transfer rules. The Information

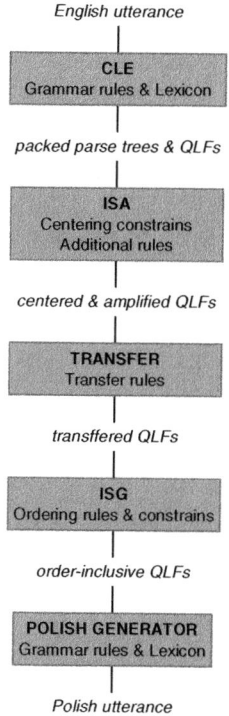

Fig. 1. General architecture of IST

Structure Generator was a post-transfer module which was compiled **with** the Polish part of the system. Polish Synthesis generates permissible Polish surface structures.

3   Information Structure Activator

ISA implemented methods of activating and centering information. Preprocessing, multi-centering and non-contextual features extraction were the three modules comprising this system (Figure 2 q.v.). The discourse history database was being updated as subsequent utterances were being processed.

3.1. Preprocessing

During the recursive traversal of the input QLF checks have been made for transitivity, markedness features and the presence of adjuncts. An appropriate construction type was assigned to the input QLF from the pool of intransitive, monotransitive, ditransitive, passive and a selected sample of pragmatically marked constructions including clefts, existentials, and fronted (right and left dislocation). Once the construction type was identified, all QLF terms representing nominals were extracted. The output of this phase was an ordered list of tagged terms within a given QLF which was then translated into an auxiliary predicate-argument construct, an *item*. Each *item* incorporated the following fields: *Surface_form, Semantics,Index,Resolution, Ferm_type_identifie, Center_value, Syntactic function* which would be instantiated by appropriate contextual and non-contextual checks in subsequent traversals.

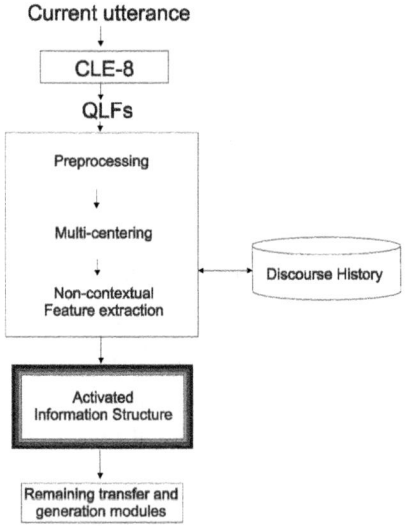

Fig. 2. Information Structure Activator

3.2 Multi-centering

The contextual processing module of ISA (Figure 3 q.v.) included the anaphora resolution phase which offered resolution of pronouns and operated on the list of unresolved *items*. Center values were calculated for each item according to the Gradation Principles ([14]). The resulting list of *items* with center value slots instantiated was then asserted in the dynamic database which kept a discourse history for successive utterances of the input text. The database was accessed each time an utterance U_i, starting with $i=1$, was being processed. For each U_i, a database handling predicate asserted the current list of *items*. At this point, center transitions ([6]) were calculated for U_i; $j=i-1$, $i-2$, …, $i-r$, where r was the maximum referential distance.

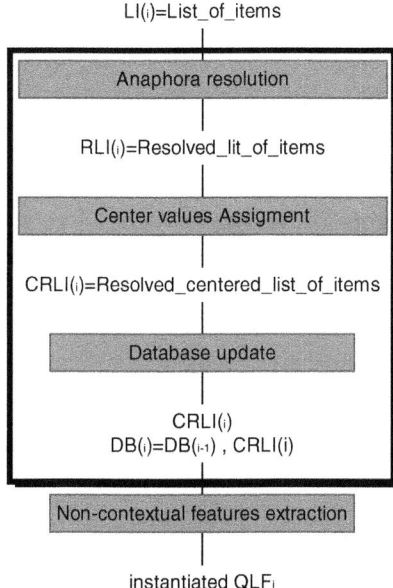

Fig. 3. Multi-centering modules

3.3   Non-contextual Features Extraction

Non-contextual features extraction complemented the interpretation phase of IST. For each successive utterance, checks were made for the occurrence of adjuncts, pronouns, specifications of syntactic functions of existing pronouns and lengths of nominal constituents. ISA instantiated the global (utterance-level) and local (nominal) fields necessary for further processing.

4 Bridging the Information Gap

Unification-based transfer formalism relied on compositionally translating the input language QLF to a QLF of the target language by matching QLF fragments against QLF pair patterns specifying transfer rules ([10]). Transfer rules were written declaratively and their left and right-hand side patterns matched the corresponding parts of English and Polish QLFs, respectively. These rules may be simple mappings (e.g. QLF constants) or recursive rules which contain allowing for transfer of a QLF expression in terms of the transfer of one or more of its sub-expressions.

Since both structural and lexical choices have to be made in translation, the transfer module differentiates between lexical (e.g. identities) and structural (equivalence and complex) transfer rules. The transfer of features related to information structure was bundled in subsequent QLFs and occurred at two levels, nominal information level associated with each term and top information level pertaining to the utterance. Each transferred QLF included contextual data needed for further processing: the generation of felicitous output orders.

5 Filtering Constituent Orders

The core filter application consisted of a series of precision points at which the initial list of S-V-O+/-A[1] permutations were being successively truncated. The method of ordering followed the multiplicity[2], restrictiveness and gradability criteria ([14]) and have been guided by a number of discourse principles and rules: Given Information Fronting Rule ([4]) Communicative Dynamism ([3]), Light-Heavy Constraint ([7]), Relative Order Principle ([14]), Zero Subject Rule ([14]). ISG was applied to a sequence of transferred QLFs. A looping structure *for i=0, 1,...,n* was entered to process the ith QLF underlying utterance *Ui*. The body of the loop was divided into five main decision points corresponding to constituent order filtering stages (Figure 4 q.v.).

5.1 Test Filters

Each successive QLF was first passed through two test filters, which checked, for emphatic markers and pronominal subject cases with shift centering transitions ([2]). If an adjunct was detected, additional placement criteria were being applied. Each path led to a unique solution.

---

[1] S-O-V+/-A (Subject Verb Object +/- Adjunct) is the prominent constituent order in English. Polish allows six contextually-motivated S-V-O permutations.

[2] Start by generating a list of all potential translation orders and restrict them by the application of successive filers. If there is more than than one order left from the initial list, scores are assigned to those based on statistical preference criteria.

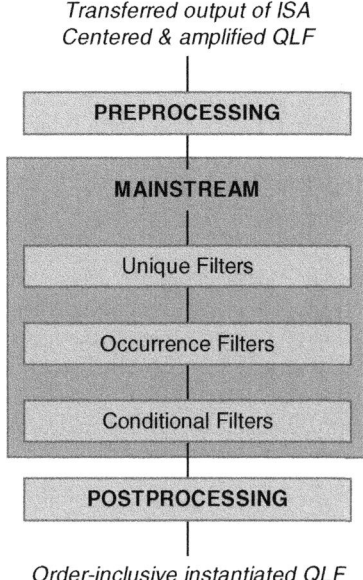

Transferred output of ISA
Centered & amplified QLF

| PREPROCESSING |
| MAINSTREAM |
| Unique Filters |
| Occurrence Filters |
| Conditional Filters |
| POSTPROCESSING |

Order-inclusive instantiated QLF

Fig. 4. First level flow chart for ISG

5.2 Occurrence Filters

If the unique solutions have not been arrived at, twelve possible paths through the occurrence filters were being pursued, as shown in figure 5.

	Path											
	f_1	f_2	f_3	f_4	f_5	f_6	f_7	f_8	f_9	f_{10}	f_{11}	f_{12}
Occurrence Filters	A+	A+	A+	A+	A+	A+	A-	A-	A-	A-	A-	A-
	S+	S+	S+	S+	S-	S-	S+	S+	S+	S+	S-	S-
	S:P+	S:P+	S:P-	S:P-	S:P+	S:P-	S:P+	S:P+	S:P-	S:P-	S:P+	S:P-
	O:P+	O:P-	O:P+	O:P-			O:P+	O:P-	O:P+	O:P-		

Fig. 5. Paths through occurrence filters

The occurrence filters checked for the presence/lack of a constituent (e.g. adjunct, zero surface subject) and identified the nature of that constituent (e.g. pronominal subject S:P+; non-pronominal object O:P-).

5.3 Conditional Filters

The resulting set of constituent orders was filtered through further discriminating criteria. Centering conditions defined by the Center Calculation Formula ([14]) were key determinants in conditional filter application. Center values defined for each nominal constituent formed a numerical progression, so that for each adjacent pair of nominal constituents the following would hold:

$$center(Term\_func1) - center(Term\_func2) >= 2.$$

Adjunct placement criteria and heaviness preferences based on statistical data from Polish corpus studies ([12]) supplemented conditional checks.

During the post-processing phase, statistical preference criteria ([12], [13]) defined the unique preferred order with the highest likelihood of occurrence as the actual output among the remaining orders.

This last stage helped to decide on the preferred translation version if more than one order remained in the candidate list.

6   Example

For utterance U_n in the following sequence

...
U_{n-1} : *A rabbit hopped across the lawn.*
U_n : *It ate a carrot.*
...

the output of ISA is IS-specific QLF:

```
QLFn-English =
[top_info(dcl, svo, na),
 form(l([it,ate,'a~',carrot]),
    verb(past,no,no,no,y),
A,
B^    [B,
    [eat_Consume,
     A,
     term(l([it]),ref(pro,it,sing,l([])),
         nom_info(1, 3, 3, rabbit_Animal, subj, 1),
         D^[impersonal,D],E,F),
     term(l(['a~',carrot]),
         q(G,a,sing),
         nom_info(2, -1, -1,carrot_DaucusCarota, obj, 2),
         I^[carrot_DaucusCarota,I],
         J,
         K)]],
    L)]
```

and the output of ISG is the order-inclusive QLF:

```
QLFn-Polish =
[top_info(dcl, svo, na, continuing, [ [v,s] ]),
 form(l(['~', zjadl, ,marchewke]),
```

```
   verb(_,_,_,_,_),
A,
B^   [B,
   [jesc_WrzucacDoZoladka,
   A,
   term(l(['~']),ref(zero_pro,on,sing,l([])),
      nom_info(1, 3, 3, krolik_Szarak, subj, 1),
      D^[impersonal,D],E,F),
   term(l([marchewke]),
      q(G,a,sing),
      nom_info(2, -1, -1,carrot_DaucusCarota, obj, 2),
      I^[carrot_DaucusCarota,I],
      J,
      K)]],
   L)]
```

A detailed description and elaborate illustration of ISA and ISG can be found [14]).

7 Evaluation

The evaluation process included program and native speaker testing of the Multi-centering and Ordering Hypotheses ([14]).

Several statistical hypotheses have been set up and tested in order to establish whether or not there have been significant differences between the quality (comprehensibility and coherence) of translations, one of which was consistent with the algorithmic paths of Multi-centering and Ordering, while the other one disregarded it. The evaluation of translation input was carried out by statistical tests of significance for difference in mean evaluation scores as well as the chi-square test of independence comparing proportions of failed translations and measuring homogeneity of texts with respect to the proportion of failed translations.

The other main category of tests included questionnaire-based native-speaker judgments of 32 original texts, complemented by statistical testing.

All tests clearly showed the importance of information structure for machine translation into free word order languages such as Polish.

8 Acknowledgments

I would like to thank David Carter, Manny Rayner and Steve Pulman for introducing me to the CLE and allowing me to use the SLT system as the backbone for this implementation. I would also like to thank Karen Sparck-Jones, my Thesis Supervisor, for many hours of insightful discussions.

References

1. Alshawi, H. (ed).: The Core Language Engine. The MIT Press. Cambridge, Massachusetts (1992)
2. Brennan, S.E., Friedman, M.W., and Pollard C.J.: A Centering Approach to Pronouns. Proceedings of the ACL (1987)
3. Danes, F.: Functional Sentence Perspective. Proceedings of the Conference on Connexity and Coherence. Amsterdam (1989) 23 – 31
4. Firbas, J.: Functional Sentence Perspective in Written and Spoken Communication. Cambridge: Cambridge University Press (1992)
5. Grosz, B.J., Joshi, A., and Weinstein, S.: Centering: A Framework *for* Modelling the Local Coherence of Discourse. Computational Linguistics 21/2 (1995) 203-227
6. Grosz, B.J. and Sidner, C.: Lost Intuitions and Forgotten Intentions. In Walker, M., Joshi, A., and Prince, E (eds.), Centering Theory in Discourse. Oxford: Clarendon Press (1998) 39-51
7. Hawkins, John A. A Performance Theory of Order and Constituency. Cambridge: Cambridge University Press (1994)
8. Rayner, M English Linguistic Coverage. In Agnas, M-S., Alshawi,H., Bretan, I., Carter, D. M., Cedar, K., Collins, M. J., Crouch, R. S., Digalakis, V., Ekholm, B., Gamback, B., Kaja, J., Karlgren, J., Lyberg, B., Price, P., Pulman, G., Rayner, M., Samuelsson, C., and Svensson, T. (eds.), Spoken Language Translator: First Year Report. SRI Technical Report CRC-043 (1994)
10.Rayner, M.: Transfer and Robust Translation. In Agnas et al. (eds.), Spoken Language Translator. Cambridge, UK: SRI technical report (1998) Chapter 12
11.Siewierska, A.: Postverbal Subject Pronouns in Polish in the Light of Topic Continuity and the Topic Focus Distinction. In . J. Nuyts, J. and de Schutter, G. (eds.), Getting One's Words into Line. Dordrecht (1987)
12.Siewierska, A.: Syntactic Weight vs. Information Structure and Word Order Variation in Polish. Journal of Linguistics 29 (1993) 233-265
13.Siewierska, A.: Subject and Object Order in Written Polish: Some Statistical Data. Folia Linguistica XXVII (1993)
14.Stys-Budzikowska, M.: A Processing Model of Information Structure in Machine Translation. University of Cambridge: Ph.D. Thesis (1998)
15.Vachek, J. Vilem Mathesius as Forerunner of Contrastive Linguistic Studies. Papers and Studies in Contrastive Linguistics 11. Poznan: A.M.University (1980) 5-15

The Effect of Source Analysis on Translation Confidence

Arendse Bernth and Michael C. McCord

IBM T.J. Watson Research Center, P.O. Box 218, Yorktown Heights, NY 10598, USA
arendse@us.ibm.com and mcmccord@us.ibm.com

Abstract. Translations produced by an MT system can automatically be assigned a number that reflects the MT system's confidence in their quality. We describe the design of such a confidence index, with focus on the contribution of source analysis, which plays a crucial role in many MT systems, including ours. Various problematic areas of source analysis are identified, and their impact on the overall confidence index is given. We will describe two methods of training the confidence index, one by hand-tuning of the heuristics, the other by linear regression analysis.

1 Introduction

Given the state of the art of Machine Translation, it is useful for an MT system to supply the user with an estimate of the translation quality for each sentence it translates. By a *translation confidence index* for an MT system, we mean a function that assigns to each source language segment a number that estimates the confidence that the MT system can translate that segment well.[1] We assume that the range of values of the index is between 0 and 10, with 0 meaning no confidence and 10 meaning complete confidence. We can also view the computation of this number as an attempt to approximate the way an expert human translator would rate the MT system's translation on a scale from 0 to 10. Of course the algorithm for the index will normally use heuristics, so that an index of 10 does not really completely *guarantee* a perfect translation! Note that the index is a measure of confidence in the translations by a *particular* MT system, not necessarily a general measure of translatability for a source text. However, ingredients used in calculating the index may apply across different MT systems, and this is true for many of the ingredients discussed in the present paper.

In [4] we described the overall design of a translation confidence index, hereinafter called the *TCI*, and in [5,6] we illustrated its use in IBM's MT system for English-German [14,9]. The TCI is fully implemented and has been integrated with the IBM MT system. This MT system is a transfer-based system, and that is reflected in the design of the TCI.

The idea of a translation confidence index is of course closely related to the idea of automatic evaluation of MT output. *Manual* evaluation of MT output

---

[1] A system that measures the translatability of a *complete* document is described in [8].

J.S. White (Ed.): AMTA 2000, LNAI 1934, pp. 89–99, 2000.

has a long history, dating back at least to the ALPAC report [15]. Since then, a number of papers have addressed various issues relating to evaluation; see e.g. [10] for an overview. Our proposal differs from previous work in that the "evaluation" is fully automatic and takes place *during* translation so that the translation process for a given segment can be abandoned as soon as the confidence falls below a user-specified threshold. Of course our index is only an estimate. If the system knew enough to make a completely accurate evaluation, it would seem to have to evaluate by comparison with a perfect translation, and then the system would be able to produce such a translation automatically.

The overall idea behind the design and implementation of the TCI is to measure the complexity of the translation process. As the complexity increases, the confidence in the translation decreases. The index for a segment is calculated during translation of that segment. We start out with a score of 10 – perfect confidence. As various situations or conditions are encountered during the translation process, this score gets penalized by subtraction of various kinds of penalties. Penalties are floating point numbers, with a larger number representing a worse problem. For convenience of use of the results, the TCI is cut off at 0 if the total penalty rises above 10. Of course the impact of the various types of problems may vary from language pair to language pair, so the exact penalties are set in a language-pair-specific profile. The profile specifies two things: (1) It selects among various types of penalties that are available with the TCI. (2) For each selected penalty, the profile specifies an *adjustment coefficient* for that penalty. The TCI engine itself computes a number associated with the penalty, and then this number is multiplied by the associated adjustment coefficient in the profile before applying the penalty to the overall TCI score.

Proper calibration of the language-pair-specific profile is a matter of great importance. This calibration can be viewed as an optimization problem. Until recently we have done the calibration totally "by hand". However, we have begun work on calibration by linear regression analysis, and have preliminary results which are better than those of the "hand" calibration, for the tests done so far. The basic idea of the regression analysis is that the adjustment coefficients in the profile are selected by the regression analysis algorithm on the basis of training data, instead of being selected by hand. We will report in this paper on both methods. In the bulk of the paper, we will report on the penalties as they are in a "hand" profile for our English-German system; they are summarized in table 1. The automatically selected coefficients are often fairly similar, so this gives a good idea anyway of the algorithm. In Section 7 we describe our process for training with regression analysis, and in Section 8 we report on the results of the regression analysis, and compare it with the hand-tuning method.

Penalties may be applied at any stage of the translation process – during source analysis, lexical transfer, structural transfer, and morphological generation. Penalty rules applied during structural transfer have the effect of penalizing certain infelicitous properties of the target tree or a precursor of it. However, *source analysis* plays the most important role in the translation process, because (1) source analysis is the most nondeterministic and most error-prone part of

Table 1. Summary of Penalties

Problem type	Penalty
Lack of Initial Capitalization of Segment	1
Abbreviations	0.1
Punctuation	0.5
Footnotes	1.5
Segment Length	(See Section 2)
Lexical Analyses L	If $L = 0$, then 0.3; else $0.01 * L * s$
Parts of Speech	$number\_of\_parts\_of\_speech * s$
Noun-Verb	$0.07 * s$
Determiner/Pronoun–Noun/Verb	$0.07 * s$
Infinitive/Imperative Verb–Noun	$0.1 * s$
Adjective/Noun–Noun	$0.5 * s$
Infinitive/Imperative Verb/Adjective–Noun	$0.1 * s$
Proper Noun–Noun	$0.1 * s$
"To"–Infinitive Verb/Noun (segment length > 3)	1.5
Coordinating Conjunction	0.5
Problematic Words	0.1
Failed Parse	5
Parse with Unfilled Obligatory Slots	1.0
Many Parses	(See Section 4)
Identical Parses with Different Word Senses	0.5
Close Parses	$0.25 * s$
Parsescore	$(0.5 * parsecore)/ segment\_length$
Missing Subject	0.1
Missing Hyphen	0.1
Lack of Subject-Verb Agreement	0.1
Wrong Comparative/Superlative	0.1
Long Noun groups	0.1
Missing "that"-Complementizer	0.05
Passive Construction	1.5
Nonfinite Verb	0.5
Potentially Wrong Modification in Subjectless VP	0.2
String of Prepositional Phrases	0.05
Double Ambiguous passives	0.1
"For-to"-Construction	0.5
Time Reference	0.2
Prepositions without Object	3
Lexical Time Usage	$(0.01 * time) / segment\_length)$
Syntactic Time Usage	$(0.002 * time) / segment\_length)$
Pointer Space Usage	$(0.00001 * space) / segment\_length)$
Character Space Usage	$(0.001 * space) / segment\_length)$

MT, and (2) errors made at this stage tend to carry over to and influence later stages. In this paper we shall give more technical detail about those aspects of the TCI that relate to source analysis. The discussion is self-contained.

The main steps of source analysis where things may go wrong are: segmentation and tokenization; lexical and morphological analysis; and syntactic analysis. We look at certain problems that may occur during these steps. Additionally, we look at the output of the parsing process to discover certain properties of the source text that may be indicative of hard-to-parse or hard-to-translate segments. These especially include certain ambiguous or complex constructions. In this paper we shall examine each of these contributions to the TCI in source analysis.

2   Segmentation and Tokenization

The first step in the translation process is segmentation and tokenization of the source text. In order to get a correct parse, it is of course crucial that this step is correct.

Lack of capitalization of the first word of the segment (as the segment is determined by the segmenter algorithm!) may imply wrong segmentation. This gets a penalty of 1.0.

Another problem is posed by abbreviations which normally end in a period. In these cases, there is usually only one period regardless of whether this is the end of the segment or not. Checking on the capitalization of the following word does not always help, because the following word may be a proper noun, or the segment may be a header where content words are capitalized. For such abbreviations the penalty per occurrence is 0.1.

Occurrences of dashes, semicolons, and double quotes may also pose problems for source analysis. The penalty per occurrence of a pair or a single punctuation is 0.5.

Although footnotes are not common in all text types, they can play havoc with segmentation. There appears to be no consistent use of footnotes; they can appear as internal parts of a segment, which need to be treated as part of the segment, or they may be separate segments, which should be treated as separate entities. And there is no clear-cut way of reliably distinguishing these two cases. The penalty per occurrence is 1.5.

Segment length (number of tokens) can be determined as soon as segmentation and tokenization are completed. This is of course an extremely important (and easy-to-determine!) indicator of potential problems. *Long* segments are famous for being difficult to parse accurately; but also *short* segments (4 words or less) can give trouble because of the lack of context available that would help disambiguate part of speech. This penalty is a function of the segment length. The basic function, *segment_length_penalty*, is coded in the engine as follows. Here N is the segment length.

$segment\_length\_penalty(N) = 1.0 \qquad (1 \le N \le 4);$
$segment\_length\_penalty(N) = 0.0 \qquad (5 \le N \le 19);$
$segment\_length\_penalty(N) = 0.7 \qquad (20 \le N \le 25);$
$segment\_length\_penalty(N) = 1.0 \qquad (26 \le N \le 29);$
$segment\_length\_penalty(N) = 1.5 \qquad (30 \le N).$

The profile specifies a constant multiplier for this function. In our tuned profile for English-German, the constant is 0.07, so that the penalty is 0.07 * *segment_length_penalty(N)*.

3   Lexical and Morphological Analysis

After tokenization, each token is given a lexical analysis. For English, this is an area with a great potential for ambiguity, which affects parsing. Of course, in most cases the sentence context helps in disambiguating the lexical choice. But some contexts are notoriously ambiguous, especially for shorter segments (4 words or less). In the previous section, we have already described a general penalty for short segments, but there is an additional penalty related to the number of lexical analyses of each word. A constant *shortseg* figures in the following penalties. In our hand-tuned profile, *shortseg* is set to 0.4. In the rest of the paper we agree that the variable *shortfactor* is equal to *shortseg* if the current segment is a short segment (4 words or less) and otherwise *shortfactor* is 1.[2]

In assigning penalties based on lexical analyses, we consider both the number of lexical analyses per word and the number of different parts of speech per word.

The first penalty is assigned as follows for each word w. Let L be the number of lexical analyses of w. Then we assign the penalty P as follows:

If $L = 0$, then $P = 0.3$;
else $P = 0.01 * L * shortfactor$.

The second penalty Q is assigned to each word w as follows. Let *NPOS* be the number of parts of speech of w in its set of lexical analyses.

$Q = NPOS * shortfactor$

Certain combinations of possible parts of speech can also be very ambiguous. We look at all pairs of words occurring in the segment. Let the first element of any given pair be called *Word1*, and the second element be called *Word2*. We look for the following combinations:

- Word1: Singular noun; Word2: Singular verb and plural noun. Example: *Asparagus spears.*
  (Penalty per occurrence of pair: 0.07 * *shortfactor*)
- Word1: Determiner and pronoun; Word2: Noun and verb. Example: *All benefits.*
  (Penalty per occurrence of pair: 0.07 * *shortfactor*).

---

[2] In table 1 *shortfactor* is abbreviated to *s*.

- Word1: Infinitive/imperative verb and singular noun; Word2: Singular or plural noun. Example: *File cabinets*.
  (Penalty per occurrence of pair: 0.1 * *shortfactor*).
- Word1: Adjective and singular noun; Word2: Singular or plural noun. Example: *Level gun*.
  (Penalty per occurrence of pair: 0.5 * *shortfactor*).
- Word1: Infinitive/imperative verb and adjective; Word2: Plural noun. Example: *Level guns*.
  (Penalty per occurrence of pair: 0.1 * *shortfactor*).
- Word1: Singular proper noun; Word2: Singular or plural noun. Example: "He gives *John trouble*".
  (Penalty per occurrence of pair: 0.1 * *shortfactor*).
- Word1 is *to*; Word2: Infinitive verb and singular noun. This only applies to segments longer than three words. Example: *. . . to market . . . .*
  (Penalty per occurrence (i.e. per sentence): 1.5).

In addition to these lexical problems, we also look for certain problematic words which do not fit neatly into any of the above categories. Coordinating conjunctions are penalized heavily: 0.5 per occurrence. Each of the following types is penalized 0.1 per occurrence: pronouns, words that are both adverbs and subordinate conjunctions, words that are both prepositions and particles, and, finally, the specific words *as, like, which, not*.

4   Process of Syntactic Analysis

The obvious thing to check for relating to syntactic analysis is of course a failed parse. Even though the ESG parser [11,12] provides a pieced-together parse in these cases, an incomplete parse still has a very tangible impact on the quality of the translation. (Penalty per segment: 5).

There are also some parses which, even though they succeed to some extent, are not good parses because not all obligatory slots have been filled. (Penalty per segment: 1).

The ESG parser does pruning of intermediate results during parsing. *Parse scores* are assigned dynamically to intermediate analyses in the chart [12,13]. Parse scoring is used for pruning the chart as well as for ranking the final parses heuristically as to likelihood of correctness. (Lower parse scores indicate better parses.) Parse space pruning results in an average of around two final parses per segment.

The TCI uses parse scores to assign penalties in several ways. The first penalty is computed as follows. Let *numparses* be the number of final parses of the segment. The higher *numparses* is, the more uncertainty there is of the correctness of the best-ranked parse. Let *parsescore* be the ESG parse score of the best-ranked parse, and let N be the number of words in the segment. We calculate the following penalty Q if *numparses* > 1. Let

$P = \max(0.03 * numparses * shortfactor, 3)$;
if $0.5 * parsescore + P > 3.0$,
    then $Q = 3 - 0.5 * parsescore/N$;
    else $Q = P$.

The second penalty is as follows. If there are two parses with identical parse scores, and the parses are the same except for differences in one or more word senses, then there could be a problem in translation of those word senses, and we assign a penalty of 0.5.

On the other hand, if the two best-ranked parses are close but not identical in parse scoring, this may also be indicative of a potential problem. In this case we assign a third penalty of $0.25 * shortfactor$.

Finally, the parse score itself is a measure of the confidence of the parse. To offset the impact of segment length on the parse score, the parse score is divided by segment length, and we assign the following penalty:

$0.5 * (parsescore / segment\_length)$.

5 Properties of the Parse Tree

Various other properties of the source text are indicative of trouble. These are related to some of the problems that EasyEnglishAnalyzer [1,2,3,5,6,7] looks for. They include sentences with missing subject (penalty per occurrence: 0.1), missing hyphens (penalty per occurrence: 0.1), lack of subject-verb agreement (penalty per occurrence: 0.1), wrong comparatives and superlatives (penalty per occurrence: 0.1), long noun groups (penalty per occurrence: 0.1), missing "that"-complementizer (penalty per occurrence: 0.05), passive constructions (penalty per occurrence: 1.5), nonfinite verbs (penalty per occurrence: 0.5), potentially wrong modification in subjectless verb phrases (penalty per occurrence: 0.2), more than one consecutive prepositional phrase (penalty per occurrence: 0.05), ambiguous double passives (penalty per occurrence: 0.1), *for-to* constructions (penalty per occurrence: 0.5), time references which may be both adverbs and nouns (penalty per occurrence: 0.2), and prepositions without objects (penalty per occurrence: 3).

6 Time and Space

Time and space used during source analysis can also be indicative of complexity and therefore of potential problems. Time is measured separately for lexical analysis (penalty: $(0.01 * time) / segment\_length$) and syntactic analysis (penalty: $(0.002 * time) / segment\_length$). Space usage is a simple indication of the number of partial analyses and associated computation during parsing. The more partial analyses, the higher the risk is of choosing the wrong final analysis. We measure the space used for pointers and numbers (penalty: $(0.00001 * space) / segment\_length$), and for characters (penalty: $(0.001 * space) / segment\_length$) separately.

7   Training with Regression Analysis

To obtain a profile with adjustment coefficients determined from regression analysis, we have so far experimented with two different training sets of sentences, one with 200 sentences selected at random from newspaper articles (online), and another with 200 sentences from web page news stories (5 stories). The English-German MT system translations of these sentences were scored by hand on our scale of 0 to 10 for translation quality. We have tried the regression analysis on both of the test sets, and on the combination, but got the best results for the web page set alone, and will report on that here.

The ideas of the regression analysis can be explained simply, as follows. Let the raw penalties calculated by the TCI for any segment x be:

$$p_1(x), p_2(x), \ldots, p_n(x)$$

The *TCI* function itself then has the form

$$TCI(x) = 10 - c_1 p_1(x) + c_2 p_2(x) + \cdots + c_n p_n(x)$$

for suitable coefficients c_j – our *adjustment coefficients*. The formula for $TCI(x)$ starts with 10 (representing a perfect score) and subtracts the weighted penalties $c_j p_j(x)$. We want to determine the weights c_j automatically by fitting the function TCI to data given by human scoring on a training set. This determination is just what the regression analysis does.

Suppose our training set of segments is:

$$\{x_1, x_2, \ldots, x_m\}$$

For $1 \leq i \leq m$, let s_i be the human score assigned to segment x_i.

The task of the regression analysis algorithm can be stated as follows: It determines values for the coefficients c_j such that the sum of squares

$$(TCI(x_1) - s_1)^2 + (TCI(x_2) - s_2)^2 + \cdots + (TCI(x_m) - s_m)^2$$

is minimized. The square root of this sum of squares is just the distance between the two points

$$(TCI(x_1), TCI(x_2), \ldots, TCI(x_m)),$$

$$(s_1, s_2, \ldots, s_m)$$

in Euclidean m-space; so we are minimizing the distance between the vector of human scores on the training data and the vector of (fitted) TCI scores on the data.

The actual input that we give to the regression analysis package[3] consists of two things:

---

[3] We found it convenient to use the regression analysis package associated with Lotus 1-2-3.

1. the $m \times n$ matrix P which has $p_j(x_i)$ in its ith row and jth column,
2. the length-m vector $S = (s_1, s_2, \ldots, s_m)$

Our TCI program can be run in a mode where the vector of raw penalties

$$p_1(x), p_2(x), \ldots, p_n(x)$$

can be output for any segment x, so this allows us to produce the matrix P.

The regression analysis package then uses the input data P and S and provides us with the coefficients c_j, which we take as the adjustment coefficients in the *regression-trained profile*, and we have the *regression-trained TCI*.

8 TCI Testing and Comparison of Regression Training and Hand-Tuning

We ran the TCI twice on a test set of 60 new sentences from web page news stories, once with the regression-trained profile and once with the hand-tuned profile.

We made a comparison based on the use of the TCI where the MT system is being used by a human translator, who will postedit the output. Of course we prefer not to bother the human translator with bad output when we can help it. Professional translators often find it easier to translate a segment from scratch than to postedit bad MT output. So a *threshold* score T is set, and the MT system's result on a sentence will not be shown to the human translator unless the TCI score is above T.

In general, the threshold could be set by the human translator, but we will report the results for a threshold of 7.0, which seems to represent a safe cut-off for usefulness of MT for a translator.

For the regression-trained TCI (and threshold 7.0), the results of interest are as follows.

% of sentences above threshold, per human scoring = 58.3%
% of sentences above threshold, per TCI scoring = 58.3%
% of sentences where human and TCI agree on side of threshold = 66.7%
% of sentences shown to user that were above threshold per human scoring = 71.4%

Notes:
(a) The fact that the same percentage (58.3%) occurs for the first two statistics is slightly coincidental. It is not the same set of sentences in the two cases, as one can see from the third statistic.

(b) The third statistic (with value 66.7%) more or less represents the accuracy of the TCI's choices (whether to call a sentence "good" or "bad" with respect to this threshold).

(c) The fourth statistic (71.4%) represents the success in the goal of not showing bad results to the user. Of course we could avoid showing bad results by not showing *any* results to the user at this threshold, so there is a tradeoff there! But in fact we see from the second statistic that 58.3% of the test sentences are shown to the user, and this is a non-trivial number. The fourth statistic says that, among those sentences shown to the user, 71.4% really *should* have been shown (for the given choice of threshold).

For the hand-tuned TCI (and threshold 7.0), the corresponding results are as follows.

% of sentences above threshold, per human scoring = 58.3%
% of sentences above threshold, per TCI scoring = 28.3%
% of sentences where human and TCI agree on side of threshold = 63.3%
% of sentences shown to user that were above threshold per human scoring = 88.2%

Notes:

(a) The hand-tuned TCI is more successful (88.2%) at not showing bad results to the user. But this is at the price of not showing as many results totally to the user (only 28.3%).

(b) Considering the overall set of statistics, we judge that the regression-trained TCI has better performance than the hand-tuned TCI, as they stand now.

9   Future Work

There is much more that can be done to improve the TCI, continuing along the lines we have started.

One issue is the exact mix of penalty types that we use. Perhaps some of them that have been selected are not worthwhile. Perhaps there are others that we should bring into the picture.

We plan to concentrate on the regression analysis approach to tuning. The most obvious need is to use much more training data, and to categorize training and profiles per subject matter. Another factor is to take more account of the fact that some of the raw penalty numbers do not vary linearly with sentence length. We plan to experiment with piecewise linear regression.

10   Conclusion

An automatic index that measures an MT system's own confidence in its translations can be extremely valuable when MT is used by human translators, since they need not bother looking at MT output with low indices. Such an index can be valuable also for casual users of MT so that they will know better when to trust the machine's output. The TCI described (in part) in this paper provides such an index. In the paper, we have concentrated on the computation of the components of the TCI that are associated with source analysis. This is a crucial part of the index because (1) source analysis is the most non-deterministic and most error-prone part of MT, and (2) errors made at this stage tend to carry over to and influence later stages. We have identified and described the various problematic areas of source analysis and, by assigning penalties, ranked them in importance. By integrating and applying this to our English-German MT system with an initial result of a TCI accuracy of around 67%, we have indications that the method shows good promise.

Acknowledgment. We wish to thank Claudia Gdaniec for many useful suggestions in this work.

References

1. Bernth, A.: EasyEnglish: A tool for improving document quality. In Proceedings of the Fifth Conference on Applied Natural Language Processing. Association for Computational Linguistics (1997) 159–165
2. Bernth, A.: EasyEnglish: Addressing structural ambiguity. In Proceedings of AMTA-98. Association for Machine Translation in the Americas (1998) 164–173
3. Bernth, A.: EasyEnglish: Preprocessing for MT. In Proceedings of the Second International Workshop on Controlled Language Applications. (1998) Carnegie-Mellon University. Pittsburgh, PA 30–41
4. Bernth, A.: A confidence index for machine translation. In Proceedings of Theoretical and Methodological Issues in Machine Translation. Chester, England (1999) 120–127
5. Bernth, A.: Controlling input and output of MT for greater user acceptance. In Proceedings 21st Conference Translating and the Computer. (1999)
6. Bernth, A.: Tools for improving E-G MT quality. In Proceedings of Theoretical and Methodological Issues in Machine Translation, Workshop on Problems and Potential of English-to-German MT Systems. Chester, England (1999)
7. Bernth, A.: EasyEnglish: Grammar checking for non-native speakers. In Proceedings of the Third International Workshop on Controlled Language Applications. Seattle, WA (2000) 33–42
8. Gdaniec, C.: The Logos translatability index. In Proceedings of AMTA-94. Association for Machine Translation in the Americas (1994) 97–105.
9. Gdaniec, C.: Lexical choice and syntactic generation in a transfer system: Transformations in the new LMT English-German system. In Proceedings of AMTA-98. Association for Machine Translation in the Americas (1998) 408–420.
10. Lewis, D.: MT evaluation: Science or art? In Proceedings 19st Conference Translating and the Computer. (1997) 1–14
11. McCord, M.: Slot Grammars. Computational Linguistics. **6** (1980) 31–43
12. McCord, M.: Slot Grammar: A system for simpler construction of practical natural language grammars. In R. Studer, (ed.), Natural Language and Logic: International Scientific Symposium, Lecture Notes in Computer Science. Springer Verlag, Berlin (1990) 118–145
13. McCord, M.: Heuristics for broad-coverage natural language parsing. In Proceedings of the ARPA Human Language Technology Workshop. Morgan-Kaufmann (1993) 127–132
14. McCord, M. and Bernth, A.: The LMT transformational system. In Proceedings of AMTA-98. Association for Machine Translation in the Americas (1998) 344–355
15. Pierce, J.R., Carroll, J.B., et al.: Language and machines: Computers in translation and linguistics. Technical Report 1416, Automated Language Processing Advisory Committee (ALPAC), National Academy of Sciences, National Research Council, Washington, D.C. (1966)

Contemplating Automatic MT Evaluation

John S. White

Litton PRC, McLean VA
White_john@prc.com

Abstract. Researchers, developers, translators and information consumers all share the problem that there is no accepted standard for machine translation. The problem is much further confounded by the fact that MT evaluations properly done require a considerable commitment of time and resources, an anachronism in this day of cross-lingual information processing when new MT systems may developed in weeks instead of years. This paper surveys the needs addressed by several of the classic „types" of MT, and speculates on ways that each of these types might be automated to create relevant, near-instantaneous evaluation of approaches and systems.

1 Introduction

One of the moments that many MT research presentations have in common is the viewgraph that makes the assertion that there is no standard method for evaluating machine translation. This observation is made by way of segue into a presentation of their own evaluation results, in which the researchers reviewed output and counted errors, or categorized output sentences as senseless or meaningful, or perfect, etc. The results are then generally represented as some percentage of some notion such as „acceptable," „correct," „fluent," and so on.

Many of these researchers would almost certainly concede that such observations leave much to be desired. There are no controls on the nature of the judgments made, often by the researchers themselves. There is no reliable prediction that these evaluation results could be replicated with a different population of subjects, nor, perhaps more importantly, that the measurements actually tell them anything they, their audience, or their sponsors really need to know.

The point of this discussion is not to enumerate the shortcomings of these ad-hoc evaluation methods, but rather to recognize the plight of the researcher who must pay some obeisance to the justifiable requirement to show some evaluation results. There are indeed many well-known MT evaluation methods ([8], [10], [7], [6], and [1], among many). But it is quite correct to assert that none are universally accepted as standards. It is also true that the useful ones take considerable effort, cost, and time to perform, and that none of the methods tell us all of the things different people might need to know about an MT system or approach.

J.S. White (Ed.): AMTA 2000, LNAI 1934, pp. 100-108, 2000.
© Springer-Verlag Berlin Heidelberg 2000

So there is no accepted standard for MT evaluation because of these two reasons, that there are different methods to measures different attributes, and these methods take more commitment than developers are able to make.

It seems obvious that both problems could be addressed by an instant, automatic evaluation that tells us exactly what we need to know at nearly zero cost. Why isn't there such a litmus strip for MT that can tell the developer, buyer, user, investor immediately what each needs to know about a system or approach? The best known example of why there isn't such a thing has to with the fact that MT, unlike information extraction, topic or document detection, optical character recognition or speech recognition, doesn't have a possible „ground truth" (i.e. no set of exactly right answers against which to compare the output of a particular MT instance). This is not because no one has bothered to devise such a set of data, but rather because it cannot be done in a straightforward way: since there are many ways to say the same thing in any language, it follows that there must be many „right" translations of any expressions. So an MT system could produce a „right" answer which is not anticipated by any „ground truth," with no way to tell whether it is an unaccounted-for right answer or a wrong answer, and even worse, how „wrong" it is.

And for the reason we have already noted, no one automatic measure would necessarily tell us what we need to know (e.g., how intelligible or faithful a translation is may not tell me whether I can actually use it for something I need to do). So it appears that the vision of instant, automatic MT evaluation has to include several different automatic methods.

All of these challenges are focused in the current requirements to create new MT systems very rapidly. We cannot spend months evaluating a system that was developed in a week.

In this paper I hope to present an organizing principle – the types of MT evaluation and their purposes, and describe in each case the potential for an automatic evaluation for that type. The survey nature of this paper necessarily will cover some ground that may be familiar to many readers (and I hope that they will bear with me on those portions), in order to show the potential for automation of MT evaluation for each evaluation type. From that presentation we will see that automatic evaluation, while very difficult, is not impossible.

2 Types of MT Evaluation

The different contexts of MT in the lifecycle of a particular approach require that people in different roles will, at different times, need to know different things about that approach and/or the system that incorporates it. The researcher putting together a proof-of-concept prototype needs to know about different things than does the same or different person once the system is in development, and the venture capitalist who wants to get involved financially needs to know different attributes still.

For the purposes of this discussion we will characterize the evaluation types in this way, based on the work of Arnold et al. ([1]), augmented by the models of van Slype ([10]) and Vasconcellos ([11]):

- Feasibility evaluation
- Internal evaluation
- Declarative evaluation
- Usability evaluation
- Operational evaluation

2.1   Feasibility Evaluation

A feasibility study is an evaluation of the possibility that a particular approach has any potential for success after further research and implementation.   Feasibility evaluations provide measures of interest to researchers and the sponsors of research. The attributes that a feasibility evaluation tests for are the coverage of sub-problems particular to a particular language pair, and the possibility of extending to more general phenomena.

Typically, a well-designed feasibility test for an MT approach uses sets of test patterns which cover the commonly recognized differences between the source and target language. These should be in the form of simple source language patterns that are „theory neutral,“ that is, descriptive in pedagogical terms rather than in terms of a particular syntactic theory whose principles could obscure the simple coverage problems being tackled at this stage.

In feasibility testing it is possible to come rather close to the „ground truth“ which is generally not possible in MT evaluation. Since the feasibility test is only trying to show whether an approach can handle very bounded set of sub-problems very well, it should be possible to design the test patterns to control all phenomena except the phenomenon being tested. So it is possible to think of a single „right“ translation in this context.

Automatic Feasibility Evaluation.   Because of this potential for a single right answer, automatic evaluation could be a simple as automatically comparing the output of the test pattern translation, character-by-character, to the expected output. Note that in doing this, absolute discipline must be maintained to avoid counting „blue bird“ serendipities which happen to be good translations but not the expected ones. This is because these outputs do not help prove the principle of the approach nor indicate its extensibility to more general problems. Automatic scoring of these patterns must only admit right and wrong as results, but if the test patterns are correctly designed, this is all we need at this point in the lifecycle.

I should note here the exceptional reuse potential for theory-neutral contrastive patterns. A corpus of such patterns could be used for early testing for any approach using that language pair. A collection of corpora for many pairs would be of considerable value for the community as a whole, for a very long time – theories and implementation approaches last a couple of years, but the contrasts between two languages can last for millennia.

2.2   Internal Evaluation

Internal evaluation occurs on a continual or periodic basis in the course of research and or development.   Internal evaluations test whether the components of a experimental, prototype, or pre-release system work as they are intended.

This evaluation needs to show coverage of the fundamental contrastive phenomena of the language pair, just like the feasibility evaluation. However, in this point in a system's lifecycle it must also be shown that the system is actually improving as a result of development, and that improvement in one area doesn't make something else worse. So in internal evaluation there is a standard set of test materials for iterative testing.

Additionally, the internal evaluations must actually demonstrate extensibility to the language phenomena that will actually occur in the system's intended sphere of usage. So internal test sets will also have training sets and test sets of actual source text to demonstrate incremental improvement without degradation.

Automatic Internal evaluation.   Accomplishing automatic internal evaluation is much more difficult than for feasibility testing, even though some of the test material is likely to be the same. This is because we are actually looking at the test results to see what went wrong, and what that implies for how to go about fixing it. It is also more difficult because of the less controlled phenomena in the extensibility part of it, where real source language text is used. In this case, many things can go wrong which appear to a different cause, as when a missing lexical item causes a cascade of syntactic errors.

It is likely that we cannot automate every aspect of internal evaluation. But we can automate perhaps more than we think we can. There are two fundamental views in internal evaluation testing: black box and glass box. The first observes the input and the output and measures the change against the expected change.   Glass box evaluations watch the process occur and determine whether each component does what it is supposed to do in the test circumstance.

It is possible to perform an automatic comparison of the expected data structures at each sub-component of a system in a glass-box view, and this can be expressed in a binary way, as long as we have characterized the expected structure for each input in the test set.   It may even be possible to automatically suggest reasons and remediations at each component where the structure deviates from the expected. However, it will still be incumbent upon the developer to interpret the results, determine whether the fault lies with the affected component or with some previous component in the stream, and figure out what it means in terms of improvement.

2.3   Declarative Evaluation

Declarative evaluation is what most of us think MT evaluation is. Conceptually it confirms to some notion we all (think we) share about the performance of MT systems. When spokespersons for a product or for the field as a whole characterizes the state-of-the-art as N% accurate, he/she is appealing to this notion. And this is one of the things that makes discussion of MT evaluation especially tricky.   Our researcher with whom we introduced this paper will make some judgments along the lines of a declarative belief and express them as feasibility results. A salesperson for an MT product will take internal results (e.g. counting errors germane to its own development approach) and represent than as declarative statistics.

The purpose of declarative evaluation is to measure the ability of an MT system to handle text representative of actual end-use. It purports to measure the actual performance of a system external to the particulars of the feasibility of the approach or of the development process. As with feasibility and internal evaluations, we look coverage of linguistic phenomena and handling of samples of real text. However, these generally do not use constrained test patterns, and they are not directly used to determine the extensibility of a system, but how good it is right now.

Declarative evaluations generally test for the attributes of *intelligibility* (how fluent or understandable it appears to be) and *fidelity* (the accuracy and completeness of the information conveyed). These attributes are particularly susceptible to the problems that prevent us from having a ground truth. Both these attributes are extremely subjective in nature. Not only are there many ways to say the same thing, you will get very many different human judgments about which of these ways to say something is actually the best way to say it (with or without a situational context). Therefore capturing a generalizable characterization of the intelligibility/fidelity of imperfect MT output requires a fairly large sample of judgments from a good number of people.

It generally appears that fidelity and intelligibility are separate attributes. After all, a translation can be perfectly understandable but wrong (e.g., when a negation in the source is left out of the target), or garbled but informative (e.g., if all I need are some key words to help me decide whether to keep the document). But they do converge at least in two places. A system that produces just dots is maximally unintelligible and as a result is maximally unfaithful. A system which is „perfect" (by which I mean produces translations that are as if they had originally been written in the target language) is maximally faithful and for the same reason maximally intelligible.

Automatic declarative Evaluation. We have already said that the best declarative evaluations involve human judgments, which in turn require human factors controls and many judgment points. Thus it should be very difficult to conceive of an automatic measurement of intelligibility and fidelity. But it may be possible after all, and a solution appears to have something to do with our observation about the convergences of fidelity and intelligibility.

The series of MT evaluations in the 1990's known as the DARPA series ([13]) needed three measures to capture a declarative evaluation of several English-target systems at the same time: „informativeness," which is rather like a reading aptitude test; „adequacy," which compares the information in small chunks of expert translation with the information in MT outputs; and „fluency," which asks readers to indicate how English-like a sentence of output is. The first two measure aspects of fidelity, while fluency measures an aspect of intelligibility.

In statistical analyses subsequent to the DARPA series of evaluations, it was possible to determine that informativeness and adequacy results were highly correlated (which is to be expected), but also that fluency results highly correlate with the other two. We know that the two attributes converge in the extreme (Fig. 1), but this finding implies that the two attributes may not greatly diverge over the whole range of there respective qualities.

Consequently, if there is an automatic measure of one of these attributes, it may be possible to predict the value of the other at the same time. There are some intriguing areas for speculation here. For example, statistical models of English based on n-grams may be said to reflect the baseline intelligibility ([5]). Automatically comparing English MT output vector-wise with a statistical model of human English will reflect the intelligibility of the output, and allow the inference of its fidelity as well.

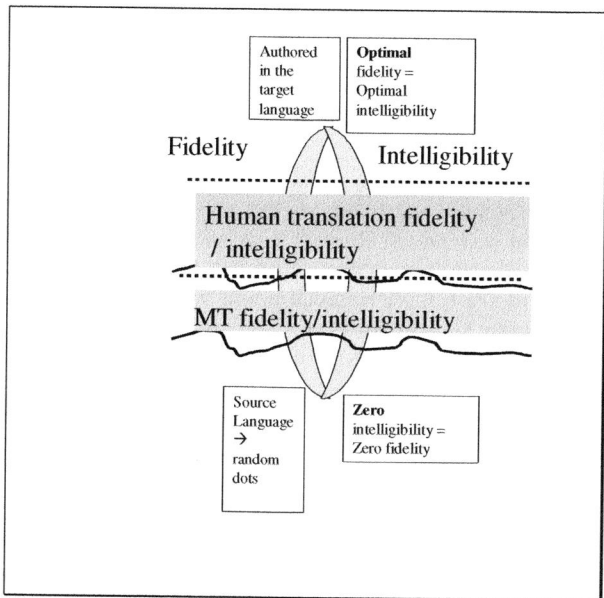

Fig. 1. Fidelity and intelligibility converge at two points, but we don't know how far they ever diverge

There is peril here, of course – the true correlation between the two attributes is not completely known, and an n-gram model might only say something about the intelligibility of word-order-intensive languages like English. But the prospect of automatic declarative evaluation is not without hope.

2.4   Operational Evaluation

Operational evaluations generally address the question of whether an MT system will actually serve its purpose in the context of its operational use. The primary factors include the cost-benefit of bringing the system into the overall process.

A variety of issues are considered here, including such things as software and hardware compatibility with the incumbent office automation system. However, the more fundamental question to ask for operational use is whether the MT system enhances the effectiveness of the „downstream" task, or whether the end-to-end process is better off without it (or indeed without any MT at all). This question lies at the crux of the current initiatives in „translingual" or „cross-lingual" information processing.

We have alluded to this idea already, when we talked about the possibility that MT which is of poor intelligibility might nevertheless be useful for certain language handling tasks that follow.   Evaluation of MT embedded into a cross-lingual information processing environment takes into account the measures that are germane to the „downstream" task.   So if we want to know whether an MT system helps information extraction, we compare the recall and precision (measures germane to extraction) of the MT-plus-extraction configuration to an expert translation-plus-extraction process, or to extraction without any translation at all. Note that we don't measure values such as fidelity and intelligibility, germane to MT in isolation, but rather the effect of MT (good or bad) on the downstream task in terms of that task's metrics.

Sadly, this is not what usually happens. Current discussions include the ability to develop rapidly MT systems of new language pairs, whose output is sufficient (whatever that means) to get the gist (whatever that means) of the source text. We have an intuitive idea that we can tell whether an MT system's output is good enough for such a thing, and we tend to believe that we share this intuition and the meaning of such things as „gist" among ourselves. But we don't have any such understanding. And even if we did share that reference point, we couldn't generalize beyond it to predict all the tasks an MT system's output might be good enough for. And to make all of this even more difficult, most automatic text handling systems are insufficiently robust to behave in a controlled way over several trials. So task-based evaluation tends to involve human judgments, this time by the experts who perform these tasks with or without automated tools.

Automatic task-based Evaluation.   As noted, there are several factors under the „operational evaluation" category, including compatibility, availability, life-expectancy of the vendor, which we have mostly ignored in this discussion. Focusing on just the task-based evaluation in a cross-lingual context, the current methodology involves collecting human judgments, with the attendant difficulties in test design, time and resources that we have already observed. The best hope for automating task-based evaluation lies in the ability to capture the expert judgments in just the sort of test patterns that are possible for feasibility testing.

The recently completed government project known as the MT Proficiency Scale ([15], [3]) elicited from users a series of judgments which enabled the establishment of a scale of text handling tasks (like information extraction, document detection, gisting, among others). This scale means that if I can establish the suitability of some MT output for one task but not another, I can also predict which other tasks it will be good enough to help and which it will not. So far, establishing this suitability has not been an automatic process, but it likely could be.   Basically, certain translation problems occur in imperfect MT output which constitutes the difference between its being only good enough for task X and not quite good enough for task Y. Capturing those phenomena and generalizing them into test patterns will be a step in the direction of automatic, task-based evaluation. Note that measuring the results of these patterns cannot be as controlled as it is for feasibility (at this point we are facing the problem of no one right translation), and thus the scoring itself is not obviously automatic. But development and dissemination of such test patterns will nevertheless serve to accelerate the evaluation process.

2.5   Usability Evaluation

The purpose of usability evaluation is to measure the ability of a system to be useful to people who are actually going to operate it. In the cross-lingual, end-to-end scenario envisioned above, users may not actually interface with the translation component at all. But the envisioned scenario will also need to be very fluid, and at different times for different problems the translation component may need to be touched directly by the information consumer. And of course, the professional translator will necessarily continue to use MT systems directly, as will non-translators who will increasingly want to translate web pages.

Usability is typically measured by attributes such as „utility" and „satisfaction" ([14]). There are quantitative metrics for each of these attributes, but often there is great reliance on users' subjective judgments (e.g., [2]). Usability for an MT application will measure such things as the time to complete a task, the number of steps required, naturalness of navigation, how easy it is to learn, and similar judgments.

Automated Usability Evaluation. Usability studies are done at the point of interface between the application and the user, and there is no obvious escaping this step of the process if we really want to claim that a particular application is usable by the people who will interact with it. However, there are some metrics that can be collected that form a corpus of knowledge from users that can be applied. Usability standards for response time, color combinations, number of keystrokes to reach a goal, etc. are relatively well known for desktop applications in general. An MT application can be algorithmically evaluated for these: all of the path threads in the interface can be followed automatically, which will give the number of steps to a goal, though it will not tell whether the end state reached was actually a useful one. This will not, of course substitute for the eventual hands-on evaluation of usability, but it may prevent systems not ready for this level of use to come up for evaluation prematurely.

3 Conclusion

This survey of the classic types of MT evaluation has amplified on the well-attested claims that there is no one established evaluation standard, in part because of he different needs for measurement of attributes of MT. And in part because of the nature of rendering expressions into semantically equivalent but formally different ones, there is no obvious automatic scoring methodology. However, it may be possible to nibble around the edges, by pursuing the aspects of each type of MT evaluation that may be partly automated, resulting ultimately in widely available, rapidly deployable test sets and scoring algorithms that will actually measure what needs to be measured and help the people who need the measurement.

Acknowledgments

Special thanks to Jennifer Doyon, who suggested this organizing principle for discussing the issues in automatic MT evaluation.

References

1. Arnold, A., Sadler, L., and Humphreys, R.: "Evaluation: an assessment." Machine Translation 8-1/2 (1993) 1-24
2. Dostert, B. User's Evaluation of Machine Translation, Georgetown MT System, 1963-1973. Rome Air Development Center Report AD-768 451. Texas A&M University (1973)
3. Doyon, J., Taylor, K., and White, J.: "Task-Based Evaluation for Machine Translation." Singapore : Proceedings of Machine Translation Summit VII '99 (1999)
4. Hovy, E., 1994. „Apples, Oranges, or Kiwis? Criteria for the comparison of MT Systems" Panel Discussion, Vasconcellos, M., moderator. In Vasconellos, M. (ed.) MT Evaluation: Basis for Future Directions. National Science Foundation (1994)
5. Jones, D. and Rusk G.: Toward a Scoring Function for Quality-Driven Machine Translation. Proceedings of Coling-2000 (2000)
6. King, M, chair. 1991. "Evaluation of MT systems panel discussion." Proceedings of MT Summit III (1991) 141-146
7. Nagao, M., Tsujii, J. Nakamura, J.: "The Japanese Government project for machine translation." Computational Linguistics 11-2/3 (1985) 91-109
8. Pierce, J., (Chair): Language and Machines: Computers in Translation and Linguistics. Report by the Automatic Language Processing Advisory Committee (ALPAC). Publication 1416. National Academy of Sciences National Research Council (1966)
9. Taylor, K., and White, J.: "Predicting what MT is Good for: User Judgments and Task Performance." Proceedings of Third Conference of the Association for Machine Translation in the Americas, AMTA98. Philadelphia, PA (1998)
10. Van Slype, G. Critical Methods for Evaluating the Quality of Machine Translation. Prepared for the European Commission Directorate General Scientific and Technical Information and Information Management. Report BR 19142. Bureau Marcel van Dijk (1979)
11. Vasconcellos, M. (ed.): MT Evaluation: Basis for Future Directions. Proceedings of a workshop sponsored by the National Science Foundation. Washington, D.C.: Association for Machine Translation (1994)
12. White, J. Toward an Automated, Task-Based MT Evaluation Strategy. Athens, Greece: Proceedings of the Workshop on Evaluation, Language Resources and Evaluation Conference (2000)
13. White, J., and O'Connell, T.: 1994. The ARPA MT evaluation methodologies: evolution, lessons, and future approaches. Proceedings of the 1994 Conference, Association for Machine Translation in the Americas (1994)
14. White, J., and O' Connell, T.: „Adaptation of the DARPA machine translation evaluation paradigm to end-to-end systems" Proceedings of AMTA-96 (1996)
15. White, J. and Taylor, K. 1998. „A task-oriented metric for machine translation." Granada, Spain: Proceedings of the First Language Resources and Evaluation Conference (1998)

How Are You Doing? A Look at MT Evaluation

Michelle Vanni[1] and Florence Reeder[2]

[1]Department of Defense, Ft. Meade, MD
mtvanni@afterlife.ncsc.mil
[2]1820 Dolley Madison Blvd., McLean VA 22102
freeder@mitre.org

Abstract. Machine Translation evaluation has been more magic and opinion than science. The history of MT evaluation is long and checkered – the search for objective, measurable, resource-reduced methods of evaluation continues. A recent trend towards task-based evaluation inspires the question – can we use methods of evaluation of language competence in language learners and apply them reasonably to MT evaluation? This paper is the first in a series of steps to look at this question. In this paper, we will present the theoretical framework for our ideas, the notions we ultimately aim towards and some very preliminary results of a small experiment along these lines.

1   Introduction

Machine Translation Evaluation (MTE) has been more magic and opinion than science. The notion of evaluating MT products results in too broad of a scope for reasonable evaluation – everything from interface, to scalability, to faithfulness of translation, to mean-time-between-failures of the system are fair game for the evaluation of MT systems. Yet, it is necessary to have a method to measure the usefulness of a system to users and equally desirable to point to places where system designers and researchers can improve system outcomes. Bowing to the notion that evaluating MT in a vacuum is like evaluating a sports team that never plays a game, the trend towards task-based evaluation provides guidelines and constraint on what to evaluate, how to evaluate and what context to use for evaluation. The long history of MTE will be described more thoroughly in the next section, but the holy grail is to have an automated evaluation method that is objective, gives reasonable measures of utility and does not rely on casts of thousands to reproduce. Therefore, we look for ways to constrain and decompose evaluation so that it provides measures that are both meaningful to developers and users and ones that indicate not only where systems will be useful but also how they can be improved.

   If we consider the history of MTE, we are coming full-circle by looking at the evaluation of language learners as a source for techniques in MTE. Language learner evaluation has had a similarly checkered career – methods for accurately measuring language competence have changed to reflect trends of pedagogy and computing ability. Language learner evaluation research, however, has developed some simple tests which have shown strong correlations to language ability and are good indicators of language competence. These are exactly the kinds of measures we are seeking for

J.S. White (Ed.): AMTA 2000, LNAI 1934, pp. 109-116, 2000.
© Springer-Verlag Berlin Heidelberg 2000

MT evaluation. The history of language learner evaluation and an outline of the principles which may be applied to MTE will be discussed in section 3.

Taking these two ideas in concert, then, we begin a program of looking at the utility of applying language learner evaluation strategies to MTE. The first step in this will be described in this paper. The next section addresses MTE research and why it has been a difficult challenge. The following section briefly highlights the evaluation of language learners and language skills. After that, we describe an initial experiment which will help the process of determining the granularity of measure appropriate for automating MTE. Finally, we will discuss the results of the experiment and look to future tests which may prove useful.

2 Overview of MTE Research

Machine Translation (MT) Evaluation (MTE) is a long-standing issue with many approaches and formalisms having been proposed throughout the years. What to evaluate, how to evaluate and what context to use in evaluation are problematic issues. Unlike some other Natural Language Processing (NLP) problems, there is no gold-standard evaluation possible. This lack of "ground truth" makes the task of automating evaluation even more challenging. The lack of agreement on the assessment of what makes a good translation, even when human translators are involved, hampered initial efforts in MTE, which compared the output of systems to renderings produced by professional translators ([9], [15]). The results of tests of adequacy, informativeness, and fluency as performed on system output were compared to the results of those performed on the human renderings. While this notion of focusing on the outcome of the translation process is a reasonable one, the implementation of the tests proved difficult and somewhat detrimental to the field. In order to assemble the amount of data necessary, such MTE programs were expensive, time-consuming and human-intensive. Requirements listed below multiplied the cost in dollars, time and human involvement exponentially:

    (1) expert renderings for each of the input texts
    (2) several tests performed on each system's output
    (3) testing by several individuals for each criterion evaluated
    (4) diagnostic tests, performed by language experts, of each system's output ([15])
    (5) the production of back translations from English for systems handling non-English input ([15])

Moreover, these programs measured only one broad aspect of the translation output at a time. Developers were left with little to go on in the way of help to improve their systems and users were left with little which would help them select an appropriate system to meet their requirements. For example, one finding of the DARPA 1994 evaluation was that larger knowledge sources were correlated with better performance ([14]) – a useful piece of information in a general sense, but not particularly helpful for specific system designers or users.

Even before the DARPA studies were completed, there was a sentiment in the community that perhaps black-box evaluations looked at the glass as half-empty rather than half-full ([3]). Since then, plans for large-scale evaluations have become more functionally oriented. For example, the MT Scale plan ([13]) sought to associate the diagnostic scores assigned to the output used in the DARPA evaluation with a scale of language-dependent tasks such as scanning, sorting, and topic identification. Linking the breakdown in a user's language-based performance of a function to some phenomenon in system output extended the usefulness of this approach ([11]). Similar types of associations were explored even further with experiments in correlating systems' handling of a set of text features with users' performance on information processing tasks ([12]) and measuring a system's performance on new text types ([10]). Consideration of variables such as the function of MT output and the complexity of MT input continued to be explored by researchers with the recognition and description of the role of the user's purpose and process ([6]).

The direction of these endeavors seems to be toward streamlining the evaluation process and equipping users with tools for carrying out their own evaluations, assessments of MT systems which are tailored to what the user requires from the MT system output. One feature of any such test will be a description of what linguistic features the system can handle reliably. Another possibility suggested during the time of functional evaluation was to look at the language models developed for language acquisition, particularly second language acquisition (SLA) errors ([4]). Research in SLA and also cognitive skills development provides us with a potential model for identifying a constellation of such features useable diagnostically to characterize the performance of a system.

3   Models of Language Learner Evaluation

Like MT, language learner evaluation has gone through a long and varied history – a reflection on pedagogical, cognitive and other changes in language learning development. Yet, it is this long history that may yield useful ideas in MTE – as we understand the language learning process better, we have developed measures of what it means to "know" a language. These measures, and the insight into language sills they provide, will lead to useful methods for measuring system abilities and, hopefully, illustrate the ways in which system performance can be improved. Before we discuss the first in a series of experiments to demonstrate this, we will highlight some aspects of language learning and learner evaluation.

Language teaching in the 18th and 19th centuries focused on the form of language rather than the function of it. Features of a language such as grammar rules and vocabulary lists were taught such as the long tables of Latin conjugations. These were memorized and translations were of texts that had existed for centuries. Greek and Latin, the primary languages taught, were not in use beyond academics and their study reflected this lack of contextualization. Some of the principles of this form of teaching exist in language pedagogy today as reflected by the drill-and-practice exercises that still proliferate.

With the expansion of language learning and the idea that language learning could provide benefit beyond academic exercise, there was a movement based on the idea that one could demonstrate a certain useful command of a language without knowing which prepositions take dative form or even what dative means.[1] This was the beginning of language learning in context which viewed foreign language abilities as they developed and identified ways of teaching useful language skills without as much emphasis on language mechanics. The "communicative language approach" ([1]) caused a reevaluation of teaching and testing methods – a trend away from the traditional, rote methodologies occurred. Instead of testing conjugation with the filling in of tables, learners were evaluated on their abilities to communicate a given point in a given situation with differing levels of sophistication.[2]

Neither trend – rote learning or totally communicative learning – is sufficient to support all levels of language learning. Additionally, neither reflects what we know about language acquisition, particularly second language acquisition. In recent years, the trend is to view language acquisition as a continuum of related skills that build upon each other. Evaluation of language learners focuses on measuring competence and performance while supporting a model of which languages features are learned in what order. One popular theory that has been computationally useful is the notion of Zones of Proximal Development (ZPD) as described in Michaud & McCoy ([8]). In this theory, language learning is seen as a scaffolded series of abilities where some abilities are at the same level and others are needed to reach the next level of development. Specific aspects of language can be tested and the correlation between these tests and the level of the student is good. This notion draws on the drill-and-practice testing methods developed under early language teaching methodology, but also attempts to also characterize the ability of the student to use language effectively. Another measure growing from language development research is the Interagency Language Roundtable (ILR) scale ([2]) used to assess government linguists. For purposes noted later, we chose the ILR scale as the first measure for our experiments.

At this point, we will discuss the commonalties between testing of language learners and MTE which lead us to the series of experiments we are enacting. The most attractive feature of learner evaluation is the multitude of automated tests, both standardized and non-standardized, which exist. If we can draw a correlation between the language skills these measure and the language capabilities translation engines provide, we have a less human-intensive measure for translation engines. Additionally, these tests can inform translation engine developers about the kinds of language features which could be improved for better translation quality. The objection may be raised that measuring language learning skills is not the same as measuring translation ability. Generally, though, advanced foreign language handling skills are associated with the students' ability to translate as well. That is, to understand what language is to be used in a situation and generate appropriate responses.

---

[1] Quick – can you define dative? As defined ([5]): "the dative mainly affects nouns, along with related words (such as adjectives and pronouns), and signals a range of meanings typically expressed in English by the prepositions *to* or *for*…"

[2] Interested readers are directed to Levy [7], for a more detailed description of language teaching evolution.

4 Experimental Design

At the roughest grain, we can look at the grading of MT system outputs as if they were language learners. While we recognize that this is too coarse a grain to provide much in the way of meaningful indicators of usefulness or areas for future development, it is a starting point to give a baseline of these measures. To this end, we found a widely-used set of criteria for evaluating foreign language students which focuses on the coherence and competency of the produced text. The ILR scale ([2]) identifies both levels of language competency and also the kinds of tasks and kinds of materials which might be mastered by a student at each of these levels. Table 1 roughly describes some each level.

In our preliminary experiment, we identified five 100 word foreign language texts (examples in Tables 2-6) of different complexity levels. We then produced expert translations of each of these texts. Following this, we submitted the initial text to two (or more) MT systems and then applied the ILR scoring methods on a 100-point scale. Table 7 shows the grading scheme for scoring.

Table 1. ILR Rating Scale

Level 0+	Level 1	Level 2	Level 3	Level 4
Survival	Orientation	Instructive	Evaluative	Projective
Traffic signs	Forms	Instructions	Analyses	Think-pieces
Calendars	Menus	News reports	Critiques	Commentary

Table 2. Level 0 Translation Exercise Example

Various	Expositions	Displays	Conferences
Reading	Cinema	Music	Opera
Circus	Theatre	Dance	Meetings
Cultural	Appointments		

Table 3. Level 1 Translation Exercise Example

Hello, how are you?	What's your name?
Very well, thank you and you?	My name is Jeanne?
Everything is going well.	And them?
Have a nice day.	Their names are Jacques and Jules.

Table 4. Level 2 Translation Exercise Example

Bill Clinton was awakened Friday, December 31, at 5:00 in the morning to learn of Boris Yeltsin's decision to leave office.

According to the White House spokesperson, in the course of a 20 minute conversation, the outgoing Russian president stated to his American counterpart that the Russians will remain faithful to their constitution, to democracy, to arms control and to the market economy.

Table 5. Level 3 Translation Exercise Example

The annual report of the Inter-Ministerial Mission Against Sects (IMLS), which was expected by the end of the year, will not be submitted to the Prime Minister before January 15th. Officially, the delay would only be due to unimportant technical adjustments. In reality, the advisors hope that the IMLS reviews its copy while correcting the wording of certain anti-sect proposals in order to avoid exaggerated reactions to the diplomatic plan.

Table 6. Level 4 Translation Exercise Example

Life goes on. The news is not good. That's probably what one must call the domino effect which is nothing other than the news. The hull cracks here, the weather there and the cold front continues. Reason finally snaps regarding this Cuban child. Because here we have this little one traveling in the belly of the political whale from now on, a symbol of the clash among those who diplomatically seek to create happiness for children through that of nations. We have to save the child, a soldier of an American-Cuban guerilla war. The child has become a hostage in the struggle which pits the Republican-majority American congress against its president and his attorney general, Janet Reno. The child is summoned to appear before the State Court of Florida on February 10th. Total absurdity. Liberty has a strong back which transports everywhere in the global village the image of a laughing child and you see how the breath of liberty is good for his complexion and his smile. One imagines the hearing if it's necessary to have one someday. Then, my little one, speak without fear. Who do you prefer? Your father or Liberty? You are free to decide – all your orphaned liberty or your six years under the influence.

Table 7. Error Assessment Scale

Error Type	Points Subtracted
Major syntactic errors significantly altering the meaning	4
Minor syntactic errors causing meaning distortions	3
Lexical, grammatical affixation	2
Stilted usage, disfluencies	1

The first stage of the experiment is the selection of materials. These were randomly selected from newspapers used for the teaching of French translation. Second, the materials were run through three translation engines of varying degrees of sophistication and completeness.[3] The resulting translations were then given to a teacher for scoring. We are reporting on this scoring, understanding that the next step is to have other teachers score the materials.

---

[3] While we will not specifically name them here, two are commercially available and the third was a government developed system.

5 Results and Discussion

The most interesting initial result is that the levels of learning on which the machine translation engines performed best were levels 02 and 03. This was consistent across all translation engines, regardless of methods of development. Levels 02 and 03 represent full sentences with developed grammars, but without inference and descriptive analytical power. This is not surprising for a number of reasons. First, translation engines work best on well-formed input text. Levels 0 and 01 represent many stages of ill-formed or under-developed language use. Level 04 represents a level of sophistication and cross-sentence processing that most translation engines do not possess. More detailed analysis will be necessary to determine which specific language features of these text levels make them more amenable to translation engines or automated processing.

Another criticism that may be leveled is that this still represents a human-intensive evaluation technique for MT. Especially when more than one teacher is needed for scoring and, to be complete, we would need translation students exercises mixed in with translation engine outputs. We recognize this and hope to use the results not to develop a new human-intensive evaluation methodology, but to show us if the language learning track is worth pursuing for MTE.

References

1. Asher, A.: Learning Another Language Through Actions: The Complete Teachers Guide-book. Los Gatos, CA: Sky Oaks Productions (1977)
2. Child, J., Clifford, R., and Pardee, L., Jr.:. Proficiency and Performance in Language Testing. Applied Language Learning. 4:1-2. (1993) 19-54
3. Church, K. and Hovy, E.: Good Applications for Crummy Machine Translation. Machine Translation 8 (1993) 239-258
4. Connor-Linton, J. 1995. Cross-cultural comparison of writing standards: American ESL and Japanese EFL. World Englishes, 14.1. Basil , Oxford (1995) 99-115
5. Crystal, D.: An Encyclopedic Dictionary of Language and Languages. Blackwell Publishers, Oxford, UK (1992)
6. Hovy, E.: Why Core Technology Evaluation Doesn't Work. Talk given at the Second Conference of the Association for Machine Translation in the Americas. Montreal, Quebec, Canada (1996)
7. Levy, M.: Computer Assisted Language Learning : Context and Conceptualization. Oxford University Press (1997)
8. Michaud, L. & McCoy, K.: Modeling User Language Proficiency in a Writing Tutor for Deaf Learners of English. In Olsen, M. (ed.): Computer-Mediated Language Assessment and Evaluation Natural Language Processing, Proceedings of a Symposium by ACL/IALL. University of Maryland (1999) 47-54
9. Pierce, J. (Chair).: Language and Machines: Computers in Translation and Linguistics. Report by the Automatic Language Processing Advisory Committee (ALPAC). Publication 1416. National Academy of Sciences National Research Council (1966)
10. Povlsen, C., Underwood, N., Music, B., and Neville, A.: Evaluating Text-Type Suitability for Machine Translation a Case Study on an English-Danish System. Proceedings of Language Resources and Evaluation Conference, LREC 98, Volume I. Granada, Spain (1998) 21-27

11. Taylor, K.B. and White, J.S.: Predicting what MT is Good for: User Judgments and Task Performance. Proceedings of Third Conference of the Association for Machine Translation in the Americas, AMTA98. Philadelphia, PA (1998)
12. Vanni, M.: Evaluating MT Systems: Testing and Researching the Feasibility of a Task-Diagnostic Approach. Proceedings of the Conference of the Association for Information Management (ASLIB): Translating and the Computer 20, London, England (1998)
13. White, J.S. and Taylor, K.B.: A Task-Oriented Evaluation Metric for Machine Translation. Proceedings of Language Resources and Evaluation Conference, LREC-98, Volume I. Granada, Spain (1998) 21-27
14. White, J.S.: Approaches to Black Box MT Evaluation. Proceedings of MT Summit V (1995)
15. White, J.S. et al.: ARPA Workshops on Machine Translation. Series of 4 workshops on comparative evaluation. PRC Inc. McLean, VA (1992-1994)

Recycling Annotated Parallel Corpora for Bilingual Document Composition

Arantza Casillas[1], Joseba Abaitua[2], and Raquel Martínez[3]

[1] Departamento de Automática, Universidad de Alcalá
arantza@aut.alcala.es
[2] Facultad de Filosofía y Letras Universidad de Deusto, Bilbao
abaitua@fil.deusto.es
[3] Depatamento de Sis. Informáticos y Programación, Facultad de Matemáticas
Universidad Complutense de Madrid
raquel@eucmos.sim.ucm.es

Abstract. Parallel corpora enriched with descriptive annotations facilitate multilingual authoring development. Departing from an annotated bitext we show how SGML markup can be recycled to produce complementary language resources. On the one hand, several translation memory databases together with glossaries of proper nouns have been produced. On the other, DTDs for source and target documents have been derived and put into correspondence. This paper discusses how these resources have been automatically generated and applied to an interactive bilingual authoring system. This tool is capable of handling a substantial proportion of text both in the composition and translation of structured documents.

1 Introduction

Over the past decade, memory-based systems have become one of the hottest growth areas in the translation and localization industry. By adopting the technology of translation memory (TM), large corporations and government administrations have considerably improved the workflow process and quality of their invariably repetitive documentation (Allen, 1999). On the one hand, such authoring tools let technical writers plagiarize texts more easily, a practice that has been deemed highly beneficial because it promotes terminological and stylistic homogeneity in technical documentation (Adolphson, 1998). On the other hand, translation memories allow for the constant recycling of material previously translated and validated, saving translators the repetition of much intellectual effort.

Good commercial software packages for authoring and managing translation memories already exist in the market. However, although these products facilitate the reutilization of aligned segments, usually sentences, they neglect any information referring to the logical structure of the text. This is a waste of potential, considering that most TM packages rely on SGML-based coding. Precisely,

J.S. White (Ed.): AMTA 2000, LNAI 1934, pp. 117–126, 2000.

one major feature of SGML (ISO879, 1996) is its ability to represent the structural composition of a document in the form of a grammar: the Document Type Definition, DTD (Figure 4). This paper presents an approach that integrates TM technology and DTD control to support bilingual authoring. Users who are composing original documents are given the opportunity to select a document type, i.e. a DTD, that will determine its logical structure. Then they are automatically given the core markup for the source text with the basic content units, which are automatically put into correspondence with units in the target text. An experimental editing tool that integrates both processes of source text composition and translation has been implemented.

The project started in 1993, shortly before the Text Encoding Initiative (Sperberg.McQueen, 1994) had made public its final set of guidelines (TEI-P3), and long before XML was designed. The first stage of the project was mainly concerned with the compilation of the corpus of bilingual legal documents in Basque and Spanish. Texts in the corpus showed regular logical structures and consistent distribution of text segments. The purpose of the second phase was to make these explicit. The corpus was processed and annotated with tags that marked up a variety of structural features. Then the corpus was aligned at different levels of translation equivalence (Martinez, 1997), (Matinez, 1998).

For the experiments, the most common type of document in the corpus, *Orden Foral*, was chosen (53% of the documents in the corpus belong to this type). We analysed some 100 tokens and hand-marked the most salient elements. The heuristics to identify these elements were later expressed in a collection of recognition routines in Perl and tested against a set of 400 tokens including the intial 100. As a result of this process of automatic tagging of structural elements we produced a TEI/SGML tagged corpus. Textual units were identified and segmented at different levels:

- Domain independent elements, such as paragraphs (`<p>`) or sentences(`<s>`), but also others as dates(`<date>`) and numbers(`<num>`).
- Structural elements. These reflect the division of documents into structural units (`<opner>`, `<div0>`, `<div1>`, `<dateline>`, `<closer>`)
- Elements that mark up textual units which are domain-dependent. These elements help define the structure of the document too.

Both structural and domain-dependent elements will compose the DTD. Figure 1 and 2 show an annotated text in Spanish and its aligned counterpart in Basque (the attributes id and correspond identify the source element and its corresponding target translation). Once the corpus has been appropriately aligned, it becomes a rich source of material that can be constantly recycled for future translations. Two different types of resources can be extracted:

- Paired DTD for each document type (see Section 2).
- Translation memories (see Section 3).

The composition strategy uses these resources to compose new bilingual documents as we will show in Section 4 and 5.

<legebi> <text> <body> <opener> <seg31 id=13ES1 corresp=13EU1> Medi-
ante </seg31> <title id=ctES1 corresp=ctEU1> Orden Foral </title> <num>
número 3607/94, </num> <date> 9 de Noviembre </date> <name id=nmES1
corresp=nmEU1> del Diputado Foral de Medio Ambiente y Acción Territorial </name> <seg3 id=13ES1 corresp=13EU1> ha adoptado la resolución
cuya parte dispositiva es la siguiente: </seg3> </opener> <div0> <div1>
Primero: Revocar el nombramiento provisional otorgado mediante Orden Foral
número <num num=60394> 603/94 </num>, de <date> 22 de febrero
</date>, a favor de doña Ana Fernández Gutierrez-Crespo para
el puesto de Tesorería del Ayuntamiento de Getxo por incapacidad laboral
transitoria de su titular, por haber fallecido este último. </div1> <seg9
id=9ES1 corresp=9EU1> Contra dicha <rs type=law id=LES12 corresp=LEU10>
Orden Foral </rs>, que agota la vía administrativa podrá inter-
ponerse recurso contencioso-administrativo ante la <rs type=organization id=0ES9
corresp=0EU11> Sala de lo Contencioso-Administrativo del Tribunal Superior de Justicia del País Vasco </rs>, en el plazo de dos meses, contado desde el día
siguiente a esta notificación sin perjuicio de la utilización de otros
medios de defensa que estime oportunos. </seg9> </div0> <closer> <dateline>
<rs type=place id=PES1 corresp=PEU1> Bilbao </rs>, <date> 9 de noviembre de
1994 </date>. </dateline> <name id=dcES1 corresp=dcEU1> El Director General
de Medio Ambiente y Acción Territorial , Ander Salaberria Amesti </name>
</closer> </body> </text> </legebi>

Fig. 1. Spanish tagged text

<legebi> <text> <body> <opener> <name id=nmEU1 corresp=nmES1> Inguru-
giro eta Lurralde Ekintzapideko Foru Diputatuaren </name> <date> azaroaren 9ko
</date> <num> 3.607/94 </num> <title id=ctEU1 corresp=ctES1> Foru Agin-
duz </title> <seg3 id=13EU1 corresp=13ES1,31ES1> bere aginte zatia honako
hau deneko erabakia hartu da: </seg3> </opener> <div0> <div1>
Lehenengoa: Titularraren aldibaterako lan ezintasunagatik Ana Fernández
Gutierrez-Crespo Andreari Getxoko Udaleko Diruzaintza lantokia betetzeko
<date> otsailaren 22ko </date> <num num=60394> 603/94 </num> Foru Agin-
duz behin-behingoraco egindako izendapena baliorik gabe uztea, titularra hil
egin delako . </div1> <seg9 id=9EU1 corresp=9ES1> <rs type=law id=LEU10
corresp=LES12> Foru agindu </rs> horrek amaiera eman dio administrazio
bideari; eta beraren aurka <rs type=organization id=0EU10> Administrazioarekiko
</rs> auzibide-errekurtsoa jarri ahal izango zaio <rs type=organization id=0EU11
corresp=0ES9> Euskal Herriko Justizi Auzitegi Nagusiko Administrazioarekiko Auz-
ibideetarako Salari </rs>, bi hilabeteko epean; jakinarazpen hau egiten den
egunaren biharamunetik zenbatuko da epe hori; hala eta guztiz ere, egokiesten diren
beste defentsabideak ere erabil litezke. </seg9> </div0> <closer> <dateline>
<rs type=place id=PEU1 corresp=PES1> Bilbon </rs> <date date=9.11.1994>
1994.eko azaroaren 9an. </date> </dateline> <name id=dcEU1 corresp=dcES1>
Lurralde Ekintzapideko zuzendari nagusiak, Ander Salaberria Amesti </closer>
</body> </text> </legebi>

Fig. 2. Basque annotated text

2   Paired DTD abstraction

SGML markup determines the logical structure of a document and its syntax in
the form of a context-free grammar. This is called the Document Type Definition (DTD) and it contains specifications to define the names and content for
all elements that are permitted to appear in a document and the order in which
these elements must appear.

Since documents were not produced using any SGML-based authoring software,
DTDs have been abstracted from the annotations that were automatically introduced in the corpus. Similar experiments have been reported before in the
literature: (Ahonen, 1995), (Shafer, 1995), (Saxon, 1999). Our method is similar
to Shafer's, but with some slight modification in order to reduce document rules
instances. A tool to obtain a DTD for all document instances has been developed
(Casillas, 1999). Our tool shares with Shafer's method three steps in the DTDs
abstraction process:

1. Extraction and generation of instances and storage of attributes and entities.
   Figure 3 shows the set of rules extracted from the annotated text in Figure
   1.
2. Reduction of instances. Figure 4 contains a part of the DTD that corresponds
   to the document of Figure 1. This DTD exhibits some divergencies with
   the actual structure of the document, as a result of the DTD abstraction
   process. What the DTD in fact reflects is the general structure shared by all
   documents of this same type.
3. Conversion of reduced instances to DTD code.

The order of logical components and translation units in Basque and Spanish is
not identical, due to the configurational differences of the two languages. Thus,
two different DTDs are induced, one for each language, and paired through a
correspondence table.

3   Derivation of Translation Memories

Four complementary language databases may be obtained at any time from the
annotated corpus: three translation memory databases (TM1, TM2, and TM3)
as well as a glossary of proper nouns. These TMs differ in the nature of the
translation units they contain. TM1 consists of aligned sentences that can feed
commercial TM software. TM2 contains translation segments ranging from whole
sections of a document or multi-sentence paragraphs to smaller units, such as
short phrases and idioms. TM3 simply hosts the whole collection of aligned bilingual documents, where the whole document may be considered the translation
unit. TM3 can be construed as a bilingual document-database. Much redundancy
originates from this TM collection, although it should be noticed that they are
all by-products derived from the same annotated bitext which subsumes them
all. Good software packages for TM1 and TM3 already exist in the market, and
hence their exploitation is beyond our interest (Trados Translator's Workbench,

$legebi \rightarrow text$
$text \rightarrow body$
$body \rightarrow opener, div0, closer$
$opener \rightarrow seg31, title, num, date, name, seg3$
$title \rightarrow \#PCDATA$
$num \rightarrow \#PCDATA$
$date \rightarrow \#PCDATA$
$seg31 \rightarrow \#PCDATA, rs, \#PCDATA$
$seg3 \rightarrow \#PCDATA, rs, \#PCDATA$
$name \rightarrow \#PCDATA, rs, \#PCDATA$
$div0 \rightarrow div1, seg9$
$div1 \rightarrow \#PCDATA, num, \#PCDATA, date, \#PCDATA$
$num \rightarrow \#PCDATA$
$date \rightarrow \#PCDATA$
$seg9 \rightarrow \#PCDATA, rs, \#PCDATA, rs, \#PCDATA$
$rs \rightarrow \#PCDATA$
$rs \rightarrow \#PCDATA$
$closer \rightarrow dateline, name$
$dateline \rightarrow rs, date$
$name \rightarrow \#PCDATA$
$rs \rightarrow \#PCDATA$
$date \rightarrow \#PCDATA$

Fig. 3. Instances extracted forma the text of Figure 1

```
<!ELEMENT LEGEBI - - (TEXT)>
<!ELEMENT TEXT - - (BODY)>
<!ELEMENT BODY - - (OPENER, DIV0, CLOSER)>
<!ELEMENT OPENER - - (SEG31, TITLE, NUM, DATE, NAME? SEG3)>
<!ELEMENT (SEG3,SEG31) - - (#PCDATA))>
<!ELEMENT (DIV0) - - (DIV1, SEG9?, SEG10?)>
<!ELEMENT (DIV1) - - (#PCDATA|RS|DATE|NUM)+>
<!ELEMENT (SEG10,) - - (#PCDATA|RS|NUM)+>
<!ELEMENT (CLOSER) - - (DATELINE?, NAME?)>
<!ELEMENT (SEG9) - - (RS|#PCDATA)+>
<!ELEMENT (TITLE, NUM, DATE, RS, NAME) - -(#PCDATA)>
<!ELEMENT (DATELINE) - - (RS, DATE)>
<!ATTLIST RS TYPE (ORGANIZATION| LAW| PLACE| TITLE |UNCAT) #IMPLIED>
```

Fig. 4. DTD para textos en castellano

Star's Transit, SDLX, Déjá Vu, IBM's Translation Manager) for TM1; and any SGML browsing tool for TM3. The originality of our editing tool lies in a design which benefits from joining the potentiality of DTDs and the elements in TM2. Translation segments in TM2 are relevant to the DTD. These have been tagged <seg1>, <seg2>... <segn>, and account for variable recurrent language patterns very frequent in the specialized domain of the corpus and whose occurrence in the text is well established.

All these translations memories are managed in the form of a relational database where segments are stored as records. Each record in the database containa four fields: the segment string, a counter for the occurrences of that string in the corpus, the tag name, and its attributes (type, id and corresp). TM2 and glossaries require a special processing in three steps:

- First, non-pertinent tags are filtered out from the annotated corpus. Tags marking sentence <s> and paragraph <p> are removed, because they are of no interest for TM2 or glossaries (recall that <s> elements are registered in TM1).
- Second, translation segments <segn>, <title> and <name> phrases and referential expressions <rs> are detected in the source document and looked up in the database.
- Third, if they are not already present in the database, they are stored each in its database, and values of the id and corresp attributes are used to set the correspondence between source and target databases.

TM3 needs no particular manipulation because it corresponds to the corpus itself. Table 1 shows how the text fragment inside the </div1>...</div0> tags of Figure 1 and Figure 2 renders three records in the database. Note how the content of the string field in the database maintains only the initial <segn> and <rs> tags. Furthermore, <rs> tagged segments inside <segn> records are simplified so that their content is dismissed and only the initial tag is kept, which is similar to approach taken by (Lange, 1997), (Brown, 1999). The reason is that they are considered variable elements within the segment (dates and numbers are also of this type). The string *Orden Foral* of record 2 in Table 1 is marked as <rs type=law> and *Sala de lo Contencioso-Administrativo del Tribunal Superior de Justicia del País Vasco* of record 3 is marked as <rs type=organization>. In this way, they need not appear as such in record 1 <seg9>, so they may serve for other instantiations of the segment. These internal elements are largely proper nouns that vary from one instantiation of the segment to another. The <rs> tag can be considered to be the name of the varying element. The value of the type attribute <rs type=law> constraints the kind of referential expression that may be inserted in that point of the translation segment.

4   Composition Strategy

In the process of generating the bilingual document, a document type must first be selected. Each document type has an associated DTD. This DTD specifies

Spanish Unit	Basque Unit
<seg9> Contra dicha <rs type=law>, que agota la vía administrativa podrá interponerse recurso contencioso-administrativo ante la <rs type=organization>, en el plazo de dos meses, contado desde el día siguiente a esta notificación, sin perjuicio de la utilización de otros medios de defensa que estime oportunos.	<seg9> <rs type=law> horrek amaiera eman dio administrazio bideari; eta beraren aurka <rs type=organization> auzibide-errekurtsoa jarri ahal izango zaio <rs type=organization>, bi hilabeteko epean; jakinarazpen hau egiten den egunaren biharamunetik zenbatuko da epe hori; hala eta guztiz ere, egokiesten diren beste defentsabideak ere erabil litezke.
<rs type=law> Orden Foral	<rs type=law> Foru agindu
	<rs type=organization> Administrazioarekiko
<rs type=organization> Sala de lo Contencioso-Administrativo del Tribunal Superior de Justicia del País Vasco	<rs type=organization> Euskal Herriko Justizi Auzitegi Nagusiko Administrazioarekiko Auzibideetarako Salari

Table 1. Source and targe language record samples in TM2

which elements are obligatory and which are optional. The composition of the source document is guided by the markup cotained in TM2 and the paired DTD, which controls the aplication of this markup. The target document is generated with the aid of the paired DTD and the translations obtained from TM2. TM1 and TM3 also take part in the composition process. The user can browse TM3 to examine how similar documents have been composed before. TM1 provides translation equivalents for elements which are not contain in TM2. The extraction of elements from the translation memories is performed by approximate matching. The composition process follows two main steps which correspond to the source document generation and the translation into the target document. The markup and the paired DTD guides the process in the following manner:

1. Before the user starts writing the source document, a DTD must be selected. This has two consequences: on the one hand, the selected DTD produces a source document template that contains the logical structure of the document and some of its contents. On the other hand, the selected source DTD triggers a target paired DTD, which will be used later to translate the document. There are three different types of elements in the source document template:

   − Some elements are mandatory and are provided to the user, who must only choose its content among some alternative usages (the user will get a list of alternatives ordered by frequency, for example <title>). Other obligatory elements, such as dates and numbers, will also be automatically generated.

- Some other elements in the template are optional (e.g., <seg9>). Again, a list of alternatives will be offered to the user. These optional elements are sensitive to the context (document or division type), and markup is also responsible for constraining the valid options given to the user. Obligatory and optional elements are retrieved from TM2, and make a considerable part of the source document.
- All documents have an important part of their content which is not determined by the DTD (<div1>). It is the most variable part, and the system lets the writer input text freely. It is when TM2 has nothing to offer that TM1 and TM3 may provide useful material. Given the recurrent style of legal documentation, it is quite likely that the user will be using many of the bilingual text choices already aligned and available in TM1 and TM3.

2. Once the source document has been completed, the system derives its particular logical structure, which, with the aid of the target DTD, is projected into the resulting target logical structure. In the target document there also exist three types of elements:
   - Elements that are handled by simple translation algorithms (<date>, <num>).
   - Elements whose source content can be found in some of the translation memories, and thus are easily retrievable (e.g. <seg9>).
   - Elements that are not controlled by the DTD and therefore may not be contained as a whole in any of the translation memories (this is the case of <div1>). Still, the user may consult particular segments such as proper nouns or phrases.

5   Evaluation

Table 2 shows the number of words that make up the mandatory and optional segments stored in TM2 from the source documents. There is a line for each of the sizes of coverted documents. We can see that the average of segments contained in TM2 is 22.5%, on a scale from 24% to only 2.4%. The amount of segments dealt with largely depends on the size of the document. Short documents (90.21) have about 24% of their text composed in this way. This figure goes down to 2.4% in documents larger than 1,000 words. This is understandable, in the sense that the larger the document, the smaller proportion of fixed sections it will contain.

Table 3 shows the percentage of words that are proposed for the target document. These translations are obtained from what is stored in TM2 and glossaries complemented by algorithms designed to translate dates and numbers. We can see that the average of document translated is 34.6%. Short documents have 36.5% of their text translated, falling to above 11.2% in the case of large documents. Table 4 shows the percentage of words that are proposed for target <div1> elements. These translations are obtained from what is stored in TM2 and glossaries complemented by algorithms to translate dates and numbers.

Word/doc.	Num. doc.	TM2 (mand.)	TM2 (opti.)	Total
0-500	378	21.3	2.6	24
500-1,000	25	9.1	2.8	11.9
More 1,000	16	1.1	1.4	2.4
Weighted mean		19.8	2.5	22.5

Table 2. Document % generated by mandatory and optional elements of TM2

Word/doc.	TM2	Glo.	Alg.	Total
0-500	24	4.84	7.7	36.5
500-1,000	11.94	2.83	6.6	21.3
More 1,000	2.45	2.40	6.4	11.2
W. M.	22.46	4.63	7.6	34.6

Table 3. Document % translated by TM2, glossaries and algorithms

6   Conclusions

We have shown how DTDs derived from descriptive markup can be employed to ease the process of generating bilingual structured documentation. On average, one fourth of the source document and one third of the target document can be automatically accounted for. It must also be pointed out that the part being dealt with represents the core structure, lay-out and logical components of the text. The parts wich are not treated can yet be managed with the aid of sentence-oriented memory systems, filling in the gaps in the overall skeleton provided by the target template. Composers may also browse TM3 to retrieve whole blocks for those parts which are not determined by the DTD. We are currently studying the adaptation of XSL stylesheets developed by TEI people (Rahtz, 2000) to allow access to the corpus by means of XML browsers. One of the clear targets for the future is to extend the coverage of the corpus and to test structural taggers against other document types. A big challenge we face is to develop tools that automatically perform the recognition of documents from less restricted and more open text types. Given a particular form of an interactive authoring process, what we have demonstrated is that SGML and TM techniques can be hybridized to produce substantial MT coverage of structured documents. All the resources needed (DTDs and TMs) were obtained from an aligned parellel corpus enriched with descriptive annotations.

Word/doc.	TM2	Glo.	Alg.	Total
0-500	2.9	3.4	5.6	12.1
500-1,000	2.4	2.8	5.5	10.8
More 1,000	1.3	2.3	5.8	9.44
W. M.	2.8	3.3	5.6	11.9

Table 4. <div1> % translated by TM2, glossaries and algorithms

References

[Adphson, 1998]   E. Adolphson Writing instruction and controlled language applications: panel discussion on standarization. *Proceedings of CLAW'98*, 191, 1998.

[Ahonen, 1995]   H. Ahonen. Automatic Generation of SGML Content Models. *Electronic Publishing*, 8(2-3):195-206, 1995.

[Allen, 1999]   J. Allen. Adapting the Concept of Translation Memory to Authoring Memory for a Controlled Language Writing Enviroment. *ASLIB-TC21*, 1999.

[Brown, 1999]   R. D. Brown. Adding Linguistic Knowledge to a Lexical Example-Based Translation System. *Proceedings of the Eighth International Conference on Theoretical and Methodological Issues in Machine Translation*, 22-32, 1999.

[Casillas, 1999]   A. Casillas, J. Abaitua, R. Martínez. Extracción y aprovechamiento de DTDs emparejadas en corpus paralelos. *Procesamiento del Lenguaje Natural*, 25:33-41, 1999.

[ISO8879, 1986]   ISO 8879, Information Processing–Text and Office Systems–Standard Generalized Markup Language (SGML). *International Organization For Standards*, 1986, Geneva.

[Lange, 1997]   J. Langé, É Gaussier, B. Daile. Bricks and Skeletons: Some Ideas for the Near Future of MATH. *Machine Translation*, 12:39-51, 1997.

[Martinez, 1997]   R. Martínez, J. Abaitua, A. Casillas. Bilingual parallel text segmentation and tagging for specialized documentation. *Proceedings of the International Conference Recent Advances in Natural Language Processing (RANLP'97)*, 369-372, 1997.

[Martinez, 1998a]   R. Martínez, J. Abaitua, A. Casillas. Bitext Correspondences through Rich Mark-up. *36th Annual Meeting of the Association for Computational Linguistics abd 17 International Conference on Computational Linguistics (COLING-ACL'98)*, 812-818, 1998.

[Martinez, 1998b]   R. Martínez, J. Abaitua, A. Casillas. Aligning tagged bitexts. *Sixth Workshop on Very Large Corpora*, 102-109, 1998.

[Rahtz, 2000]   S. Rahtz. XSL stylesheets for TEI XML. *http://users.ox.ac.uk/rahtz/tei*

[Saxon, 1999]   SAXON DTD Generator: A tool to generate XML DTs. *http://www.home.iclweb/icl2/mhkay/dtdgen.htm*

[Shafer, 1995]   K. Shafer. Automatic DTD creation via the GB-Engine and Fred. *http://www.oclc.org/fred/docs/papers*

[Sperberg.McQueen, 1994] C. Sperberg.McQueen, L. Burnard. Guidelines for the Encoding and Interchange (P3). *Text Encoding Initiative*, 1994.

Combining Invertible Example-Based Machine Translation with Translation Memory Technology

Michael Carl

Institut für Angewandte Informationsforschung,
Martin-Luther-Straße 14,
66111 Saarbrücken, Germany
carl@iai.uni-sb.de

Abstract. This paper presents an approach to extract invertible translation examples from pre-aligned reference translations. The set of invertible translation examples is used in the Example-Based Machine Translation (EBMT) system EDGAR for translation. Invertible bilingual grammars eliminate translation ambiguities such that each source language parse tree maps into only one target language string. The translation results of EDGAR are compared and combined with those of a translation memory (TM). It is shown that i) best translation results are achieved for the EBMT system when using a bilingual lexicon to support the alignment process ii) TMs and EBMT-systems can be linked in a dynamical sequential manner and iii) the combined translation of TMs and EBMT is in any case better than each of the single system.

1 Introduction

Ambiguity is one of the major challenges in MT. There are two sources for ambiguity in MT: i) to decide which representation to generate from the input and ii) how to map a source language representation into the target language. The latter ambiguity is due to multiple entries in a bilingual transfer lexicon while the former ambiguity is due to different decompositions of the input. These ambiguities are independent and the number of possible translations is the product of both.

To reduce the number of analyses, some MT-systems compute only a subset of the possible representations. The ReVerb EBMT system [4], for instance, only allows trees of depth 1 which may have arbitrary arity. Other systems e.g. [14] allow only binary trees of arbitrary depth. Still other systems allow - in principle - all possible representations of the input strings e.g. EDGAR [2], GEBMT [7]. However, since all possible representations can hardly always be computed, these systems make use of some heuristics at runtime to generate the source language representation.

Once a representation is generated from the input, it is transferred into the target language where it is specified and refined according to the target language syntax. Some MT systems percolate single items, delete or insert subtrees

J.S. White (Ed.): AMTA 2000, LNAI 1934, pp. 127–136, 2000.
© Springer-Verlag Berlin Heidelberg 2000

in representations in order to approximate the target language syntax. Other systems use a statistical model of the target language to generate the most likely output. However, it is an open problem how these transformations should be done and how a mapping from the source language into an equivalent target language representation could be achieved cf. [13].

Instead of making excessive use of tree-adaptation and modification heuristics, which quickly become intractable, we have decided to generate a bilingual grammar which maps each source representations into exactly one target language representation; ambiguity thereby reducing to the generation of the source representation. To achieve such a deterministic mapping, this paper introduces invertible bilingual grammars. Bilingual grammars generate from each source language parse tree exactly one target language string.

First the invertibility criterion for bilingual grammars is elaborated. Two variants of an algorithm to extract from a set of reference translations an invertible bilingual grammar are proposed. One method generates an invertible bilingual grammar using a bilingual lexicon for anchoring the aligned segments, another method generates an invertible bilingual grammar without such resources. In a test translation, the translation output of EDGAR [2] using these invertible grammars is compared with the translation outcome of EDGAR using a local (i.e. non-invertible) grammar and with a translation memory (TM). It is shown that a combination of TM and EDGAR performs better than any system on its own and that EDGAR performs best with a lexical anchored invertible grammar.

2   Invertible Bilingual Grammars

The concept of invertible grammars is not new. It has been shown that invertible grammars can be updated in polynomial time in the size of the input [11] and that for each context-free grammar, there exists an invertible context-free grammar such that both grammars generate the same language [8]. As yet, to my knowledge, no research has been undertaken which applies the invertibility condition to bilingual grammars inference.

Table 1	Invertibility condition

$$\left.\begin{array}{l} a \leftrightarrow x \\ b \leftrightarrow y \end{array}\right\} \implies ((a \neq b) \text{ and } (x \neq y)) \quad or \quad ((a = b) \text{ and } (x = y))$$

Table 2	Non-Invertible Translation Examples

2.1 $\left.\begin{array}{l} \text{(Gear shift lever)}_{noun} \\ \text{(Transmission Unit Gear Selector)}_{noun} \end{array}\right\} \leftrightarrow \text{(Gestängehebel)}_{noun}$

2.2 $\left.\begin{array}{l} \text{(Locate the outer cable)}_s \\ \text{(Secure the outer cable)}_s \end{array}\right\} \leftrightarrow \text{(Aussenseil befestigen.)}_s$

According to [11] a (monolingual) grammar is invertible if $A \rightarrow a$ and $B \rightarrow a$ in the set of production rules implies that $A = B$. Thus, every right-hand side of a production rule occurs only once in the grammar.

Applying this condition to bilingual grammars can be paraphrased as: if any one language side of a rule is identical to another rule, then the other language side must be identical as well. A formal definition of this is given in table 1. An invertible set of translation examples is shown in table 5 where each left-hand side and each right-hand side occurs only once in the set.

As a negative example consider table 2 where the entries are not conform to the invertibility condition. Two pairs of translation examples, 2.1 and 2.2, are of the form $a \leftrightarrow x$ and $a \leftrightarrow y$ where identical left-hand sides translate into different right-hand sides. Such translation ambiguities cannot usually be resolved during translation. Consequently, when extracting translation examples from a pre-aligned text, for each conflicting pair we retain only one translation example in order to fulfill the invertibility condition.

3   Invertible Alignment

We want to extract an invertible set of translation examples from a pre-aligned bilingual text. This reference text consists of a number of reference translations which - we assume - are typical for the text domain. The extracted invertible bilingual grammar bears holistic constraints on the of the reference text: Each rule has a number of features which makes it different to all other rules in that grammar. There are many ways to extract such an invertible set from the reference translations. For instance, provided that no two reference translation have equal source sides and different target sides, the reference text could serve as an invertible grammar.

However, at least two criteria should be considered for the inference of an invertible grammar: i) it should cover the reference text in a most compositional manner and ii) it should generate the least number of erroneous translations possible. The resulting bilingual grammar should thus contain a maximum number of useful coherent translation rules.

Two methods are described to generate an invertible set of translation examples from a reference text. The INV method makes use of the morphological analyzer MPRO [10] and the shallow syntactic processor KURD [3], while the LEX method considers in addition a bilingual lexicon.

In INV and LEX, a small number of constituents are marked in each language side of the reference translations. The marked constituents are nouns, adjectives, noun-clusters, verbal clusters, simple NPs, DPs and PPs. We assume that there is no knowledge which left-hand side constituent pairs with which right hand side constituent so that all pairing combinations are extracted as alignment. Thus, if m constituents are marked in the left-hand side of a reference translation and n constituents are marked in the right-hand side, $m \times n$ alignments are extracted and added to an alignment base AB.

In INV, each alignment $A \in AB$ is weighted according to the difference in the number of lexemes in their right-hand sides (rhs) and left-hand sides (lhs) as shown in equation 1. In addition to this, LEX takes into account a bilingual lexicon and the translation probabilities $P(lhs_i \leftrightarrow rhs_j)$ of the lexical anchors in alignments as shown in equation 2.

$$W_{INV}(A : lhs \leftrightarrow rhs) = \frac{min(lhs, rhs)}{max(lhs, rhs)} \qquad (1)$$

$$W_{LEX}(A : lhs \leftrightarrow rhs) = W_{INV}(lhs \leftrightarrow rhs) * \sum_{l_i \in lhs, r_j \in rhs} P(l_i \leftrightarrow r_j) \qquad (2)$$

An alignment where lhs has the same number of lexemes as rhs has $W_{INV} = 1$. The more the number of lexemes differ in both sides, the smaller is the weight of an alignment. An alignment which has no lexical anchor has $W_{LEX} = 0$.

Once all alignments are extracted from the reference text and each alignment is assigned a weight W_{INV} and W_{LEX}, two invertible sets EB_{INV} and EB_{LEX} are extracted from the set of alignments. A usability value U_i is computed for each alignment $A_i \in AB$ based on the number of excluding and reinforcing alignments. In case two alignments A_i and A_j violate the invertibility condition their usability values are mutually decremented and the index i of the conflicting alignment is memorized in the exclude list of alignment A_j. Then the compositionality of the alignments is checked. In case one alignment is contained in the other one, their usability value are mutually augmented. In case one hand side of an alignment is contained in the other alignment but the other hand-side isn't this alignment pair is non-compositional and their usability is mutually decreased.

```
For all alignments A_i, A_j ∈ AB  i ≠ j do
    if A_i and A_j identical then              U_i+ = W(A_j);  delete A_j from AB;
    else if A_i and A_j non-invertible then    U_i- = W(A_j);  append j to E_i;
    else if A_i and A_j compositional then     U_i+ = W(A_j);
    else if A_i and A_j non-compositional then U_i- = W(A_j);
end

For all alignments A_i ∈ AB do calculate mean usability U̅_i; end
Sort AB by U̅;
For all A_i in sorted list AB do
    include most useful alignment A_i in EB;
    For all j ∈ E_i do delete A_j from AB; end
end
Return EB
```

Fig. 1. Filter invertible Example Base EB

Once all pairs of alignments are checked, the mean usability for each alignment is calculated. The most 'useful' alignment is included in an initial example-base EB and all conflicting alignments are discarded from the AB. Then the next remaining, most useful alignment is added to EB and its conflicting alignments are excluded from AB and so forth until no more alignments are in AB. The algorithm is depicted in Figure 1

4   An Alignment Example

A reference text consisting of 13 reference translations as depicted in table 3 was given to the system. The aim is to find possible translations of German *stark*. In the examples, *stark* translate into English *strong, big, high, heavy, bad, grave, best, large* and *considerable*. In four of the reference translations *stark* translates into *strong* and once into *strongly*. The translation *stark ↔ strong* would thus be a potential candidate for a default translation to be found by the alignment procedure. The remaining eight translations of *stark* occur only once. They would need to occur with some context in order to be unique and thus conform to the invertibility condition.

From these 13 reference translations, 349 alignments were extracted including the original reference translation. There were 6 redundant alignments i.e. alignments that occur twice or more. This is due to the fact that for alignments to be identical the lemma (stem) and its part of speech are considered. Because words may have ambiguous interpretations, the same sequence can be once extracted as a a noun and once as an adjective or it can be tagged as a np and by another rule as a **noun**.

From the 349 alignments, INV extracted 55 invertible translation examples which were included in EB_{INV}. In LEX, 108 alignments had a weight $W_{LEX} > 0$ from which 37 invertible translation wincluded in EB_{LEX}.

12 of the 13 collocations of *stark* were contained in EB_{INV} and in EB_{LEX}. There are, however, more noisy translation examples in EB_{INV} such as *Maria ↔ interest, Raucher ↔ John, Regen ↔by the strong rain* among the 55 extracted translation examples. One example is decomposed in a completely misguiding way as the translation example *Beteiligung ⟷ take, starke Beteiligung ⟷ will take* etc. implies. Also a wrong adjective translation $(stark)_{adj} ↔ (smoker)_{noun}$ was extracted.

However, the result is encouraging as 2/3 of the INV alignments are correct. Moreover, erroneous alignments occur mostly for single frequency words such that one can expect reasonable translation examples as the size of the reference text grows and word occurrences increase. The most reasonable adverb-default translation *stark ↔ strongly* has been found and for almost all of the less frequent translations of *stark* the context is included in the translation example.

In LEX, the bilingual lexicon in table 4 has been used containing 10 lexical translations for *stark*. Each of the *stark* translations has the translation probability of 0.100.

Table 3	Reference Translation containing *stark*

Das ist ein **starker** Mann	⟷	This is a **strong** man
Es war sein **stärkstes** Theaterstück	⟷	It has been his **best** play
Wir Hoffen auf eine **starke** Beteiligung	⟷	We hope a **large** number of people will take part
Eine 100 Mann **starke** Truppe	⟷	A 100 **strong** unit
Der **starke** Regen überraschte uns	⟷	We were surprised by the **strong** rain
Maria hat **starkes** Interesse gezeigt	⟷	Mary has shown **strong** interest
Paul hat **starkes** Fieber	⟷	Paul has **high** temperature
Das Auto war **stark** beschädigt	⟷	The car was **badly** damaged
Das Stück fand einen **starken** Widerhall	⟷	The piece had a **considerable** response
Das Essen war **stark** gewürzt	⟷	The meal was **strongly** seasoned
Hans ist ein **starker** Raucher	⟷	John is a **heavy** smoker
Im Sommer gab es eine **starke** Nachfrage	⟷	There was a **big** demand in summer
Er hatte daran **starken** Zweifel	⟷	He had **grave** doubts on it

Table 4	Bilingual Lexicon

$$(stark)_{adv} \longleftrightarrow (strong)_{adv}$$
$$(stark)_{adv} \longleftrightarrow (bad)_{adv}$$
$$(stark)_{adv} \longleftrightarrow (good)_{adv}$$
$$(stark)_{adj} \longleftrightarrow (strong)_{adj}$$
$$(stark)_{adj} \longleftrightarrow (big)_{adj}$$
$$(stark)_{adj} \longleftrightarrow (high)_{adj}$$
$$(stark)_{adj} \longleftrightarrow (heavy)_{adj}$$
$$(stark)_{adj} \longleftrightarrow (grave)_{adj}$$
$$(stark)_{adj} \longleftrightarrow (large)_{adj}$$
$$(stark)_{adj} \longleftrightarrow (considerable)_{adj}$$

Table 5	Invertible Translation Examples

$$(stark)_{adj} \longleftrightarrow (strong)_{adj}$$
$$(stark)_{adv} \longleftrightarrow (strong)_{adv}$$
$$(starker\ Mann)_{np} \longleftrightarrow (strong\ man)_{np}$$
$$(ein\ starker\ Mann)_{dp} \longleftrightarrow (a\ strong\ man)_{dp}$$
$$(starke\ Truppe)_{np} \longleftrightarrow (strong\ unit)_{np}$$
$$(starke\ Zweifel)_{np} \longleftrightarrow (grave\ doubts)_{np}$$
$$(starke\ Regen)_{np} \longleftrightarrow (strong\ rain)_{np}$$
$$(starkes\ Interesse)_{np} \longleftrightarrow (strong\ interest)_{np}$$
$$(starkes\ Fieber)_{np} \longleftrightarrow (high\ temperature)_{np}$$
$$(stark\ beschädigt)_{np} \longleftrightarrow (badly\ damaged)_{np}$$
$$(starken\ Widerhall)_{np} \longleftrightarrow (considerable\ response)_{np}$$
$$(einen\ starken\ Widerhall)_{dp} \longleftrightarrow (a\ considerable\ response)_{dp}$$
$$(stark\ gewürzt)_{np} \longleftrightarrow (strongly\ seasoned)_{np}$$
$$(starker\ Raucher)_{np} \longleftrightarrow (heavy\ smoker)_{np}$$
$$(ein\ starker\ Raucher)_{dp} \longleftrightarrow (a\ heavy\ smoker)_{dp}$$
$$(starke\ Nachfrage)_{np} \longleftrightarrow (big\ demand)_{np}$$
$$(eine\ starke\ Nachfrage)_{dp} \longleftrightarrow (a\ big\ demand)_{dp}$$
$$(starke\ Beteiligung)_{np} \longleftrightarrow (large)_{adj}$$
$$(eine\ starke\ Beteiligung)_{dp} \longleftrightarrow (large\ number)_{np}$$
$$(auf\ eine\ starke\ Beteiligung)_{pp} \longleftrightarrow (a\ large\ number)_{dp}$$

Table 5 shows a subset of EB_{LEX} which contain *stark* in their lh-sides. 12 collocations have been found within a minimal disambiguating context. The translation examples *starke Beteiligung* ↔ *large* and consequently *eine starke Beteiligung* ↔ *large number* seems somewhat odd[1]. The most likely adjective and adverb translation *stark* ↔ *stong* and *stark* ↔ *strongly* are extracted. Almost 90% of the translation examples are correct; a single lexical anchor yields sufficient indices to determine the surrounding constituents.

---

[1] There was no rule which marked the phrase *large number of people* such that an alignment containing this translation could not be generated.

5   A Translation Experiment

In this experiment four corpus-based MT systems are compared: a string-based translation memory (STM) and three versions of the EBMT system EDGAR [2]. EDGAR was given a reference text which was aligned using three different methods: a local alignment (LOC), and two invertible alignment methods INV and LEX as described in section 3. LOC is different from INV and LEX as each reference translation is considered independent and the resulting EB_{LOC} is likely to contain translation ambiguities. LOC works similar to LEX as it makes use of the same bilingual lexicon and the phrasal tagger KURD. During alignment, LOC and LEX made use of a bilingual lexicon containing more than 400,000 entries. From each, EB_{LEX}, EB_{INV} and EB_{LOC}, a bilingual grammar was inferred as discussed in [2] which was used in EDGAR for translation of the test text.

The STM makes use of the FindLink database retrieval software distributed by CONNEX [5,9]. FindLink returns a match score MS with each translation. MS indicates the similarity of the search string - i.e. the string to be translated - and the match string - i.e. the string in the memory. MS is scaled from 0% and 100% where 100% means greatest similarity of the search string and the match string.

Each system, STM, LOC, LEX and INV, was trained with a reference text containing 303 German-English reference translation as produced by a car ma-nufacturer. The test text contains 265 test translations from the same company and the same sub-domain (repair instructions). The length of the translations ranges from 1 up to 100 words is length containing single numbers and words, short imperative sentences, noun phrases and whole sentences with subordinate clauses. The test text and the reference text are from the same domain, with similar vocabulary and similar phrase structure.

The test translations were fully automatic evaluated where the generated translations are checked against an "ideal" translation contained in the test text. [12] claim that fully automatic evaluation methods can be used to validate enhancement efforts in MT systems to re-ensure that incremental changes of a system are for the better rather than for the worse. They propose an evaluation function which computes the ratio between the complement of the intersection set of the generated translation T and the ideal translation I ($|\overline{I \cap T}|$) and the combined length of these two ($|I + T|$) as shown in equation 3.

$$TS = \frac{|\overline{I \cap T}|}{|I + T|} \qquad (3)$$

A generated translation T which has no word in common with the ideal translation I has a translation score 1 because the complement of the intersection $|\overline{I \cap T}|$ is equivalent to the length of the concatenation $|I+T|$. On the other hand, if the generated translation is identical to the ideal translation the complement of their intersection is empty and thus, the translation score yields 0. For the calculation of the translation score TS only lexemes of the content words are considered.

134   M. Carl

6   Discussion

The graphs in Figure 2 show the translation outcome of STM, LOC, LEX and INV. The left-hand graph shows the translation score TS achieved for the percentage of the test text. The four systems produce between 20% and 25% ideal translations (i.e. $TS = 0$) and between 18% and 7% wrong translations, (i.e. $TS = 1$). Most ideal translations are produced by LEX (24.1%), STM (23.7%), INV (21.8%) and LOC (20.7%). At $TS = 0.5$ a jump in translation quality of about 6% and 9% for LEX and LOC can be observed.

The graph on the right-hand side in Figure 2 aims to outline the benefits of the linkage of TMs and EBMT. The four upper dotted lines depict the mean TS of the four single systems INV (0.472), LOC (0.445), STM (0.438) and LEX (0.396). The three lower dotted lines show the mean of the minimum TS for the combinations STM+LOC (0.335), STM+LEX (0.344) and STM+INV (0.374). For instance, the mean of the minimum TS for STM+INV was obtained based on the better of the STM and the INV translations according to the formula:

$$\sum_{i=1}^{N} min(TS(STM_i), TS(INV_i))/N$$

where $N = 265$ and STM_i and INV_i represent the ith translation of STM and INV. These results show that we can expect an increased mean TS of 15%, 24% and 22% if we can chose between between STM and INV, STM and LOC or STM and LEX translations compared to STM translations alone. Obviously, for every combination, there is a subset of test translations which is better translated by EDGAR and another subset which is better translated by STM.

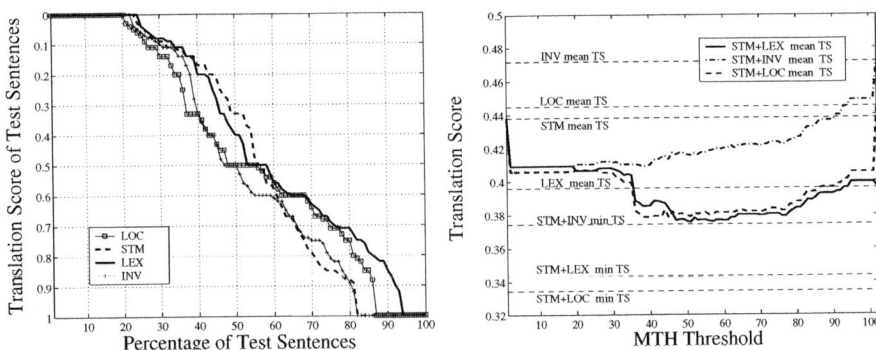

Translation Result of single systems (left) and combined systems (right): String-Based Translation Memory (STM) and EDGAR using local alignment (LOC), invertible alignment (INV) and lexical anchored invertible alignment (LEX)

Fig. 2. Translation Result of single and Combined Systems

In order to automatically separate the test translations into one set to be translated by STM and one set to be translated by EDGAR, we make use of the match score MS. If MS is less than an MS-threshold MTH translations are produced by EDGAR, otherwise the STM translation are considered. The mean TS of the combined systems is depicted in bold lines in Figure 2 (right). At $MTH = 0$ all translations are produced by STM and the curves start with the combined minimum $TS = 0.452$. At $MTH = 1$ the mean minimum TS of the combined systems is already about 8% lower than the STM output only. That is, translation quality can be increased considerably if STM produces translations for $MS \geq 1$ and EDGAR produces translations for $MS = 0.00$. A further significant gain in translation quality for STM+LEX and STM+LOC can be observed around $MTH = 40\%$. This gain in translation quality can be traced back to the use of lexical anchored alignments in LEX and LOC. For $MS = 40\%$ some parts of the test text match the reference translations. Due to compositional translation in EDGAR, these parts are correctly translated by LEX and LOC while this is not the case for STM and precision in INV seem not high enough for short segments. This jump in performance is also traced in the left-hand graph in Figure 2, where LEX and LOC produce better at $TS \leq 0.5$.

Roughly, between $40\% < MS < 80\%$ the STM+LOC and STM+LEX curves remain around a combined minimum $TS = 0.38$. For $MTH > 80\%$, the combined minimum TS increases again. At $MTH = 101\%$ all translations are produced by EDGAR and the combined mean TS join the dashed lines indicating the LEX, LOC and INV mean TS.

Note that around $MTH = 95\%$ the combined mean TS for STM+LEX is worse than the mean TS for the LEX system alone. Obviously, LEX produces more ideal translations than STM for $MS > 95\%$. The explanation to this is related to the availability of most frequent default translations contained in the invertible grammar used by LEX, while STM has no means which one to select amongst ambiguous translations. If, for instance, *Gear shift lever*, as in table 2, occurs more frequently in the reference text than *Transmission Unit Gear Selector*, LEX choses choses the first translation, while STM may only selecet a hazardous translation. Provided a similar distribution of translations in the reference text and the test text, LEX will more likely produce more ideal translations than STM.

7   Conclusion

This paper introduces invertible bilingual grammars and presents two variants of an algorithm, LEX and INV, to extract an invertible set of translation examples from a pre-aligned reference text. These invertible translation examples are used in the EBMT-system EDGAR for the translation of a test text. The translation result is compared with a string-based translation memory (STM) and with EDGAR translations based on non-invertible translation examples (LOC).

As a single system, LEX produced best overall translation results. The comparison of the translation results show that STM achieved highest translation quality when near matches are found. If the reference text does not contain similar translation example(s) such that STM match score (MS) falls below 80%, LEX, LOC and INV produced higher translation quality than STM.

A way is shown to combine STM+LEX, STM+INV and STM+LOC to produce better translations than each of the single systems. Best performance is observed with the STM+LEX combination.

This allows the following conclusions: i) bilingual grammars for EBMT yield best translation results if a bilingual lexicon is used in the alignment process. ii) the use of invertible bilingual grammars outperforms a local alignment method iii) STM and EBMT technologies can be combined in a way such that the combined output is in any case better than the output of each single system.

In contrast to the Multi-Engine Machine Translation (MEMT) scenario [6, 1], it can also be concluded that if we know the special characteristics of each single translation system, a sequential combination can be found such to exploit the individual features in an optimized way.

References

1. Brown, R.D.: Example-Based Machine Translation in the Pangloss System. In COLING-96. (1996)
2. Carl, M.: Inducing Translation Templates for Example-Based Machine Translation. In MT-Summit VII. (1999)
3. Carl, M., Schmidt-Wigger, A. and Hong, M.: KURD - a Formalism for Shallow Postmorphological Processing. In Proceedings of the NLPRS, Phuket, Thailand. (1997)
4. Collins, B.: Example-Based Machine Translation: An Adaptation-Guided Retrieval Approach. PhD thesis, Trinity College, Dublin. (1998)
5. CONNEX, Hildesheim, Germany: CONNEX: WORKSHOP (1996)
6. Frederking, R. and Nirenburg, S.: Three heads are better than one. In Proceedings of ANLP-94, Stuttgart, Germany. (1994)
7. Güvenir, H.A. and Cicekli, I.: Learning Translation Templates from Examples. Information Systems. **23(6)** (1998) 353–363
8. Harrison, M.A.: Introduction to Formal Language Theory. Addison-Wesley, Reading. (1978)
9. Heitland, M.: Einsatz der SpaCAM-Technik für ausgewählte Grundaufgaben der Informatik. PhD thesis, Universität Hildesheim, Fachbereich IV, Hildesheim, Germany. (1994)
10. Maas, H.D.: MPRO - Ein System zur Analyse und Synthese deutscher Wörter. In R. Hausser, (ed.), Linguistische Verifikation, Sprache und Information. Max Niemeyer Verlag, Tübingen. (1996)
11. Mäkinen, E. On the structural grammatical inference problem for some classes of context-free grammars. Information Processing Letters. **42** (1992) 1–5
12. Meyers, A., Yangarber, R., Grishman, R., Macleod, C. and Moreno-Sandoval, A.: Deriving transfer rules from dominance-preserving alignments. In Computerm, First Workshop on Computational Terminology, Montreal, Canada. (1998)
13. Nagao, M.: Machine Translation Through Language Understanding. In MT Summit 6, San Diego. (1997) 41–48
14. Wu, D.: Grammarless extraction of phrasal translation examples from parallel texts. In TMI-95. (1995)

What's Been Forgotten in Translation Memory

Elliott Macklovitch and Graham Russell

RALI, Université de Montréal
{macklovi,russell}@iro.umontreal.ca

Abstract. Although undeniably useful for the translation of certain types of repetitive document, current translation memory technology is limited by the rudimentary techniques employed for approximate matching. Such systems, moreover, incorporate no real notion of a document, since the databases that underlie them are essentially composed of isolated sentence strings. As a result, current TM products can only exploit a small portion of the knowledge residing in translators' past production. This paper examines some of the changes that will have to be implemented if the technology is to be made more widely applicable.

1   Introduction

The term "translation memory" admits of at least two different definitions, one broad and one narrow. The narrower, but more widely used, definition corresponds to the characteristics of a popular set of commercial products that includes *Translator's Workbench* from Trados, *Transit* from Star AG, *Déjà-Vu* from Atril and IBM's *TranslationManager/2*. According to this definition, a translation memory (abbreviated henceforth as TM) is a particular type of translation support tool that maintains a database of source and target-language sentence pairs, and automatically retrieves the translation of those sentences in a new text which occur in the database.

The broader definition regards TM simply as an archive of past translations, structured in such way as to promote translation reuse.[1] This definition, notice, makes no assumptions about the manner in which the archive is queried, nor about the linguistic units that are to be searched for in the archive. The narrower definition, by contrast, fixes the sentence as the privileged processing unit of TM systems and presumes automatic look-up as the privileged processing mode. It would thus exclude from the class of TMs an interactive bilingual concordancing tool like the RALI's *TransSearch* system[2], where the initiative for querying the archive resides with the user and not the system, and where any linguistic unit — full sentence, word or expression — may be submitted to the system's bi-textual database [8].

---

[1]   This generic definition of TM is quite similar to that provided in the final report of the EAGLES Evaluation of Natural Language Processing Systems [3].

[2]   http://www-rali.iro.umontreal.ca/TransSearch/

J.S. White (Ed.): AMTA 2000, LNAI 1934, pp. 137–146, 2000.

While fully subscribing to Pierre Isabelle's assertion that "existing translations contain more solutions to more translation problems than any other available resource" [6], we contend that the current generation of commercial TM systems exploits only a small portion of the translational knowledge that resides in translators' past production. In this paper, we attempt, first, to clarify the limitations of these systems and, second, to elucidate the challenges that will have to be met in order to overcome these limitations and produce more powerful and more broadly applicable translation memories.

2   The Limitations of Current TM Systems

All the better-known commercial TM systems basically function in the same manner. A new text to be translated is first segmented into units which are generally sentences but may also include titles, headings, table cells, and other "stand-alone" elements. As the translator works his way through the new text, each successive segment is looked up in a database of past translations, or, to be more precise, a bi-textual database of aligned source and target translation units. When a match is found for a new source language (SL) segment, the system retrieves the associated target language (TL) segment from the database, which the translator may accept as is or alter as necessary. In this way, the vendors of TM systems claim, the translator need never translate the same sentence twice.

A first question that may be raised about this technology is what exactly is meant by the expression "same sentence" in this context. That is, what qualifies as an exact match between a new SL segment and the contents of the TM database? The answer is not as obvious as one might think. For example, are two SL units considered identical if they contain exactly the same wording but differ in their formatting attributes? Some TM systems discard all formatting and store only the plain text content, while others claim to offer the user the choice of whether or not to match on formatting attributes. Is a new sentence identical to a stored sentence if the wording of the two is identical except for certain non-translatables, e.g. proper names, dates or other types of numerical expressions? Trados' *Translator's Workbench* (henceforth TWB) will in fact treat the two sentences as an exact match and can, moreover, automatically replace the values of certain non-translatables in the retrieved TL sentence with the appropriate values from the new source sentence.[3] What about two SL sentences that are composed of the same lexical units, although some of these are inflected differently, say, for tense or number? In this case, few of the major TM systems will recognise the two sentence as constituting an exact match. Indeed, as Planas and Furuse [9] point out, unless a TM system can do morphological analysis, it will have difficulty recognising that sentence (3) below is more similar to input sentence (1) than sentence (2) is:

---

[3]   Other TM products may be able to do so as well. For the purposes of this paper, we have been able to actively experiment with TWB, which we take to be representative of the commercial state of the art. Our knowledge of other TM systems is more limited.

(1) The wild child is destroying his new toy.

(2) The wild chief is destroying his new tool.

(3) The wild children are destroying their new toy.

In particular, a system such as TWB whose notion of similarity is based on the number of shared characters (or, more generally, edit distance between strings) will conclude the contrary, since (2) differs from (1) by only 4 letters while (3) differs from (1) by 9 letters.

In a sense, such qualifications to the notion of "identical sentence" can be seen as attempts by TM developers to come to grips with a fundamental problem faced by this type of repetitions processing technology, and that is that, outside the particular context of document revisions or updates, and perhaps certain types of technical maintenance manuals, the verbatim repetition of complete sentences is relatively rare in natural language texts. Given that the overwhelming demand for translation today is not made up of revisions and updates, this imposes a serious limit on the applicability of these systems. Despite the enthusiastic welcome accorded TM technology by translators and professional translation services, one can imagine that certain users are nevertheless frustrated with existing systems precisely because of the relative rarity of full-sentence repetition in the bulk of the texts they translate, and because they are convinced, furthermore, that their archives actually contain much useful information on a sub-sentential level that is not being exploited by these systems.

Why can't existing systems retrieve repetitions below the level of the full sentence? As the discussion of examples (1)–(3) suggests, the bi-textual databases underlying these systems are composed of essentially unanalysed sentence strings. Rather than parsing a sentence into units at a finer level of granularity and attempting to align those units across the two languages, today's TM systems typically accommodate non-identical sentences within the input text by means of some notion of 'fuzzy' or approximate matching. How exactly do these fuzzy matching algorithms work? It is difficult to say with certainty because TM vendors, although they do illustrate the concept in their promotional literature and demos, do not generally provide a formal definition of the similarity coefficient that users may specify in order to constrain the search for approximate matches. Hence, it is not at all obvious just how the results of a 70% match will differ, say, from a 74% match or an 81% match. According to Planas and Furuse [9] (p. 338), "the notion of similarity ... in Trados [is] based on the number of similar characters". While this is undoubtedly true, it is not the whole story, for systems like TWB may lower the value of a match when the stored translation unit has been produced by an automatic alignment program or by a machine translation system, or when the source segment has multiple target equivalents; not to mention the opaque effects of word-order differences on the matching coefficient. Combining several distinct and incomparable factors into a single numerical measure may appear to simplify things for the user, but as a consequence users are left with a vague and ill-defined comprehension of a parameter that is central to the system.

In any event, the important point to underline is that in all cases, what these fuzzy matching algorithms are evaluating is the degree of similarity between complete sentences. When no sufficiently close match can be found for a new input sentence, current TM systems are unable to "back off" and retrieve examples of clauses or other major phrases, even though such units may well be present in the database. Allow us illustrate with a simplified, schematised example. Suppose that example (4) below is a new input sentence made up of twenty words, each five characters long. The TM database contains no exact match for (4) but does contain the SL sentence in (5). The two sentences, notice, share an identical sub-string $w_1 \ldots w_5$ which in both cases is marked off from the rest of the sentence by a comma. However, since this sub-string contains only 25% of the sentence's total number of characters, it is doubtful that any current TM system would be able to retrieve it among its fuzzy matches; for users are generally advised not to set the similarity coefficient too low, to avoid being swamped by dissimilar and irrelevant examples.

(4) $w_1 \; w_2 \; w_3 \; w_4 \; w_5, \; w_6 \ldots w_{20}$.
(5) $w_1 \; w_2 \; w_3 \; w_4 \; w_5, \; w_{21} \ldots w_{35}$.

Calculating similarity in terms of a simple character count is clearly unproductive and indeed counter-intuitive here. In the following section, we will discuss some of the strategies that could be employed by a more flexible TM system in order to reliably locate this kind of sub-sentential repetition and retrieve its stored translation. The point we want to make here is that current TM systems have little to offer in this kind of situation. The best they can do is back-pedal on the level of automation and allow the user to manually select and submit a word or phrase to the bi-textual database via a *TransSearch*-like concordancing tool.[4]

Another weakness in current TM systems that can be traced to the nature of the underlying database structure is the fact that in these systems, the very notion of a document is lost. Not only are the segmented units in a new text extracted from their context and submitted to the database in isolation, but the contents of the database are also stored as isolated sentences, with no indication of their place in the original document. As every competent translator knows, however, it is not always possible to translate a sentence in isolation; the same sentence may have to be rendered differently in different documents, or even within the same document, as Bédard [1] convincingly argues. It is not hard to come up with examples of phenomena that are simply not amenable to translation in isolation: cross-sentence anaphora is one obvious example, but there are many others. Sceptics may argue that such problems are relatively rare, but they are missing the point. In order to evaluate a translation retrieved from memory, translators routinely need to situate that target sentence in its larger context. Current TM systems offer no straightforward of doing this because, unlike full document archiving systems, they archive isolated sentences.

---

[4] And even here, the graphic interface to the concordancer in TWB is such that the user can only submit a single contiguous sequence of input tokens. While this is sufficient for (4) and (5), it precludes Boolean or proximity-based searching of the kind that would be necessary to locate discontinuous translation units.

The above-mentioned article by Bédard also contains an interesting analysis of different configurations of repetition, not all of which, he maintains, warrant recourse to a TM system. In particular, if all the repetitions in a text are grouped together in a readily identifiable block, e.g. a page of introduction or the numbered clauses of a boiler-plate contract, or if the repetitions are limited to a small number of sentences, each of which recurs very often, then there may be more efficient ways to proceed than strict successive sentence-by-sentence processing.[5] Similarly, when an updated document has undergone only a few changes, it will often prove simpler to use a document comparison program to locate those source-language changes and then modify only the corresponding sentences in the previous translation rather than to resubmit the full document to TM. On the other hand, when the repetitions range over a large number of different sentences and these are dispersed unpredictably throughout the text, the type of repetitions processing that current TM products offer may well constitute the best solution.

To summarise: There is no denying the usefulness of current TM systems, particularly for texts that display a high degree of sentence-level repetition. On the other hand, existing TM systems are certainly far from optimal; in particular, their restriction to complete sentences as the sole processing unit, and their rudimentary character-based algorithms for locating approximate matches mean that these systems can exploit only a small part of the translational knowledge lying dormant in past translations. We now turn to the question of what will have be done in order develop more powerful TM technology.

3   Matching and Equivalence

3.1   Kinds of Equivalence

As we have seen, the "narrow" TM system organizes its contents on two levels: text is stored and accessed in sentence units, and similarity is evaluated principally in terms of shared characters. Neither of these is optimal from the user's perspective. Although sentences have a clear semantic basis in a way that characters do not, their variability, reflecting what some linguists think of as the "creativity of natural language", results in lower frequency rates than one might expect. Even when a sentence is composed largely of formulaic phrases, these can be combined with other material in novel and unpredictable ways and thus defeat present search mechanisms.

In this section we consider what steps might be taken to remedy this situation by extending the capacity of TM technology. The central issue is the behaviour of the system when confronted with a sentence to be translated: what criteria of

---

[5] Some TM systems also offer a batch mode alternative in the form of a pre-translate function. But, of course, there is no guarantee that the automatically inserted translations will be appropriate, especially if the TM database is composed of a wide variety of documents. For one translator's particularly severe assessment of this pre-translation function, see Falcone [4].

equivalence are used in selecting candidate matches from its database, and how pertinent are these criteria for translation?

The discussion in Sec. 2 leads us to the following observation: Strict matching based on string identity between sentences yields high precision but low recall; high precision, since any result means that the entire query sentence exists verbatim in the TM and must therefore be relevant; low recall, since other relevant sentences will not be extracted owing to the low rate of verbatim repetition. The challenge is to improve the latter without significantly diminishing the former. A general approach to this problem involves establishing equivalence-classes of source-language expressions. This is the role of approximate matching; retrieving (3) as a reliable result for the query (1) implies treating *children* as equivalent to *child*. And as we saw earlier, if equivalence is defined purely in terms of edit distance it is impossible to exclude spurious matches such as that between *child* and *chief*. This section considers other more useful notions of equivalence, obtained by ignoring inflectional variation, conflating expressions of certain well-defined types, and identifying shared subsequences. These extensions require the ability to perform a more detailed analysis of source-language texts.

3.2 Inflection

One obvious step towards a useful definition of equivalence is to allow inflectional variants of a word to match (so *child* would match *children* but not *chief*). The underlying assumption here is that, for a user who wishes to find translations of a sentence containing some word w, the translation of any sentence containing an inflectional variant of w will be potentially informative, despite whatever minor adjustments need to be made to accommodate the variation.

A popular solution to an apparently similar problem in information retrieval is stemming [5]; here, different word-forms are reduced to a common stem using little or no linguistic knowledge, sometimes yielding erratic results. Assuming that a relatively complete morphological description of the source-text language exists, more powerful models of the desired equivalences are available and seem advisable.

Let F be a mapping from inflected forms of words to their canonical base-forms.[6] What the latter are is not important here — for English, we can take the bare infinitive of verbs, singular of nouns, etc. Non-inflecting forms map to themselves. For example, $F(\texttt{lamps}) = \texttt{lamp}$, $F(\texttt{lamp}) = \texttt{lamp}$, $F(\texttt{between}) = \texttt{between}$, $F(\texttt{eaten}) = \texttt{eat}$, and so on. This is simply the basic function required for dictionary lookup in many NLP contexts, minus the various types of grammatical information that might be associated with a word-form.

The inverse of F, denoted by F^{-1}, performs the reverse mapping: $F^{-1}(\texttt{eat}) = \{\texttt{ate}, \texttt{eat}, \texttt{eaten}, \texttt{eating}, \texttt{eats}\}$. The composition of F with F^{-1} then has the effect of finding all inflectional variants of a word, using its base form as a pivot:

---

[6] Although the presentation refers to inflectional variation, the approach could be extended to deal with derivation.

$$F^{-1}(F(\texttt{ate})) \; = \; F^{-1}(F(\texttt{eats})) \; = \; F^{-1}(F(\texttt{eating})) \; = \; \dots$$
$$= \; F^{-1}(\texttt{eat})$$
$$= \; \{\texttt{ate}, \texttt{eat}, \texttt{eaten}, \texttt{eating}, \texttt{eats}\} \; .$$

In the present context, we are interested less in generating all variants than in determining the equivalence of some pair of word-forms. This can be done quite straightforwardly: $x \equiv y$ iff $x \in F^{-1}(F(y))$. The obvious implementation of this technique is to compose a finite-state transducer encoding the relation F with its inverse F^{-1} [7], and make matching conditional on acceptance of both strings by the resulting composite transducer.

In some cases, the classes so defined will be too inclusive. For example, many English words are categorially ambiguous: *last* as adjective, noun and verb will all be mapped by F onto the same string $\texttt{last}$, even though they will be translated differently. As a result, irrelevant sentences will be retrieved. This problem could be avoided by tagging the input sentence and stored source-language texts with part-of-speech information, and defining equivalence via a mapping G, like F but with category information at the pivot. However, it is a special case of the more general problem arising from multiple word-senses; in general, perfect performance in this area could only be obtained by correctly disambiguating each potentially ambiguous word.

Rather than complicating the matching and searching process, one might consider simply applying F, lemmatizing source-language texts as they are stored in the TM and the query sentence before it is looked up, so that the sentences in (1) and (3) above would both be presented to, and represented in, the system as *The wild child be destroy* .... However, this solution has the disadvantage of losing information; in some circumstances a user might want results ranked in a way that privileges inflectional identity and this cannot be done unless the relevant distinctions have been preserved. Both lemmatized and 'raw' text representations could be stored in a multi-level TM of the kind suggested by Planas and Furuse [9], albeit at some cost in space.

3.3   Named Entities

A rather different kind of equivalence is displayed by sentences containing dates, times, proper names, numerical expressions, monetary amounts, etc. Such expressions tend to require special treatment, being either invariant in translation (e.g. most company and personal names) or subject to specific conversions (e.g. some place names, number formats). Moreover, they can largely be handled in a modular fashion; the treatment of a date or place-name is independent of the linguistic context in which it appears (although it may be subject to stylistic constraints), while the exact date or place-name used in a sentence has little effect on how the remainder of that sentence is translated. This property permits another refinement in TM functionality: if all possible dates are conflated into a single "archidate" representation, certain sentence pairs which are distinct when judged by edit-distance or the identity up to inflectional variance discussed in

Sec. 3.2 can be treated as equivalent. The same applies to monetary amounts, names, and so on.

The Trados TWB goes some way towards this goal, recognizing some numerical and other expressions, copying or converting them automatically into the target text, and ignoring them for matching purposes. However it is not capable of handling the full range of modular expressions discussed here. Expressions of this kind are known as "named entities" in the information extraction community[7] and it is likely that techniques under development for their detection and classification could be adopted with advantage for use in more sophisticated TMs. For names in particular see Coates-Stephens [2].

3.4   Parsing

As examples (4) and (5) in Sec. 2 illustrate, a matching criterion based on edit distance will not in general be able to retrieve relevant sentences in which even a significant subsequence is shared with the input, if the identical text forms less than a given proportion of the total. Inflectional merging and named-entity conflation may help here, but only incidentally, by altering the ratio of shared text. They are orthogonal to the the central problem, which is that the edit-distance model has no built-in conception of adjacency or constituency. Recognizing that $w_1 \ldots w_5$ form a coherent textual unit which may well be associated with one or more reusable translations is therefore beyond its ability.

Ideally, an advanced TM system would be able to analyse a source language text into units at a finer level of detail than the sentence. Since a complete parse of unrestricted input, even where feasible, is generally too expensive, techniques of shallow parsing or chunking [10,11] should be considered. The input sentence would then be broken into phrases or pseudo-phrases which, because they are shorter and inherently less variable, are more likely to be present in the TM than the entire sentence, and which, because they correspond to syntactically defined expressions, are more likely than a random subsequence of the same length to yield a relevant translation.

Note that this does not necessarily imply the abandonment of the sentence as the basic storage unit; only the matching criterion is changed, edit distance now playing a smaller role, if any.

4   The Suprasentential Level

In the previous section, we criticized current TM technology for its inability to provide a principled treatment of repetition at the sub-sentential level. Another area in which TM limitations are felt is their inability to process text in units longer than the sentence: paragraphs and even entire documents have a role to play in the storage and retrieval of previous translations. It is to these higher-level units that we now turn.

---

[7]   See http://cs.nyu.edu/cs/faculty/grishman/NEtask20.book_3.html for a description of the MUC-6 "Named Entity Task".

A document is more than just a collection of sentences; it has global properties that are not easily associated with its lower-level components. Administrative information concerning who originally translated a certain document, when, for which client, as part of which project, who revised and approved the translation, etc. is properly treated as applying to the text as a whole rather than separately to each individual sentence. While TWB allows for similar annotations to be made at a sentential level, this cannot be regarded as more than a matter of expedience. Current TM systems provide little or no support for document management and archiving.

Even where the core functionality of a TM is concerned, namely detection of existing (partial) translations of a new document, sentence-based storage has the weakness noted in Sec. 2 of lacking a uniform treatment of extended matching passages.

A TM system which represented documents explicitly, or at least was able to reconstruct them from smaller units, would provide its users with far more flexibility than the narrow TM model permits, including the ability:

1. to search on the document-level logging information mentioned above, in order to find the most recent documents translated for this client, etc.;
2. to retrieve similar documents and their translations for use in preparatory background reading;
3. to identify and process extended passages, removing the need to treat each sentence separately;
4. to examine the context in which proposed matches for the current sentence appear.

Support for this functionality relies on full-text indexing similar to that provided by the mg system of Witten et al.c̃itemg, or any of several commercial packages. In our view, these same functionalities need to be extended to the context of parallel documents and fully integrated with TM technology. A partial solution is adopted by the Translation Service of the European Commission, where TWB is used as a front-end to a full-fledged document management system [12].

5   Conclusions

There is a certain tension between the main selling point of current TM systems ("your translations are full of repetitions — save time and money by exploiting them") and the facilities that they actually offer: most repetitions are subsentential and are difficult to locate without sorting through large numbers of irrelevant results, while others may extend over several paragraphs, making the sentence-based processing mode unnecessarily laborious.

This paper has drawn attention to some of the limitations of present TM technology and outlined a number of modifications that could be made in order to remedy them. Some of these (inflectional merging, recognition of and conflation of certain named entities) are relatively straightforward, while others (proper name recognition, shallow parsing) are matters for continuing research. Readers may be surprised at the fact that we have made no mention of research into finer-grained alignment methods. The reason is that reliable sub-sentential alignment is less crucial for TM technology than it is, say, for example-based MT where there may be no human in the loop. The critical challenge for better TMs, in our view, is not in linking components of a source-language sentence to their target-language counterparts, but rather in finding more efficient ways of locating source-language repetitions at levels both above and below the sentence.

Current TM systems are limited for good reasons: the choice of sentence-based storage and edit distance as the main matching criterion permits efficient implementation, and makes for a program which is intuitively accessible for users. Nevertheless, we believe that there is room for more advanced TM technology, providing access to stored source texts at levels other than the sentence, and allowing more linguistically informed search. The objective, one under investigation at RALI, is something that one might call "Full Text Translation Memory".

References

1. Bédard, C.: Les mémoires de traduction: une tendance lourde. Circuit. **60**. (1998) 25–26
2. Coates-Stephens, S.: The Analysis and Acquisition of Proper Names for Robust Text Understanding. PhD thesis, City University, London. (1992)
3. EAGLES Evaluation of Natural Language Processing Systems, Final Report. EAGLES document EAG-EWG-PR.2 (1995). Section E.3.1: Design and Function of Translation Memory, 140–145. Also available at http://issco-www.unige.ch/ewg95/
4. Falcone, S.: Translation Aid Software: Four Translation Memory Programs Reviewed. Translation Journal **2(1)** (1998) http://accurapid.com/journal/03TM2.htm
5. Frakes, W.B.: Stemming Algorithms. In Frakes, W.B. and R. Baeza-Yates (eds.) Information Retrieval: Data Structures and Algorithms. Prentice Hall (1992) 131–160
6. Isabelle, P., Dymetman, M., Foster, G., Jutras, J-M., Macklovitch, E., Perrault, F., Ren, X., Simard, M.: Translation Analysis and Translation Automation. Proc. TMI'93. (1993) 201–217
7. Kaplan, R.M., Kay, M.: Regular Models of Phonological Rule Systems. Computational Linguistics **20(3)** (1994) 331–378
8. Macklovitch, E., Simard, M., Langlais, P.: TransSearch: A Free Translation Memory on the World Wide Web. Proc. LREC 2000 **III**. (2000) 1201–1208
9. Planas, E., Furuse, O.: Formalizing Translation Memories. Proc. MT Summit VII. (1999) 331–339
10. Ramshaw, L.A., Marcus, M.P.: Text Chunking using Transformation-Based Learning. Proc. Workshop on Very Large Corpora. (1995) 82–94
11. Skut, W., Brants, T.: A Maximum-Entropy Partial Parser for Unrestricted Text. Proc. Sixth Workshop on Very Large Corpora. (1998) 143–151
12. Theologitis, D.: Translation Technology from Theory to Practice. Presentation at NLP2000, Patras. (2000)
13. Witten, I.H., Moffat, A., Bell, T.C.: Managing Gigabytes: Compressing and Indexing Documents and Images. Morgan Kaufmann (1999)

Understanding Politics by Studying Weather:
A Cognitive Approach to Representation of Polish Verbs of Motion, Appearance, and Existence

Barbara Gawronska and Hanna Duczak

University of Skövde, Box 408, S-541 28 Skövde, Sweden
barbara.gawronska@isp.his.se

Abstract. The paper deals with the question whether representations of verb semantics formulated on the basis of a lexically and syntactically restricted domain (weather forecasts) can apply to other, less restricted textual domains. An analysis of a group of Polish polysemous verbs of motion, existence and appearance inspired by cognitive semantics, especially the metaphor theory, is presented, and the usefulness of the conceptual representations of the Polish motion/appearance/existence verbs for automatic translation of texts belonging to less restricted domains is evaluated and discussed.

Introduction

The work presented here is related to two NLP projects: one of them is a system for automatic translation of weather forecasts between Swedish, English, and Polish; the second one is an experimental system for multilingual summarization of news reports. Both domains have been investigated by a considerable number of computational linguists [3, 10, 11, 12, 23, 24, 25, 31, 32,]. While the domain of weather forecasts does not seem to draw the theorists' interest any longer, the task of translation or summarization of political and economical news still poses a lot of difficulties, most of them related to anaphora resolution and word sense disambiguation. Especially the problem of identifying and representing the semantics of verbs has been the subject of a lot of theoretical work [4, 7, 8, 18, 19, 21, 22, 30, 39].

Our goal was to investigate if the experience of translating texts belonging to such a restricted domain as weather forecasts could be useful for choosing translation equivalents of motion verbs, verbs of appearance and existence/location verbs in the much broader domain of news reports. More exactly, we were interested in checking whether the semantic representations of certain motion, appearance and existence verbs established on the basis of data from our weather forecast corpus can apply to other domains as well, or whether different, domain specific lexical representations are to be preferred.

J.S. White (Ed.): AMTA 2000, LNAI 1934, pp. 147-157, 2000.
© Springer-Verlag Berlin Heidelberg 2000

2   Polish Motion Verbs in the Domain of Weather Forecasts

The huge amount of work on verb semantics includes purely logic-based approaches [28], corpus-based approaches [6], cognitive interpretations [9, 17] and – especially in the recent years – very impressive work on lexical knowledge combining issues in corpus linguistics, psycholinguistics, cognitive semantics, syntax, and pragmatics [2, 18, 19, 20, 21, 22, 25, 26, 27, 30, 38, 39]. Our approach is to a great extent related to the work performed on WordNet and EuroWordNet, and probably even more influenced by cognitive semantics [9, 13, 14, 15, 16, 35, 36], and by categorial grammar. The formalism we use is not incompatible with HPSG [5], but aimed at a simplified notation and a simplification of lexical transfer in translation.

The MT-system used as our starting point is a hybrid interlingua-transfer-example system. The monolingual lexical entries are provided with interlingua codes, and word order changes are triggered by transfer rules; the lexicons are augmented by correctly translated sentences. The number of lexemes (excluding proper names, stored in an onomasticon) per language is ca. 800 (for Swedish 220 common nouns, 46 verbs, 150 adjectives, 300 adverbs, 98 words from closed classes). During the first phase of the system development, the system performed only Swedish-to-English translation, and the lexical choice of translation equivalents was based on an English-centered interlingua. This meant, for example, that those Swedish verbs that could be translated as 'move' (*förflytta sig, röra sig, förskjutas*) were provided with the code 'move', according to such simplistic DCG-rules as:

```
slex('move',v,vintr,pres) → [förflytta,sig] ; [röra,sig] .
```

This resulted in comprehensible and grammatically correct outputs; however, the first translation alternative usually showed too little stylistic variation. In the course of system testing, the default choices exemplified above have been improved by matching them against a human-post-edited example base. The Swedish-to-English output could actually not be distinguished from a translation by a human (recall and precision about 95%). When introducing Polish into the system, however, we decided to develop more elaborated verb representations. This was partially caused by the lack of post editors; partially by the quite intricate nature of semantic differences between the Slavic verbs and the verbs in both Germanic languages, which, combined with the relatively free word order in Polish, would require a much larger example base than the one used for Swedish and English; and, finally, by our plan to test the possibility of applying the results of the analysis of weather forecasts to other textual domains.

The most frequent motion verbs in the corpus of Polish weather forecasts we have investigated (12000 words), are the following (470 occurrences, i.e. 42% of all verb occurrences): *napływać, nasuwać się, przesuwać się, przemieszczać się.*

All four verbs can be used as translations of *move*, as in a-d below.

    a.   opady deszczu **przemieszczają się** z frontem atmosferycznym
           fall   of-rain   'move'   with   front   atmospheric
           'showers move with the front'
    b.   wilgotne powietrze znad Islandii **napływa** nad południową Szwecję
           moist   air   from-over Island 'move' to-over southern Sweden
           'moisture over Island moves into southern Sweden'

c. chłodny front znad   Finlandii **przesuwa się** nad Szwecję
    cold   front from-over   Finland   'move' to-   over Sweden
    'cold front over Finland moves into Sweden'
d. od wschodu **nasuwa się** zatoka wyżowa
    from east   'move'   ridge of low pressure
    'a ridge of high pressure is moving from the east'

However, *przesuwać się, nasuwać się* and *napływać* cannot be used interchangeably in most contexts; cf e-h, where g. and h. are ungrammatical.

e. obszar niżowy   **przemieszcza się** na północ
    low pressure area   'move'   northwards
f. obszar niżowy   **przesuwa się** na północ
    low pressure area   'move'   northwards
g. *obszar niżowy   **napływa**   na północ
    low pressure area   'move'   northwards
h. *obszar niżowy   **nasuwa się**   na północ
    low pressure area   'move'   northwards

All four verbs have a lot of other possible translation equivalents in English. For example, the verb *napływać* can, according to the Great Polish-English Dictionary [34] be rendered as *flow in, gush forth, well up, come, arrive, approach, flow, flock and pour in*. In the domain of weather forecast, however, the most frequent equivalents of *napływać* are *stream, flow, approach* and *move*. The English equivalents of *napływać* belong thus to two types in Levin's [19] classification: verbs of appearance (*stream, flow, come, arrive*) and motion verbs (*move, approach*). The verb *flock* is classified by Levin as an existence verb, but here it shall be treated rather as a verb of appearance, since the 'flock'-meaning of *napływać* is synonymous to 'come in great number'. The combination of appearance and movement seems to be a general feature of Polish verbs consisting of the prefix *na-* and a motion verb (*pływać* = *swim, float*) [1], while the verbs *przesuwać/przemieszczać się* are primarily pure motion or 'transport' verbs [37].

3 Conceptualization of the Subjects of the Polish Motion, Appearance, and Existence Verbs

As shown in a-h above, the four motion verbs differ with regard to their semantic valence restrictions: all "movable weather objects" are not combined with all motion verbs. In table 1 we show nouns denoting "weather objects" that occur as subject heads with the considered verbs. The difference between the four subject groups seems to be possible to explain by means of Talmy's [35, 36] notion of quantity disposition. The possible intersections of the four quantity distribution attributes - dimension, plexity, boundedness, and dividedness - are schematized in [36] as in figure 1.

Table 1. Most frequent subjects of the Polish motion/appearance verbs

napływać	powietrze (air)
nasuwać się	zatoka (ridge)
przesuwać się	wyż, niż, obszar, front (low/high pressure, area, front)
przemieszczać się	niz, wyż, obszar, front, zatoka (low/high pressure, area, front, ridge)

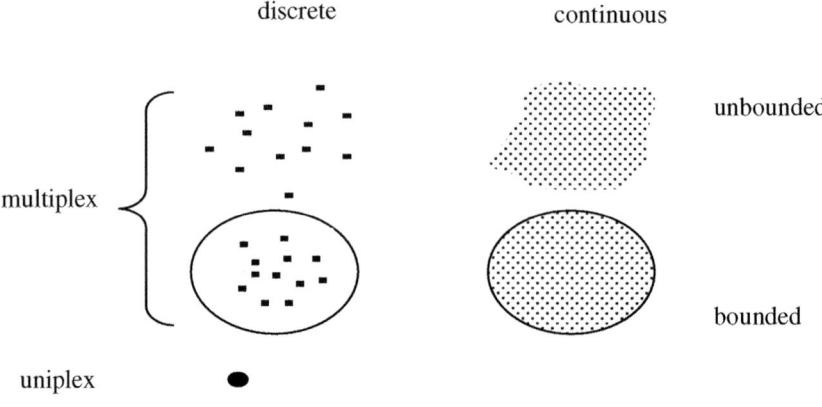

Fig. 1 Quantity distribution attributes as schematized in [36], p. 181

It is easy to notice that *napływać* occurs in our material only with subjects with the features +continuos and –bounded, *nasuwać się* with +bounded subjects (the Polish noun *zatoka* means prototypically *bay* – an object with clear limits), while *przesuwać się* and *przemieszczać się* allow both bounded and unbounded subjects. The classification of the noun *obszar* (*area*) as + or – bounded depends to a great degree on the semantics of the genitive attribute: *obszar Polski* (*the area of Poland*) is +bounded, while *obszar opadów* (*rain area*) or *obszar ciśnienia* (*pressure area*) - rather unbounded because of their diffuse limits. Still, even *obszar opadów* or *obszar ciśnienia* can refer both to bounded objects, depending on the context (the referent may be converted to a bounded object if its limits are specified by adverbial phrases).

The bounded/unbounded distinction alone does not explain the impossibility of use of the noun *powietrze* (*air*) with the verbs *nasuwać się* and *przemieszczać się*. Our first hypothesis - later tested on texts from other domains, cf. section 4 - is that these selectional restrictions are due to the conceptual metaphor [15,16] AIR is FLUID (remember the semantics of the stem *pływ* – *swim, float*). The same metaphor is present in English and Swedish, although their manifestations are not distributed in exactly the same way as in Polish. Thus, our assumption was that the subject of the verb *napływać* must refer to objects that can be conceptualized as fluids.

The analysis of motion, appearance and/or existence verbs in Polish weather forecasts is shown in table 2. The subjects taken into consideration were only nouns referring to "movable weather objects" that actually occur in the Polish corpus as subjects of finite verbs. Nouns like *rain, snow, thunderstorms* etc. are not included in the table since, in the forecasts, they never occur as heads of subject NPs, but only as genitive modifiers (*obszar deszczu* – lit. *rain+gen area – rain area* or *opady deszczu* – lit. *fall of rain*) or in verbless constructions (*jutro deszcz – tomorrow rain*). The descriptions in the last column are to be understood as "conceptualized in Polish as…(fluid, container, etc.)".

Table 2. Motion, appearance and/or existence verbs in Polish weather forecasts

Polish verbs	English equivalents in weather forecasts	Other English equivalents in bilingual dictionary	Classes according to Levin	Most freq-uent subject heads	Impossible subjects	Conceptual features of the subject
napływać	stream, flow, move, approach	come, pour in, flock, arrive, approach,	appear, motion	air	area, front system, ridge,	–bounded + fluid
pokrywać	cover, range	roof, adjust	existence, putting	area, system	front	a flat object with large horizontal surface
zalegać	cover	fill, surge, occupy, brood, be overdue	appear, change of state	system	air	preferably +bounded
nasuwać się	move	creep, glide,over-lap, arise, emerge, occur	appear, motion	ridge	air	a flat object with large horizontal surface, + bounded
sięgać	range	reach, grasp, strive	appear, change of state	ridge	air	a flat object, with large horizontal surface, +bounded
rozciągać się	spread, range, scatter	lengthen, dilate, run out, reach, stretch,	appear, change of state	area	air	a flat object with large horizontal surface, –bounded

Polish verbs	English equiva-lents in weather forecasts	Other English equiva-lents in bilingual dictionary	Classes according to Levin	Most freq-uent subject heads	Impos-sible subjects	Conceptual features of the subject
obejmować	spread, range	grasp, hug, clasp, enfold, encircle, border, embrace, surround, envelop, overcome overwhelm comprise, include, contain, embody	appear, existence, 'hold and keep', social interaction	area, system	air front	container
prze-suwać się	move	shift, pass, slip through	motion, sending and carrying'	front, area	air	+/- bounded, - fluid
przemiesz-czać się	move	shift	motion, sending and carrying	front, area	-	no restrictions

4   Testing the Lexical Representations of "Weather Forecast Verbs" in Other Textual Domains

The assumptions about the semantic representations of the analyzed verbs were tested on sentences from sample texts concerning political and economic news. Similarities between weather forecasts and stock market reports have been analyzed in [31, 32], although with focus on syntax and such verbs of state change like *increase*, *rise* and *fall*; in the world news, appearance, motion and existence verbs are frequent in the subdomains of military conflicts and peace talks. Before testing, the lexical verb representations had to be completed with regard to the possibility of taking subjects referring to uniplex objects (all weather objects are multiplex). The Prolog format for a completed lexical entry is exemplified below:

```
lexentry(naplywac, Codelist,[intr,imp,d14],
    subj(np, multiplex, unbounded,conc(fluid)),
        opt([source([prep(z,gen),prep(znad,gen)),
            [appear,motion]).
```

The variable Codelist refers to a list containing lexical codes of possible translation equivalents. Slot 2 contains grammatical information (transitivity, aspect value, inflectional pattern). In the valence frame, optional arguments are marked by the functor 'opt' and, if they may be realized as PPs, provided with information about the form (z, na...) and the case demand (gen, ack) of the preposition. In the last slot, we encode Levin-based verb classes of those translation equivalents that correspond to the use of the verb within the valence frame specified in the third and fourth slot. This means that e.g. the verb *obejmować* is coded as two lexical entries: one representing the motion/appearance variant, one – the 'keep and hold' and 'social interaction' variant. The motion/appearance entry does not allow the instrument role, which can be optionally realized in the 'keep and hold' entry. Furthermore, the 'keep and hold' variant allows uniplex subject referents, while the motion/appearance variant requires multiplex entities as subjects.

The next step in lexicon augmentation was to identify and encode the possible conceptualizations of nouns. On the basis of examples from the entries a monolingual Polish dictionary [33], the following metaphors have been implemented: AIR is FLUID, POPULATIONS are FLUIDS, INFORMATION is FLUID, MONEY is FLUID, AREAS are CONTAINERS.

From the news reports samples (ca. 5000 words), we selected sentences containing the Polish verbs listed in table 2 (148 sentences). Below, we show some sample sentences:

Badania   **obejmują** tylko przedsiębiorstwa zatrudniające powyżej   50 osób
Investigations 'spread/range' only companies   employ+prt   more-than 50 persons
'The investigations include only companies that employ more than 50 persons'

Napływają gratulacje z Zachodu
'move/float' congratulations from West
'Letters of congratulation are coming from the West'

Jeszcze większa liczba Romów **napływa** do Wielkiej Brytanii.
Yet   greater number of-Gypsies 'move/float' to Great Britain
'A yet greater number of Gypsies is moving into the U.K.'

Nasuwa się pytanie...
'move/occur'   question
'A question arises...'

The sentences were translated into English by a human translator and then translated again into Polish by the MT-system. In the first and the second test, the augumented lexical entries were not utilized. In the first test, only the simple interlingua codes from the original Swedish-to-English weather forecast system and some information about the semantic classes and the grammatical valence frames of the Polish verbs were used. It means that for example the verb *nasuwać się* could be associated only with the English verb *move,* and not with the other possible equivalents (*creep, glide, overlap, arise, emerge, occur*). In the second test, codes of all possible English equivalents of the Polish verbs were added, but no selectional restrictions concerning the subject were used. In the third test, we utilized the augmented lexicon described above. In all three tests, we let the system produce all possible outputs. The results are shown in table 3. By correct verb choices we mean not only those outputs that are identical with the original Polish input, but also those translations that do not sound odd to a native speaker of Polish.

Table 3. Test results

Test	Translated input sentences	Correct verb choices	Incorrect verb choices	Recall	Precision
1.	106	108	52	73%	68%
2.	140	142	52	96%	73%
3.	140	142	5	96%	97%

5   Conclusions and Further Research

The tests included only re-translation of Polish sentences containing the nine verbs under consideration; the English input did not contain all possible translation equivalents listed in Table 2, column 3. Drawing more general conclusions as to the disambiguating capacity of the lexical representations presented here would require more tests performed on less limited material. However, the results are quite encouraging, as the number of incorrect verb choices decreased drastically in tests 3. Three of the five incorrect choices are second translation alternatives, where the first alternatives were correct. The remaining two wrong choices are due to a too general specification of the source and goal arguments in the valence frame. The sentences that have not been translated in test 2. and 3. contained verbs and lexical phrases that had not been coded in the lexicon as possible translation equivalents. Thus, the quality of translation of our limited material has been certainly improved by combining the interlingua codes and the information about semantic classes of translation equivalents with subject descriptions based on Talmy's notion of quantity disposition and the notion of conceptual metaphor. We can also conclude that analyzing a limited text domain – like weather forecasts – is a good starting point for understanding the semantics of a certain verb group and that contrastive analyses of restricted domains could be incorporated into larger statistically based or definition based lexicon acquisition systems as a useful tool. In a domain with a restricted number of possible event and object types, the basic semantic distinctions between verbs belonging to the same semantic class are often more clearly manifested than in a heterogeneous corpus. Obviously, a larger corpus must be used to test the hypotheses.

The next step in the testing procedure will be to develop lexical representations of all Polish verbs that can be translated as English motion/appearance/existence verbs and to use them both in re-translation and in translation of original English texts. If the tests confirm the usefulness of the lexical representation format proposed here, a further subgoal will be to develop a semi-automatic procedure for lexical acquisition

[29,39] involving: 1) extraction of translation equivalents of Polish verbs from bilingual dictionaries (a quite simple task, as all English verbs listed in a lexicon article will be copied); 2) classification of the English verbs based on Levin's work; 3) extraction of knowledge about grammatical and semantic valence from informants, preferably using examples from restricted, homogenous domains; and 4) testing results on large heterogeneous corpora. It follows from the approach suggested here that in 3), the informants would primarily concentrate on the semantics of nominal complements, which has several practical advantages (fewer linguistic instructions required, the possibility of using simple non-ambiguous pictures on the interface, probably a higher agreement rate in answers).

An interesting goal for further theoretical research would be to investigate if there is a systematic correlation between the English verb classes and alternations defined by Levin and semantico-syntactic patterns of Polish verbs. In our very limited material, the same syntactic pattern of a Polish verb and the same semantic restrictions on the subject corresponded to translation equivalents belonging to classes 'motion' and 'appearance', or 'existence' and 'appearance', while English verbs belonging to other classes require slightly different patterns. A systematic exploration of possible regularities between Germanic verb classes and the semantics of Slavic verb is both of theoretical and practical (i.e. MT-related) interest.

References

1. Agrell,S.: Aspektänderung und Aktionsartbildung beim polnischen Zeitworte. PhD thesis, Lund University (1908)
2. Atkins, S., Fillmore, C.: Starting where the Dictionaries Stop: the Challenge of Corpus Lexicography. In: Atkins, B, Zampolli, A. (eds.): Conceptual Approaches to the Lexicon. Oxford University Press, Oxford (1994)
3. Blåberg, O. On Machine translation of Finnish Weather Forecasts. Fackspråk och översättningsteori, VAKKI-seminarium. Vörå (1991) 22-27
4. Boguraev, B., Pustejovsky, J.: Corpus Processing for Lexical Acquisition. MIT Press:Cambridge, Massachusetts (1996)
5. Copestake, A., Briscoe, T.: Semi-Productive Polysemy and Sense Extension. Journal of Semantics 12. Oxford University Press (1995) 15-67
6. Dagan, I., Itai, A.: Word Sense Disambiguation Using a Second Language Monolingual Corpus. Computational Linguistics, 20(4). (1994)
7. Dorr, B. J.: Machine Translation: a View from the Lexicon. The MIT Press, Cambridge, Massachusetts, London (1993)
8. Dorr, B. J., Garman, J.,Weinberg, A.: From Syntactic Encodings to Thematic Roles: Building Lexical Entries for Interlingual MT. Machine Translation 9 (1995) 221-250
9. Fillmore, C., Atkins, B.: Toward a Frame-based Lexicon: The Semantics of RISK and its Neighbors. In: A. Lehrer & E. Kittay (eds.): Frames, Fields, and Contrasts. Hillsdale/N.J.:Lawrence Erlbaum (1992) 75-102
10. Gawronska, B., House, D.: Information Extraction and Text Generation of News Reports for a Swedish-English Bilingual Spoken Dialogue System. In Proceedings of ICSLP-98, Sydney,1 1998. International Conference on Spoken Language Processing. (1998)
11. Goldberg, E., Kitredge, R., Polguére, A .: Computer Generation of Marine Weather Forecasts. Journal of Atmospheric and Oceanic Technology, vol 5, no 4 (1988) 472-483
12. Hovy, Eduard H : Generating Natural Language under Pragmatic Constraints. New Jersey: Lawrence Erlbaum Associates (1988)

13. Jackendoff. R.S.: Semantics and Cognition. MIT Press, Cambridge, MA (1983)
14. Jackendoff. R.S.: Semantic Structures. MIT Press, Cambridge, MA (1990)
15. Lakoff, G. & Johnson, M.: Metaphors We Live By. Chicago: The Univ. of Chicago Press (1980)
16. Lakoff, G.: The Contemporary Theory of Metaphor. In Ortony, A. (ed.): Metaphor and Thought, 2d ed., Cambridge: Cambridge University Press (1993)
17. Langacker, R. :Concept, Image, and Symbol. The Cognitive Basis of Grammar. Berlin/New York: Mouton de Gruyter (1991)
18. Leacock, C., Miller, G., A., Chodorow, M.: Using Corpus Statistics and WordNet Relations for Sense Identification. Computational Linguistics, vol. 24 nr 1 (1999)
19 Levin, B.: English Verb Classes and Alternations. The University of Chicago Press, Chicago/London (1993)
20. Mahesh, K., Nirenburg, S., Beale, S.: If You Have It, Flaunt It: Using Full Ontological Knowledge for Word Sense Disambiguation'.In: Mitkov, R., Nicolov, N., Nicolov, N. (eds): Proceedings from Recent Advances in Natural Language Processing. Tzigov Chark, Bulgaria (1997)
21. Miller, G., A. (ed): WordNet: An On-Line Lexical Database. International Journal of Lexicography, vol. 3. Oxford University Press (1990)
22. Miller, G., A. WordNet: An On-Line Lexical Database. Communications of the ACM, 38(11) (1995)
23. Mitkov, R.: Generating Public Weather Reports. Proceedings of Current Issues in Computational Linguistics. Penang, Malaysia (1991)
24. Mitkov, R.: Multilingual Generation of Public Weather Forecasts. Proceedings of SPICIS-92. Singapore (1992)
25. Nirenburg, S., Raskin, V.: Universal Grammar and Lexis for Quick Ramp-Up of MT Systems. Proc. of COLING'98, 10-14 August 1998, Montreal, Canada (1998) 975-979
26. Onyshkevych, B., Nirenburg, S. The Lexicon in the Scheme of KBMT Things. Memoranda in Computer and Cognitive Science, MCCS, Las Cruces, N.M.:New Mexico State University (1994) 94-277
27. Pustejovsky, J.: The Generative Lexicon. The MIT Press, Cambridge, Massachusetss London (1995)
28. Reichenbach, H.: Elements of Symbolic Logic. New York: The Free Press (1966)
29. Sanfilippo, A., Poznanski, V.: The Acquisition of Lexical Knowledge from Combined Machine-Readable Dictionary Resources. In Proceedings of the Applied Natural Language Processing Conference, Trento, Italy (1992) 80-87.
30. Sanford Pedersen, B.: Systematic Verb Polysemy in MT: A Study of Danish Motion Verbs with Comparisons to Spanish. Machine Translation, vol. 14 (1999) 39-86
31. Sigurd, B. Willners, C., Eeg-Olofsson. M., Johansson, C. Deep Comprehension, Generation and Translation of Weather Forecasts (Weathra). Proc. of Coling '92, Nantes, Aug. 23-28, 1992, vol.2 (1992) 749-755
32. Sigurd, B., Eeg-Olofsson, M., Willners, C. & Johansson,C. Automatic Translation in Specific Domains: Weather (Weathra) and Stock Market (Stocktra, Vectra) (1992)
33. Skorupka, S., Auderska, H., Łempicka, Z. (eds.): Maly S•ownik Jzyka Polskiego. Państwowe Wydawnictwo Naukowe, Warszawa (1969)
34. Stanisławski, J.: The Great English-Polish Dictionary. Wiedza Powszechna, Warszawa (1986)
35. Talmy, L.: Force Dynamics in Language and Cognition. Cognitive Science 12. (1988) 49-100
36. Talmy, L.: The Relation of Grammar to Cognition. In: Rudzka-Ostyn, B. (ed.): Topics in Cognitive Linguistics. Amsterdam/Philadelphia: John Benjamins (1988) 165-205
37. Viberg, Å.: The Meanings of Swedish 'dra'-'pull': a Case Study of Lexical Polysemy. EURALEX'96. Proceedings. Part I.239-308. Göteborg University, Department of Swedish (1996)

38. Wilks, Y., Fass, D., Guo, C.M., McDonald, J., E., Plate, T., Slator, B., M.: Machine Tractable Dictionary Tools. In: Pustejovsky, J. (ed.): Semantics and the Lexicon. Kluwer, Dordrecht (1993)

39. Zajac, R.: Habanera, a Multipurpose Multilingual Lexical Knowledge Base. NLPRS Workshop on Multilingual Information Processing Pacific Rim Symposium 1997, 1-4 December, Phuket, Thailand (1997)

Small but Efficient: The Misconception of High-Frequency Words in Scandinavian Translation

Pernilla Danielsson[1] and Katarina Mühlenbock[2]

[1] Språkdata, Dept of Swedish, Göteborg University, Sweden
pernilla@svenska.gu.se
[2] Nordisk Språkteknologi Holding AS, Voss, Norway
katarina.muhlenbock@gri.no

Abstract. Machine translation has proved itself to be easier between languages that are closely related, such as German and English, while far apart languages, such as Chinese and English, encounter much more problems. The present study focuses upon Swedish and Norwegian; two languages so closely related that they would be referred to as dialects if it were not for the fact that they had a Royal house and an army connected to each of them. Despite their similarity though, some differences make the translation phase much less straight-forward than what could be expected. Taking the outset in sentence aligned parallel texts, this study aims at highlighting some of the differences, and to formalise the results. In order to do so, the texts have been aligned on smaller units, by a simple cognate alignment method. Not at all surprising, the longer words were easier to align, while shorter and often high-frequent words became a problem. Also when trying to align to a specific word sense in a dictionary, content words rendered better results. Therefore, we abandoned the use of single-word units, and searched for multi-word units whenever possible. This study reinforces the view that Machine Translation should rest upon methods based on multiword unit searches.

1 Introduction

Scandinavian languages are very similar, in fact some dialects of Swedish and Norwegian are so close that it is hard for the unfamiliar to separate them. The present border between the countries is in fact established as recently as 1905. Still, it is not true that Swedes in general understand all Norwegians or vice versa. In fact, it is quite often the case that groups of Scandinavians turn to English for help or to a sort of Scandinavian, which is a lame version of all the Scandinavian languages combined. The Norwegian linguist Einar Haugen [6] has coined the term 'semi-communication' as a description of the linguistic situation in Scandinavia. In fact, there is a high level of 'code noise', which hampers communication but doesn't bar it.

Translation between the languages is important since the countries are each other's most frequent business partners. The cultures are very similar and an industrial product or a literary work adapted for one nation is usually also suitable for the other.

J.S. White (Ed.): AMTA 2000, LNAI 1934, pp. 158-168, 2000.
© Springer-Verlag Berlin Heidelberg 2000

In such an environment one could expect machine translation to do well, but at present date no Scandinavian MT-system can be found on the market, or even in the academic society. One reason could be that it is thought of as such an easy task no one needs to bother. In this study, we aim to highlight the difficulties arising in translation between "sibling languages" and suggest a solution.

We will focus upon two languages, Swedish and Norwegian, and our investigations will be based upon parallel, aligned, text between the two languages.

2 Swedish and Norwegian; Sibling Languages

Swedish and Norwegian are genetically that closely related to be defined 'siblings', and share a common ancestor in the language spoken in Norway, Denmark and Sweden during the first 500 years A.D. Language historians describe two branches successively developing from this ancient Scandinavian, namely East and West Scandinavian, to which we can assign Swedish and Danish to the former and Norwegian to the latter branch.

Several efforts to bring the Scandinavian languages back together have been made during the last centuries. In the 19th century attempts were made to harmonize orthography, as for instance the phonetically-based distribution of vowels, which for Swedish resulted in a proposal to replace *ä* with *æ*. This initiative, however, failed to gain public approval.

Nowadays, a common vocabulary seems to be the most interesting topic of discussion among Scandinavian linguists. Spontaneous loans have always existed, and are difficult to trace due to the closeness of the languages. A modest Scandinavian terminology planning is concentrating on improving mutual comprehension and preventing the languages to drift further apart. One of the major contributions in this field is the collection of huge corpora in the three major Scandinavian languages, presently in progress at *Nordisk Språkteknologi* in Norway. Balanced corpora are compiled, primary for the purpose of being a resource for the language modelling for software development, but with an enormous potential for further research projects. As present, the Norwegian corpus amounts to 1,000 millions, Danish to 800 millions and Swedish to 550 million words.

Naturally, the situation in Scandinavia is similar to that of most other regions of the world, in that the impact of English is dominating far more than loan terminology from other languages. The *Nordisk Språksekretariat (Nordic Language Secretariat)* tries to take measures against unnecessary differences within the languages in this process. As an example, let us take the concept 'computer', which according to Vikør [12] in Danish became *datamat*, in Swedish *dator* and in Norwegian *datamaskin.* Even the public has raised attacks both in Sweden and Norway against the negative impact of English on the indigenous languages.

3 The Object of Study; The Parallel Texts

The object of study here is parallel texts, a type of research material which have gained in popularity over the last decade, much thanks to new technology. The parallel text, consisting of an original text and one or more translation into other languages, can serve as a base for researchers interested in contrastive linguistics, translation theory, machine translation, bilingual lexicography and more, and is an endless source of information. A word of warning when using the parallel texts could be that a translation is just one person's interpretation of a text, and thus cannot be said to conquer the one and only truth, if such ever exists. But at the same time one should recall that a translator, at least the professional translator, is indeed a trained and skilled language user, which might be more than one can attribute the author of the original text. Anyone can write, but not anyone will be given the opportunity to translate.

In earlier projects involving compiling parallel corpora in Scandinavia, such as the Pedant corpus [2], [3], or the English Norwegian Parallel Corpus [7], the obvious choice has been to put a Scandinavian language in contrast or comparison with one or more of the five commercial languages; English, French, German, Spanish and Italian. In the light of comparison, one cannot avoid commenting upon how much more straightforward it is to align Scandinavian texts, thanks to the shared structure of both texts and of sentences in Swedish and Norwegian, giving an almost complete agreement. Sometimes it is hard to differentiate between the language versions, as can be seen from Example 1 below. The quoted text consists of samples from two Swedish novels and each of their Norwegian translations. The material consists of 150,000 words per language.

SW: Det hade varit på vägen mot Tomelilla, en tidig vårkväll.
NO: Det hadde vært på veien mot Tomelilla, en tidlig vårkveld.
(*'It had been on the way to Tomelilla, an early evening in Spring'*)

Example 1. Language example Swedish – Norwegian in order to show similarities

In addition to the parallel texts, the previously mentioned large corpora of monolingual texts were used to support the hypothesis made.

4 Aligning Words

Many computational linguistic algorithms have been put forth over the last years for word alignment, and the work of Melamed [10] has been most influential. The thought of retrieving bilingual dictionaries out of parallel texts is very appealing, and could enhance the work in Machine Translation. However, the work on single-word units in NLP manifests the problems of word sense disambiguation, a problem neglected in many NLP applications, but one that MT cannot escape. While most NLP systems of today avoid confronting "meaning" in language, it is hard to do translation without it. Therefore, any type of method that seems to increase the amount of ambiguity into language most be avoided. Before discussing the creation of ambiguity in text, we should mention the possibility to use machine-readable dictionaries (MRD) in Scandinavian MT.

Since the lexicon modules in NLP systems are well known bottlenecks it has become acceptable to re-use machine readable versions of published dictionaries. This is used to some extent also in MT, even though bilingual dictionaries are known to have a much less stable theoretic framework and the selection of words and translations must be said to be more *ad hoc*. If one would follow this line also in a Swedish-Norwegian MT system one must be aware of special features of these MRDs. First of all, since very many words are identical in the two languages, these words are not listed in a dictionary. Also words that are almost the same, such as *häst* and *hest*, are excluded for the same reason. Therefore, in a lexicon look-up all unknown words, or rather words not present in the machine-readable dictionary, are most probably the same in the two languages, though there are no absolute guarantee for this.

Common for most dictionaries are the listings on a single-word basis, and as will be shown in this study, even though the single words might be easy to translate it is often the patterning around a word that will differ, for instance different use of prepositions.

4.1   Single and Multi-word Units

How is the ambiguity increased by the use of single-words? This question is rather tricky since we have to distinguish between the fact that our software might still want to process the input word by word, or letter by letter, but the problem we are discussing addresses the actual analysis which is different. Let us think of the problem as one of tokenization. If we already when we tokenise can differentiate between single and multi-word units, then the computer algorithm does not need to check for all possible senses of each and every word in the case of multi-word units.

To illustrate the multi-word units we can use an example from Norwegian, *bli kvitt*. If we consult a Norwegian corpus we will find that while *bli* ('become') can collocate with almost any word, *kvitt* is almost exclusively found after *bli*. The whole lexical unit means *'get rid of'* and there is no possible word-by-word translation between English and Norwegian. In our parallel texts, we find an instance of *bli kvitt* where the Swedish corresponding unit is *göra sig av med* (lit. 'make oneself off with'). It should be noted though that Swedish has a corresponding unit *bli kvitt*, which is much less commonly used than *göra sig av med*.

SW: Det var en minnesbild han aldrig hade lyckats göra sig av med.
NO: Det var et minne han aldri hadde greid å bli kvitt.
(*'It was a memory he never succeeded to get rid of'*)

Example 2. Example of *bli kvitt* and *göra sig av med*

When looking at high-frequency words in dictionaries or when consulting linguistic theories, the general impression is that they are insufficiently described. This becomes obvious in projects aiming at aligning words from a corpus to corresponding dictionary senses, where it is much harder to find a definition that corresponds to the word's function and meaning in the text for the high-frequency words. This can easily be transferred into analysis of translated text, where the content words of the text might be adequately translated but the short words, i.e. the function words, such as prepositions, auxiliary verbs, verbal complement etc, are often incorrect.

We have categorized the relation between Swedish and Norwegian words in three ways (as follows):

1. Identical, as to content and form
2. Partly similar, when the words have the same content, but differ with regard to form in a systematical way
3. Different, when the words are completely without connection to each other, but are functionally related.

A major part of the partially similar words only differ with regard to their orthographic form. This is the case especially with the vowels, which have different graphical form. We have therefore considered only the consonants when aligning the partially different words. A variation of one character was also allowed.

4.2   Cognate Aligning in Scandinavian Texts

The cognate aligning algorithm was constructed in three steps; (a) The first focused upon words that are identical in the two languages. (b) The second phase focused upon words that would be identical in positioning in the text and in its consonants. (c) Everything left unaligned was suggested as corresponding units to each other.

The first phase was very straightforward, and was made possible mainly due to the close relation between the two languages. The result from this phase includes words such as:
- names
- some short function words which the languages share; such as pronouns
- content words, up to about 10% are exactly the same in the two languages.

Words identified in the first phase were considered to be *perfect match anchor words* (henceforth 'anchors') from which the successive alignment process could start.

In the examples below, the aligned perfect matches between two sentences has been highlighted in italics:

SW: Inte dimman *som smyger* in från *Hanöbukten*.
NO: Ikke tåken *som smyger* seg inn fra *Hanöbukten*.
(*'Not the fog creeping in from Hanöbukten'*)

SW: Plötsligt märkte *han* att *han* oftare än vanligt kastade en blick *mot* backspegeln.
NO: Plutselig merket *han* att *han* oftere enn vanlig gløttet *mot* bakspeilet.
(*'He suddenly realized that he more often than usually had a look in the rear-view mirror'*)

Examples 3 and 4. Examples of perfect matches

The next phase was intended to find "fuzzy matches", words with identical position and near-identical orthography. The similar positions were assessed in relation to the perfect match anchor words. The fuzzy match was at first calculated as the number of matching consonants allowing for one mismatched character, since it became obvious that only the vowels differed between the languages in many cases.

Table 1. Cognate alignment on consonants, allowing for one mismatched character

Swedish	Norwegian	English translation
från: fr	fra: fr	from
plötsligt: pltslgt	plutselig: pltslg	suddenly
! backspegeln: bckspgln	bakspeilet: bksplt	rear-view mirror
! Inte: nt	Ikke: kk	not
vanligt: vnlgt	vanlig: vnlgt	usual
märkte: mrkt	merket: mrkt	noticed
att: tt	at: t	that/to

Two of the examples in Table 1 above did not fit with this alignment, backspegeln/bakspeilet ('rear-view mirror') and *inte/ikke* ('not'), but since they were isolated, they could be aligned on position instead. In order to illustrate the results from the second phase of the alignment algorithm, we have highlighted the words in bold:

SW: **Inte** dimman *som smyger* **in från** Hanöbukten.
NO: **Ikke** tåken *som smyger* seg **inn fra** Hanöbukten.

SW: **Plötsligt märkte** *han* **att** *han* **oftare än vanligt** kastade en blick *mot* backspegeln.
NO: **Plutselig merket** *han* **at** *han* **oftere enn vanlig** gløttet *mot* bakspeilet.

Examples 5 and 6. Examples of fuzzy matches.

The third phase would then give us the most important information from the text, namely where the two languages differ the most. As could be expected we found differences on the lexical level, such as the Swedish word *dimman*, which becomes *tåken* in Norwegian; a word that could easily be misunderstood in the two languages, since they resemble other words in the corresponding language; *tåken* in Norwegian can often be misunderstood as *taken* in Swedish. This is a good example of the frequently occurring *false friends*, i.e. commonly misunderstood words between the two languages. Many of these are words deriving etymologically from a common stem, but resulting in different meanings, the classic example being *rolig*, which means *fun* in Swedish and *calm, quiet* in Norwegian.

Some words seem to have no correspondence at all, such as the Norwegian word *seg*, however, reconnecting to the data we find that the Swedish verb *smyger* ('sneaks') needs a reflexive pronoun in Norwegian.

The most interesting results, though, were all the multi-word unit that did not have a word-by-word translation, such as the Swedish *kastade en blick*, which was translated into Norwegian as *gløttet*.

4.3   High-Frequency and Low-Frequency Words in Translation

From the method we chose above, we found that we could construct machine readable dictionaries fairly easily due to the many similarities between the two languages. As much as 30% of the text consisted of word and its equivalent with exactly the same representation in the text, and as much as 43% had only differences in the vowels.

Among the words that were very different, we found our retrieval method especially useful in cases where:

(a) they occurred between two anchor words
(b) they occurred between the beginning of a sentence and an anchor word
(c) they occurred between the anchor word and the end of a sentence.

This worked best for low-frequency words. Among the high-frequency words it is much harder to discuss what is an equivalent, since it is hard to define what meaning the high-frequency word carries. In many theories, the high-frequency words are described only as function words, which would not contribute to the meaning but only structure. More recent investigations around high-frequency words have shown a much richer and interesting patterning than we at first might expect, and in studies by Renouf [11] high-frequency words have been shown to carry meaning indeed, when in combination with other high-frequency words. Also studies by Altenberg [1], have shown that language can be seen as consisting of a wide set of multi-word phrases. In fact, as much as 70% of the London-Lund corpus turned out to be repetitive phrases of two or more words, mostly high-frequent words, such as "of the" or more meaningful utterances as "at the end of the" and "thank you".

Also in our study we soon found the high-frequency words to be the most interesting, simply because they did not allow for a straightforward translation, which seems to be the case with all other words. We could differentiate between:

(a) high-frequency words that did not correspond to an obvious, similar, high-frequency word in the other language,
(b) high-frequency word in one language but no corresponding word in the other,
(c) complete multi-word units with unique meaning, translated into a single word unit in the corresponding language.

Table 2. Non-similar words retrieved from the parallel text

Swedish	Norwegian	English
dimman	tåken	'the fog'
sprattlat	sprellet	
förlamad	lammet	'lame'
kände	følte	'felt'
lugnare	roligere	'calmer'
fortfarande	fremdeles	'still'
Minnas	huske	'remember'

When we found two different high-frequency words, we could usually formalise a rule as to when a certain high-frequency word in one language would correspond to something different in the other language. For example, the use of high-frequency word in relation to time, as in the example below, it was possible to formalise rules as to when a certain translation should be applied.

SW: Klockan var nio *på* kvällen den 11 oktober 1993.
NO: Klokken var ni om kvelden den 11. oktober 1993.
(*'It was nine o'clock in the evening on the 11ᵗʰ October 1993'*)

Example. 7 Different prepositions when referring to date.

Both *på* and *om* can be found in Swedish and Norwegian, and often used in the same way, though not in the above example. In reference to a certain part of the day, such as morning, evening, night, the Swedish language uses the preposition *på* where the Norwegian uses *om.*

SW: Klockan var sju minuter *i* tio.
NO: Klokken var sju minutter *på* ti.
(*'It was seven to ten'*)

Example 8. Different preposition in use when referring to time.

The Swedish word *vid* ('at') has a corresponding unit also in Norwegian, and contrastively the Norwegian *til('to')* has a corresponding word *till* in Swedish.

SW: Jag vänjer mig aldrig *vid* den.
NO: Jeg venner meg aldri til den.
(*'I never get used to it'*)

Example 9. The multi-word units *'vänjer mig vid'* and *'venner meg til'*.

Some variations are lexically governed, and though the Swedish *vid* are found correspond to the Norwegian *ved*, and the Norwegian *til* correspond to the Swedish *till*, they can never be replaced in combination with the verb *vänja/venne* ('get used to'). If we avoid the single-word unit thinking, we can here say that the unit consists of three parts, where the middle part is a reflexive pronoun which can alter. Thus the Swedish unit *vänja sig vid* corresponds to the Norwegian unit *venne seg til* ('get oneself used to'). By stating that it is an overall unit, we have not added to the number of possible translation for the high-frequent words, and thus not increased the amount of ambiguity in the text.

Some words seem to demand a high-frequency word in one language, though not in the other. This is the case in the example below, where the Swedish expression *på hemväg* consists of a noun governed by a preposition, denoting an act of movement towards a goal. In Norwegian, the preposition *hjemover* expresses the same thing.

SW: Han satt i bilen *på hemväg* mot Ystad och hade just passerat Brösarps Backar när han körde rakt in i det vita.

NO: Han satt i bilen hjemover mot Ystad og hadde nettopp passert bakkene ved Brösarp, da han kjørte rett inn i det hvite.

('He was driving on his way home towards Ystad and had just passed the hills at Brösarp when he ran into the white')

Example 10. Multi-word unit in Swedish, '*på hemväg*', corresponds to single-word, '*hjemover*', unit in Norwegian.

Supporting Renouf [11], we found several high-frequency multi-word units to connect into meaningful units. In languages as similar as the Scandinavian many of the multi-word units can in fact be word-by-word equivalent, though we found several not to be.

The separable verb particles in the Scandinavian languages merit a discussion of its own. Even though this specific feature is common for both Norwegian and Swedish, there is no absolute agreement in the use of particles. In the example below, the Swedish participle verb *burit* ('carried') corresponds to the Norwegian participle *hatt* followed by the particle *på* and the reflexive pronoun *seg*. This construction could very well be directly transferred into Swedish, resulting into the phrase *haft på sig*, and consequently into a proper cognate alignment.

SW: Men mannen som kom emot honom hade varit solbränd, han hade *burit* en mörkblå kostym och alldeles säkert inte varit över femtio år gammal.

NO: Men mannen som kom mot ham hadde vært solbrent, han hadde *hatt på seg* en mørkeblå dress og helt sikkert ikke vært over femti år gammel.

('But the man approaching him had been tanned, had worn a dark blue suit and had definitely not been over fifty years old')

Example 11. Single-word unit in Swedish, '*burit*', with multi-word unit translation in Norwegian, '*hatt på seg*'.

SW: Sedan hade han stannat och *stigit ur* bilen.
NO: Så hadde han stanset og gått ut av bilen.
('He had stopped and got off the car)

Example 12. The multi-word units '*stigit ur*' in Swedish and the corresponding '*gått ut av*' in Norwegian.

In the following example, the Swedish participle verb *stigit* together with the particle *ur* ('get off') belongs to a group of movement verbs usually separated in all forms. Its' Norwegian counterpart is very similar, except that the verb *gått* is followed by a particle *ut* and the preposition *av*.

5 Conclusion

In this study, we have examined two closely related languages, Norwegian and Swedish, from a MT perspective, in order to understand where the problems will be encountered. Since the syntactical behaviour of the two languages is highly similar, we found the lexical aspects to be more interesting.

Swedish-Norwegian bilingual dictionaries only cover "difficult words", by which they refer to words not obviously equivalents. Much of the vocabulary in the two languages have the same graphical representation or is so similar and distinct from other words that could take the same position, that there would be no reason to list them in a dictionary. From a machine translation perspective, this makes the bilingual dictionaries less useful as data supplier from an MRD to a MT lexicon. This is not necessarily a negative thing though, since the re-use of MRDs into NLP must be a much questioned method of efficiency. In fact, it is argued here that all work manifesting the single-word units as the base units of language will only increase the amount of problems into language automation rather than making it efficient.

We found the approach to work on multi-word units very attractive and efficient to solve the problems encountered in parallel texts. The multi-word units also eliminate the problem of handling high-frequency words, since the high-frequency words are hard to describe in their singularity. Though this could be taken as an indication that high-frequency words, or function words as they are sometimes referred to, do not carry meaning, our expectations were different. As indicated by works of other researchers, we expected to find multi-word units consisting only of high-frequency words with very distinct meaning, and this hypothesis proved to hold also in our study.

References

1. Altenberg, B.: "Speech as linear composition". In Caie, G., Haastrup; K., Lykke Jakobsen, A., Nielsen, J-. E., Sevaldsen, J., Specht, H., Zettersten A.: Proceeding from the fourth Nordic Conference for English Studies. University of Copenhagen (1989)
2. Danielsson, P.: The base units of language - for automatic language treatment. Doctoral thesis (forthcoming 2000)
3. Danielsson, P., Ridings, D.:Pedant - Parallel texts in Gothenburg. Research report from Department of Swedish, Gothenburg University (1996)
4. Ekman, K.: Händelser vid vatten. Bonnier, Stockholm (1994)
5. Ekman, K.: Hendelser ved vann. Translated from Swedish by Gunnel Malmström. Aschehoug, Oslo (1997)
6. Haugen, E.: Semicommunication: The Language Gap in Scandinavia. In Sociological Inquiry 36 (1996) 280-297
7. Johansson, S., Hofland, K.: Towards an English-Norwegian Parallel Corpus. In Fries U., Tottie G., Schneider P. (eds) Creating and Using English Language Corpora. Rodopi: Amsterdam (1994)
8. Mankell, H.: Mannen som log. Ordfront Förlag, Stockholm (1999).
9. Mankell, H.: Silkeridderen. Translated from Swedish by Kari Bolstad. Gyldendal Norsk Forlag ASA, Oslo (1999)
10.Melamed, D.: Empirical Methods for Exploiting Parallel Texts. Doctoral Thesis. Manuscript.University of Pennsylvania (1998)

11.Renouf, A.: What do you think of that: A pilot study of the phraseology of the core words in English. In Leitner, G. (ed.) New Directions in English Language Corpora: Methodology, results, Software developments. Mouton de Gruyter, Berlin (1992)
12.Vikør, L.S.: The Nordic Languages. Their Status and Interrelations. Novus Press, Oslo (1995)

Challenges in Adapting an Interlingua for Bidirectional English-Italian Translation

Violetta Cavalli-Sforza[1], Krzysztof Czuba[2],
Teruko Mitamura[2], and Eric Nyberg[2]

[1] San Francisco State University, Department of Computer Science
1600 Holloway Avenue, San Francisco, CA 94132
vcs@Sfsu.edu
[2] Language Technologies Institute, Carnegie Mellon University
5000 Forbes Avenue, Pittsburgh, PA 15213
{kczuba, teruko, ehn}@cs.cmu.edu

Abstract. We describe our experience in adapting an existing high-quality, interlingual, unidirectional machine translation system to a new domain and bidirectional translation for a new language pair (English and Italian). We focus on the interlingua design changes which were necessary to achieve high quality output in view of the language mismatches between English and Italian. The representation we propose contains features that are interpreted differently, depending on the translation direction. This decision simplified the process of creating the interlingua for individual sentences, and allows the system to defer mapping of language-specific features (such as tense and aspect), which are realized when the target syntactic feature structure is created. We also describe a set of problems we encountered in translating modal verbs, and discuss the representation of modality in our interlingua.

1   Introduction

In this paper, we describe our experience in adapting an existing high-quality, interlingual, unidirectional machine translation system for a new domain and bidirectional translation. We concentrate on some of the changes in the interlingua design that were necessary to ensure high quality output.

KANT [7] is an interlingua-based software architecture for knowledge-based machine translation. The CATALYST project used the KANT technology for translation of technical documentation in the domain of heavy equipment from English to several European languages. At present, systems for translation to Spanish, French and German are in production use, and a Portuguese system for the same domain is almost fully developed. Prototypes of varying coverage for different domains have been developed for languages as diverse as Italian, Chinese, Japanese, Turkish, and Arabic [2], [6], [4].

In the CATALYST system, translation is unidirectional, from English to other languages, and not all of the target languages were known before the interlingua was designed. Although the interlingua design does represent the

J.S. White (Ed.): AMTA 2000, LNAI 1934, pp. 169–178, 2000.

meaning of the input by abstracting away from the surface details, it is somewhat isomorphic to the semantic structure of English [3], [1].

In this paper we discuss our experiences in the MedTran project, an application of KANT technology to bidirectional English-Italian translation of medical records. The goal of the project was to facilitate communication between monolingual physicians and medical staff working in an international facility. Very little source material was available in Italian. For English we had access to a sizeable corpus of transcribed documents. The input was not controlled, could be ungrammatical, and might contain structures which are not part of common written English. Ambiguous constructions might require interactive disambiguation to promote high-quality translation. In addition, the medical domain emphasizes different concepts and constructions than the domains for which the KANT interlingua was designed originally.

We began by implementing a proof-of-concept demonstration system that translated from English into Italian. Building the prototype forced us to focus on a number of linguistic issues that were not as significant in the original KANT domains. Based on this experience, we redesigned the interlingua, taking into consideration specific issues that arose when translating from English into Italian and vice-versa. We review briefly a few of the key findings, sketch our approach, and draw some general conclusions from our experience.

2   System Architecture

The general architecture of KANT is shown in Fig. 1 . Translation is performed on one sentence at a time, with separate analysis and generation phases.

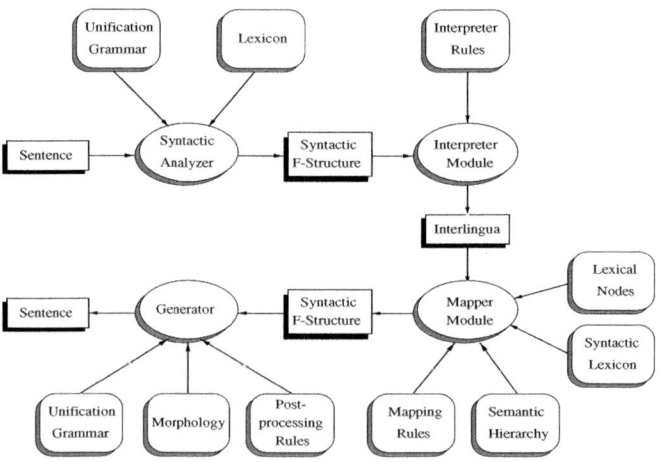

Fig. 1. The KANT system architechture

During the analysis phase, each sentence is first converted into tokens. Using a lexicon enriched with syntactic information, a morphological analyzer, source language grammar rules, and optionally semantic information, the tokenized sentence is parsed into a feature structure (FS), a recursive list of feature-value pairs that reflects the syntactic structure of the input. Using a set of analysis mapping rules, the interpreter converts the FS into a tree-structured interlingua representation (IR), which abstracts away many of the syntactic details of both source and target language, while conveying the meaning of the source [3].

In the generation phase, generation mapping rules convert the IR into a FS that reflects the syntactic structure of the target language. The mapper recursively traverses the IR, converting subtrees to FS constituents and terminal concept nodes to target lexical items. The mapper uses general mapping rules, bilingual data structures called 'lexical nodes', and a syntactic lexicon for the target language. The FS is then processed by the generator, which uses target language grammar rules and morphological generation rules to produce a preliminary target language output. In the final generation step, post-processing rules clean up spacing and punctuation, and handle surface-level issues such as elision and contraction of words.

3   Input Characteristics

The input in the MedTran project consists of various kinds of notes made by physicians (progress notes, discharge summaries, radiology reports, etc.), traditionally dictated and transcribed. For the development of the proof-of-concept prototype system we used five examples of medical texts drawn from two document types, discharge summaries and progress notes, for a total of approximately 110 distinct phrases and sentences. The texts are semi-structured, with labels usually identifying different sections of the text (e.g., *Cardiovascular, Respiratory, Renal*). This structure reflects the sequence in which medical examinations are performed and can be used for disambiguation purposes in the MT system.

On the linguistic side, the texts included idioms that could not be translated literally and required some restructuring, as illustrated in Example 1.

Example 1.
(a) This is a 60 year old male who is end stage liver disease.
(b) *Questo è un maschio di 60 anni che è affetto da malattia epatica terminale.*
(c) This is a male of 60 years who is affected by end stage liver disease.

In this example, the English phrase "end stage liver disease" (*malattia epatica terminale*) is used as a predicate in (a). In the Italian translation, shown in (b), the sentence must be changed to a passive construction. The literal word-by-word translation into English of the Italian output is shown in (c). The underlined segments of the sentences show the effect of the required restructuring.

Since the texts were mostly dictated by non-native speakers of English, minor adjustments to the input were required in a small number of cases in which the input was not only ungrammatical but also difficult to understand even for a human reader. Other changes we made were in the use of tenses (e.g., *The liver enzymes continued to be rising.*), prepositions, and punctuation.

Another characteristic of the texts was ample use of a range of tenses, temporal modifiers and other expressions implying the time dimension. Time turned out to be an important issue in interlingua design for the medical domain, whereas it had been less important in previous applications of the KANT technology.

4   Interlingua Design: Issues and Approach

The KANT interlingua representation (IR) contains features that are purely semantic and features that are primarily grammatical in nature. In some cases, grammatical features are used by the generation module to produce a maximally accurate target translation. In the MedTran system, the IR also contains grammatical features. However, because translation is bidirectional, and English and Italian differ in significant ways, the information that must be represented in the IR might not be identical for the two languages. This issue arose in the representations of mood, tense, aspect, and modality. We addressed this by choosing a set of IR features that are shared by the two languages, but that are interpreted somewhat differently during translation. In some cases, the same features are interpreted differently because they are used to represent different linguistic concepts. In other cases, one language uses only a subset of the features, or of the values defined for a particular feature. Examples of all cases are given below. With this approach, the IR encodes as much information as possible from the source language, allowing the generation phase to use this information as needed to produce an appropriate target language output. Another important modification is the introduction of new features to better capture the use of temporal and location modifiers, which must be generated with special care in domains where time is an important component of the information conveyed by the text. This section describes the challenges we encountered in the abovementioned areas, and sketches the solutions we developed.

4.1   Verb Mood, Tense and Aspect

Although the tense and aspect systems of English and Italian show some similarities, there are also many differences that make mapping tenses between the languages difficult in an MT system.

The feature verb-mood (with values subjunctive, conditional, indicative, imperative, infinitive, gerund and participle), is used to represent the mood of the verb. The feature verb-mood is distinct from the feature sentence-mood (with values declarative, interrogative, exclamative, and imperative). In Italian, it is possible for an imperative sentence to use different verb moods, for example: a subjunctive, to indicate a formal command; an imperative, for informal commands; or an infinitive, common in product instructions and manuals.

The tense and aspect system also differs between the two languages. In English, most verbs can be marked independently for the progressive and perfective aspect and for tense. For example, "he examines" is a simple present, neither perfective nor progressive; "he has been examining" is both perfective and progressive; "he is examining" is only progressive; and "he has examined" is only perfective. The same combinations of perfective and progressive exist for the past and the future tenses. To encode this information, when translating from English to Italian, the IR uses the features tense, with values present, past, and future, and the features perfective, and progressive with the values + and -.

In Italian, the distribution of aspect is not entirely independent of the distribution of tense, especially with respect to the expression of progressive aspect. The indicative mood has eight tenses, four simple tenses (present, past, imperfective, future), and four compound tenses (explained below). The subjunctive mood has two simple tenses (present and imperfective) and two compound tenses. The conditional mood has only one simple and one compound tense. In each mood, compound tenses are formed by using an auxiliary verb (normally *avere* "to have" or *essere* "to be") in one of the mood's simple tenses followed by a past participle. The IR features tense and perfective are used differently when going from Italian to English. A simple verb uses only the tense feature, with the same values as English plus the value imperfective. A compound verb is encoded using tense to capture the tense of the auxiliary verb, plus the feature perfective set to +. For example, *avesse mangiato* (roughly "that he had eaten"), an example of the Italian subjunctive compound tense pluperfect, uses the imperfective of "to have" (*avesse*) and the past participle of *mangiare* ("to eat"); it would be encoded as (verb-mood subjunctive), (tense imperfect), (perfective +).

The relationship of progressive aspect in English and Italian is complex. The indicative imperfective tense is sometimes used to convey habitual or repetitive actions in the past – where English might use a past progressive form or a different construction (Example 2) – or an ongoing action – where English might use a progressive or a simple past (Example 3). The verb ending -*ava* is a third person singular masculine or feminine indicative imperfective ending.

Example 2.
Fumava un pacchetto di sigarette al giorno.
S/he was smoking/used to smoke a pack of cigarettes a day.

Example 3.
Parlava mentre il dottore lo visitava.
He was talking/talked while the doctor was visiting/visited him.

The imperfective is also used to express enduring states in the past (Example 4), whereas a simple or compound past is used with point events (Example 5).

Example 4.
Ieri la temperatura era 37,5.
Yesterday the temperature was 37.5.

Example 5.
Ieri le entrate <u>sono state</u> 3,4 litri e le uscite <u>sono state</u> 4,6 litri.
Yesterday input <u>was</u> 3.4 liters and output <u>was</u> 4.6 liters.

Progressive constructions in Italian are used to convey being in the process of acting or experiencing and are used more rarely than in English. They are formed using the verb *stare* (literally 'to stay') as an auxiliary and the gerund of the main verb, as in Example 6: *stiamo* is the present indicative first person plural of *stare*, *dando* is the gerund of *dare* ("to give").

Example 6.
<u>*Gli*</u> *<u>stiamo dando</u> insulina.*
<u>We are giving</u> <u>him</u> insulin.

The progressive feature with value + is used exclusively to indicate this type of construction. The tense feature indicates the tense of the auxiliary *stare*, which can only be a simple tense. Hence, in representing an Italian input, the features progressive and perfective never co-occur.

4.2   Modals

The design of the IR for modal verbs was one of the more complex issues we had to address. English modals (e.g., "may", "can", "should") are not full-fledged verbs. In Italian, however, modal verbs (e.g., *potere*, *dovere*) are fully conjugated verbs that require a non-perfective or perfective infinitive form of the main verb. Because of these differences, and the ambiguity generated by the use of modals, the IR captures the value(s) of modality expressed by the modal verb in a special feature. It also captures tense, mood, and aspect information present in the input for both main and modal verbs. Translation from English uses a subset of the features used required by Italian.

The mandatory IR feature for representing modals is modality, which can take on several values. The modality habit encodes the modal "would" as used in the sentence "The patient would walk a few minutes every morning", which would be translated as an imperfective of the verb "to walk" (*passeggiava*). The modality hypothetical is used for the modal "should" in the sentence "Should the patient improve, we will decrease the dose", which would require a hypothetical construction with *se* ("if") in translation. The values ability, permission, and possibility are used for the modals "can" and "could", among others. The values expectation, necessity, obligation are used for the modal "should", among others. Since it is frequently difficult to distinguish among these modalities, and not always necessary for correct translation, they frequently occur as a disjunctive value (e.g., (:or necessity obligation)).

Other features may be present as well. The feature occurrence (with values certain, uncertain, or unrealized), combines with modality to encode different shades of modality. The features modal-tense (mostly for Italian) and modal-perfective (only for Italian), with values + and -, encode tense and aspect for the modal verb. The verb features described in Section 4.1 encode the main verb.

In the remainder of this section we provide a few examples of use of these features in both directions of translation.

The Modals "can" and "could". The modals "can" and "could" are responsible for much ambiguity in English. The uses of "can" in Example 7 cannot be disambiguated without extensive semantic analysis; however they can all be translated into Italian with the verb *potere* followed by a non-perfective infinitive, maintaining the same ambiguity. In these cases the IR would have (modality (:or ability permission possibility)).

Example 7.
The patient can open his eyes. (ability)
The patient can go home tomorrow. (permission)
The tumor can metastasize. (possibility)

Uses of "could", however, must be disambiguated in order to produce a correct translation.

"Could", used as the past of "can", as in the example "We could not identify the source of the bleeding", is translated with an appropriate past tense of *potere*. The IR uses (modality (:or ability permission possibility)) and (modal-tense past).

"Could", followed by a non-perfective infinitive, as in Example 8, may express higher uncertainty than "can" and is encoded in the IR with (occurrence uncertain). The Italian translation requires the present conditional of *potere* followed by a non-perfective infinitive.

Example 8.
Questo potrebbe essere dovuto a un'epatite.
This could be due to hepatitis.

"Could", followed by a perfective infinitive (encoded as (perfective +)), in some contexts expresses uncertainty in the past, encoded with (occurrence uncertain). It must be translated into Italian with the present conditional of *potere* (*potrebbe*) followed by a perfective infinitive (e.g. *avere avuto*, from *avere* "to have"), as in Example 9.

Example 9.
Potrebbe avere avuto un piccolo infarto.
He could have had a small infarction.

In other contexts, "could" followed by a perfective infinitive expresses unrealized ability, possibility or permission, which is encoded as (occurrence unrealized). This is translated in Italian with a past conditional of *potere* (*avremmo potuto*) followed by a non-perfective infinitive (e.g. *operare* "to operate"), as in Example 10.

Example 10.
Avremmo potuto operare ieri.
We could have operated yesterday (but we didn't).

The Modal *Dovere* in Italian. Ambiguity in modal use is possible in translating from Italian to English as well. The modal *dovere* in Italian conveys expectation, necessity and obligation. While obligation and necessity modalities do not need to be distinguished from each other, in some cases they need to be distinguished from expectation, as shown in Example 11 below. (*Dobbiamo* and *devono* are present indicative first and third person plural respectively of *dovere*).

Example 11.
Dobbiamo informare la famiglia. (obligation)
We <u>must</u> inform the family.

Dobbiamo operare il paziente in settimana. (necessity)
We <u>must</u> operate the patient within the week.

I risultati <u>devono</u> arrivare in settimana. (expectation)
The results <u>will/should</u> arrive this week.

As an example of modal encoding in the IR when translating from Italian, the past conditional modal *avremmo dovuto* in Example 12 is represented by (modal-tense present), (modal-perfective +), (occurrence unrealized).

Example 12.
Avremmo dovuto operare prima.
We <u>should</u> have operated earlier (but we didn't).

4.3   Time and Location Modifiers

Modifier Positioning. The IR design considers a number of clausal and sentential modifiers, including subordinate clauses, adjoined modifiers (e.g., *if necessary*), discourse markers (e.g., *actually, nonetheless*), adverbial phrases, noun phrases, and prepositional phrases. The IR for modifiers includes the feature position, which can take on at least the values initial, if the modifier occurs at the beginning of the clause, and end if it occurs at the end of the clause. For some kinds of modifiers, other internal positions are also possible in English, depending on the presence of auxiliary verbs and other syntactic characteristics, as illustrated by Example 13 [8]. A similar range of options is available for modifier positioning in Italian.

Example 13.
By then, the patient should have been feeling better. (initial)
The patient, by then, should have been feeling better. (initial-medial)
The patient should, by then, have been feeling better. (medial)
The patient should have, by then, been feeling better. (medial-medial)
The patient should have been, by then, feeling better. (end-medial)
The patient should have been feeling, by then, better. (initial-end)
The patient should have been feeling better, by then. (end)

While it is not strictly necessary to generate modifiers in all possible positions, in order to obtain more faithful translations it is important to record modifier position on input and choose the position on output accordingly. In Italian, as in English, initial positioning is more "neutral", while modifiers positioned at the end of a sentence carry more emphasis and modifiers positioned right after the subject are somewhat parenthetical. Time expressions, in particular, appear to be widely used in the medical domain. Their positioning can carry subtle shades of meaning. Consider the following sentences:

Example 14.
(a) Tomorrow Dr. Boyle will request chest X-rays for Mr. Smith.
(b) Dr. Boyle will request chest X-rays for Mr. Smith tomorrow.
(c) Dr. Boyle, tomorrow, will request chest X-rays for Mr. Smith.

In Example 14, the initial position of "tomorrow" in (a) is unremarkable, while the end position in (b) emphasizes the adverbial and suggests a contrast with another time, for example "later today". In (c), "tomorrow" is added almost as an afterthought.

In our sample input, mostly dictated by non-native speakers of English, temporal modifiers were sometimes placed a little anomalously. To remain as faithful as possible to the original input, we did not correct positioning in generation unless it violated positioning rules for the target language. For example, in English an adverbial modifier cannot be positioned between a verb and its direct object, but it can follow the direct object. In Italian both positions are often possible, but positioning between the verb and the direct object is preferable.

Example 15.
L'infermiera chiamò immediatamente il Dott. Boyle.
*The nurse called immediately Dr. Boyle.

L'infermiera chiamò il Dott. Boyle immediatamente.
The nurse called Dr. Boyle immediately.

Co-positioning of Temporal and Location Modifiers. We found it desirable to keep time and location modifiers together but separate from other types of modifiers. Isolating them gives greater control over their positioning. Joint handling is motivated by the observation that they often appear together in the input and are frequently related. Extracting time modifiers and positioning them separately from location modifiers can easily lead to breaking subtle but important ordering relationships. Consider the following examples.

Example 16.
(a) Tomorrow at the hospital, Dr. Boyle will visit the patient.
(b) Dr. Boyle will visit the patient tomorrow at the hospital.
(c) Dr. Boyle will visit the patient at the hospital tomorrow.
(d) Tomorrow, Dr. Boyle will visit the patient at the hospital.
(e) At the hospital, Dr. Boyle will visit the patient tomorrow.

In (a) there is more emphasis on the visiting, in (b) on the time and place. In (b) and (d) there is more emphasis on the place, in (c) on the time, while (e) is somewhat anomalous. The combination of placing the time and location modifiers in the same IR slot, recording their position, and keeping them in the same relative order in which they appeared in the source sentence, facilitates generating them in the correct place and order in translation.

5   Conclusions

In this paper we have described some of our experiences with adapting an interlingua representation for a unidirectional MT sytem when moving to bidirectional translation between English and Italian and a different domain. While, by definition, an interlingua representation abstracts away the syntactic details of the source language, an effective interlingua may need to represent grammatical information present in the input if this information captures important semantic and functional distinctions that are made by each language. We took the approach of using a common set of features for the two languages, which allows the representation to be language independent, as an interlingua should be. At the same time, we allowed the features to be used differently or not used at all depending on the direction of translation. This approach allows us to capture specific feature sets which more accurately represent degrees of meaning in the source language. The finer detail can be utilized by specific target language generators to produce more accurate translations when the target language supports the same feature set.

References

1. Czuba, K., Mitamura, T., and Nyberg, E.: Can practical interlinguas be used for difficult analysis problems? In: Proceedings of AMTA-98 Interlingua Workshop (1998).
2. Hakkani, D., Tür, G., Oflazer, K., Mitamura, T., and Nyberg, E.: An English-to-Turkish interlingual MT system. In: Proceedings of AMTA-98 (1998).
3. Leavitt, J., Lonsdale, D., and Franz, A.: A reasoned interlingua for knowledge-based machine translation. In: Proceedings of CSCSI-94 (1994).
4. Li, T., Nyberg, E., and Carbonell, J.: Chinese sentence generation in a knowledge-based machine translation system. Technical Report CMU-CMT-96-148, Carnegie Mellon University (1996).
5. Mitamura, T., and Nyberg, E.: Controlled English for knowledge-based MT: Experience with the KANT system. In: Proceedings of TMI-95 (1995).
6. Nyberg, E., and Mitamura, T.: A real-time MT system for translating broadcast captions. In: Proceedings of MT Summit VI (1997).
7. Nyberg, E., and Mitamura, T.: The KANT system: Fast, accurate, high-quality translation in practical domains. In: Proceedings of COLING-92 (1992).
8. Quirk, R., Greenbaum, S., Leech, G., and Svartvik, J.: A Comprehensive Grammar of the English Language Longman, London New York (1985).

Text Meaning Representation as a Basis for Representation of Text Interpretation

Stephen Helmreich and David Farwell

Computing Research Laboratory
New Mexico State University
Las Cruces, NM 88003 USA
{shelmrei, david}@crl.nmsu.edu

Abstract. In this paper we propose a representation for what we have called an interpretation of a text. We base this representation on TMR (Text Meaning Representation), an interlingual representation developed for Machine Translation purposes. A TMR consists of a complex feature-value structure, with the feature names and filler values drawn from an ontology, in this case, ONTOS, developed concurrently with TMR. We suggest on the basis of previous work, that a representation of an interpretation of a text must build on a TMR structure for the text in several ways: (1) by the inclusion of additional required features and feature values (which may themselves be complex feature structures); (2) by pragmatically filling in empty slots in the TMR structure itself; and (3) by supporting the connections between feature values by including, as part of the TMR itself, the chains of inferencing that link various parts of the structure.

0 Introduction

In this paper, we propose a representation for what we have called, in other work, an interpretation of a text. The basis of the proposed representation is a text meaning representation (TMR). This interlingual representation language was developed at the Computing Research Laboratory at New Mexico State University under the direction of Sergei Nirenburg to support interlingual Machine Translation. (see http://crl.nmsu.edu/Research/Projects/mikro/index.html for more information about TMR). A TMR consists of a complex feature-value structure with the feature names and value fillers, (and some additional structure), drawn from an ontology, in this case ONTOS, constructed for the same project to interact with TMR. Our proposal for the representation of an interpretation of a text builds on that structure in several ways. First, additional features and feature values must be added to the basic TMR structure. Second, empty slots in the TMR structure must be pragmatically filled. Third, we suggest including, as part of the TMR itself, chains of inferences that link various parts of the structure.

The use of feature structures to represent pragmatic information is not new (see, for example, [12]). What is unique about this proposal is that it is not simply pragmatic constraints that are encoded, but actual contextual background information used to

J.S. White (Ed.): AMTA 2000, LNAI 1934, pp. 179-188, 2000.
© Springer-Verlag Berlin Heidelberg 2000

interpret the utterance. In addition, we suggest that the choice of which information to include is guided by the interaction between the semantic representation of the utterance and the representation of the world knowledge as represented in the ontology.

In the first section, we summarize previous work, leading to a characterization of an interpretation of a text. In the second section, we discuss in more detail how a TMR is constructed from a text, focusing on those aspects of TMR structure and construction relevant to the enhanced interpretation representation proposed here. We specify the types of enhancement necessary so that an enhanced TMR can be characterized as an interpretation as outlined in section one. In section three, we exemplify each of the enhancements by means of examples. The reader might find it useful to read sections two and three in parallel, rather than consecutively. Section four provides a conclusion.

1 Background

In a series of papers that examine translational variants, ([11], [8], [9], [10], [12]; see [7] for a summary) we have argued that it is not the semantic content of a text or utterance that translators use as the basis of translation, but rather that translators base their translation on an interpretation of the text, a situated understanding of the language and semantic content of the text, situated within a set of assumptions (beliefs) about the purpose of the communication and the extra-linguistic and extra-semantic world knowledge presupposed by the author. An interpretation can be described as broadly equivalent to the author's communicative intent in making the utterance. It is thus also broadly equivalent to the understanding of the text that is reached by the intended addressees of the utterance, or at least the understanding of the text that is presumed (by the author) to have been reached by the intended addressees.

Interpretations are greatly underdetermined by the semantic content of an utterance and thus will often vary from interpreter to interpreter, since the background knowledge brought to the task of interpretation varies from person to person (and, in fact, may be inconsistent from person to person). We have suggested, therefore, that the task of translation is best characterized as providing an equivalent utterance, that is, one from which the same interpretation(s) can be derived, given that the target language audience has different beliefs and brings a different context to the task of interpretation.

In these various papers, we have suggested a number of things that need to be represented in an interpretation.

In [11] we have argued that an interpretation of an utterance in a dialogue must include the semantics of the utterance, a representation of the communicative intent (which we identified roughly with the illocutionary act) and a representation of the purpose of the utterance (which we identified roughly with the perlocutionary effect). We also argued that the chains of inference leading from the semantics to these other representations needed to be included in the representation as well.

In [8] we again focus on representation in the interpretation of the actual referent of a phrase (not merely its semantic content), and the chain of inferences that leads to the resolution of that referent, in order to justify translational variants.

Other papers ([13] and [9] focus on the necessary representation in an interpretation of larger-scale attitudes of the author: in one case, the understanding of the author about the larger purpose of the newspaper article, in the other case, on the author's understanding of the economic and political background against which the events of the article take place.

In all these papers we have assumed machinery which would permit construction of a Text Meaning Representation from input text, such as the Mikrokosmos system ([2], [5]), a default inferencing mechanism or some other kind of reasoning mechanism for moving logically from a TMR to an interpretation (e.g., [4] and an encapsulated representation system of belief spaces, such as ViewGen ([3]), by which differing and perhaps inconsistent beliefs and interpretations of text and events could be held by different communicating agents represented in the text and also by the different participants in the translation process itself. We also assumed a lexicon (representing common linguistic knowledge), an ontology (representing shared general knowledge), and an episodic data base of facts (representing the part of the context, namely, those facts or beliefs -- sometimes shared -- about particular concrete events or situations). We continue to assume these mechanisms in this paper, but focus here on the resultant representation and how these mechanisms can be guided to produce that representation.

2 TMR Construction

In this section, we look in more detail at how a TMR is constructed from ontological and lexical information. We extend and modify that method to construct a representation of an interpretation showing how this new method may produce multiple plausible and coherent interpretations, among them ones similar to those that humans make.

In the first phase of analysis, syntactic, morphological, and lexical information in the input text is used to construct a TMR (an interlingual representation) of the input. In a very simplified view, lexical items point to particular concepts or nodes in an ontology, while syntactic and/or morphological information determines how these concepts are merged into a single TMR structure. Well-formedness constraints on the structure of the TMR may also require additional features and values to be present.

For a very simplified example, in analyzing the sentence *John is sleeping*, the lexical entry for the English lexical item *sleep* is accessed. This entry contains syntactic information that *sleep* in English requires a subject and that it points to the SLEEPING event node in the ontology. It also contains the information (taken from the ontology) that the SLEEPING event has an AGENT, and that this AGENT is to be identified with the subject of the verb. The analysis also identifies John as the subject of the sentence, identifying it with an instance of the ontological category HUMAN and then placing it as the value of the AGENT feature of the SLEEPING event in the TMR. The TMR also must contain additional information, such as a TIME feature, to indicate the time that the event occurs.

This approach, involving (1) a lexicon with pointers to concepts in (2) an ontology, which are then hooked together according to (3) the requirements for well-formedness of a TMR by means of (4) the analysis program, could be said to be a common underlying structure for most interlingual systems.

Two aspects of this process are worthy of note. The first is that, in addition to the material that derives directly from the lexical items and the ontology, the well-formedness constraints for TMRs requires the presence of some other features and values that are not so directly derived, but indeed, must be filled on the basis of some kind of inference or default mechanism. For example, there is a FORMALITY feature, whose filler is derived from a more global examination of the properties of the lexical items in the text. There are COREFERENCE features to indicate that two instantiations are the same. There are temporal features which indicate the time of occurrence of each event in the TMR and further features which indicate temporal relation between these events.

We would propose that at least two additional features be required for every TMR, if it is also to count as an interpretation: one feature which takes as value a representation of the communicative intent (the illocutionary force) of the utterance, and a second, which is filled with a representation of the intended effect (the perlocutionary effect) of the utterance. It is important to note that these will not be simple features. The communicative intent of an utterance, in our view, cannot be simply described by picking one from a list of possible speech acts, but is a complex representation of the information that the author intends to communicate. As such it may be as complex as the initial TMR that represents the semantic content of the utterance.

We do not claim to have a formal description of exactly what this communicative intent looks like, nor do we have a procedure for automatically deriving it from the initial TMR input. However, it would seem that the latter would involve minimally encoding in the ontology an analysis of categories of communicative intent, as well as the encoding in a reasoning module rules that relate utterances and communicative intent. So, for example, a taxonomy of speech acts is encoded in the ontology, while rules that relate aspects of utterances to categories of speech act are stored within the reasoning module.

Second, as a result of this process of TMR construction, some empty features may appear in the finished TMR (or filled only with some non-specific value). This is because of a mismatch between the bits of TMR connected to lexical items, so that not all feature values are filled from the information provided by the text. For example, a verb usually points to an event node in the ontology. Every event has certain thematic roles attached to it, as a consequence of the semantic character of the event, e.g., it may have an agent role or an experiencer role. Usually these thematic role features are filled by entities instantiated by other lexical elements in the sentence -- the subject or object, for instance. However, in a passive sentence, the agent may be unexpressed, so that the final TMR has an AGENT feature attached to the event which has no value. Similarly, nominalizations may be treated as events and thus also may give rise to unfilled feature values, if no specifier or modifiers appear in the text to fill the roles of event AGENT or THEME.

We propose that one aspect of interpretation building is filling in these empty feature values with pragmatically appropriate fillers (or specifying them if they instead simply have a non-specific value). Different interpretations then will arise when these feature values are filled (or filled out) differently by different interpreters. Of course, not all empty slots need to be filled to produce an interpretation. Only those that are used in constructing a coherent interpretation of the speaker's intent need be filled in, and then perhaps only as other text (other TMR portions) motivates it.

In the analysis of text and construction of TMR, it should be clear that the construction of the initial TMR requires an evaluation step. There are many different TMRs that can be constructed from a single input text, either because some lexical items are ambiguous (leading to the introduction of different ontological nodes into the TMR), or have different subcategorization frames (leading to the introduction of different thematic roles into the TMR) or because the inferencing to fill certain non-lexical slots (such as coreference, temporal relations, formality) produces more than one result.

These possible TMRs are be reduced in number (ideally to only one) by evaluating each TMR for plausibility. The fillers of connected features in a TMR are evaluated by applying constraints, that are stated in the ontology, to the fillers of the connected features, to see whether or how well they fit the constraints. This is usually performed by means of graph traversals within the ontology. For example, if a certain EVENT node in the ontology has an AGENT, that agent is likely constrained to be a HUMAN. In evaluating a particular TMR, the value of the AGENT feature is checked to see if it is, indeed, of category HUMAN, usually by seeing whether the entity node of which the subject is an instantiation is a descendant of the HUMAN node.

Each step of this graph traversal can be seen as a compressed inference (such as e.g., "Spot ISA DOG," "a DOG ISA MAMMAL," "If A ISA B, and B ISA C, then A ISA C," therefore "Spot ISA MAMMAL") and the entire graph traversal as an inference chain. The existence of such an inference chain indicates that the feature value plausibly fills that feature value slot. In Mikrokosmos, each link also contributes a weight to the chain, so that the chain has a total weight, conceived as providing a measure of the plausibility of that particular chain forming part of a TMR.

Thus, behind each TMR (so to speak) is a set of ontology graph traversals (or, equivalently, inference chains) which link the feature values of connected features, and which rate the connection on the basis of plausibility. We propose that these traversals be included as part of the TMR itself, rather than discarded after a "best" TMR is selected. They are, in fact, part of what we would call the interpretation. They are a way of situating the TMR within a real-world context, namely that of the ontology itself. Each chain represents a set of inferences made by the interpreter, connecting the feature values in the TMR.

We would further propose that additional connections (inference chains) might be deduced and stored as part of the TMR, further solidifying the interpretation. By including these chains of inference, we increase the coherence of the interpretation, since elements are logically connected, and, at the same time, provide another avenue by which interpretations might differ -- by following different chains of inference.

For example, in addition to simply showing that the agent of an action fits the appropriate constraints on such agents, a more fine-grained connection might be required, one that would provide an actual chain of cause and effect between the agent and the event. Differences in how these chains are constructed would also result in different interpretations. For example, the difference between the relationship of Nixon and bombing in "Nixon bombed Hanoi" (indirect causation through orders carried out by subordinates) and the relation of the pilot and Hiroshima in "The pilot of the Enola Gay bombed Hiroshima" (direct causation) has to do with the causal chain connecting the agent in each case with the event.

Even unconnected features in a large TMR might trigger a chain that would attempt to connect them. For example, the value of a communicative intent feature or of a perlocutionary effect feature should undoubtedly be logically connected in some way (through a theory of discourse and/or a theory of action) with the same slot fillers in TMRs derived from preceding and subsequent text.

Thus, in examining the structure and construction of a typical TMR, we have isolated three aspects which, if appropriately enhanced, would, we feel, make that TMR a representation of the interpretation and not just of the semantics. First, some additional slots and fillers would need to be added to TMR structure. Second, certain empty slots in the TMR structure would need to pragmatically filled. And, third, connected slots would need to be "supported" by additional chains of reasoning, which are themselves incorporated directly into the TMR itself.

3 Examples

In this section we illustrate through example how the TMR will need to be extended in order to accommodate pragmatic information that will transform it from a text meaning representation to a text interpretation representation. We look first at some examples of the need to fill empty slots in TMRs as they are currently envisioned. We then look at the need for extending the representation to include the illocutionary and perlocutionary aspects of communication. Finally, we exemplify the need for and approach to representing the inference chains that are used in order to establish the pragmatic aspects of communication, in particular, its coherence.

Interpretation as Filling in Empty Feature Values

As one example of the need for filling empty feature value slots in TMRs as they are currently being generated, consider the following sentence, treated at length in [14] (pp. 135-146):

Dresser Industries said it expects that major capital expenditure for expansion of U.S. manufacturing capacity will reduce imports from Japan.

Here, each nominalization (expenditure, expansion, manufacturing, imports) introduces an event concept having an implicit agent, none of which is indicated overtly. However, in order to establish coherence between the various events referred to (a spending, an expanding, a manufacturing, an importing), these agents need to be identified. The task, then, is to infer who the spender is, who the expander is, who the manufacturer is and who the importer is. It is possible that Dresser itself is in all cases that agent. But alternatively, based on prior text, it appears that the capital expenditure will be made by a new joint venture between Dresser and Komatsu Ltd., if not by the Japanese firm on its own or by Dresser and Komatsu individually as part of the divestiture process. On the other hand, it is clearly the new construction equipment joint venture which is expanding its own manufacturing capacity. As for who the importer is, it appears to be buyers of construction equipment in the US since the sentence above appears to encapsulate the argument the joint venture partners are putting to the US government in order to seek the government's approval of the deal. There are, of course, other reasonable interpretations of the fillers of these slots, but what is key here is that these slots need to be filled in order to establish a coherent connection between the events described. Filling these slots requires inferencing from world knowledge and facts reported in the prior text.

As a second example of the need to fill empty feature value slots in current TMR, consider the two translations into English of the Spanish expressions del tercer piso (on the third floor) and el segundo piso (the second floor) described in detail in [8].

> ... the 300 square meters of the third floor were available ..., but they were rented .... All that is left is the second floor ....

> ... the 300 square meters on the fourth floor were available, but they were rented ...; only the third floor remains ....

Where one translator has used the expression third and second as equivalents, the other has used the expressions fourth and third. Both translations are possible. What is happening is that an ordering of elements has been implied by the semantics of tercer (third) and segundo (second) and that with each ordering, the TMR requires the introduction of an associated convention for determining how the elements are ordered. Here, there are at least two possible conventions for how to count the floors of a building, one beginning with the ground floor and continuing on with the first floor (typically used in Europe) and one beginning with the first floor and continuing on with the second floor (typically used in the US and elsewhere). In order to establish a coherent interpretation in this case for translation, selecting one or the other of the floor-naming conventions is necessary and that process requires relativized default reasoning based on knowledge of the world and facts reported earlier in the text.

Interpretation as Filling New Feature Value Slots in an Extended TMR

To exemplify the need for representing the illocutionary and perlocutionary aspects of the text as well as the semantic, first consider the subtitled equivalent of:

    Hein, on va pas   jouer   une scène de Feydeau
         We are not acting out a scene   from Feydeau

which was provided by a translator for the film Jesus of Montreal ([1]):

    This is not a bedroom farce

We have argued ([11]) that the semantic content of this subtitle is equivalent to the illocutionary aspect (communicative intent) of the original French expression and that it is this illocutionary aspect of the original expression that serves as the basis for the translation. If this is correct, then the communicative intent of utterances must be represented as well as the semantic content and, consequently, TMR will have to be extended to accommodate it. What the communicative intent of any given utterance is or how it is established is by no means obvious. But it is clear that the process involves inferencing from world knowledge and information in the context of the utterance.

In a separate study reported in [10] we described how the lexical choices in each of two different translations into English of the same Spanish text on events related to a possible earthquake in Chile fell into two different patterns which reflected differing underlying interpretations of the translators as to the author's purpose in writing the text. For one translator, the author's purpose was to show that the media had acted irresponsibly and thus caused public panic and the lexical choices reflect this by emphasizing the irrationality of the reaction of the population and the preparations of the government while de-emphasizing the likelihood and magnitude of the possible earthquake. For the second translator, the author's purpose was to show that the government has acted irresponsibly and thus caused a panic and the lexical choices reflect this by emphasizing the imminence and magnitude of the possible earthquake while de-emphasizing the irrationality of the reaction of the population and the preparations of the government. The relevance of this is that to establish these patterns of lexical choice in the translations, the author's purpose must be identified and represented. Again, it is not obvious what the purpose of any given text is or how it is established. It is clear, however, that the process involves inferencing from world knowledge and information in the context of the utterance.

Interpretation as Chains of Inferences between Feature Value Slots

Returning to the Dresser example presented above, it turns out that there is an instrument slot associated with the reducing event, corresponding to will reduce, which the semantics will fill with the concept corresponding to major capital expenditure. Although this is, in fact, an appropriate analysis, it is nonetheless under-informative. It is vital for establishing coherence to infer how the expenditure will, in fact, cause the reduction. One possible line of reasoning, for instance, concerns the finiteness of funds (i.e., if money is spent on expanding manufacturing capacity, it cannot be spent on imports and so imports go down). Another possible line of reasoning concerns preferences for and availability of locally produced goods (i.e., if consumers can buy US-made products, they will and so, if the availability of US-made products is increased, consumers will buy them and consequently they will not import them from Japan and imports from Japan will decrease). The point is that different inference chains connecting the same two slots in the representation represent different interpretations of the text. Therefore, in order to represent differing interpretations, TMR must be extended to allow for the representation of such inference chains.

An additional example of the relevance of representing the inferencing related to interpretive process as part of the interpretation itself can be found [6]. In this presentation of an interlingual-based approach to reference resolution, the focus is on attempting to decide whether the filler of a given functional relation (e.g., the agent of an action) is the same as any prior mentioned or implied slot filler. If it is, a coreference link is established between the two fillers. If it cannot be connected to any of the prior mentioned or implied slot filler, then the filler is assumed to introduce a new referent into the context

This process is one of inferencing on the basis of knowledge of the world and facts introduced earlier in the discourse. As an example, consider the resolution of Productos Roche SA in the text segment below.

El grupo Roche, a través de su compañía en España, adquirió el laboratorio
    the Roche Group through   its company in Spain   purchased the pharmaceutical
    farmacéutico Doctor Andreu, ...
    laboratory   Doctor Andreu

...la operación   realizada entre   Productos Roche SA y   Unión Explosivos ...,
    the transaction carried out between Productos Roche SA and Union Explosivos
    hasta ahora mayoritaria en   el accionariado.
    until now majority holder among the shareholders

As it turns out, the referent of Productos Roche SA is the same a that of su compañía en España. To establish the connection between the two referents it is necessary to first resolve the reference of la operación (the transaction) to the purchase described by the first clause (... adquirió ...). This can be done by inferring on the basis of ontological knowledge that a purchase is a type of transaction. Since the purchase referred to in the first clause is the only transaction in the utterance context, it must be the same as the referent of the definite description la operación. Next, it is necessary to identify form ontological knowledge that a purchasing involves a buyer, a seller, a thing bought and a sum of money used for buying it. From the first clause it is apparent that Roche's company in Spain was the buyer and that Doctor Andreu was the thing bought. From the second segment it is apparent that Productos Roche was involved the purchase as either the buyer or the seller and that Union Explosivos was involved as the other party. All this apparent information is derived from semantic analysis. The final step, then, is to infer that, since Union Explosivos has until now been the majority share holder, presumably of Doctor Andreu, and that by implication it no longer is, it must be the seller. Therefore, Productos Roche SA must be the buyer, that is to say Roche's company in Spain. But this is not the only reasoning chain that might be used for making the connection. So, again, interpretations may vary due to differing chains of inferencing and, as a result, the chains of inferencing must be represented as part of the interpretation.

4 Conclusion

In this paper we have suggested certain methods for expanding a TMR (a text meaning representation) so that it can include additional pragmatically inferred information (an interpretation of the text). This additional information, we have claimed elsewhere, is necessary to account for observed variation in human translation. We suggest that it is incorporated within the current structure of the TMR in three ways -- first by pragmatically filling in empty feature values in the representation, thus connecting the elements of the text in coherent ways with surrounding text and the non-linguistic context;   second by inclusion of additional features in the TMR, most prominently ones that reflect conclusions drawn about the communicative intent and intended effect of the utterance;   and finally by incorporating "behind" the TMR inference chains that provide support for coherent interpretations of the semantics of the utterance. We have further exemplified from previous work how each of these aspects is necessitated by evidence from variants in human translations.

References

1. Arcand, D.: Jesus of Montreal. Miramax: Orion Home Video (1989)
2. Attardo, D. MIKROKOSMOS TMR Builder's Guide. Internal Memo, Computing Research Laboratory, New Mexico State University, Las Cruces, NM (1994)
3. Ballim, A., and Wilks, Y.: Artificial Believers: the Ascription of Belief. Hillsdale, NJ: Lawrence Erlbaum (1991)
4. Barnden, J., Helmreich, S., Iverson, E., and Stein, G.: An Integrated Implementation of Simulative, Uncertain and Metaphorical Reasoning about Mental States. In Doyle, J., Sandewall, E., and Torasso, P. (eds.), Principles of Knowledge Representation and Reasoning: Proceedings of the Fourth International Conference,. San Mateo, CA: Morgan Kaufmann (1994) 27-38
5. Carlson, L., and Nirenburg, S.: World Modeling for NLP. Technical Report 90-121, Center for Machine Translation, Carnegie-Mellon University, Pittsburgh, PA (1990)
6. Farwell, D., and Helmreich, S.: An Interlingual-based Approach to Reference Resolution. Paper presented at the NAACL/ANLP Workshop on Applied Interlinguas. Seattle, WA. (2000)
7. Farwell, D., and Helmreich, S.: Pragmatics and Translation. *Procesamiento del Languaje Natural*, 24 (1999) 19-37
8. Farwell, D., and Helmreich, S.: What floor is this? Beliefs and Translation. Proceedings of the 5th International Colloquium on Cognitive Science, (1997) 95-102
9. Farwell, D., and Helmreich, S.: Assassins or Murders: Translation of Politically Sensitive Material. Paper presented at the 26th Annual Meeting of Linguistics Association of the Southwest, University of California at Los Angeles, Los Angeles, CA (1997)
10. Farwell, D., and Helmreich, S.: User-friendly Machine Translation: Alternate Translations Based on Differing Beliefs. Proceedings of the Machine Translation Summit VI (1997) 125-131
11. Farwell, D., and Helmreich, S.: This is Not a Bedroom Farce: Pragmatics and Translation. Proceedings of the 4th International Colloquium on Cognitive Science (1995) 73-82
12. Green, G.: The structure of CONTEXT: The representation of pragmatic restrictions in HPSG. In J. Yoon, (ed.), Proceedings of the Fifth annual meeting of the Formal Linguistics Society of the Midwest. Urbana, IL.: Studies in the Linguistic Sciences (1996)
13. Helmreich, S., and Farwell, D.:   Translation Differences and Pragmatics-based MT. *Machine Translation,* 13(1) (1998)17-39
14. Nirenburg, S., and Raskin, V.: 2000. Ontological Semantics. Unpublished manuscript (2000)

MT-Based Transparent Arabization of the Internet TARJIM.COM[1]

Achraf Chalabi[2]

Sakhr Software
B.P. 11771
Sakhr Building, Free Zone, Nasr City, Cairo , Egypt
ac@sakhr.com
http://www.sakhr.com

Abstract. As is known, the majority of the actual textual content on the Internet is in English language. This represents an obstacle to those non-English speaking users willing to access the Internet. The idea behind this MT-based application is to allow any Arabic user to search and navigate through the Internet using Arabic language without the need to have prior knowledge of English language. The infrastructure of TARJIM.COM relies on 3 basic core components : 1- The Bi-directional English<>Arabic Machine translation Engine, 2- The intelligent Web page layout preserving component and 3-The Search Engine query interceptor.

Bidirectional English<>Arabic Machine Translation Engine

This is the Core of TARJIM.COM. The MT engine is based mainly on the transfer model.

Due to the complexity of Arabic language automatic processing, the analysis module, which is the heart of the MT component has been developed in the first place to handle Arabic, then the same techniques have been successfully applied to handle English language.

One of the aspects making Arabic language more complex, from NLP viewpoint, than English is the absence of diacritics (vowels) in written Arabic text. It's as if English or French were written without vowels. This represents a challenge one order of magnitude bigger than handling Latin-based language counterparts.

Another major problem faced in handling Arabic computationally is the rare use of punctuation marks. Although punctuation is present in Arabic, it is rarely used in written text thus making the automatic sentence segmentation process a mandatory one during the analysis phase for Arabic text.

A 3rd concern in handling Arabic is that Arabic is a highly inflectional and derivational language, thus making the morphological analysis a much tougher process than just stemming or lemmatizing.

---

[1] TARJIM.COM is a trademark of Sakhr Software company (http://www.tarjim.com)
[2] Head of MT Research Department, Sakhr Software (http://www.sakhr.com)

J.S. White (Ed.): AMTA 2000, LNAI 1934, pp. 189-191, 2000.
© Springer-Verlag Berlin Heidelberg 2000

With an average accuracy of about 65% for the translated text, the MT engine was ready to serve in TARJIM.COM, the Internet Arabization application, whose main target is to convey the general meaning (gist) of any Web page to the Arabic user.

During source language analysis, the MT engine consults an automatic theme prediction module whose role is to deduce whether the input sentence subject to translation is biased towards a specific theme yes or no. If it happens to be, the theme predictor specifies that dominant theme out of 20 predefined themes including economics, politics, sports, computer, medicine, etc.

Using available thematic information carried over the word senses, a repeated theme is assumed dominant if its frequency is high enough with respect to the sentence length to which it will be assigned. The predicted theme, if any, is used in subsequent processing to resolve word-sense ambiguity. Based on what preceded, the thematic predictor would assign for following sentence : "*A Reuters team in the area, saw Yugoslav army tanks and anti-aircraft guns blasting suspected positions*", a dominant theme equals to "*military*", this will result in the selection of the "*vehicle*" sense for the word "*tank*".

So far the results of the automatic theme predictor are only efficient on the word-sense disambiguation level, but are expected to reach a level of accuracy that will permit their positive contribution on morphological disambiguation level in the near future.

While the default behavior on TARJIM.COM is to assume automatic theme prediction, the user still has the option to bypass automatic prediction and specify manually the theme in case he has prior knowledge about the nature of the pages he will translate. It was found that user-defined theme, when selected accurately, usually enhances the translation accuracy by an average of 10%.

The Application's core, the MT engine, is the result of intensive R&D work in NLP achieved in Sakhr Software over the last 10 years. Based on the transfer model, the MT engine performance has been boosted considerably by a statistical language model contributing to the lexical and morphological disambiguation of the source language, in addition to enhanced word selection in the target language.

The Sakhr language statistical model is supported by two balanced Corpuses, one for English and another one for Arabic (~200 millions words).

During source language analysis, morphological disambiguation is achieved through a morphological analyser and a homograph resolver with an accuracy reaching 80% for Arabic. Syntactic analysis is performed via a single-stack, bottom-up parser, driven by a multi-pass grammar and hand-shaking with a shallow semantic analyser supported by intensive selection restrictions information.

In addition to the regular lexical and syntactic transfer, the engine takes care of most of the non-isomorphic aspects on both levels between Arabic and English including lexical conflation, verb arguments swapping, and others.

Arabic morphological generation of the output is performed through a morphological synthesizer supported by morpho-syntactic features produced during syntactic transfer and generation.

Preserving the Web Page Layout

Usually Web pages contain more than pure text, such as images, hyperlinks, formatting tags, etc.

Preserving the layout of a source page while translation is a major advantage in such a service, but this added value has a tradeoff in translation accuracy. This negative impact on translation accuracy results from the fact that 'natural' sentence segmentation is interrupted by many 'artificial' segmentation rules required to preserve hyperlinks, text formats, image locations, etc., thus distorting the syntactic analysis of the sentence.

In TARJIM.COM, we overcome this tradeoff by intelligently mapping HTML tags between the source and target Web pages during translation. Although the small overhead on the performance, the user will get the original layout preserved without any impact on the translation accuracy.

The Search Engine Query Interceptor

In order to open the door to the Arabic user to one of the most useful tools on the Internet which is the search engine, TARJIM.COM allows the user to submit his query in any Web search engine in Arabic language. The user can even build his query in mixed Arabic and English and get the search results in Arabic, then continue his navigation in Arabic language.

In order to implement this, TARJIM.COM intercepts any search query, parses it and extracts the text to be searched. In case the text is Arabic, it is automatically translated using the Arabic to English direction of Sakhr MT engine, then the query is reconstructed and resent to the destination server to process it. Search results which are in English are translated to Arabic via the English to Arabic direction of Sakhr MT engine, then forwarded back to the user.

The KANTOO Machine Translation Environment

Eric Nyberg and Teruko Mitamura

Language Technologies Institute, Carnegie Mellon University
5000 Forbes Avenue, Pittsburgh, PA 15213
{ehn, teruko}@cs.cmu.edu

Abstract. In this paper we describe the KANTOO machine translation environment, a set of software services and tools for multilingual document production. KANTOO includes modules for source language analysis, target language generation, source terminology management, target terminology management, and knowledge source development. The KANTOO system represents a complete re-design and re-implementation of the KANT machine translation system.

1   Introduction

KANTOO is a knowledge-based, interlingual machine translation system for multilingual document production. KANTOO includes: a) an MT engine, the result of fundamental redesign and reimplementation of the core algorithms of the KANT system [2, 4]; and b) a set of off-line tools that support the creation and update of terminology and other knowledge resources for different MT applications. Several workflows are supported by KANTOO (see Figure 1):

- **Controlled-language authoring and checking**, performed by the source language author(s). Authors use the Controlled Language Checker (CLC) tool for vocabulary and grammar checking on each document they produce. The KANTOO Analyzer is used as a background server which handles individual check requests.
- **Batch document translation**, performed as part of the document production workflow. The KANTOO Analyzer and Generator are utilized as standalone batch servers.
- **Knowledge creation and update**, performed by the domain and language experts. The Knowledge Maintenance Tool (KMT) is used by system developers to edit grammars, structural mapping rules, and other rule-based knowledge in the system.
- **Source terminology creation and update**, performed by domain experts. The Lexical Maintenance Tool (LMT) is used to maintain source terminology in a relational database structure.
- **Target terminology creation and update**, performed by domain translators. The Language Translations Database (LTD) tool is used by translators to create target translations of new source terminology.

J.S. White (Ed.): AMTA 2000, LNAI 1934, pp. 192–195, 2000.

KANTOO Clients   **KANTOO Servers**   **KANTOO Knowledge**

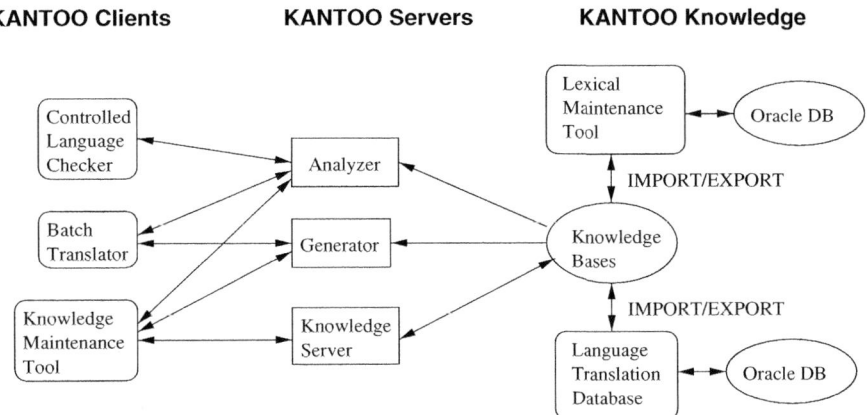

Fig. 1. KANTOO Architecture.

The KANTOO architecture is scalable; several domains, languages, and versions of their knowledge sources can be maintained and executed in parallel. The PC delivery format of the LTD and LMT allow those tools to be used by third-party translations vendors to develop terminology resources. These tools are in daily use at an industrial document production facility [1] for Spanish, French, and German.

2   KANTOO Modules

- **Analyzer**. The Analyzer module performs tokenization, morphological processing, lexical lookup, syntactic parsing with a unification grammar, and semantic interpretation, yielding one or more interlingua expressions for each valid input sentence (or a diagnostic message for invalid sentences). The same Analyzer server can be used simultaneously by the CLC, Batch Translator and KMT[1].
- **Generator**. The Generator module performs lexical selection, structural mapping, syntactic generation, and morphological realization for a particular target language. The same Generator executable can be loaded with different knowledge bases for different languages. The same Generator server can be used by the Batch Translator an KMT in parallel.
- **Lexical Maintenance Tool (LMT)**. The Lexical Maintenance Tool (LMT) is implemented as an Oracle database and Forms application which helps

---

[1] Space limitations preclude a discussion of a) the Controlled Language Checker, which has been discussed at length in [3], and b) the Batch Translator, which is a simple piece of driver code that uses the KANTOO servers to translate entire documents.

users to create, modify, and navigate through large numbers of lexical entries. The LMT brings together the various kinds of lexical entries used in NLP development, including words, phrases, and specialized entries such as acronyms, abbreviations, and units of measure.

- **Language Translation Database (LTD)**. The LTD is the target language counterpart to the LMT, and is also implemented using Oracle and Forms. The LTD includes productivity enhancements which provide the translator with partial draft translations taken from similar translated terms.

- **Knowledge Maintenance Tool (KMT) and Knowledge Server**. The Knowledge Maintenance Tool (KMT) is a graphical user interface which allows developers to test their knowledge changes in the context of a complete working system. Users can trace or edit individual rules or categories of rules. The KMT operates in conjunction with the Knowledge Server, which provides distributed network access to a version-controlled repository of KANTOO knowledge sources.

3   Knowledge Update in KANTOO

There are two main types of knowledge update in KANTOO: a) terminology updates, which include both source and target language vocabulary; and b) knowledge base updates, which include enhancments and bug fixes made to source and target grammars, mapping rules, etc. to improve translation coverage and quality.

- **Terminology Updates**. When a new version of the source language terminology is released, the contents of the LMT are synchronized with the contents of the LTD. Both databases share a virtual data model, and use the same primary key; the synchronization process ensures that each target language database includes entries for all the new (untranslated) terminology. The individual databases are then distributed to translators, who provide translations for the new terms. Both the LMT and LTD databases are then exported to the machine-readable lexicon format used by KANTOO. Once a set of new lexicons have been created and tested, they are integrated into the production workflow by updating the production knowledge repository. The KANTOO analyzer and generator servers automatically incorporate these knowledge updates when they are restarted.

- **Knowledge Base Updates**. A variety of rule-based knowledge sources must be maintained in the KANTOO system. Chief among them are the syntactic grammars for the source and target languages. The biggest challenges for updating rule-based knowledge sources effectively rest in the potential complexity of the debug/test cycle. Changing a particular rule might result in widespread changes in grammar coverage, or regressive failures. The Knowledge Maintenance Tool (KMT) is used by the developer to test individual updates, with recourse to full regression testing on various reference corpora. All changes to the knowledge are managed under explicit version control, so that it is straightforward to synchronize the knowledge sources for different releases. The KMT also includes an interactive tracing and debugging environment which utilizes the KANTOO analyzer and generator servers.

4 Current Status and Future Work

KANTOO is implemented in C++ (Analyzer, Generator, Knowledge Server), Java (KMT) and Oracle/Forms (LMT, LTD). KANTOO has been deployed under AIX and Linux, and is currently being tested under Windows NT. The flexibility of the KANTOO client-server architecture supports distributed, parallel development of new applications and robust, scalable deployments. Our current research focuses on the issues related to deploying the KANTOO architecture in an environment where document authoring and document translation are performed by third-party vendors external to the customer site. This architecture is particularly well-suited for the deployment of authoring and translation as distributed internet services, available over the network 24 hours a day.

5 Acknowledgements

We would like to acknowledge David Svoboda and Michael Duggan for their work on the KANTOO Analyzer and Generator; Anna Maria Berta for her work on LTD and LMT; and David Svoboda, Michael Duggan and Paul Placeway for their work on KMT. We also would like to thank Kathy Baker, Margarida Bolzani, Violetta Cavalli-Sforza, Peter Cramer, Eric Crestan, Krzysztof Czuba, Enrique Torrejon, and Dieter Waeltermann for their work on the development of different KANTOO applications.

References

1. Kamprath, C., Adolphson, E., Mitamura, T. and Nyberg, E.: Controlled Language for Multilingual Document Production: Experience with Caterpillar Technical English. In: Proceedings of the Second International Workshop on Controlled Language Applications (1998)
2. Mitamura, T., Nyberg, E. and Carbonell, J.: An Efficient Interlingua Translation System for Multi-lingual Document Production. In: Proceedings of the Third Machine Translation Summit (1991)
3. Mitamura, T. and Nyberg, E.: Controlled English for Knowledge-Based MT: Experience with the KANT System. In: Proceedings of TMI-95 (1995)
4. Nyberg, E. and Mitamura, T.: The KANT System: Fast, Accurate, High-Quality Translation in Practical Domains. In: Proceedings of COLING-92 (1992)

Pacific Rim Portable Translator

John Weisgerber, Jin Yang, and Pete Fisher

SYSTRAN Software, Inc.
7855 Fay Avenue
La Jolla, CA 92037
(858) 459-6700
(858) 459-8487

Army Research Laboratory
2800 Powder Mill Rd.
Adelphi, MD 20783
(301) 394-4302
(301) 394-2682

jweisgerber@systransoft.com
Jyang@systransoft.com
Pfisher@arl.mil

Abstract. ARL's FALCon system has proven its integrated OCR and MT technology to be a valuable asset to soldiers in the field in both Bosnia and Haiti. Now it is being extended to include six more SYSTRAN language pairs in response to the military's need for automatic translation capabilities as they pursue US national objectives in East Asia. The Pacific Rim Portable Translator will provide robust automatic translation bidirectionally for English↔Chinese, Japanese, and Korean, which will allow not only rapid assimilation of foreign information, but two-way communication as well for both the public and private sectors.

1 Introduction

This paper briefly describes the extension to the Army Research Laboratory's Forward Area Language Converter (FALCon), which is being developed by SYSTRAN Software, Inc. as part of the Dual Use Science & Technology Program. The FALCon's integrated OCR/MT capabilities are being extended to include bidirectional English to Chinese, Japanese, and Korean, and this version of the FALCon is being referred to as the Pacific Rim Portable Translator. Because this paper describes an integrated suite of systems, the emphasis has been placed on the process and capabilities of the whole rather than the architecture or methodology of the components.

J.S. White (Ed.): AMTA 2000, LNAI 1934, pp. 196-201, 2000.
© Springer-Verlag Berlin Heidelberg 2000

2 Background

2.1 The FALCon System

The Forward Area Language Converter (FALCon) permits users with no foreign language experience to evaluate the content of foreign language documents. With FALCon technology, non-linguists can provide support for linguists and translators by triaging foreign language documents. This process reduces the burden on linguists/translators by removing non-significant documents from the evaluation process. In addition, FALCon can provide the linguist/translator with an initial conversion of the foreign language document to English, thus jump-starting the translation process. Army Research Laboratory (ARL) has been delivering FALCon systems to the Army for pilot field-testing since May of 1997, with as many as seven systems in Bosnia at a time. FALCon serves as a testbed for the multilingual program at ARL.

2.2 Motivation for Extension

Being a Dual-Use project, whereby the cost is split between the government sponsor and the private contractor, the development of the Pacific Rim Portable Translator serves a twofold purpose:

1. Automatic translation in East Asian languages is needed to support military missions in the Pacific Rim. Human linguists proficient in Chinese, Japanese, and Korean are in short supply and are heavily overburdened. This software suite can be integrated into military operations at any echelon from strategic command, control, communications, computer and intelligence (C4I) networks to tactical support systems such as FALCon. This system will enable troops to evaluate captured enemy data in real time and enhance their ability to communicate in a coalition environment.
2. SYSTRAN has the opportunity to develop an English to Chinese system, which was the only missing element of the suite, and to enhance its Asian language pairs concurrently in order to more effectively improve translation quality and ensure their commercial viability.

3 System Description

3.1 The Pacific Rim Portable Translator

The core translation technology of this system consists of a suite of robust, general-purpose, bi-directional English-Chinese, Japanese, and Korean MT engines (six SYSTRAN language pairs), each with a relatively high rate of accuracy and a basic specialization in military terminology. These language pairs have been integrated into the preexisting FALCon architecture, which is described below.

Two configurations of the FALCon system are available: An integrated software suite that can be added to existing personal computer (PC) platforms; An integrated system consisting of a PC, document scanner, and power supply integrated into a briefcase and loaded with the software suite. This permits FALCon to be run as either a stand-alone package, or be integrated into existing systems.

As shown in figure 1, the FALCon system processes documents using three successive software modules. Scanner software is used to acquire a document image from the scanner. Optical character recognition (OCR) software then converts that image to text in the foreign language. Machine translation (MT) software then converts the foreign language text to English. In addition, the MT software can search the resulting translation for keywords from a keyword list file specified by the user. Keywords that are found are highlighted and the number of keywords found is displayed. All three of the software modules are commercial-off-the-shelf (COTS) products. As a result, they all have independent controls for setting the selected language for processing. In order to simplify the use of FALCon, ARL developed a user interface that permits the user to specify the source language and the keyword list in one place. The user interface then configures the language and keyword settings for all three software modules.

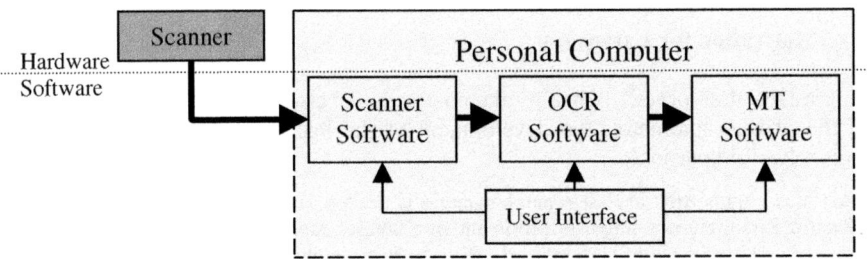

Fig. 1. FALCon System Process

Two processes are available for the operation of FALCon, „one button" operation, or step-by-step. In either case the user interface must first be used to set the source language and the keyword list to be used. Next the user feeds the document of interest through the scanner. The scanner software automatically acquires the document image and displays it. The user then uses the mouse to click on the FALCon button to start the cascade process of OCR, conversion, and keyword search. At the end of this process the PC screen shows the source document (OCR output), resulting conversion, and the results of the keyword search in one window. For the step-by-step process the software flow matches the process of the one button operation as described above, but the user now executes each process and can view and correct the output of each software module. Step-by-step operation is provided so that errors that result from the scanning and OCR processes can be corrected prior to conversion of the document to English. While the step-by-step and correction process is more time consuming, the elimination of errors prior to machine translation can result in greatly improved document conversion and improved understanding of the original document.

3.2   SYSTRAN's CJK MT Engines

The translation engines in this system all utilize SYSTRAN's patented MT technology, which has consistently been highly rated in robustness and accuracy throughout its long history.   Specifically, the Pacific Rim Portable Translator is comprised of six SYSTRAN language pairs: Chinese-to-English (CE), English-to-Chinese (EC), Japanese-to-English (JE), English-to-Japanese (EJ), Korean-to-English (KE), and English-to-Korean (EK).

SYSTRAN's MT engines are written in ANSI C or C++ and tested for portability to the major UNIX variants and PC operating systems. This suite of software will be made available for Windows 9x/2000/NT, UNIX SunOS, UNIX Solaris, and HP UNIX.

SYSTRAN's Asian language pairs support the input and output of each of the most common encoding schemes for Chinese, Japanese, and Korean. These are managed by mapping them to the Unicode standard, which SYSTRAN has adopted internally for its language pair development. The supported encodings are as follows:

1. For Chinese, these schemes include: (a) the "Big 5" scheme used for traditional characters in Taiwan, (until recently) Hong Kong, and most expatriate Chinese communities abroad and (b) the GB and HZ schemes used for "Simplified" characters in the Peoples Republic of China.
2. For Japanese, these schemes include: the standard encoding for Japanese, "JIS" (Japanese Industrial Standard) and its 2 common variants, shift-JIS and EUC. These will enable input to be handled in any or a combination of three scripts: (a) Hiragana - a phonemic syllable-based script used primarily for function words, inflectional affixes, and very common words. (b) Katakana - a phonemic syllable-based script designed for transcribing foreign loan words, and now used for textual emphasis as well. (c) Kanji - a subset of the Chinese ideographic lexicon used for most content words.
3. For Korean, the scheme is KSC, which handles the single phonemic script, Hangul, with occasional use of Chinese characters for proper nouns. In addition to the KSC encoding, SYSTRAN's Korean MT systems also support the input and output of the SKATS transliteration system (a.k.a. Morse transliteration), which is commonly used in the military signals intelligence community.

The component that most distinguishes the CJK-to-E systems from the familiar SYSTRAN MT architecture is the Word Boundary program.   Word Boundary tokenizes the Chinese, Japanese, or Korean text using the data available in the system dictionary and rules defined by the CJK system developers. Some of the useful features of the Word Boundary program include:

1. Support for Customer Specific Dictionaries and additional word lists (e.g. names list);
2. Conversion of CJK number conventions to Arabic numerals before analysis;
3. Accessible and customizable segmentation rules.

3.3   CJK OCR Integration

The OCR input capability is a major part of the tactical value of the FALCon system. COTS OCR packages are being evaluated for Chinese, Japanese, and Korean to determine their accuracy and their portability to the FALCon framework. Once selected, a commercial OCR product for each language will be integrated into the FALCon architecture to reduce the effort required for system operation.

4 Scope of Development

4.1   Performance Objectives

The FALCon system has so far been primarily used for the rapid assimilation of foreign information. For effective two-way communication, on the other hand, reliably high quality MT output is required. This is a challenge for any MT system, but is especially so when dealing with the combination of English and Asian languages. At the beginning of the project, SYSTRAN already had five of the required six MT engines operating at a browse-quality level or better. In addition to general quality improvements, this project allowed for focused development in each language on authentic military data to customize the system for military applications. By training the systems on authentic text corpora, we can achieve the quality level necessary to enable effective bidirectional communication in English and Chinese, Japanese, or Korean for the military subdomains in which they have been trained.

4.2   Rapid Development of SYSTRAN's English-to-Chinese MT System

As noted above, at the beginning of this project SYSTRAN only had five of the six required MT engines operational. Theoretically, transfer-based MT systems are at a disadvantage when porting to new languages due to the fact that new transfer modules are required for each new system. In contrast to this generally accepted theory, SYSTRAN was able to rapidly develop an English-to-Chinese system by reusing applicable technology that was already established for other language pairs. Development of each of the English-source systems was also enhanced by the unique opportunity for concurrent development that this project provides, allowing the E-CJK systems to cooperate on the handling of a number of linguistic phenomena common to all three target languages.

5 Notes

The development of the Pacific Rim Portable Translator has highlighted a number of important issues related to MT development, such as the possibility of rapidly developing a transfer-based MT system through technology transfer and the added value of developing related languages concurrently. We hope to illustrate these issues in detail in future conference papers.

The integrated technologies in this system provide a unique suite of MT software that will significantly facilitate the ever-increasing interactions between the governments and businesses of the East and West. Field testing of the Pacific Rim Portable Translator is planned for the near future, similar to that conducted for previous versions of FALCon (see the paper by Holland, Schlesiger, and Tate in these proceedings).

6 Acknowledgments

SYSTRAN would especially like to thank Dr. Melissa Holland of ARL and Mr. Dale Bostad of NAIC, for their support of this project. The system described in this presentation was prepared through an Agreement sponsored by the U.S. Army Research Laboratory under Agreement No. DAAD17-99-3-0074. The views and conclusions contained in this presentation are those of the authors and should not be interpreted as presenting the official policies or position, either expressed or implied, of the U.S. Army Research Laboratory or the U.S. Government unless so designated by other authorized documents. Citation of manufacturer's or trade names does not constitute an official endorsement or approval of the use thereof. The U.S. Government is authorized to reproduce and distribute reprints for government purposes notwithstanding any copyright notation hereon.

LabelTool
A Localization Application for Devices with Restricted Display Areas

Jimmy C.M. Lu[1], Lars Åkerman[1], and Karin Spalink[2]

[1]Scheelev. 17 SE-223 70 Lund, Sweden
Email: {jimmy.lu, lars.akerman}@ausys.se

[2]Ericsson, HFID
PO Box 13969
8001 Development Drive
Research Triangle Park, NC 27709, USA
Email: karin.spalink@ericsson.com

Abstract. The LabelTool/TrTool system is designed to administer text strings that are shown in devices with a very limited display area and translated into a very large number of foreign languages. Automation of character set handling and file naming and storage together with real-time simulation of text string input are the main features of this application.

System Description

Purpose of the System

The LabelTool/TrTool-translator/TrTool-validator suite was developed by AU-system, under the supervision of Ericsson, to administer menu texts translated into 40 languages. The Ericsson translation process involves three steps:

1. Text collection
2. Text translation
3. Text validation

The texts are strings (single words, phrases, sentences, paragraphs) that will be displayed on the screen of mobile telephones. Each text string is attached to a label which in turn is used as a resource marker in the software program. The texts are collected from specification documents and entered into LabelTool. Once the English text have been approved they are sent out to the translators for translation. Translated texts are validated in the target countries to ensure use of current and widely accepted terminology.

Although the system is mainly designed to handle texts that appear in cellular phones the concept is applicable to all devices with a limited display area.

The system consists of:

- LabelTool, the administrative tool to organize labels with their constraints in a SQL database, the administrator generates files to be translated and imports the translated files back into the database upon the completion of the translation process.
- TrTool-translator, the tool that the translators utilize in order to view and translate the files generated by LabelTool.
- TrTool-validator, the tool used by validators to validate the translated texts.

In LabelTool constraints such as width, height and alignment can be set for each label or a group of labels. The constraint parameters are exported with the files as they are generated for the TrTool-translator as well as the TrTool-validator. Administrators, translators and validators are able to view the text in a simulated phone screen as they work on them. Color codes are used to indicate different status of the texts.

System Requirements

- LabelTool:
    - PC system with CPU speed equivalent to Pentium II 233MHz.
    - 128 MB primary memory.
    - WinNT 4.0 and above.
    - MS SQL server 7.0.
- TrTool:
    - PC system with CPU speed equivalent to Pentium 133MHz.
    - 64 MB primary memory.
    - Win95, Win98 or WinNT 4.0 and above.

Feature Set

- Use of Unicode: the tool suite uses Unicode to address all text input and storage issues. Unicode makes handling of all languages possible.
- Unicode keyboard: the system provides a Unicode software keyboard for input, this feature allows the user to map any key on the keyboard to a specific Unicode and its glyph. By defining an optional set of keys the translator will be able to produce translations in any language without using any third party software or being forced to install a specific language version of Windows.
- Unicode support for Search and Replace functions.

- Language support handling bi-directional input and display conversion according to Unicode standard.
- Font file: the tool suite uses Ericsson defined fonts for display and text constraint measurement. The very same font file is used by the cellular phone. Font file and Unicode usage is tightly integrated.
- Simulator: the tool suite shows texts as they will appear on the cellular phone screen to give translators a realistic view.
- Language handling: since Unicode is used to address the texts, it makes it possible to handle all 40 languages at the same time. To view as well as to manipulate them.
- Filing system and file naming: the system has a predefined storage structure handling all outputs from the system. Users can choose a starting point from where the structure will be defined by the system. The naming process of the outputs is also handled automatically by the system.
- Translation production is independent of any Windows language environment.
- Basic feature set.
- Version handling is tightly integrated in the system, it makes it possible to track all changes throughout the translation process.
- All columns can be sorted in ascending or descending order.
- Own file format with following controls:
    - Checksum to prevent transmission error.
    - Version control.

Future Features (Short-Term)

- Web-based version
- Automatic generation of a first draft
- Spell checker
- Input method for Chinese characters in a non-Chinese environment

Future Features (Long-Term)

- Interface to other software applications
- Integration with documentation production
- Integration with terminology database

Demonstration

Introduction

LabelTool was developed to administer the creation and display of restricted texts in more than forty different languages. The main features of the tool focus on the automation of character set handling for input and for display. LabelTool takes advantage of those features internally by providing a simulator that lets the operator see in real-time whether the intended text (source or target) will fit into the allotted space and how it will display on the screen. When translating into so many languages, file handling also becomes a real challenge. The Ericsson translation process includes a validation step, i.e. in addition to a set of translation files we also have a set of validated translation files. LabelTool automates file naming and storing.

Input

LabelTool requires the following information in order to be able to apply its character set and file handling automation capabilities:
- the actual text string to be displayed
- the display parameters for each of those text strings
- the language(s) the text string is to be displayed in
- the font file that is used to display the characters

The source for this information is the set of specifications that is created by the Human Factors group.

The actual text string to be displayed in the phone is referred to in LabelTool as the 'master text'. Each master text is identified through a '(text) label' which will be used by software as a reference to the resource file. Since English is the official language at Ericsson, all master texts, independent of country of creation, are generated in English. The text label consists of three parts: a prefix, the label itself and a suffix. The prefix describes the function within the phone, e.g. PHB for Phonebook. The label describes the master text, e.g. ADD_ENTRY, which is a list item that the user chooses when he or she wants to enter another number to the phonebook. The suffix identifies the text type, e.g. TTL for title or HLP for help text.

The display parameters are:
- the designated screen size, i.e. 'width' and 'height'
- the text alignment
- the font used

Not all screens use the entire physically available screen. For aesthetic or usability reasons the area that is used to display text may be smaller than the physical screen size. It could also be that the text to be displayed is larger than the screen size in which case functions like scrolling or panning will be invoked.

The screen size may be defined in actual pixel numbers or as a GUI object. The display parameters of GUI objects are defined in the specifications. For example: a TITLE on a GUI object MENU is defined as centered and occupying one line only, no matter how wide the phone's display screen is. Furthermore, the MENU TITLE will always be shown in size 12 font. A HELP TEXT, on the other hand, is left aligned and shown in a box with borders that is offset from the edge of the screen by 5 pixels and HELP TEXT uses size 7 font.

Display parameters can be defined for individual labels or for groups of labels such as menu or help texts. In addition to width, height and alignment parameters the font that the characters will be shown in also has to be defined.

LabelTool uses the same font files that the phone software uses to display characters of all languages. The characters in each font file are based on a pixel grid enabling the application to determine how many characters can display on a line and to center text horizontally.

The languages have to be defined before the LabelTool file is sent to the translators. Defining a language for a project embeds the Unicode range specific to the chosen language. The embedded character set information frees the LabelTool administrator, the translator and the translation company from ever having to deal with code pages and other character set-related issues.

In addition to the automation of character set handling LabelTool provides support to the translator in the form of descriptions and comments. Since the texts that are

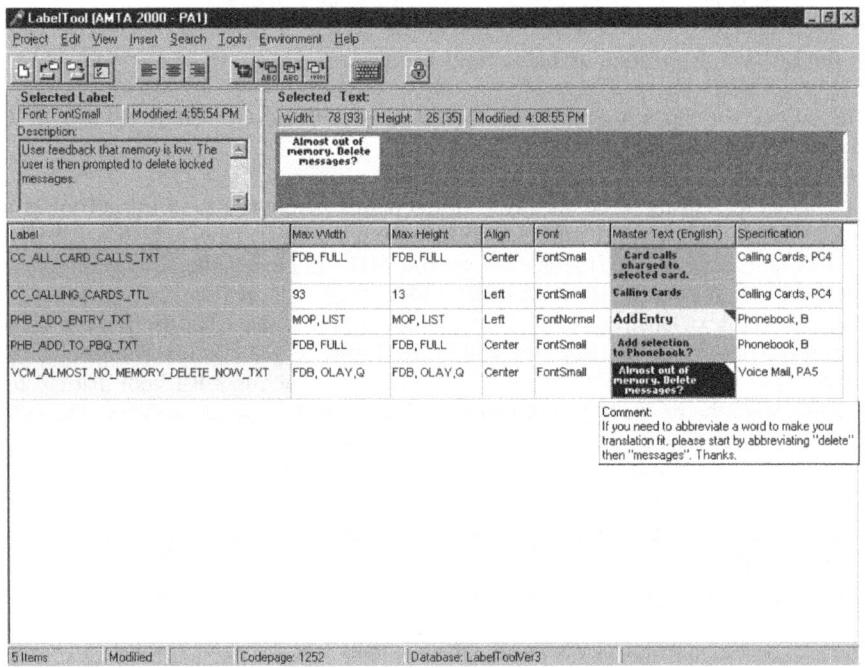

displayed in telephones have to be very concise, they often do not provide enough context for the translators to enable them to do a quality translation. To this end LabelTool also provides descriptions for each label. The descriptions are written to help the translators understand what the text means to the end user. They include information about the text's function and position within the framework of the menus in the phone. If label-specific instructions have to be communicated to the translators, those can be added as comments to the master text field belonging to that specific label. A comment is indicated through a small colored flag.

Since the human factors group and software development will be making changes until the very last moment it is important that those changes also find their way into the LabelTool file. For this purpose we also attach specification information to each label. As new specification revisions are released, we sort our LabelTool project file by specification and compare our labels to the change information in the specification. Once the final changes are implemented the LabelTool file is ready for translation.

Processing

Once all the information has been collected from the specifications, all properties have been set and the master text has been checked for size, spelling and style guide compliance, the file can be exported to the translator. The system attaches the corresponding two-letter ISO language code to each file it creates.

The translators import this file into their abridged version of the LabelTool called TrTool-translator. The translator can only write to the translation column, all other columns are read-only. This avoids accidental modifications which can lead to substantial rework requirements further downstream in the production process. The translator can attach comments to each translation, communicating concerns and questions back to the translation company or the LabelTool administrator.

Any changes made to the original project file are shown in color. Different types of changes are shown in different colors. Once the translations have been completed the translators export files for validation.

The validators use a tool similar to the translator's tool, called the TrTool-validator. The validator can only write to the validation column, all other columns are read-only, avoiding accidental overwrites and reconciliation procedures. The validated file is returned to the translator who will then implement any suggested changes if necessary. The validated translation file is imported back into LabelTool, enabling us to produce output that is suitable for use in the phone software.

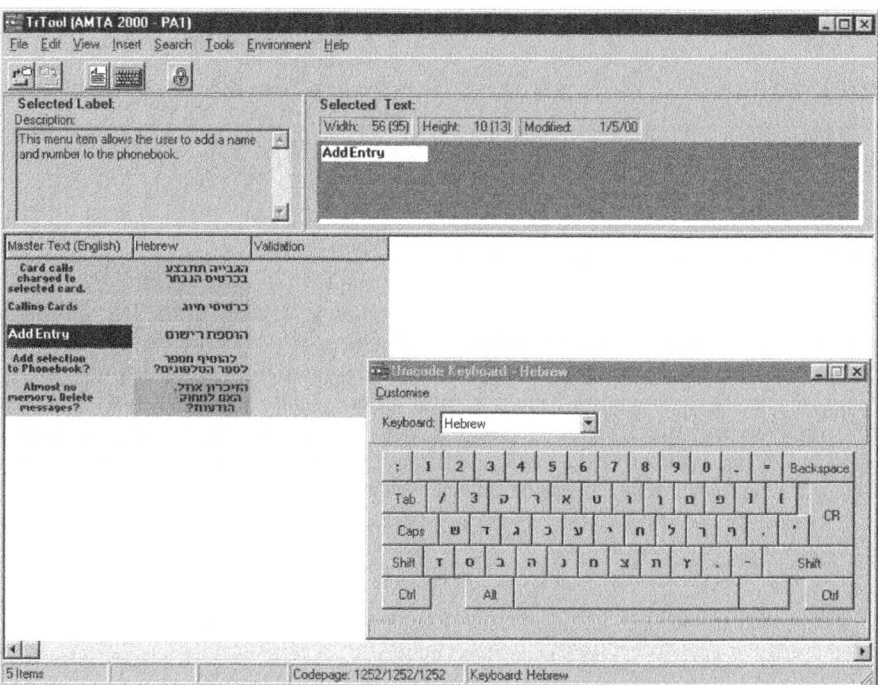

Output

LabelTool creates the resource files that the phone software refers to whenever a text display has been requested by the user. One resource file is created for each language.

LabelTool also outputs all language files for display in HTML format, creating a .jpg file for each master text and each translation. At Ericsson USA we use this feature to publish all master texts and their translations on our internal website for the verification/quality control department. They will compare the actual phone displays with the LabelTool output to ensure that they match.

English Output to Software	Latin American Spanish Output to Software

// String Table
//
STRINGTABLE English
BEGIN
CC_ALL_CARD_CALLS_TXT "Card calls\ncharged to\nselected card."
CC_CALLING_CARDS_TTL
"Calling Cards"
PHB_ADD_ENTRY_TXT   "Add Entry"
PHB_ADD_TO_PBQ_TXT
"Add selection\nto Phonebook?"
VCM_ALMOST_NO_MEMORY_DELETE_
NOW_TXT
"Almost no\nmemory. Delete\nmessages?"
// **********************************
// Export to software file end.
END
	// String Table
	//
	STRINGTABLE Latin American Spanish
	BEGIN
	CC_ALL_CARD_CALLS_TXT
	"Llams tarjeta\ncon cobro a\ntarj. seleccionada"
	CC_CALLING_CARDS_TTL
	"Tarj. de llamada"
	PHB_ADD_ENTRY_TXT
	"Agreg entrada"
	PHB_ADD_TO_PBQ_TXT
	"¿Agreg. sel\nen agenda?"
	VCM_ALMOST_NO_MEMORY_
	DELETE_
	NOW_TXT
	"Casi sin memoria.\n¿Borrar \nmensajes?"
	// *******************************
	// Export to software file end.
	END

Conclusion

With the elimination of language-specific technical aspects from the translation process we can focus on the translation itself. The production and display of foreign language versions has become a one-time painless event that eliminates rework. The next step in the automation of the translation process will be to improve re-use rates by implementing a translation memory function that will propose full and partial matches to the translator for acceptance or modification. A more long-term goal is to integrate the master text translation with the user manual translation.

The LogoVista ES Translation System

Nan Decker

Language Engineering Corporation, 385 Concord Avenue, Belmont, MA 02478
nan@lec.com

Abstract. The LogoVista ES translation system translates English text to Spanish. It is a member of LEC's family of translation tools and uses the same engine as LogoVista EJ. This engine, which has been under development for ten years, is heavily linguistic and rule-based. It includes a very large, highly annotated English dictionary that contains detailed syntactic, semantic and domain information; a binary parser that produces multiple parses for each sentence; a 12,000+-rule, context-free English grammar; and a synthesis file of rules that convert each parsed English structure into a Spanish structure. The main tasks involved in developing a new language pair include the addition of target-language translations to the dictionary and the addition of rules to the synthesis file. The system's modular design allows the work to be carried out by linguists, independent of engineers.

1 Introduction

The LogoVista ES system uses the same parser, English dictionary, and shell for synthesis rules as LogoVista EJ. Its non-binary grammar is converted to binary form for use by a chart parser. Parse trees for each sentence are evaluated by a set of probabilistic experts that apply to grammar rules, lexical entries and other components. The user is presented with the top 20 translations ranked in order of likelihood. The system's modular design allows linguists to work on different language pairs independently of each other and of the engineers.

The LogoVista system has been under development for more than ten years. Translation quality has steadily improved as a result of incremental improvements to the dictionary, grammar, synthesis rules, and parser, rather than as the result of any major design changes.

2 Dictionary

LogoVista ES contains a very large, richly annotated English dictionary that includes many phrases, idiomatic expressions, and multiple senses of words. There are more than 289,000 English inflected forms in the dictionary and more than 140,000 Spanish translations. Improvements are made on a daily basis by a team of linguists and professional translators. Multiple senses of a word are ranked by frequency of occurrence.

J.S. White (Ed.): AMTA 2000, LNAI 1934, pp. 209-212, 2000.
© Springer-Verlag Berlin Heidelberg 2000

2.1 Semantic Information in the Dictionary

Each sense of each adjective in the dictionary is coded with selectional restrictions that describe the semantic types of the nouns it can modify. Each noun is coded with semantic features that specify its semantic category. The match between the adjective's selectional restrictions and the noun's semantic features is scored, and translations with better scores tend to appear in higher-ranked parses. The following examples show how LogoVista's semantics affect translation. Results from five other well-known systems are given for comparison:

- **a hard test**
  LogoVista: una prueba difícil
  The noun "test" has the semantic feature +mental_object and the "difícil" translation for "hard" has the selectional restriction +mental_object. Compare with:
  Sys 1: una prueba difícil   Sys 2 & 3: una prueba dura   Sys 4: una prueba importante
  Sys 5: un análisis/ensayo/prueba difícil

- **a hard floor**
  LogoVista: un piso duro
  "piso" has the semantic feature +artifact and "duro" has the selectional restriction +artifact.
  Sys 1: un piso difícil   Sys 2, 3, 4: un piso duro   Sys 5: un mínimo/suelo duro

2.2 Syntactic Information in the Dictionary

Likewise, each verb is coded with selectional restrictions that specify the kinds of arguments it takes. These match semantic features on nouns to give better translations. Verbs are also subcategorized according to the syntactic structure of their arguments:

- **She turned on the lights. („on" is a movable particle)**
  LogoVista: Encendió las luces.
  Sys 1: Ella conectó las luces.   Sys 2: Ella prendió las luces.   Sys 3: Ella encendió las luces.   Sys 4: Conectó las luces.   Sys 5: Encendía las luces.

- **She turned on the sidewalk. (verb + PP)**
  LogoVista: Dobló sobre la acera.
  Sys 1: Ella conectó la acera.   Sys 2: Ella prendió la acera.   Sys 3: Ella encendió la acera.   Sys 4: Puso la acera.   Sys 5: Giraba en la acera.

- **She turned on her friend. (verb + PP)**
  LogoVista: Atacó a su amigo.

Sys 1: Ella conectó a su amigo.   Sys 2: Ella prendió a su amigo.   Sys 3: Ella encendió a su amiga.   Sys 4: Se volvió en contra de su amigo.   Sys 5: Excitaba a su amigo.

- **Her future turned on the outcome. (Note imperfect translation of stative verb)**
  LogoVista: Su futuro dependía del resultado.
  Sys 1: Su futuro conectó el resultado.   Sys 2: Su futuro prendió el resultado.
  Sys 3: Su futuro encendió el resultado.   Sys 4: Su futuro puso el resultado.
  Sys 5: Su futuro dependía del resultado

2.3   Coverage of Idioms

Both frozen-form idioms and non-literal uses of words and phrases are covered in the dictionary:

- **He kicked the habit.**
  LogoVista: Dejó el hábito.
  Sys 1: El dió patadas el hábito.
  Sys 2: Él pateó el hábito.
  Sys 3: Él dio de puntapiés el hábito.
  Sys 4: Pateó la costumbre.
  Sys 5: Dejaba la costumbre.

- **He looked through me.**
  LogoVista: Miró sin verme.
  Sys 1: Él me miró(examinó).
  Sys 2: Él me examinó.
  Sys 3: Él parecía a través de mí.
  Sys 4: Miró por mí.
  Sys 5: Me ojeaba.

- **He looked through the book.**
  LogoVista: Revisó el libro.
  Sys 1: Él miró(examinó) el libro.
  Sys 2: Él examinó el libro.
  Sys 3: Él parecía a través del libro.
  Sys 4: Miró por el libro.
  Sys 5: Hojeaba el libro.

3 Grammar

The non-binary grammar is converted to binary form for the chart parser. The parser reports up to 20 parses to the user. These are ranked according to scores from a number of experts, which include the semantic feature matching expert, and dictionary probability and grammar rule probability experts. There are more than 12,000 context-free grammar rules and the grammar's coverage is continually being expanded.

- **She dressed and cooked the turkey.**
  Parse #1: She [dressed and cooked] the turkey. -> Aliñó y cocinó el pavo.
  Parse #6: She [dressed] and [cooked the turkey]. -> Se vistió y cocinó el pavo.

- **The news that she left was erroneous.**
  Parse #1: Las noticias que dejó eran erróneas. (relative clause parse, „left" is transitive)
  Parse #6: Las noticias de que partió eran erróneas. (factive parse, „left" is intransitive)

The user interface also gives the user the option of guiding the parser by setting the part of speech for a word or phrase and by grouping words so that they are not interrupted by other constituent boundaries.
  Dialectal differences are supported. The user can control the informal translation of „you" (tú/vosotros, vos/ustedes, tú/ustedes) and request the „voseo" conjugation of verbs:

- **You sing it → Vos lo cantás.**

Dialect settings also influence word choice. The user can request preference for peninsular translations at this time.

- **Her pocketbook has been stolen.**
  Su cartera ha sido robada. (default setting)
  Su bolso ha sido robado. („Spain" dialect setting)

- **Did you get your your train on time?**
  ¿Usted tomó su tren a tiempo? (default setting)
  ¿Usted cogió su tren a tiempo? („Spain" dialect setting)

The parser can be run with one or more domains set to influence word choice. There are over three dozen domains, such as computers, legal, finance, medical, sports. For example, with no domain set, „browsers" is translated as „curiosos." With the computer domain set, it is translated as „navegadores."

LogoVista ES runs on any Intel platform, using any Windows operating system.
Contact systems operations specialist Taro Ikai for further information: taro@lec.com.

L&H Lexicography Toolkit for Machine Translation

Timothy Meekhof and David Clements

Lernout & Hauspie Speech Products
4375 Jautland Drive
San Diego, CA 92121
tmeekhof@lhs.com

Abstract. One of the most important components of any machine translation system is the translation lexicon. The size and quality of the lexicon, as well as the coverage of the lexicon for a particular use, greatly influence the applicability of machine translation for a user. The high cost of lexicon development limits the extent to which even mature machine translation vendors can expand and specialize their lexicons, and frequently prevents users from building extensive lexicons at all.

To address the high cost of lexicography for machine translation, L&H is building a Lexicography Toolkit that includes tools that can significantly improve the process of creating custom lexicons. The toolkit is based on the concept of using automatic methods of data acquisition, using text corpora, to generate lexicon entries. Of course, lexicon entries must be accurate, so the work of the toolkit must be checked by human experts at several stages. However, this checking mostly consists of removing erroneous results, rather than adding data and entire entries. This article will explore how the Lexicography Toolkit would be used to create a lexicon that is specific to the user's domain.

Using the Toolkit

The process of using the Lexicography toolkit begins with corpus creation. The user must gather up a large number of human-translated documents and place them in the toolkit's corpus repository. The corpus repository is a SQL database where documents are represented as tables of sentences. Parallel documents are represented with an additional table that provides alignment links between the sentences that are translations of each other. For those users that have used translation memory systems such as Trados in the creation of their documents, this alignment information is readily available. For others, the toolkit can generate the sentence alignment information between documents automatically.

Once the corpus database is built, the user will use the corpus to create a terminology database. At the end of the process, this database will include all those words and phrases that are unique to the user's documents, or are used differently from their more general meanings.

The first tool used to build the terminology database is the Glossary Maker. The Glossary Maker scans the user's corpus, lemmatizes the words, and counts the number of times each word appears. Then each word is assigned a score defined as

J.S. White (Ed.): AMTA 2000, LNAI 1934, pp. 213-218, 2000.
© Springer-Verlag Berlin Heidelberg 2000

the ratio of the probability of finding the word in the user's corpus versus the probability of finding the word in a more general corpus, supplied as part of the toolkit. The word list is sorted by this score, and the highest scoring words are recorded in the Terminology Database. The user has the option of reviewing the list of words, adding to it or removing erroneous entries.

The second tool in the process of building the terminology database is the Multi-word Lexeme Tool. The job of this tool is to extract a list of the likely multi-word lexemes that appear in the user's corpus. These multi-word lexemes are added to the terminology database, after being reviewed by the user.

The next step in the process of building a terminology database is to determine the appropriate translations for each term. The toolkit includes the Translation Association Tool, which generates a list of likely translations for each entry in the term database. These translations should be verified by a lexicographer. In addition, the Translation Inference Tool will add translation frequency data to the Terminology Database, ensuring that the final MT system will prefer the most common translation of a term according to the user's actual usage.

A final step in the process of building the terminology database is to look for the most problematic words—terms like the word *suit*, which for a clothing retailer could refer to either a legal action or a product for sale. For ambiguous words like these, the toolkit provides a Context Based Sense Disambiguation Tool. This tool looks through the user's corpus, saving information about the local word-usage around each occurrence of an ambiguous word. The aggregate word-usage information is saved in a special table, along with the ambiguous word and its translation. Later, when the MT system needs to decide which of the possible translations to use in a document, it compares the words in the user's document to those stored in disambiguation databases and chooses the translation with the closest match.

Mausoleum – A Corpus Repository

The core of the toolkit is the corpus repository, which stores and provides access to all of the data that the other tools use. The repository is implemented as a SQL database, using Microsoft's SQL Server. A document in the Mausoleum is stored one sentence per record, and a set of relational links is maintained associate each sentence of a document and its translation in another document. These links between sentences can be 1-1, 1-many, and many-1.

The user interface for the mausoleum provides tools to import documents. As part of the importing process, all special formatting information is removed—only the text is relevant to the lexicography toolkit.

Document Alignment Tool

Often, users will have parallel documents, but will not have the documents aligned by sentences. For this reason, the Mausoleum includes a document alignment tool. The alignment tool works in a manner similar to that used in Meyers *et al*, 1998. It scans through both documents, pairing sentences according to a correspondence score. This correspondence score is itself based on the presence of matching translations in a machine translation lexicon.

Glossary Maker – Glossary Generation Tool

As a prerequisite for further lexicographic work, the user must determine the set of terms that are particularly meaningful to the domain of their corpus. To do this, the Miramar Toolkit includes a Glossary Maker. This tool will scan through the corpus, lemmatizing words, and counting their occurrences in the corpus. It will then produce two tables of words. The first is a table of words that the glossary tool does not recognize, often proper nouns and specialized vocabulary. The second table contains words that seem to occur more frequently in the user's corpus than in a base corpus.

At this time, the base corpus is still in development, but table 1 shows a list of the first few words returned running some L&H product manuals through the Glossary Maker:

Table 1: A list of Words Generated by Glossary Maker

L&H	grammar
translation	spelling
translate	noun
translator	verb
menu	Text-to-Speech
dictionary	directory
trademark	dialog
MTP	phrase
text	accurate
edit	inflection
Source/Target	headword
pair	online
entry	Hauspie
pane	German
button	Lernout

Many of the words are of obviously unique interest in discussing L&H's machine translation products. Not surprisingly, *L&H* appears first on the list, and it contains several other words that are of particular importance to L&H products, such as *noun*, *verb*, *inflection*, and *headword*. In addition, words like *menu*, *pane*, and *button* show up on the list because the text comes from a software product manual.

The terminology table returned by the Glossary Maker should be reviewed by a lexicographer, to weed out any erroneous entries. Also, if a user has already created a glossary of important terms, these can be imported into the terminology database as well.

Multi-word Lexeme Tool

Many specialized document domains make heavy use of multi-word terms like *machine translation*. The toolkit provides a tool that will search the corpus and produce a list of the multi-word sequences that are likely to be multi-word lexical units. Table 2 contains a list of some of the interesting word sequences that were found in one of L&H's user manuals:

Table 2: A list of multi-word lexemes

User's Guide	Language Pair
CD-ROM drive	online help
Lernout & Hauspie	Source/Target Language
Restricted Rights	English to/from
Processor Files	Windows NT
United States	registered trademarks
Speech Products	upper pane
Technical Support	Translation Quality
dialog box	Power Translator
Word Processor	Translation Utility

The multi-word lexeme tool uses mutual information to estimate the association level between the words in any sequence of words. Mutual information is given by the following formula:

$$\text{mi} = \log\frac{\Pr(w_1...w_n)}{\Pr(w_1)...\Pr(w_n)}$$

This technique is similar to that used by Brown, *et al* [2], in their discussion of Sticky Pairs. One difference however, is that the Multi-word lexeme tool has the option of working on lemmatized word sequences.

Translation Association Tool

The Translation Association tool uses the parallel nature of the user's corpus. It attempts to match each occurrence of a term in the corpus with its corresponding translation. One important feature of the translation tool is that it does not attempt to discover an entire translation lexicon, since we already have a general-purpose translation lexicon. Instead, it only looks for translations of those terms that the Glossary Maker and the Multi-word Lexeme tool have shown to be of particular interest to the user.

The Translation Association Tool works by building a list of association hypotheses. Table 3 shows a list of the possible association hypotheses for the term *energy problem* and the following sentence pair:

The energy problem has become a major challenge.
Das Energieproblem ist zu einer grossen Herausforderung geworden.

Table 3   A List of One, Two, and Three Word Association Hypothesis for *energy problem.*

Das	Das *Energieproblem*	Das *Energieproblem ist*
Energieproblem	*Energieproblem ist*	*Energieproblem ist zu*
ist	*ist zu*	*ist zu einer*
zu	*zu einer*	*zu einer grossen*
einer	*einer grossen*	*einer grossen Herausforderung*
grossen	*grossen Herausforderung*	*grossen Herausforderung geworden*
Herausforderung geworden	*Herausforderung geworden*	

The next step in the process is to eliminate many of the hypotheses that have reasonable alternative explanations, or that only contain closed-set entries. Thus, possibilities like *ist*, and *zu einer* will be removed immediately. Secondly, the algorithm looks at the other words in the sentence, and uses the existing translation lexicon to establish alternative hypothesis. Thus, it would eliminate *Herausforderung* as a possible association for *energy problem*, because *Herausforderung* is very strongly associated with *challenge* in the translation lexicon.

When the processing is completed on a single sentence, the algorithm will be left with a normally small list of hypotheses, some reasonable and some not. After performing this process on every sentence that contains the key phrase, the translation association tool will produce a database of translation hypotheses and the number of times that each hypothesis was observed in the corpus. The list will then be trimmed to include only those hypotheses that occurred often. These hypotheses are presented to a lexicographer for verification, and frequency information is kept, so that the most common translation of a term is the one most likely to be picked during translation.

Word Sense Disambiguation from Word Context

Many times, simply choosing the most common translation of a term is not sufficient, as homonyms are common even in highly specialized text. A good example of this would be a clothing retailer whose documents contain the word *suit*, referring to clothing or litigation. When words like this appear in the user's glossary of terms, the user can optionally use a word sense disambiguation tool to provide additional information to the translation lexicon.

The first step in using Word Sense Disambiguation is to identify those terms on which it should be used. Usually, these are the terms that the Translation Association Tool frequently associated with more than one translation. Using this list of terms, the disambiguation tool scans through the corpus, and records the lemmatized form of all words that occur in the vicinity of the term in the source language text. These words form a word vector that is associated with the term and its translation. Thus, for the two meanings of the word *suit*, the following words may be in the word vectors:

> suit/*Anzug* – rack, price, tag, shirt, tie, shoes, jacket, etc...
> suit/*Verfahren* – plaintiff, defendant, case, action, etc...

In addition to the words, the number of times that they appear in the context of each term/translation pair is also recorded, so that often-used terms are given greater weight than seldom used terms. Finally, these vectors are normalized to make unit vectors and saved in a separate disambiguation database.

At translation time, the machine translation system will need to decide which definition of the word *suit* should be used. To do so, it will take the all of the words that appear in the vicinity of the word *suit* and build another context vector. This context vector is also normalized to unit length and its dot product is taken with the context vectors of each sense of suit, as stored in the disambiguation database. The sense chosen will be one whose context vector results in the largest dot product with the context of the database. The dot product is defined as the product of the lengths of the vectors and the cosine of their angle. Since the vectors have unit length, choosing the largest dot product is choosing the sense whose vector has the smallest angle in the n-dimensional word space.

Much of the methodology used for word sense disambiguation is based on the work of Yarowski ([3]). However, there is a significant benefit in basing word sense disambiguation on the observed translation. In fact, it is not really so much word sense disambiguation that we are doing as context based translation choice. If two languages happen to have the same sense ambiguity, that ambiguity is not necessarily resolved. Of course, getting the correct translation is the actual goal of machine translation.

Conclusion

One of the things that a user of machine translation can do to improve its quality is to extend the translation lexicons to include the terms that are specific and important to the user. Unfortunately, this often requires expensive lexicography efforts. The Lexicography Toolkit provides a set of tools that can help identify the important simple and multi-word terms and suggest translations for those terms. This does not eliminate the need for lexicographers, but provides them with excellent data from which to work. Additionally, the toolkit provides the ability to use context-based disambiguation to address those words that are frequently ambiguous in the user's documents.

We hope that these techniques will significantly streamline custom lexicography efforts for users of machine translation. Furthermore, we hope that new and better domain specific lexicons will be constructed, using these concepts of mining parallel corpora.

References

1. Meyers, A., Kosaka, M., and Grishman, R.: A multilingual procedure for dictionary-based sentence alignment. In Farwell, d., Gerber, L., and Hovy, E. (eds.), Machine Translation and the Information Soup: Proceedings of AMTA'98. Berlin: Springer (1998) 187-198
2. Brown, P.F., Della Pietra, V.J., deSouza, P., Lai, J., and Mercer, R.: Class-based n-gram models of natural language Computational Linguistics, 18(4) (1992) 467-479
3. Yarowsky, D.: Word-sense disambiguation using statistical models of Roget's categories trained on large corpora. *Proceedings of COLING-92* (1992)

A New Look for the PAHO MT System

Marjorie León

Pan American Health Organization
525 23rd Street, N.W.
Washington, D.C. 20037 USA
leonmarj@paho.org

Abstract. This paper describes some of the features of the new 32-bit Windows version of PAHO's English-Spanish (ENGSPAN®) and Spanish-English (SPANAM®) machine translation software. The new dictionary update interface is designed to help users add their own terminology to the lexicon and encourage them to write context-sensitive rules to improve the quality of the output. Expanded search capabilities provide instant access to related source and target entries, expressions, and rules. A live system demonstration will accompany this presentation.

1 Background

The PAHO MT systems have been in use since 1980. They were originally developed exclusively to meet in-house translation needs. We agreed to make the software available to our first outside user only because their mainframe environment matched ours exactly. The code was converted from PL/1 to C in 1992 when PAHO decided to move its user applications off the mainframe computer. The resulting PC version carried us into the year 2000, and it still works well in PAHO's current environment (Novell NetWare and Windows 95). Our outside users, however, had voiced their desire to have a 32-bit Windows version of the software that would be fully compatible with Windows NT and its future incarnations. Recognizing the importance of MT as a tool for the dissemination of health and biomedical information, PAHO's Director authorized a second conversion (from C to Visual C++) in 1999. Now we finally have a graphical user interface worthy of our translation engine.

2 System Requirements

- Windows 95, 98, NT 4.0 or later
- Pentium processor (or faster) and a minimum of 32 MB of RAM
- CD-ROM drive
- 100 MB of available hard-disk space (ENGSPAN and SPANAM)

J.S. White (Ed.): AMTA 2000, LNAI 1934, pp. 219-222, 2000.
© Springer-Verlag Berlin Heidelberg 2000

3 New Features

The 32-bit Windows version of PAHO's MT systems contains many new features requested by our translation users, network administrators, dictionary coders and trainers, and system developers. The GUI components are written in Microsoft's Visual C++ with MFC. The master dictionaries are stored in Faircom's C-Tree data format for access in multi-user non-server mode. New fields were added to the dictionary record for syntactic and semantic codes, microglossaries, and record history information. The installation CD-ROM includes a utility to convert a current user's dictionaries to the new format.

3.1   For the Translation User

- Spanish or English interface selectable at runtime
- Bilingual context-sensitive help and tooltips
- Macros for translating selected terms or passages in any Word document
- Ability to copy and paste from the MT dictionaries

3.2   For the Network Administrator

- Installation from CD-ROM
- Customizable client setup with silent option
- Hardlock security compatible with TCP/IP and IPX
- UNC or mapped drives and individually customizable work folder
- Automatic detection of user names and centralized usage information

3.3   For Dictionary Coders and Trainers

- Online coding manuals and context-sensitive help in English and Spanish
- Convenient display of all related source and target entries (Fig. 1)
- New search functions to retrieve phrases and rules (Fig. 2)
- Search function to find all instances of a target item
- Dialogs and wizards for adding new dictionary entries
- Only relevant controls displayed for each type of entry
- Translation rules displayed in narrative form
- Automatic nesting of phrases in long expressions
- Utility to import terminology
- Utility to merge the master and user dictionaries

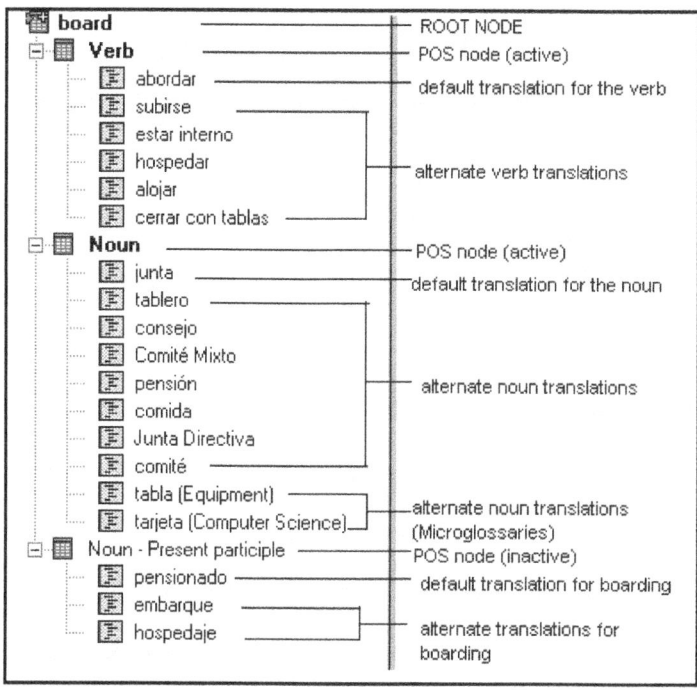

Fig. 1. This panel displays the lexical entry for the English word *board* in a tree control with clickable nodes.

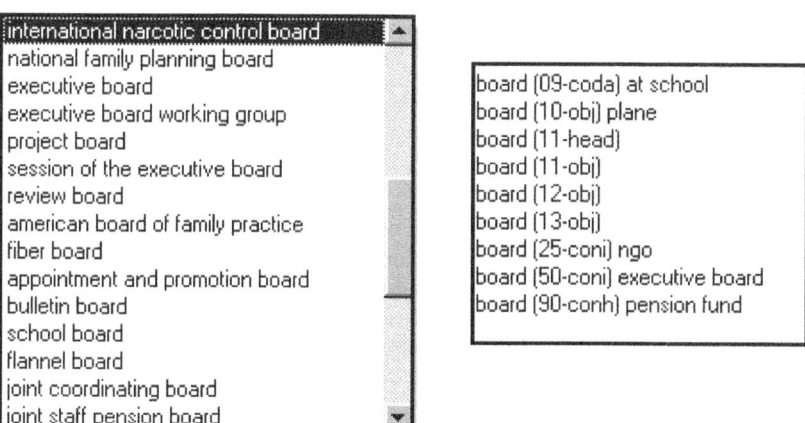

Fig. 2. The panel on the left shows a partial list of phrases containing the word *board*. The panel on the right contains the ordered list of translation rules triggered by *board*. Any item in the list can be displayed by clicking on it.

3.4   For System Developers

The bonus for PAHO's development team is that now we get to use the new dictionary update interface ourselves. We have already begun to improve the ordering of rules and to locate and remove obsolete or redundant entries. The integrated testing environment makes it possible to test new dictionary entries using the appropriate runtime parameters. The new programming environment is helping us diagnose errors and will speed up our efforts to add linguistic enhancements to the software. The functionality of the translation engine has been packaged in a COM object which can be called from a number of scripting languages in order to incorporate translation into other applications.

4   Some Things Remain the Same

The PAHO MT systems are still maintained by language professionals for use by language professionals. They are fully automatic machine translation systems and have fully customizable dictionaries. They are used by PAHO's translation unit to produce faster and more economical translations, and they provide a dependable machine translation tool on the desktop of every PAHO staff member at Headquarters.

The translation engine is still fast and robust, and it produces some of the best quality English-Spanish and Spanish-English raw MT output available. The format of the original file is preserved in the translated file. Along with each raw translation, the program generates PAHO's traditional side-by-side output with diagnostic flags. The dictionary coder has an option to save a listing of the parse and the context-sensitive rules triggered for a sentence for later inspection or transmittal to PAHO. Since postediting is still a necessary step, we continue to provide our popular postediting macros for Word.

5 Acknowledgements

The new version of the PAHO MT systems was made possible through special funding by the Pan American Health Organization and the revenue received from licensing the software. The bulk of the coding was done by a certified Microsoft Solutions Provider under a contract supervised by the author. The new dictionary interface was the brainchild of Julia Aymerich, who also developed the dictionary merge utility. She and Graciela Rosemblat did most of the testing and created the bilingual online help.

Is MT Software Documentation Appropriate for MT Users?

David Mowatt and Harold Somers

UMIST, Manchester, England
{DMowatt,Harold}@fs1.ccl.umist.ac.uk

Abstract. This paper discusses an informal methodology for evaluating Machine Translation software documentation with reference to a case study, in which a number of currently available MT packages are evaluated. Different types of documentation style are discussed, as well as different user profiles. It is found that documentation is often inadequate in identifying the level of linguistic background and knowledge necessary to use translation software, and in explaining technical (linguistic) terms needed to use the software effectively. In particular, the level of knowledge and training needed to use the software is often incompatible with the user profile implied by the documentation. Also, guidance on how to perform more complex tasks, which may be especially idiosyncratic, is often inadequate or missing altogether.

All trademarks are hereby acknowledged.

1 Introduction

It has been said that "MT evaluation is, for all its faults, probably in better shape than MT itself" [1], and indeed a lot of attention has been paid in recent years to the question of evaluating MT software from many different perspectives. One area which, however, we believe has been neglected is the documentation which accompanies MT software.

All software that is produced for the mass market needs to provide adequate documentation so that any difficulties which are encountered by users may be resolved without needing to contact the authors of the software themselves. The case of MT software (and probably numerous other applications), offers a particular scenario where a novice user will be expected both to perform specialist tasks and to be *dependent* on the documentation to learn how to perform these tasks. Elsewhere [2] we propose a methodology for evaluating the adequacy of such documentation, focusing on the particular application area of MT and looking at different commercial software products as a case study. A positive evaluation depends on whether the users, with the aid of the documentation, are able to perform necessary tasks that they were previously unable to perform. The evaluation itself is designed to emphasise what improvements should be made, rather than score different sets of documentation against each other.

J.S. White (Ed.): AMTA 2000, LNAI 1934, pp. 223–238, 2000.

In [2], we consider various aspects of our evaluation method in detail. For the purposes of the present paper, due to space limitations, we focus in particular on the issue of technical expertise, and on the question which forms the title of this paper. A recurring theme is the incompatibility between the level of expertise (especially linguistic expertise, broadly viewed) apparently needed and expected of the users, and the level at which the documentation describes the tasks to be performed.

1.1   Types of Documentation

In the early days of computer science, computer users were often highly trained experts, but soon computer use spread so that, nowadays, access to or even ownership of a computer is no more remarkable than is the case for a television or a car. Users also now expect to be able to use new software as easily as they can use a new car or TV set. Traditionally, and to some extent still at the present time, information about the software is provided in the form of a *user's manual*, originally a printed document packaged separately from the software, though now increasingly (and sometimes exclusively) provided in electronic format as part of the software.

The way this information is presented has changed over the years, and in particular schools of thought about *how* best to present documentary information have evolved. In the early days, the tendency was to describe in exact detail all the functions of the software, the descriptions often being organised in a way that reflected the organisation of the software itself. Carroll [3] calls this the "systems approach", and characterises such documentation as extremely long, decomposing tasks into largely meaningless sub-tasks. Farkas & Williams suggest that this approach "is an outmoded and largely abandoned documentation model" ([4]:182), but one can still find manuals which laboriously take the reader through each of the items in the drop-down menus, sometimes with infuriatingly tautological explanations such as

Cut: Cuts text to the Windows clipboard. ([5]:37).

We can contrast this approach with the "tutorial approach", which involves "realistic task sequences, focused on relevant goals broadly similar to what users will be trying to accomplish with the product" ([4]:183). Here, explicit and exhaustive listing of the functions of the software is replaced by examples of task-oriented procedures, organised according to users' probable needs rather than the software's internal structure. The tutorial is often complemented by a "user's guide", which more thoroughly lists all the functions of the software, but again this may be organised from a task-oriented rather than software-oriented perspective. These two complementary pieces of documentation are often accompanied by a third type, the "quick start" manual. This is generally rather brief, somewhat superficial and, as its name suggests, intended to allow users *quickly* to start to use the software, covering perhaps the most elementary of the software's functions. It is assumed that the user will soon acquire sufficient expertise, either through practise or by following the tutorial, to graduate to the more thorough user's guide.

The idea of the user acquiring expertise by *using* the software is reflected in the "minimalist" approach, pioneered by Carroll's [3] concept of "Exploratory Learning" and the "Minimal Manual". The idea here is that users are impatient to make a start on the task for which they have acquired the software. This is the thinking behind "plug and play": users want to turn immediately to a real task, and will learn as they go along, dipping into the documentation as they feel fit, in an unstructured (modular) manner, exploiting their experience of and expectations from similar software that they have used before, relying on helpful error messages and robust recovery from error on the part of the software.

In fact, there is of course no incompatibility between these approaches. In the modern era of extensive file space, most software comes packaged together with on-line documentation in various formats (a traditional contents page, a structured tutorial as well as an indexed search facility, and help balloons, addressing problems from both the "How do I do this?" and "What is this for?" points of view).

1.2   Types of User

It should not be forgotten that users differ just as much as software does. The distinction between novice and highly trained users can be understood in different ways. The "novice" user may be generally new to computers, or just new to the particular type of task in question. "Highly trained" may imply experience in use of computers in general, or this type of software, or may simply mean a domain expert. This is an important distinction we will come back to. Note also the impact of "house style": the learnability of a piece of software may be enhanced if it belongs to a suite of software tools which share certain design characteristics. This can be seen in the now standardised lay-out of Microsoft Windows software, with the most general functions always to be found in the same place on the (default) toolbars and linked to the same hotkeys.

In particular, it should be noted that not all tasks are equally complex. A lot of the research on documentation and usability has been with generic software tools like word-processors and spread-sheets. These tools have a very wide applicability, and can expect to be used by a wide variety of users. These users will come to the software with expectations and experience, as well as, crucially, an intuitive understanding of the task domain. If their intuitions are mirrored by the software, well and good.

Now consider our own area of interest: MT. Here we have a quite different scenario. The limited software that is currently available shows a tremendous variety of functionality, intended use, appearance, and so on. Users too cannot be easily characterised. Some, but not all, are translators. Few will have had much training in linguistics, and especially not computational linguistics. Experience of using computers may differ. Certainly, expectations of what the software can do will be vastly divergent (depending on what they have read or heard, and what the software vendor claims).

2   Methodology

In [2], we develop a set of criteria by which software documentation can be judged. In parallel, we present results from a pilot case study, in which we evaluated a number of commercially available MT systems: in the present paper we focus on two versions of *French Assistant* [5,6], and the English–Spanish version of *T1* [7]. These systems will be referred to respectively as FA1, FA2,[1] and T1. In the present paper we focus on the technical aspects of the software use and how the documentation[2] addresses these.

The primary concern of our evaluation is that it should be able to say whether the given documentation will allow users to perform certain tasks that would otherwise be difficult or impossible, and if not, why not. Thus we may term it an evaluation that is primarily concerned with *adequacy*. We prefer to make constructive qualitative points, rather than propose a quantitative scoring method. Our methodology did not involve experimental evaluations using volunteers to gain objective scores, though an expert in the domain performing hands-on testing was used.

The secondary concern is that the information can be understood by the user, in our case typically novice users of MT software. This means that we should measure both how easy it is to use, and how effectively it improves performance of the task in question (translation). As mentioned above, the differences in level of expertise and experience of the users in the various relevant domains (translation, linguistics, computer use) mean that clear explanation of terms and choices will be given particular attention. Using MT software essentially involves not just getting texts translated but also customising the software (in particular the lexicon).

Finally, the evaluation should be sensitive to the fact that the paper manuals and on-line help files play different roles and often contain different information. Help files are excellent at providing immediate help with the task currently being performed and at displaying hyperlinked related information. They may also be the *only* source of help for network installations of the program. Manuals are particularly useful at the side of the computer when learning specific tasks, particularly when the program and help file cannot be fitted on the screen at the same time. It is important to know in the course of the evaluation if information is contained in both or only one documentation medium.

We will focus on these three aspects.

3   Criteria and Evaluation

3.1   Level

Here we consider the technical expertise assumed by the documentation. Three factors need to be considered: (i) the competence of the *typical user* in various

---

[1] Where both versions are similar, they are referred to collectively as FA.

[2] We shall use the term "manual" throughout to mean paper documentation, and "on-line help" to mean electronic documentation.

areas, (ii) the competence *stated as being necessary* by the documentation and (iii) the competence *actually needed* to understand the documentation. The profile of the user needs to be established to determine whether the level of expertise required by the documentation matches that of the user of the application.

User profile. To determine the profile of the user, the documentation is examined to see whether it explicitly states that a user needs to possess certain skills. The issue of whether it is *reasonable* for the producers of the software to expect this level of expertise in a typical user is not strictly relevant to an evaluation of the documentation, but it is clearly an issue in software evaluation in general. This level of competence is then compared to the level actually *required* to carry out the relevant tasks when we look at quality and completeness. Knowledge of the operating system, knowledge of the foreign language or competence as a translator, and knowledge of linguistics and grammar, are all examined.

For obvious commercial reasons, MT software is presented in a way that aims to appeal to as wide a range of users as possible. Users are expected to have knowledge of the Windows environment and familiarity with standard menus and conventions, and this is stated explicitly in most of the manuals. Under the heading "What You Should Know Before You Begin", FA1 states:

> You should know the basics of how to operate your computer system, including how to locate files in directories and subdirectories. You should also know how to highlight and select items on the screen with a mouse.

> French Assistant uses the Windows environment. If you are familiar with other Windows applications, you will recognize many of the menus and commands in French Assistant. If you are not familiar with Windows applications, consult your Windows manuals for information on how to use standard Windows commands. (FA1, p. 3)

T1 hedges its bets a little, stating "for *optimum* use of the program, users should be familiar with handling applications under Windows" (p. 20, emphasis added), while elsewhere, these basics are not assumed, as is inferred by the explanation of one of the most elementary tasks shown in Figure 1.

Expertise as a translator. In none of the products surveyed have we found the *linguistic* expertise required to be stated explicitly however. It is assumed that if the users can supply the linguistic information (see below) for words both in the source and target language, then they are sufficiently competent to update the lexicon. This of course is very different from being a translator, who needs not only to know the most common translations of words (as is needed for MT), but nuances between related (though still different) translations, how to structure (and reorder the structure of) sentences, how to vary the translation according to the style of the text, and so on.

Some indication of the perspective taken by the software developers comes from what they say about the software in the first place:

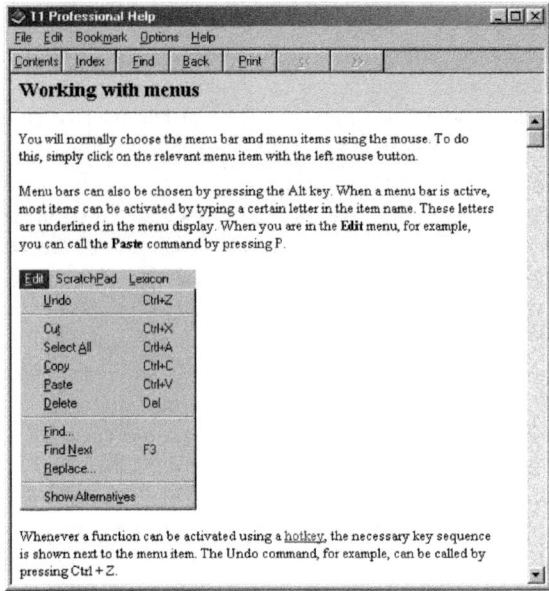

Fig. 1. T1 on-line help file "Working with Menus"

> French Assistant for Windows provides sentence-by-sentence translation to
> *help* you translate English documents into French and French documents
> into English. (FA1, p. 1; emphasis added)

In FA1, this is the nearest we get to any mention of competence as a translator,
though the user is elsewhere warned to "take care" when updating the lexicon
because "good translations rely on the accuracy of the dictionary" (p. 76), and
is warned that the software does not produce "perfect translations". Advice
given on "What You Should Do Before You Translate" (p. 50f) includes using
a spell checker, specifying the direction of the translation, choosing British or
American spelling, checking if the (French) text is correctly accented, and finally,
"if you wish", checking for unknown words and updating the dictionary. We find
it striking that suggestions like these are deemed appropriate, considering what
the user is expected to do elsewhere. Imagine if the user manual for a printer
explained to the user that they need to load paper, or the instructions for a
mobile phone explained how you can only talk to someone if you know their
"telephone number".

Elsewhere in the manual (though not in the on-line help) are "translation
tips" which suggest ways in which the input text can be "structured" to improve
the translation. Interestingly, in FA1, the hints for French-to-English translation
seem to assume that the user is probably not the author of the text, and is
more likely to use the interactive option, while for English-to-French there are
two full pages of explicit suggestions about grammatical constructions that are
(dis)favoured. To be fair, these match the obvious uses which an English-speaking

user (who is not a professional translator) might be expected to make of the software. No mention at all is made of "post-editing" in FA1: all that is said about "What to do with Your Translated Project" (*sic*, p. 60) is that it can be exported to a word processing file and/or printed out.

T1 is also explicit about the quality of the translation ...

> **T1** cannot replace the human translator, but it will produce draft transla-tions from a wide range of texts and documents. The quality of the draft translation will often be *perfectly adequate for your purposes*. If not, it can serve as the basis for a polished final version. (T1, p. 20; emphasis added)

... and the manual writers seem to have a certain kind of user in mind with the second and third sentence. T1 is to be commended for including in its documen-tation some paragraphs explaining what MT is, and what aspects of translation are particularly difficult for the computer:

> Any computer system (*or indeed any human*) attempting to translate at the surface level of a language (*word-for-word translation*) is doomed to failure and ridicule. The results will often be gibberish. [...] What the com-puter needs to be able to do is analyze the surface structures of a sentence in the source language, categorize them, recognize the underlying "deep structures", and transfer these into the surface level equivalent in the target language.

> You might think that this is the sort of thing a computer should be good at. After all, it can easily remember the translations of hundreds of thousands of words. But although a computer is good at remembering things, it is bad at making decisions. And many of the decisions a human makes when translating a particular sentence are simplified by his or her knowledge of the world. (T1, p.20f; italics original)

Expertise as a linguist. Regarding lexicon-editing, the FA1 documentation states that users should "understand how to assign the correct part of speech or attribute to a particular dictionary entry" (p. 78). Linguistic knowledge is required to update the lexicon, and a guide to basic grammar is provided in an appendix, and also under its own "French Grammar" menu in the on-line version. This suggests that the documentation is aimed at people who are familiar with language but who might have no training in formal grammar, though this is not stated explicitly anywhere. One bizarre shortcoming in both versions of FA is that the Glossary in the French Grammar help section contains just one entry, an explanation of the term "conjunction". In FA2, no reference is given to any linguistic knowledge requirements.

The competence required for updating the lexicon in T1 is minimal, and one gets an insight into the sort of user they have in mind when they say, about adding new words to the lexicon, the following:

> Many users, still haunted by memories of grammar classes at school, will be daunted by this idea. But with **T1** there's really no need to worry. Special user-friendly interfaces permit you to work in the lexicon *with a minimum of knowledge and effort.* (T1, p. 102; emphasis added)

Compare the assumed (lack of) linguistic knowledge behind the following explanations of translation options:

> The default setting for the form of Address is Formal. To change the setting to Familiar, Formal-Plural, or Familiar-Plural, click on the circle next to the appropriate setting. [...] When you click on [the Formal] option, the *vous* form is used when the subject is the English word, *you.* ... (FA1, p.64)

> The translation of *you* into Spanish can vary depending on whether the text is written in a familiar style (*tú* or *vosotros*) or a more formal style (*Usted, Ustedes*), and on whether *you* forms in the text are singular or plural. (T1, p. 92)

In general, while the level of required computer competence stated or implicit in the documentation broadly did correspond to the level actually needed, the same cannot be said of linguistic or translation competence. In all the systems evaluated there was a huge variance in this: some very basic linguistic points were explained in great detail, while other, sometimes theory-specific, terms were left unexplained. Paragraphs like the this one, from FA1, were surely not written with novice linguists in mind.

> Slot phrases are used in two distinct situations. The first is for translating prepositional phrases (multiple word prepositions, i.e. [*sic*] up to can be added as a lexical phrase with preposition as the part-of-speech). These slot phrases are similar to lexical phrases, but create more complete internal tree structures. (FA1, p. 94; wording and (lack of) punctuation or font distinction as in original)

Such unhelpful instructions are not to be found in FA2, since all linguistic details are removed and lexicon editing is not explained at all. It is debatable whether useless information is preferable to no information. (see Completeness, section 3.3).

3.2   Quality

Here we are concerned whether all the information that is present in the documentation is described in clear language[3] and whether the number of examples is sufficient to help the user understand the processes or options which are mentioned. Quality of explanations is clearly related to the assumed expertise of the user, and we have already seen some variation in this.

There is much literature about how to measure the effectiveness of what is written or explained in the documentation. Mirel [8] writes:

---

[3] The way the documentation is laid out is also an important question which we consider in [2], though lack of space prevents us from discussing this here.

Three types of questions characterise experimental usability research: 1) does a given manual feature have an effect? 2) how and why does that effect occur? and 3) among manuals that have proven to be effective, which one works best? (p. 110)

Answering such questions would obviously imply that some form of experimental research would be needed to measure "retention of skills" ([4]:187), "speed of overall task performance; number of tasks completed; accuracy; frequency and types of errors" ([8]:111) – but this is not the approach taken here. We consider whether the documentation is (subjectively) clear or not, but will *not* address the issue of what writing style or method should be followed, nor invoke the need for experimental testing. More objectively, the readability and intelligibility of the documentation could be assessed by well-known instruments (also used in evaluating MT output!) such as the Flesch scale [9] or Cloze testing [10] to name just two of many. Another issue to consider in the context of on-line documentation is the use of text colours and background textures, a subject on which there is also a considerable literature (e.g. [11]).

Complexity of the language used. In general, the documentation should be checked for excessively long sentences and paragraphs as well as for clarity of English and the frequency of the use of terms. Any term which is mentioned should be used consistently and explained where it appears: in a glossary (in the paper manual) or in a pop-up window (in the help file). When procedures are being described, potentially ambiguous elliptical style should be avoided, for example:

Connect printer to computer and turn on.

The text from the FA help file was analysed using Microsoft Word's grammar checker and was found to have approximately 1.7 sentences per paragraph and 16 words per sentence. This compares to a very similar 1.9 sentences per paragraph and 15.4 words per sentence for T1's help file. Both though gave results very similar to those of Microsoft Word's own help file and that of the On-line Collins French–English Dictionary, and significantly better (assuming that shorter sentences and paragraphs are easier to read and spread out the information well) than *Visual Basic* and *SkyMap* [12,13] applications, which average approximately 3 sentences per paragraph and 20 words per sentence. Although the text of the paper manuals cannot be analysed as readily, they contain almost identical sentences and are thus, presumably, equally easy to read.

The documentation assumes greatest importance with the most complicated and least intuitive procedures of a program. The only way the user can proceed is by consulting the documentation. Technical details or subtle differences in choices should be explained so that the user can fully understand all the details and nuances. The information in tables, lists and diagrams should be fully explained, with the aid of examples and step-by-step guides to their usage, if necessary. The evaluator should judge whether the examples and explanations given cover all of the technical details that are presented in the documentation.

Use of jargon. As mentioned above, the FA manual states explicitly its expectation that the user is familiar with the Windows environment. Unfamiliar computer terminology is dealt with well, with most concepts being explained or paraphrased in general language. Jargon such as "scroll" and "dialogue box" is occasionally used, but very few other computer terms are employed and so users inexperienced with Windows applications would have no problems. T1's manual also generally explains computer jargon well, and makes particularly good use of screenshots to illustrate terms such as "iconised" and "dialog (box)".

The FA1 manual has a chapter on English grammar which contains explanations of linguistic terms. This is not available on-line, whereas on-line there is a French grammar help file. Neither of these is directly linked to the lexicon editing task however, and, incredibly, they do not even use the same terminology. Linguistics novices may find the use of terminology overwhelming because so many new linguistic terms and concepts are being used in such abundance, as in this example:

> **Root{PofS}** Words with an indicated part of speech will match on any inflection consistent with that part of speech. (FA1, p. 95)

Some linguistic terminology is used but not explained, such as "root" and "inflection" in the above example (which may be familiar to some language learners), and other terms which are more specialised, such as "transformation" and "internal tree structure". Even linguistically trained users will find much of the terminology idiosyncratic, such as "Slot Phrase". As already mentioned, the Glossary in FA has only one entry!

In contrast, T1 makes very good use of examples and screenshots to help explain the different linguistic options, such as for semantic information (e.g. a concrete noun). Even novice users will be able to understand idiosyncratic categories such as "3rd Person Translation settings" which are very well explained.

FA2's online documentation has less complete (though broadly similar) explanations of Windows-based concepts and procedures, but with no section on updating the lexicon, it simply does not mention any linguistic concepts and so its linguistic content cannot be evaluated. Nor does it use pop-up windows to explain terminology. It employs jargon and concepts unfamiliar to a novice user. No guidance (in the on-line help file) is given as to what things are, what the implications of choosing options are, whether it is necessary to enter the information.

> 5. Enter the correct *word class* in the Word Class column (the leftmost column) by clicking the mouse in the text box at the top of the column ...

> 6. You must now enter the appropriate *rule code* to tell the Language Assistant what kind of word or phrase you are adding to the dictionary. Click on the button with the three dots immediately to the right of the text box. The Rules dialog box will appear. *Select the appropriate rule.* (FA2, on-line help file "Edit Dictionary", emphases added)

In fact, the on-line help file directs the user to "Refer to the Language Assistant's User's Guide, chapter 8, for a complete description of the process of adding and modifying words in the dictionary ...", which is of limited benefit to the user who does not have instant access to the printed documentation, as mentioned above.

T1 however has a glossary with excellent coverage of terms which, when they occur elsewhere in the help file, are hyperlinked to the glossary. Jargon is explained with the same consistency in the on-line help as it is in the manual. On the other hand, we found unexplained jargon in error messages such as the following (when we tried to add to the lexicon the phrase *lead a dog's life* = *llevar una vida de perro*):

> Canonical form not possible for this category. Please change the canonical form or the category.

Explanation of procedures. The explanation of technical details[4] is one area where the FA documentation is particularly poor. Simple details and simple tasks are well explained with ample use of step-by-step guides. Procedures ranging from translating a "project" to loading and saving files are explained in this way, but the use of step-by-step guides and examples for explaining more complicated matters, such as how to update the lexicon, is minimal. There are guides which demonstrate how to create simple entries, but totally *inadequate* explanation is given concerning the details of creating the more complicated multiple-word entries. The main failures and criticisms of the FA1 version are listed below:

- The number of example lexicon entries is minimal and in no way comprehensively covers all the different features and details.
- The significance of examples that *are* included is often incomplete. For example, the translation of *baguette* as *wand* in *baguette magique* is shown thus (p. 94):
  baguette   Fem   baguette* magique*: magic wand*
  without any indication that the asterisk indicates which words in the compound can be inflected. Misleadingly, on the next page we see an example where the asterisk has a slightly different interpretation:
  root* Words with an asterisk will match on any inflection. Thus "child*" will also match on "children".
- No information is given as to why the user should enter one thing as opposed to another and what the implications or benefits would be (e.g. why enter "literal" as a translation attribute?). The same example on p. 94 gives no indication why the part of speech (PofS) for *ice* is Noun, but for *baguette* is Fem (it turns out that the French and English dictionaries use different parts of speech).

Headword	PofS	Translation
ice	Noun	ice cream*: glace*(F)
baguette	Fem	baguette* magique*: magic wand*

---

[4] In our case study, "technical" can be taken as meaning "linguistic".

T1 performs much better. All possible options which may be selected by the user are well explained both by a definition and by using plenty of examples:

Intransitive verbs do not require a direct object.

Examples of intransitive verbs are: English *sleep* ⇒ *dormir*, *tumble down* ⇒ *desmoronar*, *fall over* ⇒ *caer*. You sleep. Something tumbles down. You fall over. Spanish: *vivir* ⇒ *live*, *acacecer* ⇒ *happen*, *brillar* ⇒ *shine*. Alguien vive. Algo acaece. Algo brilla. (T1, p. 134f)

Thus where FA's documentation used terms unfamiliar to the user without explaining them, T1's documentation contained thorough explanations aimed at novice users. Procedures telling the user where to click and type in order to create a lexicon entry are well described in both, but the technical details of what to actually enter in the various fields are well explained only in T1.

3.3 Completeness

While "quality" is concerned with whether the information that was provided was adequately explained, this section examines whether all the information necessary for using the software is actually present. This is an obvious requirement of software documentation, but it is hard to give a general indication of how to go about evaluating it. In our case study, we made an extensive hands-on evaluation of lexicon-editing tools.

Difficulties may be encountered that cannot be resolved by reference to the documentation. Information may be missing because the author of the documentation has tried to keep the "chunks of information" concise. For example, when giving step-by-step instructions for a task, the author may choose the most common activities as examples. The author will be unwilling to make the example cover every eventuality as this will render the example difficult to follow and understand. Alternatively, information in tables or lists is often reduced to keypoints as more complete explanations will not fit in the given space. This can lead to important points being insufficiently explained or to less common tasks, problems, or issues being omitted.

A practical evaluation of updating the lexicon in both FA and T1 was undertaken to verify that all the necessary information was indeed in the lexicon. The evaluation attempted to transfer the entire entry for *dog* from a printed bilingual English–French dictionary into the lexicons of the systems under review. Full details of this exercise cannot be given here, but some indicative examples are included.

Entering single words in both applications was easy and the correct translations were obtained. However, only trial and error led to the conclusion that FA required the user to enter a translation in both directions, e.g. *dogwood* = *cornouiller* in the English–French lexicon and the converse in the French–English lexicon, if inflected forms of both words (e.g. *cornouillers*) are to be found. This information should have been in the documentation. Similarly, *I like dog shows* translated incorrectly as *J'aime des exposition canins* (rather than *canin<u>es</u>*) because *exposition = show* was not entered in the lexicon.

Compound nouns caused more problems for FA, while T1 showed itself to be very flexible in this area. In FA1, when the expressions *dog collar* and *dog biscuit* were entered into the lexicon under the entry for *dog*, the singular forms translated correctly but the plural forms did not. If the lexicon entry for *dog collar* is taken out of the entry for *dog* and put into the entry for *collar* then both plural and singular forms translate correctly. It is not clear why this should be the case, and nothing about this is explained in the documentation. In FA2, interestingly, these problems did not arise, which suggests that they may have been due to faults in the software and not to poor documentation. Evaluations of software documentation must therefore always be extremely careful not to assume that things not working the way they should are due to poor or insufficient documentation – this *may* be the case, but bugged software can be an equally likely cause.

More complicated expressions often caused problems in FA. A "Slot Phrase" in FA is a type of lexicon entry consisting of a verb and its objects, such as: *be* dogged by ill fortune: être* poursuivi* par la malchance.* The * indicates the words which inflect and agree. However, *she is dogged by ill fortune* translates as *elle est pour<u>suit</u> par le* [sic] *malchance* (should be *pour<u>suivie</u>*) or, if the lexicon entry is constructed differently, as *elle est poursuivi par la malchance.* We did not manage to create an entry successfully, even though it was theoretically possible. This discrepancy might again be put down either to poor documentation (because agreement in slot phrases is not explained in the documentation) or to poor software.

All in all, the information required to create moderately complex lexicon entries was *simply not present* in FA1, and the FA2 documentation was even less helpful, lacking information even about more simple tasks. The only, very unsatisfactory, option is to try and infer how to create entries by looking at existing entries.

T1 did not allow such complex forms. As mentioned above, trying to enter *lead a dog's life = llevar una vida de perro* gave an error message. The documentation therefore failed to mention its limitations, i.e. that while compound nouns (e.g. *washing machine*) or verbs (e.g. *copy edit*) could be encoded, entries for verbs with their subjects or objects could not (e.g. *to be top dog = ser el gallo del lugar*).

Inaccurate information. Perhaps worse than missing information is information that is incorrect: this is a very obvious point, but one where for example FA1 fails. The "translation attributes" for nouns, for example, include a check box for Neuter as well as Masculine and Feminine, though this attribute is not included in the documentation: the screen shot shown (Figure 2) is not exactly like the screen that actually pops up (Figure 3).[5]

---

[5] There are some other, though trivial, differences.

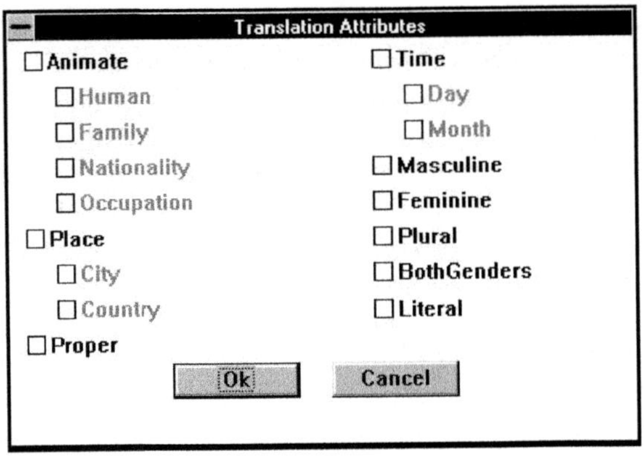

236   D. Mowatt and H. Somers

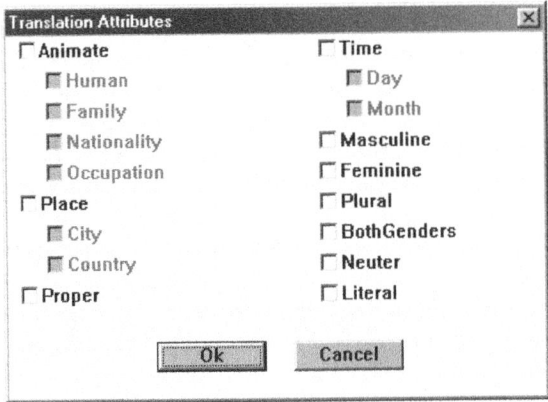

Fig. 2. Translation Attributes window as shown in FA1, p. 86.

Fig. 3. Translation Attributes window as it actually appears

Information about limitations. Given that some users will be less able at completing the task than others, there should be a list of questions and answers that the user can consult if needed.[6] If the limitations of the software are going to cause problems for the user, the documentation should both explain what is and what is not possible with the software, as well as presenting solutions for working round the limitations. This is not necessarily what happens most in practise:

---

[6] Note that some products, such as Microsoft Word, can now allow users to search the on-line documentation not by keywords but also by asking questions, which are then analysed and a list of possible answers given. Such "intelligent" assistance cannot yet be expected from anything but the largest of programs.

Manuals must map the myriad tasks presented in the manual to their own particular goals, and [the users] very often have goals that are not precisely supported by the procedures in the manual. [4]:184.

Note that this is a particularly interesting requirement since, from a marketing point of view, it may not be in the interests of the software producers to be explicit about their software's shortcomings. Yet this kind of information is almost as valuable as details of what the software *can* do. Furthermore, it can be argued that such information would only be discovered by most users *after* they buy the product as it would reside inside the documentation and not on the outside of the packaging.

As was illustrated above, it is apparent that some of the difficulties are not due to the user but to the limitations of the system. The only mention of possible shortcomings is where the documentation mentions that translations may not be "perfect". Other programs, including many from Microsoft, have documents that list known bugs and problems; sometimes these are available on a web page which is regularly updated, accompanied by a "frequently asked questions" page. FA1 has such a section, but the questions are thinly disguised rewordings of previously covered functions. To be fair, it must be difficult, when producing a new type of software, to predict what sort of questions will be frequently asked.

4 Conclusion

Evaluation of documentation is not a new idea, though we are not aware of any other studies evaluating documentation of MT systems. This paper has not been particularly formal in its approach, yet we hope to have raised awareness of some difficult problems, in particular the question posed by our title: Is MT software documentation appropriate for MT users? We feel that our most important finding has been that the answer to this question is more or less negative. In fact we have been quite shocked at the way the documentation (and packaging?) have given the impression that this is software that can be used by a complete novice, whereas in truth what is needed is a quite considerable understanding of what translation involves from at least a philosophical point of view, if not form a linguistic and above all computational linguistics point of view.

Of course, we are not the first to comment on the importance of MT software vendors' honesty and openness about their products. This seems to have been interpreted by most vendors as requiring them to admit that the systems cannot be guaranteed to provide a good translation. But it might be more accurate to observe that in fact the software works best in the hands of someone with quite sophisticated background knowledge and understanding of language(s) and linguistics. It would be interesting to see if the distinction made by many vendors between products aimed at casual vs. "professional" users (which often boil down to size of dictionary, and of course, price tag) are reflected in the way the documentation addresses its readership. There is, we believe, a place in the market for "quick and dirty" MT systems; but we think that more sophisticated users should be catered for not only with a different product but also with a different level of documentation.

It is interesting to compare MT documentation with the manual accompanying character-set software such as Macintosh's Japanese Language Kit [14], which quite reasonably assumes from the very first sentence that the user understands and is familiar with the peculiarities of the Japanese writing system (though not with the Macintosh operating system, for example). We hope that software developers might find some of our observations useful and indicative, so that MT system documentation may be better in the future.

References

1. Wilks, Y.: Developments in machine translation research in the US. Aslib Proceedings. **46** (1994) 111–116
2. Mowatt, D., Somers, H.: Criteria for evaluating MT documentation. In prep.
3. Carroll, J. M.: The Nurnberg Funnel: Designing Minimalist Instruction for Practical Computer Skill. MIT Press, Cambridge, MA. (1990)
4. Farkas, D. K., Williams, T. R.: John Carroll's The Nurnberg Funnel and Minimalist Documentation. IEEE Transactions on Professional Communication. **33** (1990) 182–187
5. French Assistant for Windows User's Guide. Globalink, Inc., Fairfax, VA. (1995)
6. French Assistant Deluxe For Windows User's Guide. Lernout & Hauspie. (1999)
7. Langendscheidt's T1: Text Translator for PC English–Spanish Spanish–English. GMS Gesellschaft für multinguale Systeme mbH/Langenscheidt KG, Berlin. (1997)
8. Mirel, B.: Critical Review of Experimental Research on the Usability of Hard Copy Documentation. IEEE Transactions on Professional Communication. **34** (1991) 109–122
9. Flesch, R.: The Art of Readable Writing. Harper Brothers, New York. (1949)
10. Taylor, W. L.: "Cloze Procedure": A New Tool For Measuring Readability. Journalism Quarterly. **30** (1953) 415–433
11. Hill, A. L., Scharff, L.F.V.: Readability of computer displays as a function of colour, saturation, and background texture. Proceedings of the Second International Conference on Engineering Psychology and Cognitive Ergonomics. Oxford, England. (1998)
12. Visual Basic v. 3.0. Microsoft Corporation. Redmond, WA. (no date)
13. SkyMap (shareware program). Chris Marriott. Cheshire, U.K. (no date)
14. Macintosh Japanese Input Method Guide. Apple Computer Inc. Cupertino, CA. (1993)

Evaluating Embedded Machine Translation in Military Field Exercises

M. Holland, C. Schlesiger, and C. Tate

Army Research Laboratory
2800 Powder Mill Road
Adelphi, MD 20783
mholland@arl.mil, cschles@arl.mil, ctate@arl.mil

Abstract. "Embedded" machine translation (MT) refers to an end-to-end computational process of which MT is one of the components. Integrating these components and evaluating the whole has proved to be problematic. As an example of embedded MT, we describe a prototype system called Falcon, which permits paper documents to be scanned and translated into English. MT is thus embedded in the preprocessing of hardcopy pages and subject to its noise. Because Falcon is intended for use by people in the military who are trying to screen foreign documents, and not to understand them in detail, its application makes low demands on translation quality. We report on a series of user trials that speak to the utility of embedded MT in army tasks.

1 Introduction

"Embedded" machine translation ([14]) refers to an end-to-end computational process in which input goes through stages of processing that include MT. Integrating these processes and evaluating the whole has proved to be problematic, due in part to the difficulty of predicting error interactions across stages of processing ([10], [14], [15]). In this paper, we report data and illustrate problems in evaluating embedded MT in job tasks, drawing on our experience with a prototype document translator known as Falcon (Forward Area Language Converter).

Following the insight of Church and Hovy ([4]) that MT is best assessed not in terms of absolute features of the output but in terms of how well the output serves an application, task-based MT evaluation has received growing attention ([11]; [12]; [13]; [15]). To date, the tests conducted and the methodology developed involve laboratory studies that reproduce selected dimensions of real-world tasks and of embedding processes. In fact, laboratory studies appear necessary at this point to control for the multiple interacting factors that characterize an application. Nevertheless, lessons can be drawn from observing embedded MT in use by people doing jobs. The data we report come from a series of army exercises into which Falcon was inserted.

J.S. White (Ed.): AMTA 2000, LNAI 1934, pp. 239-247, 2000.
© Springer-Verlag Berlin Heidelberg 2000

2 Falcon: An Embedded MT System

2.1 System Goals and Fit to Task

Falcon is a hardware-software prototype developed for the U.S. army that permits paper documents in selected languages to be scanned, processed by optical character recognition (OCR), and automatically translated into English ([7]). Thus, MT is embedded in the preprocessing of hardcopy pages and the noise that OCR errors create. Falcon is intended for use by people in the military who encounter documents in languages they do not understand. Instead of calling on a human translator in every case, they can use Falcon to screen – that is, to predict the informational relevance of a document. Only documents identified as relevant need be sent to human translators, thereby conserving a valuable army resource.

Relevance screening corresponds to the lowest points on the scale proposed by Taylor and White ([12]), which ranks text-handling tasks in terms of the quality of MT demanded. Filtering, which consists of discarding irrelevant documents, is ranked as least demanding (most tolerant of MT errors), followed by detection, which consists of finding documents of interest. Relevance screening combines filtering and detection. Because of its low demands, we felt that screening would make an apt application of *embedded* MT: that it would be robust to errors cascading through the linked processes of scanning, OCR, and translation.

2.2 System Design

Hardware. Falcon couples an off-the-shelf laptop computer with a scanner, battery pack, and power cables. These parts are protected in a padded metal case, ruggedized to withstand use in field environments. The current hardware weighs about 25 pounds.

Software components. Documents are processed in three phases, each with a separate software package: (a) scanning, (b) OCR, and (c) translation, which converts source text to English text and supports key word searches. Different off-the-shelf or experimental packages can be inserted. The version of Falcon reported on here uses a mix of commercial products designed for the PC. Languages addressed in the exercises we observed include Arabic, Croatian, Russian, Serbian, and Spanish. To cover this range, Falcon integrates two distinct products for OCR with two for translation. A fifth product performs scanning.

Software integration. The first purpose of Falcon integration is to allow simple, quick operation in the stress of a field environment. Toward this end, integration reduces the software packages with which the user must interact to a single interface. Currently, a user indicates the source language of the document to be input and the list of keywords to use for searching. The interface then sets each software package appropriately, and the user begins scanning. Eventual inclusion of automatic language identification should further simplify the procedure.

Another purpose of integration is to give a second, more flexible level of processing: Paths are provided by which users can correct and edit the results of scanning and OCR to reduce error build-up before translation.

A third purpose is to keep the three main components modular. Thus, new modules can be inserted to upgrade existing software or to test different products for OCR and MT. Modularity further permits users to enter at any stage of processing. Given electronic text, for example, users can go straight to translation. (For more information on Falcon, see Weisgerber, Yang, & Fisher, this volume.)

3 Evaluating Embedded MT: Emerging Results

The software components of Falcon are being evaluated in the lab, individually and in interaction, using linguistic output measures ([15]). At the same time, Falcon has been inserted in full into U.S. army field trials. These trials are of two kinds. First are *international missions* flexible enough to allow informal tryouts of new technologies. Users send back comments to developers. Second are *domestic exercises* in preparation for international missions. These exercises afford on-site data collection with formal instruments like opinion surveys. We present a series of observations from both kinds of trials, conducted over a three-year period.

3.1 User Comments on Falcon in International Missions

Falcon was tried in Bosnia, Haiti, and Central America between 1997 and 1999. Each tryout was preceded by a brief training period to familiarize operators with the system. Missions dealt with peacekeeping, disaster relief, refugee processing, intelligence collection, and coalition operations. Documents processed included memos from coalition partners, personal identity papers, open-source materials like newspapers, and local records like police files and hospital reports.

Laboratory findings. To prepare for the 1997 tryout in Bosnia, Falcon was equipped with OCR and MT for Serbian and Croatian ([6]). The OCR and MT were pre-commercial. Tests in the lab suggested that performance of these components would be adequate to support document screening. First, OCR testing on a small set of native documents showed that, despite errors rates of >50% on two low-frequency characters in Croatian and two low-frequency characters in Serbian, overall page error rates were low enough (<5%) to yield sufficient text for translating key words. Second, although there are no standard metrics for MT quality, the commercial developer of the Serbian and Croatian MT ranked the delivered system at 40%, or "pre-prototype quality" – an internal company benchmark for measuring progress in one language and comparing the status of different languages. Because the developer began with military and technical vocabulary, more significant for topic identification than core vocabulary (cf. [13]), we felt that the system could serve screening.

Comments from the field. A small group of soldiers tried the prototype in Bosnia. Their synopsis indicated that "the present configuration [with OCR errors going to MT] translated less than 50% of a document, which does not permit a good analysis of the document...or even whether it may be of value for translation." Conversely, when OCR errors were corrected by hand, "…[MT] translated about 80% of the text," or sufficient for screening, although "some key words were not translated such as 'police.' " Common in our experience with user feedback, the translation rates cited were derived by feel rather than by counting. To illustrate their observations of Falcon performance *with OCR errors*, users provided an article from a 1997 Serbian newspaper together with the OCR result and the English output, judged not good enough for screening (Fig. 1 shows the first paragraph). To illustrate their observations of Falcon performance *with OCR correction*, users provided a 1997 Croatian magazine article together with the English output, judged good enough for screening (Fig. 2 shows the first paragraph).

---

3 >>Njn >>chlrstog the representation Serbian >>to nl~~io~~al~~ih of interest, .>>mr MomchiloKrajis^iik, president from >>To re~~u6like >>Srpsks in The presidency >>To biH, from >>to med~u~~arod~~ih of negotiator, >>pa and from the authority of Belgrade, got >>nadimlk >>@Mmsg >>No@.

[Human translation: Mr. Moncilo Kravicinik, President of the Serb Republic (SR), in the joint Bosnia Herzogovina (BH) Presidency, has received the nickname "Mr. No" from international negotiators and even from Belgrade authorities because of his strong advocacy of Serb national interests.]

Fig. 1. MT-produced English (*without* OCR error correction) judged unacceptable for screening (NOTES: ~ signals characters not recognized by OCR; >> signals words not found by MT; Cyrillic in Serbian source displayed as ASCII in 1997 prototype.)

The Armed Forces Of the republic Serbian in >>ponedjeljak celebrated The day army in Prijedor, where is kept military parade with 2,500 soldiers >>VRS, for that >>Sfor issued >>odobrenje. >>@lako all soldiers will carry weapon, ammunition is not permitted, as not heavy armament.

[Human translation: SFOR approved an Army parade by Serb Republic forces on Monday in Prijedor. 2,500 soldiers will take part and will carry weapons, although they will not be allowed to carry ammunition nor heavy weapons.]

Fig. 2. MT-produced English (*with* OCR error correction) judged acceptable for screening (see NOTES to Fig. 2)

The end result for embedded MT was users' judgement that manual OCR correction took so long, it rendered "the current system…less than desirable for the intended function." Nevertheless, these users wanted automation: "The concept of the Falcon computer is still valid."

The MT bottleneck: Noisy input. We inferred that when MT is embedded in a system with real-world documents as input, even the limited screening function can be impeded by OCR errors. Compared with documents we tested in the lab, the documents encountered in Bosnia were lower quality for many reasons. Some arrived as "pocket litter" or "desk litter" – creased, smeared, torn, wet, soiled, or otherwise compromised. Moreover, as is typical of third-world, developing, or conflict-torn regions, documents are often produced through substandard printing processes with poor quality paper like onion skin. Samples of documents from Haiti had similar characteristics.

Noisy input of this kind appears to demand some combination of pre-OCR image enhancement, improved OCR, and stronger MT. Later versions of Falcon for Serbian and Croatian have included improvements to OCR and MT.

Supporting our notion of the OCR bottleneck were tryouts of Falcon in Central American. There, soldiers processed mainly electronic texts, bypassing OCR. Moreover, the Spanish MT they used was a commercial product, ranked at 80%, or "production quality," by the same developer as for Serbian and Croatian. These users, some of whom were trained in Spanish, deemed Falcon adequate, as summarized here: "The translation software applied to the 50-page Chapter 6 [of a technical manual]...has received several very positive reviews...The software took 6.5 minutes to complete the translation. Considering the very short time...to translate, it was one huge leap.... the product offers about an 80-85% translated version."

We drew preliminary conclusions from these field trials:

1. The most troublesome embedding factor in Falcon is noisy images produced by low-quality documents. This noise is not predictable from a small set of documents used to test performance in the lab.
2. Applied to clean text, commercial MT of varying grades is acceptable to soldiers screening and even translating documents. Pre-commercial quality is acceptable given a lexicon of domain-relevant terms.

3.2 Opinion Surveys of Falcon in Domestic Field Exercises

Falcon was among several prototype technologies inserted into three military field exercises conducted sequentially in the U.S. during 1999 and 2000.[1] The main purpose of these exercises was to train soldiers in operational scenarios that they might encounter overseas. Although more controlled than a mission like Bosnia, the exercises were still removed from laboratory experiments: They were conducted continuously over days or weeks rather than in one or two discrete sessions; they took place outdoors or in tents or temporary quarters; they treated a range of authentic documents, often shipped from overseas sites; finally, they featured variations in users, tasks, and input that complicate comparisons and conclusions.

For the field exercises, Falcon software was installed on a range of Windows-based platforms, from a small palmtop computer to a large portable office system fielded specifically for army intelligence.

---

[1] These technologies were selected by the U.S. Counterintelligence-Human Intelligence (CI-HUMINT) Advanced Concepts Technology Demonstration, begun in 1999 to assess tools for intelligence collection across the services.

An independent evaluator (Detachment 1, Air Force Operational Test and Evaluation Center, or AFOTEC) surveyed users' opinions of the prototype technologies at the end of each exercise ([1], [2]). Data collection centered on the question, "Do the participant technologies demonstrate potential military utility for counterintelligence-human intelligence operations?" This question was probed on three dimensions, standard in military assessments: the *effectiveness*, *usability*, and *suitability* of each tool or device.

A uniform questionnaire was used in each exercise, with minor tailoring for specific technologies. The 18-item questionnaire for Falcon contained six questions on effectiveness, covering aspects such as translation capability, support for decision-making processes, ability to enhance the mission, and vulnerabilities. Thirteen questions on usability and suitability addressed human factors and logistical aspects such as simplicity of set up, ease of learning, ease of use, speed of operation, ruggedness, transportability, and inter-connectivity. Operators were asked to rank each aspect on a four-point Likert scale (Strongly Agree, Agree, Disagree, Strongly Disagree). They also wrote comments to elaborate their opinions.

3.2.1 The Fort Bragg Exercise

Setting. The first domestic field exercise, conducted at Fort Bragg, North Carolina, during October and November, 1999, targeted Arabic and Serbian/Croatian documents. To provide this capability, Falcon incorporated MT and OCR software from four different commercial developers. True to the dynamism of field exercises, the scenario early on shifted away from document translation and toward oral interaction. Thus, users' opinions were based on limited experience, and not all the 12 operators polled answered every question.

Results. Summed across the 13 questions on usability and suitability, 72% of the responses were positive. Examination of individual questions showed unanimous satisfaction with speed of operation, ease of use, and clarity of the interface -- aspects that had been the focus of development of Falcon's integration software.

Responses to the six questions on effectiveness were less conclusive. When responses were aggregated, only 53% percent were positive. Examination of individual questions revealed common dissatisfaction with the Arabic capability, as opposed to the Serbian or Croatian. Users experienced crashes every time they tried an Arabic translation, crashes that did not appear during software testing in the lab. Behind this instability were problems indigenous to Arabic processing software. Both the OCR and the MT products were written for the Arabic Windows operating system, whereas Falcon and army-standard platforms use English windows. When installed on English Windows, the Arabic products do not display Arabic script. A modification of the Falcon integration incorporating Microsoft's Internet Explorer 5.0 solved the problem in our laboratory but led to incompatibilities with security software on the army portable office system used in the exercise. The effectiveness of Arabic character recognition and translation was therefore not tested. Nevertheless, for the single question pertaining to Falcon's enhancement of the mission, all opinions were favorable. This question appears to have been interpreted as one of overall potential rather than current function.

3.2.2 The Fort Huachuca Exercise

Setting. The second field exercise, conducted at Fort Huachuca, Arizona, during March, 2000, targeted Serbian, Croatian, and Spanish documents. Unlike the Fort Bragg exercise, this one involved processing of nearly 50 documents. Five operators participated in document translation tasks and answered the Falcon survey.

Results. Responses to questions on all dimensions were overwhelmingly positive. Aggregate responses were 96% favorable on usability and suitability questions and 95% favorable on effectiveness questions. These high ratings can be attributed in part to the relatively strong, stable software components for the pertinent languages. The Spanish OCR and MT packages were production-quality and commercially successful. The Serbian and Croatian OCR and MT had been improved since the Bosnia tryout, resulting in more accurate recognition of infrequent characters and in MT ranked at 55%, or "prototype level," by company-internal metrics. In addition, documents were less compromised in quality than some collected in Bosnia in 1997.

Users appreciated the utility of imperfect MT: "Enough was usually translated to allow for an effective first screening...A real linguist would have to do the actual translation." Users demonstrated ownership of embedded MT by inventing new software configurations and performance measures. For example, they installed Falcon software on a palm PC Casio Fiva platform and reported processing 40 Serbian and Croatian documents end to end in 9 ½ minutes, with a perceived translation accuracy of 80%. They estimated that it would take much more time for one of their language specialists to provide equivalent translations. In addition, when faced with wrinkled and rolled papers that would not scan, they tried a Sony PC 100 mini-digital video camera to capture JPEG images for input to Falcon, yielding an OCR and translation accuracy rate they deemed good enough for document screening.

3.2.3 The Fort Gordon Exercise

Setting. The third exercise, conducted at Fort Gordon, Georgia, in May, 2000, targeted Arabic and Russian documents. A large part of the exercise was devoted to document exploitation, that is, extracting intelligence information from texts. Provided for exploitation were hundreds of Arabic documents captured in the Gulf War and a smaller set of Russian documents. The typical user in this exercise was a specialist in the relevant language. The screening task, preceding full exploitation, required identifying specific kinds of information and appeared closer to extraction tasks on the Taylor and White scale. In support of the Fort Gordon test, fixes had been made to Falcon's Arabic configuration, which failed in the first exercise.

Results. Aggregated over nine users, 82% of responses were favorable on usability and suitability questions. As in the other exercises, opinions on ease of learning, ease of use, and clarity of interface were uniformly positive. However, only 68% of responses were favorable on effectiveness. These responses differed by language. For example, only 33% of respondents said Arabic translation was adequate, whereas 100% said Russian was adequate. Even respondents trained in Russian found less-than-perfect translations useful: "Being a Russian linguist, I could use Falcon to identify items in one document while I translate another," wrote one. "It could save lives," wrote a second.

The poor showing of Arabic was due to a combination of factors. The 10-year-old Gulf War documents presented an array of noise for OCR – aging paper, pages with bullet holes, handwriting mixed with print. The MT system, still young, was not strong enough to compensate for OCR errors. Inherent features of Arabic script, orthography, and syntax make this language less tractable than other languages for both OCR and MT. Moreover, laboratory tests of the components did not predict what the exercise showed. For example, Kanungo, Marton, and Bulbul ([9]) measured performance of the Arabic OCR product at approximately 85% accuracy on a large set of authentic documents. Doyon, Taylor, and White ([5]) measured performance of the MT product (actually, a less mature version than the one used at Fort Gordon) by comparing it to human translators. They found the MT output equivalent in informativeness (as measured by a comprehension test) to a "novice translator," a skill level comparable to many Arabic specialists in the army. Our prediction had been that linking these components would be good enough for screening.

Ownership of embedded MT was again demonstrated when operators faced with oversize pages in Russian acquired a Hewlett-Packard hand-held scanner to stitch together sections of a page, then input the scanned images wirelessly to Falcon on a Fiva. The English output, they judged, was adequate for screening.

4 Inferences about Embedded MT

Field trials present uncontrolled and often unknown variations – in users' backgrounds, the nature of their tasks, the languages employed, the quality of the documents processed, the requirements of the scenario. These variations hinder comparisons and conclusions. Nevertheless, we can draw preliminary inferences about embedded MT from data obtained informally and formally from soldiers trying Falcon outside the lab:

- The most problematic embedding factor in Falcon is noisy images from scans of low-quality documents. Although degradation models can predict OCR performance on some low-quality pages ([8]), it is not clear that these apply to the range of noise that we observed.
- Component measures obtained in the lab, even on statistically reliable samples, do not necessarily predict component performance in embedding contexts (a point emphasized by Voss & Van Ess-Dykema, [15]).
- Soldiers, even those who are language specialists, may be ideal customers for embedded MT. They differ from the analysts described by, e.g., Vanni ([13]) and Taylor and White ([12]): Soldiers want automated translation; they are tolerant of lower quality translations; they can apply such translations to document screening; they create new forms and configurations for embedded MT on the fly to fit changing contexts.

References

1. AFOTEC, Det 1: CI-HUMINT Collection Demonstration: Final Report. Kirtland Air Force Base, NM (December, 1999)
2. AFOTEC, Det 1: CI-HUMINT Demonstration - Southern Knight: Demonstration Report. Kirtland Air Force Base, NM (June, 2000)
3. AFOTEC, Det 1: HICIST Demonstration C4ISR Rock Drill: Demonstration Report. Kirtland Air Force Base, NM (March, 2000)
4. Church, K., Hovy, E.: Good Applications for Crummy Machine Translation. In: Neal, J., Walter, S. (eds.) Proceedings of the Natural Language Processing Systems Evaluation Workshop. Calspan-UB Research Center (1991)
5. Doyon, J., Taylor, K., White, J.: The DARPA Machine Translation Evaluation Methodology: Past and Present. Proceedings of the Workshop on Embedded Machine Translation: Design, Construction, and Evaluation of Systems with an MT Component. In conjunction with the Association for Machine Translation in the Americas Annual Meeting. Langhorne, PA. (1998)
6. Fisher, F., Voss, C.: Falcon, an MT System Support Tool for Non-linguists. Proceedings of the Advanced Information Processing and Analysis Conference, McLean VA (1997)
7. Holland, M., Schlesiger, C.: High-Mobility Machine Translation for a Battlefield Environment. Proceedings of NATO/RTO Systems Concepts and Integration Symposium, Monterey, CA. Hull, Canada: CCG, Inc. (ISBN 92-837-1006-1) (1998) 15/1-3
8. Kanungo, T., Haralick, R.M., Phillips, I.: Nonlinear Local and Global Document Degradation Models. Int'l. Journal of Imaging Systems and Technology 5 (1994) 220-233
9. Kanungo, T., Marton, G.A., Bulbul, O.: OmniPage vs. Sakhr: Paired Model Evaluation of Two Arabic OCR Products, Proceedings of SPIE Conference on Document Recognition and Retrieval (VI), San Jose, CA (1999) 3651
10. Reeder, F., Loehr, D.: Finding the Right Words: An Analysis of Not-Translated Words in Machine Translation. In: Farwell, D. et al. (eds.), Machine Translation and the Information Soup: Proceedings of the Association for Machine Translation in the Americas Annual Meeting. Springer-Verlag (1998) 356-363
11. Resnik, P.: Evaluating Multilingual Gisting of Web Pages. UMIACS Technical Report. University of Maryland Institute for Advanced Computer Studies, College Park, MD. (1997)
12. Taylor, K., White, J.: Predicting What MT is Good for: User Judgments and Task Performance. In: Farwell, D. et al. (eds.), Machine Translation and the Information Soup: Proceedings of the Association for Machine Translation in the Americas Annual Meeting. Springer-Verlag (1998) 364-373
13. Vanni, M.: Evaluating MT Systems: Testing and Researching the Feasibility of a Task-Diagnostic Approach. Proceedings of Conference of the Association for Information Management (ASLIB): Translating and the Computer 20 (1998)
14. Voss, C., Reeder, F. (eds.): Proceedings of the Workshop on Embedded Machine Translation: Design, Construction, and Evaluation of Systems with an MT Component. (In conjunction with the Association for Machine Translation in the Americas Annual Meeting, Langhorne, PA). Adelphi, MD: Army Research Lab. (1998)
15. Voss, C., Van Ess-Dykema, C.: When is an Embedded MT System "Good Enough" for Filtering? Proceedings of the Embedded Machine Translation Workshop II. In conjunction with the Applied Natural Language Processing Conference, Seattle (2000)

Machine Translation Systems: E-K, K-E, J-K, K-J

Yu Seop Kim[1], Sung Dong Kim[1], Seong Bae Park[2], Jong Woo Lee[2],
Jeong Ho Chang[2], Kyu Baek Hwang[2], Jang Min O[2], and Yung Taek Kim[3]

[1] Research Institute of Advanced Computer Technology, Seoul National University, Seoul,
Korea
yskim, sdkim @nova.snu.ac.kr
[2] School of Computer Science and Engineering, Seoul National University, Seoul, Korea
{sbpark, jongwoo, jhchang, mrmyself, jangmin}@nova.snu.ac.kr
[3] School of Computer Science and Engineering, Seoul National University, Seoul, Korea
ytkim@comp.snu.ac.kr

Abstract. We present four kinds of machine translation system in this
description: E-K (English to Korean), K-E (Korean to English), J-K (Japanese
to Korean), K-J (Korean to Japanese). Among these, E-K and K-J translation
systems are published commercially, and the other systems have finished their
development. This paper describes the structure and function of each system
with figures and translation results.

1 E-Tran: English-Korean MT System

E-Tran is an English-Korean machine translation system to translate English
sentences into Korean on Microsoft Windows environment, and is composed of two
versions, a text version and an Internet version. The Internet version interacts with
web browsers, such as Internet Explorer from Microsoft and Netscape Navigator,
translates English sentences into Korean, and shows translated results through the
browser. Figure 1 shows E-Tran Internet version with its interface and translation
results. The left part of the window shows the source web document and the right part
shows the translated document. The text version supports the translation of user
specified files. With the text version, users can translate sentences. The User
Dictionary enables users to add specific noun or adverb words to the translation
system. And there are 15 special domain dictionaries; such as politics, economics,
computer science, etc.

E-Tran translates documents through several steps as below. The 1st step and the 7th
step are only needed in the Internet version. The 1st step is an HTML document preprocessing: E-Tran takes HTML documents as input and picks out sentences to be
translated. In the 2nd step, input sentences are tokenized into word stems (Lexical
Analysis). In the 3rd step, idiomatic expressions in sentences are recognized and
translated into Korean directly. This step makes the system distinguishable among
other systems. The 4th step is for Syntactic Analysis: The syntactic structure of a
sentence is analyzed. In the 5th step, the English syntactic structure is transferred into
Korean syntactic structure. The 6th step is Korean Generation step: Korean sentences

J.S. White (Ed.): AMTA 2000, LNAI 1934, pp. 248-251, 2000.
© Springer-Verlag Berlin Heidelberg 2000

corresponding to Korean syntactic structure are generated. And the last step is for HTML document post-processing: A Korean HTML document is generated by combining translated results and HTML tags from the 1ˢᵗ step.

Fig. 1. SEQARABISCHInterface and translation results of E-Tran Internet version

2   KJ-Tran: Korean-Japanese MT System

KJ-Tran is a Korean-Japanese machine translation system, which is composed of an Internet version and text version like E-Tran. This system composed of several steps similar to E-Tran except syntactic analysis. Japanese and Korean have similar syntactic structure for each other, which makes it possible to omit the syntactic analysis step. For example, the Korean sentence, "나(I)는 학교(school)에(to) 갑니다(go)." ("I go to school") is translated into a Japanese sentence "私(I) は 學校(school) に(to) 行きます(go)."

Figure 2 shows an example of interface and translation result of KJ-tran Internet version.

3   K-Tran: Korean-English MT System

The *K-Tran* is a machine translation system that translates Korean into English. It consists of several subprocedures as follows:

Fig. 2. SEQARABISCHInterface and translation results of KJ-Tran Internet version

1. Morphological Analyzer: It first tokenizes a Korean sentence into eojols and then finds the base form of words in each eojol. With POS-tagging, the two most probable candidate is remained in this step.
2. Pattern Matcher: It determines various kinds of lexical patterns to solve the problems arising from free order language like Korean. The pattern matcher provides much information on structural gaps between two languages.
3. Syntax Parser: It just identifies the dependency between eojols.
4. Structural Transfer: It takes the parsing result of a Korean sentence as input and outputs structural information of the corresponding English sentence. Table 1 shows some examples of translation result from K-Tran.

Table 1. SEQARABISCHTranslation result from K-Tran

Input sentence	Translation result
우리가 어디로 가고 있는지 알겠니?	Do you know where we are going?
그 비행기는 곧 김포 공항에 착륙할 것이다.	The airplane will land at Kimpo airport soon.
비가 올 것 같다.	It is going to rain.

4   JK-Tran: Japanese-Korean MT System

JK-tran is the rule-based Japanese to Korean machine translation system. The system has three major parts. The first part is the morphological analysis part (Japanese Morphological Analyzer). The second part is the transfer part. And the generation part is the last.

1. Japanese Morphological Analyzer (JMA): JMA segments the input sentence into morphemes. JMA uses rules and dictionaries for analysis.
2. Structure Transfer: This part is composed of two steps: rule transfer and dictionary transfer. The rule transfer step translates each grammatical member of the Japanese morphemes' list into appropriate Korean morphemes. The dictionary transfer step translates the morphemes that were not translated in the rule transfer step.
3. Korean Generation: The generation step transforms the list of Korean morphemes into the Korean sentence.

Table 2 shows translation results from JK-Tran.

Table 2. SEQARABISCHTranslation Result from JK-Tran

Input sentence	Translation result
マカオ返還により `西歐諸國がアジアに植民地を持っていた狀態が終了する 。	마카오 반환에 따라, 서구 여러 나라가 아시아에 식민지를 가지고 있던 상태가 종료한다.
植民地最後の日となった１９日 `市街地はお祭り氣分の大勢の市民らでにぎわった 。	식민지 최후의 날이 된 19일, 시가지는 마쯔리(축제) 기분의 대세의 시민들에서(로) 활기찼다

4 Conclusion

We have developed 4 machine translation systems. Two of them are being sold on the market and the others are now being prepared for release. We used an Idiom-Transfer approach which uses idiomatic expressions for parsing and the transfer step. Although it can solve ambiguity problems during translation, it needs much effort from human beings. We now focus our study on the atomization in collection of idiomatic information and other statistical information.

References

1. Kim, S. D. and Kim, Y. T.: Sentence Segmentation for Efficient English Syntactic Analysis. Journal of Korea Information Science Society, 24(8) (1997) 884-890 (in Korean)
2. Yu Seop Kim, Y. S. and Kim, Y. T.: Semantic Implementation based on Extended Idiom for English to Korean Machine Translation. Journal of the Asia-Pacific Association for Machine Translation, (21) (1998) 23-39
3. Park, S-B. and Kim, Y. T.:, Semantic Role Determination in Korean Relative Clauses Using Idiomatic Patterns, In Proceedings of ICCPOL 97 (1997) 1-6
4. Chang, J. H.: Meaning Selection of Auxiliary Verb Phrase in English-Korean Machine Translation. Master Thesis (1997)
5. Hwang, K. B. Bayesian Network-based Translation of Japanese Particles in Japanese to Korean Machine Translation. Master Thesis (1999)
6. Lee, J.-W., Zhang, B.-T., and Kim, Y. T.:. Compound Noun Decomposition using a Markov Model. MT Summit 1999 35(10) (1999) 38-47

Author Index

Abaitua, Joseba	117	Kim, Sung Dong	248
Åkerman, Lars	202	Kim, Yu Seop	248
		Kim, Yung Taek	248
		Kipper, Karin	54
Badler, Norman	54	Kittredge, Richard	40
Bernth, Arendse	89	Korelsky, Tanya	40
Budzikowska, Margo	80		
Carl, Michael	127	Lavoie, Benoit	40
Casillas, Arantza	117	Lee, Jong Woo	248
Cavalli-Sforza, Violetta	169	León, Marjorie	219
Chalabi, Achraf	189	Levow, Gina-Anne	1
Chang, Jeong Ho	248	Lin, Dekang	1
Clements, David	213	Lopes, Gabriel	30
Cohen, Robin	25	Lu, Jimmy C.M.	202
Czuba, Krzysztof	169		
		Macklovitch, Elliot	137
		Martínez, Raquel	117
Danielsson, Pernilla	158	McCord, Michael C.	89
Decker, Nan	209	Meekhof, Timothy	213
Dorr, Bonnie J.	1	Mexia, João	30
Duczak, Hanna	147	Mitamura, Teruko	169, 192
		Mowatt, David	223
		Mühlenbock, Katarina	158
Farwell, David	179		
Fleming, Michael	25		
Fisher, Pete	196	Nyberg, Eric	169, 192
Fujii, Atsushi	13		
Gawronska, Barbara	147	Palmer, Martha	40, 54
		Park, Seong Bae	248
Habash, Nizar	68		
Han, Chung-hye	40	Rambow, Owen	40
Helmreich, Stephen	179	Reeder, Florence	109
Holland, M.	239	Ribeiro, António	30
Hwang, Kye Baek	248	Russell, Graham	137
Ishikawa, Tetsuya	13		
		Schlesiger, C.	239
		Schuler. William	54
Jang, Min O		Somers, Harold	223
		Spalink, Karin	202
Kim, Myunghee	40		
Kim, Nari	40	Tate, C.	239

Vanni, Michelle   109

Vogler, Christian   54

Weisgerber, John   196

White, John S.   100

Yang, Jin   196

Zhao, Liwei   54

Lecture Notes in Artificial Intelligence (LNAI)

Vol. 1791: D. Fensel, Problem-Solving Methods. XII, 153 pages. 2000.

Vol. 1792: E. Lamma, P. Mello (Eds.), AI*IA 99: Advances in Artificial Intelligence. Proceedings, 1999. XI, 392 pages. 2000.

Vol. 1793: O. Cairo, L.E. Sucar, F.J. Cantu (Eds.), MICAI 2000: Advances in Artificial Intelligence. Proceedings, 2000. XIV, 750 pages. 2000.

Vol. 1794: H. Kirchner, C. Ringeissen (Eds.), Frontiers of Combining Systems. Proceedings, 2000. X, 291 pages. 2000.

Vol. 1804: B. Azvine, N. Azarmi, D.D. Nauck (Eds.), Intelligent Systems and Soft Computing. XVII, 359 pages. 2000.

Vol. 1805: T. Terano, H. Liu, A.L.P. Chen (Eds.), Knowledge Discovery and Data Mining. Proceedings, 2000. XIV, 460 pages. 2000.

Vol. 1809: S. Biundo, M. Fox (Eds.), Recent Advances in AI Planning. Proceedings, 1999. VIII, 373 pages. 2000.

Vol. 1810: R. López de Mántaras, E. Plaza (Eds.), Machine Learning: ECML 2000. Proceedings, 2000. XII, 460 pages. 2000.

Vol. 1813: P.L. Lanzi, W. Stolzmann, S.W. Wilson (Eds.), Learning Classifier Systems. X, 349 pages. 2000.

Vol. 1821: R. Loganantharaj, G. Palm, M. Ali (Eds.), Intelligent Problem Solving. Proceedings, 2000. XVII, 751 pages. 2000.

Vol. 1822: H.H. Hamilton, Advances in Artificial Intelligence. Proceedings, 2000. XII, 450 pages. 2000.

Vol. 1831: D. McAllester (Ed.), Automated Deduction – CADE-17. Proceedings, 2000. XIII, 519 pages. 2000.

Vol. 1834: J.-C. Heudin (Ed.), Virtual Worlds. Proceedings, 2000. XI, 314 pages. 2000.

Vol. 1835: D. N. Christodoulakis (Ed.), Natural Language Processing – NLP 2000. Proceedings, 2000. XII, 438 pages. 2000.

Vol. 1836: B. Masand, M. Spiliopoulou (Eds.), Web Usage Analysis and User Profiling. Proceedings, 2000. V, 183 pages. 2000.

Vol. 1847: R. Dyckhoff (Ed.), Automated Reasoning with Analytic Tableaux and Related Methods. Proceedings, 2000. X, 441 pages. 2000.

Vol. 1849: C. Freksa, W. Brauer, C. Habel, K.F. Wender (Eds.), Spatial Cognition II. XI, 420 pages. 2000.

Vol. 1856: M. Veloso, E. Pagello, H. Kitano (Eds.), RoboCup-99: Robot Soccer World Cup III. XIV, 802 pages. 2000.

Vol. 1860: M. Klusch, L. Kerschberg (Eds.), Cooperative Information Agents IV. Proceedings, 2000. XI, 285 pages. 2000.

Vol. 1861: J. Lloyd, V. Dahl, U. Furbach, M. Kerber, K.-K. Lau, C. Palamidessi, L. Moniz Pereira, Y. Sagiv, P.J. Stuckey (Eds.), Computational Logic – CL 2000. Proceedings, 2000. XIX, 1379 pages.

Vol. 1864: B. Y. Choueiry, T. Walsh (Eds.), Abstraction, Reformulation, and Approximation. Proceedings, 2000. XI, 333 pages. 2000.

Vol. 1865: K.R. Apt, A.C. Kakas, E. Monfroy, F. Rossi (Eds.), New Trends Constraints. Proceedings, 1999. X, 339 pages. 2000.

Vol. 1866: J. Cussens, A. Frisch (Eds.), Inductive Logic Programming. Proceedings, 2000. X, 265 pages. 2000.

Vol. 1867: B. Ganter, G.W. Mineau (Eds.), Conceptual Structures: Logical, Linguistic, and Computational Issues. Proceedings, 2000. XI, 569 pages. 2000.

Vol. 1881: C. Zhang, V.-W. Soo (Eds.), Design and Applications of Intelligent Agents. Proceedings, 2000. X, 183 pages. 2000.

Vol. 1886: R. Mizoguchi, J. Slaney (Eds.), PRICAI 2000: Topics in Artificial Intelligence. Proceedings, 2000. XX, 835 pages. 2000.

Vol. 1898: E. Blanzieri, L. Portinale (Eds.), Advances in Case-Based Reasoning. Proceedings, 2000. XII, 530 pages. 2000.

Vol. 1889: M. Anderson, P. Cheng, V. Haarslev (Eds.), Theory and Application of Diagrams. Proceedings, 2000. XII, 504 pages. 2000.

Vol. 1891: A.L. Oliveira (Ed.), Grammatical Inference: Algorithms and Applications. Proceedings, 2000. VIII, 313 pages. 2000.

Vol. 1902: P. Sojka, I. Kopeček, K. Pala (Eds.), Text, Speech and Dialogue. Proceedings, 2000. XIII, 463 pages. 2000.

Vol. 1904: S.A. Cerri, D. Dochev (Eds.), Artificial Intelligence: Methodology, Systems, and Applications. Proceedings, 2000. XII, 366 pages. 2000.

Vol. 1910: D.A. Zighed, J. Komorowski, J. Żytkow (Eds.), Principles of Data Mining and Knowledge Discovery. Proceedings, 2000. XV, 701 pages. 2000.

Vol. 1919: M. Ojeda-Aciego, I.P. de Guzman, G. Brewka, L. Moniz Pereira (Eds.), Logics in Artificial Intelligence. Proceedings, 2000. XI, 407 pages. 2000.

Vol. 1925: J. Cussens, S. Džeroski (Eds.), Learning Language in Logic. X, 301 pages 2000.

Vol. 1932: Z.W. Raś, S. Ohsuga (Eds.), Foundations of Intelligent Systems. Proceedings, 2000. XII, 646 pages.

Vol. 1934: J.S. White (Ed.), Envisioning Machuine Translation in the Information Future. Proceedings, 2000. XV, 254 pagcs. 2000.

Vol. 1937: R. Dieng, O. Corby (Eds.), Knowledge Engineering and Knowledge Management. Proceedings, 2000. XIII, 457 pages. 2000.

Lecture Notes in Computer Science

Vol. 1899: H.-H. Nagel, F.J. Perales López (Eds.), Articulated Motion and Deformable Objects. Proceedings, 2000. X, 183 pages. 2000.

Vol. 1900: A. Bode, T. Ludwig, W. Karl, R. Wismüller (Eds.), Euro-Par 2000 Parallel Processing. Proceedings, 2000. XXXV, 1368 pages. 2000.

Vol. 1901: O. Etzion, P. Scheuermann (Eds.), Cooperative Information Systems. Proceedings, 2000. XI, 336 pages. 2000.

Vol. 1902: P. Sojka, I. Kopeček, K. Pala (Eds.), Text, Speech and Dialogue. Proceedings, 2000. XIII, 463 pages. 2000. (Subseries LNAI).

Vol. 1903: S. Reich, K.M. Anderson (Eds.), Open Hypermedia Systems and Structural Computing. Proceedings, 2000. VIII, 187 pages. 2000.

Vol. 1904: S.A. Cerri, D. Dochev (Eds.), Artificial Intelligence: Methodology, Systems, and Applications. Proceedings, 2000. XII, 366 pages. 2000. (Subseries LNAI).

Vol. 1905: H. Scholten, M.J. van Sinderen (Eds.), Interactive Distributed Multimedia Systems and Telecommunication Services. Proceedings, 2000. XI, 306 pages. 2000.

Vol. 1906: A. Porto, G.-C. Roman (Eds.), Coordination Languages and Models. Proceedings, 2000. IX, 353 pages. 2000.

Vol. 1907: H. Debar, L. Mé, S.F. Wu (Eds.), Recent Advances in Intrusion Detection. Proceedings, 2000. X, 227 pages. 2000.

Vol. 1908: J. Dongarra, P. Kacsuk, N. Podhorszki (Eds.), Recent Advances in Parallel Virtual Machine and Message Passing Interface. Proceedings, 2000. XV, 364 pages. 2000.

Vol. 1910: D.A. Zighed, J. Komorowski, J. Żytkow (Eds.), Principles of Data Mining and Knowledge Discovery. Proceedings, 2000. XV, 701 pages. 2000. (Subseries LNAI).

Vol. 1912: Y. Gurevich, P.W. Kutter, M. Odersky, L. Thiele (Eds.), Abstract State Machines. Proceedings, 2000. X, 381 pages. 2000.

Vol. 1913: K. Jansen, S. Khuller (Eds.), Approximation Algorithms for Combinatorial Optimization. Proceedings, 2000. IX, 275 pages. 2000.

Vol. 1914: M. Herlihy (Ed.), Distributed Computing. Proceedings, 2000. VIII, 389 pages. 2000.

Vol. 1917: M. Schoenauer, K. Deb, G. Rudolph, X. Yao, E. Lutton, J.J. Merelo, H.-P. Schwefel (Eds.), Parallel Problem Solving from Nature – PPSN VI. Proceedings, 2000. XXI, 914 pages. 2000.

Vol. 1918: D. Soudris, P. Pirsch, E. Barke (Eds.), Integrated Circuit Design. Proceedings, 2000. XII, 338 pages. 2000.

Vol. 1919: M. Ojeda-Aciego, I.P. de Guzman, G. Brewka, L. Moniz Pereira (Eds.), Logics in Artificial Intelligence. Proceedings, 2000. XI, 407 pages. 2000. (Subseries LNAI).

Vol. 1920: A.H.F. Laender, S.W. Liddle, V.C. Storey (Eds.), Conceptual Modeling – ER 2000. Proceedings, 2000. XV, 588 pages. 2000.

Vol. 1921: S.W. Liddle, H.C. Mayr, B. Thalheim (Eds.), Conceptual Modeling for E-Business and the Web. Proceedings, 2000. X, 179 pages. 2000.

Vol. 1922: J. Crowcroft, J. Roberts, M.I. Smirnov (Eds.), Quality of Future Internet Services. Proceedings, 2000. XI, 368 pages. 2000.

Vol. 1923: J. Borbinha, T. Baker (Eds.), Research and Advanced Technology for Digital Libraries. Proceedings, 2000. XVII, 513 pages. 2000.

Vol. 1924: W. Taha (Ed.), Semantics, Applications, and Implementation of Program Generation. Proceedings, 2000. VIII, 231 pages. 2000.

Vol. 1925: J. Cussens, S. Džeroski (Eds.), Learning Language in Logic. X, 301 pages 2000. (Subseries LNAI).

Vol. 1926: M. Joseph (Ed.), Formal Techniques in Real-Time and Fault-Tolerant Systems. Proceedings, 2000. X, 305 pages. 2000.

Vol. 1927: P. Thomas, H.W. Gellersen, (Eds.), Handheld and Ubiquitous Computing. Proceedings, 2000. X, 249 pages. 2000.

Vol. 1931: E. Horlait (Ed.), Mobile Agents for Telecommunication Applications. Proceedings, 2000. IX, 271 pages. 2000.

Vol. 1766: M. Jazayeri, R.G.K. Loos, D.R. Musser (Eds.), Generic Programming. Proceedings, 1998. X, 269 pages. 2000.

Vol. 1791: D. Fensel, Problem-Solving Methods. XII, 153 pages. 2000. (Subseries LNAI).

Vol. 1932: Z.W. Raś, S. Ohsuga (Eds.), Foundations of Intelligent Systems. Proceedings, 2000. XII, 646 pages. (Subseries LNAI).

Vol. 1933: R.W. Brause, E. Hanisch (Eds.), Medical Data Analysis. Proceedings, 2000. XI, 316 pages. 2000.

Vol. 1934: J.S. White (Ed.), Envisioning Machine Translation in the Information Future. Proceedings, 2000. XV, 254 pages. 2000. (Subseries LNAI).

Vol. 1937: R. Dieng, O. Corby (Eds.), Knowledge Engineering and Knowledge Management. Proceedings, 2000. XIII, 457 pages. 2000. (Subseries LNAI).

Vol. 1938: S. Rao, K.I. Sletta (Eds.), Next Generation Networks. Proceedings, 2000. XI, 392 pages. 2000.

Vol. 1939. A. Evans, S. Kent (Eds.), «UML» – The Unified Modeling Language. Proceedings, 2000. XIV, 572 pages. 2000.